BUSINESS POLITICS IN

STEFFEN HERTOG
GIACOMO LUCIANI
MARC VALERI

(*Editors*)

Business Politics in the Middle East

HURST & COMPANY, LONDON

First published in the United Kingdom in paperback in 2013 by
C. Hurst & Co. (Publishers) Ltd.,
41 Great Russell Street, London, WC1B 3PL

Printed in the United Kingdom

A Cataloguing-in-Publication data record for this book is available from the British Library.

ISBN: 978-1-84904-235-2

www.hurstpublishers.com

This book is printed on paper from registered sustainable and managed sources.

CONTENTS

ACKNOWLEDGEMENTS

This book is the result of a rather lengthy process, during which multiple debts were accumulated.

It started off in 2007 as a research project on "The Role of the Private Sector in Promoting Economic and Political Reform", generously funded by the Arab Reform Initiative (ARI) and the Gulf Research Center Foundation (GRCF). Hence our first debt of gratitude is to the ARI and personally to Bassma Kodmani who expressed an immediate personal interest in the project; and to Abdulaziz Sager, Chairman of the Gulf Research Center Foundation and generous supporter of its initiatives. We also wish to thank Rachida Amsaghrou for her management of the project in its early stages.

The preparation of several papers was funded under the first stage of the project. These papers constituted the backbone of the discussion at the workshop convened in the context of the first Gulf Research Meeting at Cambridge University in July 2010, jointly directed by Bassma Kodmani and Giacomo Luciani. We wish to thank Dr Christian Koch, Dr Oskar Ziemelis, Mrs Sania Kapasi and all others who contributed to the great success of the first Gulf Research Meeting, as well as to subsequent meetings in 2011 and 2012. Certainly our project greatly benefited from the opportunity: additional papers were presented at the workshop in response to a new call, out of which the final collection included in this volume was compiled.

Then came the Arab Spring, and the process of editing the volume was interrupted in order to allow all authors to take into account the latest developments. We are grateful to our authors, who have been asked to revise their papers not only once but several times. In the end, we believe this collection offers a timely, informed and analytically challenging perspective on a dimension of the region's political evolution that would deserve a lot more observation.

We are also indebted to Michael Dwyer at Hurst for his forbearance with slipped deadlines and continued interest in the project: without his continuing encouragement we might indeed have been tempted to give up.

In the final stages of the project, Giacomo Luciani was able to leverage the support and facilities of Princeton University, which appointed him Princeton Global Scholar for the years 2011–13.

As usual, the responsibility for all shortcomings belongs exclusively to the three co-editors.

Steffen Hertog, Giacomo Luciani and Marc Valeri

1

INTRODUCTION

THE ROLE OF MENA BUSINESS IN POLICY MAKING AND POLITICAL TRANSITIONS

Steffen Hertog

This book is the result of a project on Middle East and North Africa (MENA) business politics that started in 2008. At the time, the leading topic for political scientists working on MENA was the enduring authoritarianism of the Arab world, a region bypassed by successive international waves of democratization. Some authors saw "crony capitalism"—tight, informal and exclusive networks between leading regime actors and select capitalists—as a pivotal ingredient of authoritarian stability.[1]

From the outset, the editors of this volume were less concerned with macro-questions like the impact of business on authoritarian survival. We instead focused on understanding the little-documented politics of MENA business in its own right: How have the increased capacities of MENA businesses shaped their negotiation stances vis-à-vis regimes? How do the resulting state-business relations affect economic policy decisions and outcomes, and through which formal and informal channels are these relations conducted? How are the social roots of different sections of business reflected in their relations with the region's regimes?

After the tumultuous events of 2011 and 2012, explaining Arab authoritarian survival is less topical—and it turned out that at least in several Arab republics, business cronyism was not enough to keep veteran dictators in place. At the same time, understanding capacities and motivations of MENA businesses and their relationship to the state, both individually and collectively, has become more important than ever.

As "crony capitalist" theories would predict, business appears to have been marginal in the region's uprisings. Yet most of the regimes in the region, whether old or new, face a potential fiscal and employment crisis, unfolding against the background of heightened popular expectations and weak administrative apparatuses. MENA regimes will inevitably have to rely on local capitalists to provide public services and combat widespread un- and underemployment. The legacies of business politics analyzed in this volume will have a strong impact on the possibilities and limits of such mobilization and the attendant bargaining processes.

The countries included in the chapters of this volume are Egypt, Syria, Iran, Kuwait, the UAE, and—in the shape of a statistical survey—the other four GCC countries. The individual topics of the country case studies vary, spanning issues as diverse as economic policy-making, the role of business in civil society, and regime patronage over religious business elites. Yet there are several common themes that emerge from the book as a whole and are moreover likely to travel beyond the cases at hand to other countries not included as case studies, notably the middle-income countries Algeria, Jordan, Morocco and Tunisia.

All across the region, demographic growth and the crisis of statist development have resulted in increasing demands on the private sector to contribute to national capital formation and employment, share in the delivery of public services and welfare, and serve as interface with international business and, sometimes, international organizations and civil society. Arab business elites have also been called on to act as political intermediaries to represent wider social and political constituencies in an age of renewed social inequality and mass demobilization. At the same time, small strata of privileged businesses have been prominent recipients of regime patronage and conduits of intra-elite rent recycling—not a new phenomenon in the region's monarchies, but a novelty in scale and scope in the formerly socialist republics.

While capacities and tasks have shifted between state and business, the relationship has remained lopsided. As formal corporatist institutions of interest representation are often empty husks, state-business negotiations have frequently remained informal and purely reactive, with the vast majority of businesses excluded from them. Modern business-supported "civil society" organizations have often done the regime's bidding, operated primarily for an international audience, and developed limited resonance in local society. Levels of trust between state and business below the top echelon have remained low. The deep formal and informal involvement of the state in Arab economies has deformed and fragmented the capitalist class, a class which regimes have utilized for patronage, rent-seeking and façade modernization at least as much as for meaningful diversification and development.

The remainder of this chapter will spell out these cross-cutting themes in more detail, drawing on the contributions in this volume as well as available wider literature. It will elaborate how republican and monarchical business classes have remained somewhat distinct, with the latter enjoying a more accepted and secure—though not independent—social status and a relatively reduced need to operate in the shadows and engage in blatant corruption. It will then put the weak role of Arab business in the recent uprisings into international comparative perspective and conclude with some observations about the potential future role of Arab business in the post-revolutionary age against the background of its complex legacy.

A universally growing need for business capacities

Since at least the 1980s, Arab regimes have increasingly relied on the private sector as a driver of economic growth and job creation. Outside the rich and sparsely populated GCC countries, state-provided job guarantees have been increasingly thinned out while the quality of public services such as education has increasingly declined, leading to the emergence—by default rather than by design—of private providers for the minority of consumers able to pay the requisite fees. Public industry in the region's low- to middle-income countries turned out to be loss-making and unsustainable. Its expansion stopped and enterprises in the more economically liberal regimes were slated for privatization.[2] Bureaucracy in most MENA countries gets bad scores on international "governance" indicators and is often seen as a hindrance to development rather than the driver it was once supposed to be.[3]

While the direct role of the state in the economy in many cases increased into the 1970s, since then government consumption as a share of GDP has been on a downward trend across most of the region. Private enterprise has come to be present in many sectors traditionally dominated by public entities, including strategic areas like banking, heavy industry and utilities. While it remains largely focused on low-technology production, it has taken over a much larger share of the economy from the state.[4]

Even in the GCC, where the material pressures towards private-led development have been less acute, regimes have left increasing room for private players as part of their diversification and public service delivery strategies from the 1990s on.

The chapter by Hodson in this volume provides detailed and impressive data demonstrating the increased role of Gulf business in local capi-

Graph 1: Share of government consumption in GDP, non-GCC MENA countries.

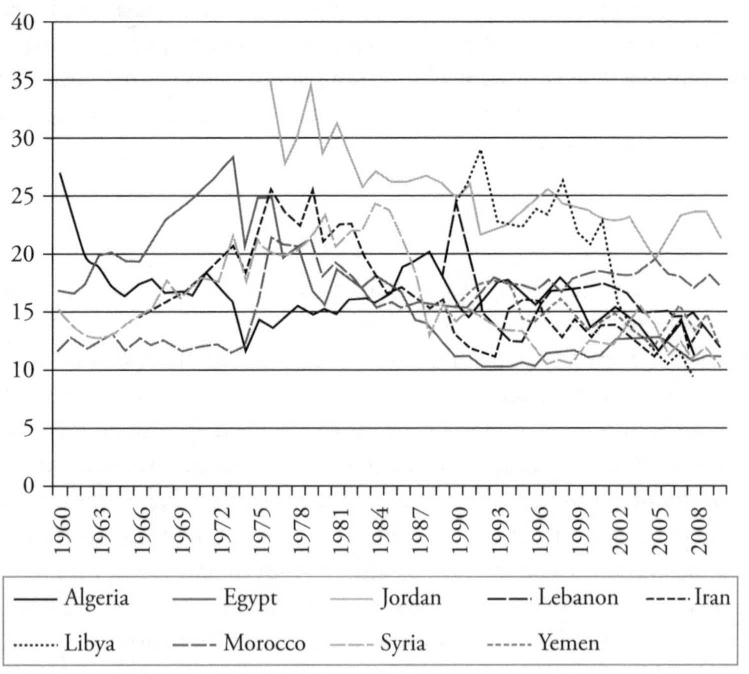

Source: World Bank Development Indicators.

Graph 2: Share of government consumption in GDP, GCC.

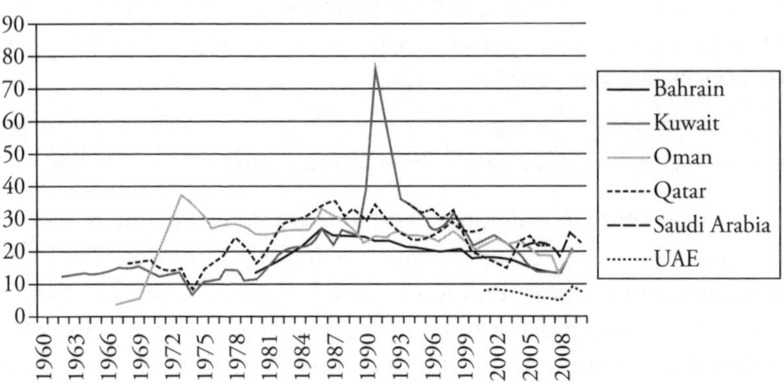

Source: World Bank Development Indicators.

tal formation and financial market development, its reduced dependence on state spending, and its leading role in regional investment.

All across the region, policy reforms have led to a superficial convergence of economic strategies and regulatory regimes on global capitalist standards, which has meant a significant turnaround particularly in the republics with a heavy statist legacy. Most economic sectors are now open to private local and foreign investment, trade has been liberalized, the share of the public sector in total employment has declined, and populist social and political institutions supporting workers and peasants have been progressively hollowed out.[5]

Even for formerly socialist Syria, Selvik in this volume documents the local "private sector's newfound status as 'development partner' for the Syrian state", reflecting a grudging but fundamental ideological reorientation, and a secular shift in capacities between state and business. Among the region's authoritarian systems, Iran's alone remains ensconced in the old populist, statist and "third worldist" paradigm, even if, as Harris shows in this volume, much of the Iranian system is a product of historical exigency rather than ideology.

A new role for business does not mean new business players: barriers against entry to MENA markets are traditionally high,[6] and as several of the chapters in this volume show, private networks and family conglomerates have dominated high-level state-business interaction in both monarchies and republics. Many leading capitalists across the MENA region have their origins as rentiers or fixers for senior regime actors.[7] Yet, as Luciani's concluding chapter argues, an important proportion of them have come to operate more serious and sometimes internationalized businesses over time.[8]

Continuing co-optation and top-down orchestration of business politics

Do a larger capacity and a more visible role amount to a more serious role for business in economic policy-making? On the formal level, the evidence for this is weak. Business is mostly organized through corporatist, state-licensed mechanisms of interest representation, including both traditional chambers of commerce and new elite business clubs and groups, all of which are usually dominated by large players close to power (see the chapters of Zintl and Selvik on Syria, Springborg on Egypt, and Valeri on Bahrain and Oman). As Zovighian's chapter shows, even an SME interest group organized with aid from foreign donors in Egypt quickly became part of the state-controlled corporatist system in which it was granted a monopoly position but came under increasing administrative control.

The influence of formal business organizations on policy outcomes appears to remain limited. As Almezaini's chapter on the UAE and Valeri's chapter on Bahrain and Oman show, lobbying tends to focus on defending existing privileges rather than engaging with policy problems in a proactive way. Across the region, there are few exceptions to this rule.[9] More broadly, deep and unaccountable state intervention tends to lead to individual deals between business and regime players instead of collective action, a process that has also been documented for Latin American cases.[10]

On the informal level too, co-optation rather than an even-handed relationship seems to characterize state-business relations. As Azoulay's chapter demonstrates, this is the case even in semi-democratic countries like Kuwait that enjoy a deep tradition of merchant politics. The only partial exception to this lopsided relationship appears to be Oman, documented in Valeri's chapter, where a limited number of merchant families around the Sultan have gained control over strategic parts of government—a unique situation in which neither an omnipresent security apparatus nor an extensive ruling family has been able to control the levers of power and distribution.

Façade civil society and the role of business elite in it

The vast majority of Arab businesses are de facto excluded from sectoral interest group politics. The same is true of "civil society" activities more broadly, important parts of which have been under direct or indirect regime control. In the activities where businesses have played a role—such as the "corporate social responsibility" agenda in Syria, documented by Selvik's chapter—this has often served to project an image of liberal modernity to international donors and organizations. It is part of "authoritarian upgrading"[11] rather than genuine interest group politics, and again follows a corporatist logic in which the regime grants monopoly functions to specific charities or groups. Differing from the old authoritarian-populist corporatism of unions and syndicates, however, this camouflaged corporatism is elitist and exclusionary, as it has no real social reach or commitment to large-scale redistribution. As with the SME group in Egypt, the resonance of Syria's new, regime-endorsed charities among the wider business class or local society at large is strictly limited. And as in the Gulf, important parts of Syria's charitable sector supported by business have close personal links to the ruling family, in particular the President's wife.

Zintl in this volume shows how Western-educated Syrian entrepreneurs with close regime connections have helped to "blue-wash" or "white-wash" the repressive local regime in the international arena by creating a façade civil society. Ironically, the "modern" elements of the Syrian bourgeoisie who hold Western degrees and have adopted the Western phraseology of civil society and corporate social responsibility appear altogether more likely to be cronies. Selvik shows that it is more traditional businessmen focusing on Islamic, *zakat*-based charities who are relatively independent of the regime and who enjoy real social legitimacy—and thereby could play a more prominent role in a post-Asad future.

'Coerced charity' and other means of delegating some public service and welfare provision

Stephen King has described civil society activities of business in the MENA's authoritarian republics as "coerced charity",[12] a sort of stealth tax: as the regime's capacity to provide welfare for the wider population has declined, charitable giving by capitalists is expected in return for continued political support, or limited interference, in their business operations. In the words of one industrial manager cited by Selvik: "the government wants to rid itself of all kinds of responsibilities and push it on the private sector ... it will apply the new rules of the social market economy to force the private sector to pay even more".[13]

Donations to charities patronized by regime members are especially encouraged. "Coerced charity" as a de facto means of privatizing public services is less of a concern in the rich GCC. Nonetheless, there can be considerable pressure on businesses to contribute to princely charities after a ruling family member has provided—often modest—seed money for an institution in his or her own name.[14] Regime-endorsed charity usually reflects a hierarchical view of society: it is a top-down gesture rather than a result of social solidarity, and hence plays to business elites' interest in underlining their privileged status.[15]

Successful and failed attempts to set up elite business players as social elites

While regime-endorsed civil society activity among businessmen is not necessarily meant to strike societal roots, there have also been some attempts to set up politically connected capitalists as a new social elite with wider power. In the colonial and early post-colonial era predating mass politics, much of MENA politics was conducted by elite clans representing and speaking on behalf of wider social communities.[16] It seems that with their attempts to empower select businessmen as a new political elite, some regimes in the region have attempted to resuscitate such a stratum of "notables".

These attempts have met with very mixed success. Gamal Mubarak in Egypt tried to position businessmen clients of his as new power brokers in Parliament and the National Democratic Party, gambling on their (relatively) autonomous material resources and local power as landlords or factory owners. In fact, many businessmen candidates failed in the elections and the NDP had to reintegrate into its parliamentary group old party strongmen or non-NDP businessmen who had run as independents with better entrenched (if also often declining) networks of local patronage.

As Zintl shows, even in previously anti-bourgeois Syria, a considerable number of businessmen were allowed to enter Parliament under Bashar. But here too, their performance has been lacklustre and has focused on their individual agendas more than representing a cohesive group with autonomous political resources.

As Springborg describes, the supposedly powerful Egyptian crony business elite was sidelined and in several cases publicly sacrificed by the military apparatus early on in the revolution. Crony capitalists in Syria and Tunisia have been even more closely linked to the ruling circles, and have played no independent role in a domestic struggle where the presidents and security agencies have determined regime strategy.

During the uprisings, the crony bourgeoisies have proved weaker and more fragmented than many analysts of the new "neo-liberal" MENA authoritarianism had thought. Economically liberalizing republics like Egypt, Syria and Tunisia had come to rely on small coteries of business clients that were not representative of the capitalist class at large, maintained a small social basis and remained at the whim of the presidential family or the security sector.

While most other businesspeople did not engage in opposition, neither were they loyal supporters of the regime—instead, many tried to remain as independent as possible by staying clear of politics like Syria's conservative, *zakat*-paying entrepreneurs. The fragmentation of the business class—discussed in more detail in Luciani's concluding chapter—has been accentuated by the "missing middle",[17] that is, the weak presence of middle-sized companies that could have either given the regimes a broader basis or served as an organized pillar of opposition.

MENA monarchies have a longer history of economic openness and deeper traditions of integrating business elites into their ruling coalitions,[18] sometimes going back centuries as in Kuwait or Morocco. While republican cronies often appeared out of nowhere after the anti-bourgeois policies of the populist era were reversed, there is more of a tradition of "politics of notables" in the region's monarchies. Of course their origins, albeit going further back in time, are sometimes as "crony" as those of their younger republican peers. Monarchical regimes moreover remain perfectly capable of creating new business elites ex nihilo, as individual examples from Kuwait and Bahrain in this volume demonstrate. But many of the large business clans have deeper social roots and status in the monarchies.

While business and especially state-business transactions remain personalized across the whole region, the whiff of corruption is worse in the republics.[19] Ironically, the more egalitarian and statist legacy of an earlier age seems to have brought out the very worst of capitalism in the age of liberalization, having undermined legitimate business and pushed transactions into the shadows, dependent on omnipresent state networks. Springborg's chapter shows how even in Egypt, a country with a long pre-Nasserist history of capitalist development, the historical legitimacy of Egyptian business remains limited. In populist Iran, as shown in Harris' chapter, business is particularly marginalized; corrupt deals are not even transacted through private sector lackeys, but remain largely within the fragmented state apparatus.

Most capitalists' levels of trust vis-à-vis the state have been correspondingly low in the republics, as is vividly illustrated in the chapters on Syria and Iran in this volume. In the monarchies, links and cooperation between the state and "old money" are closer, as both the UAE and Kuwaiti case studies show. The state acts more predictably towards a larger stratum of established businesses. While there are serious corruption problems in the monarchies as well, and no large business player can thrive if he (or, rarely, she) draws the ire of the rulers, many of the senior players are less dependent on individual patrons in the regime.

While business elites have a more solid social standing in the monarchies, their political status is less clear. Their function as "notables" representing larger social strata has also eroded as a larger and more educated middle class has started to get politically organized. While landowning notables remain powerful in the Moroccan countryside,[20] the propertied urban elites' clout has been eroding, and business cronies around the King have drawn the ire of protestors.[21]

Azoulay's chapter describes how members of Kuwait's ruling family have managed to create a number of Shi'i business notables almost from scratch in the 2000s. The then Prime Minister successfully deployed these new intermediaries to defuse political conflicts on behalf of the wider Shi'i community in Kuwait, drawing on both deep pockets and a long tradition of elite clans that allowed the regime to dress up an essentially modern, neo-patrimonial strategy in traditional garb. Even in Kuwait, however, this strategy has been contingent on the minority status of the Shi'i and seems to have run into trouble in the wake of middle class protests against regime corruption. Big Sunni merchant families in Kuwait continue to be socially respected, but have little political clout and have been marginalized in parliament since the 1970s.

The role of large business clans in the even quieter UAE, analyzed in Almezaini's chapter, is closer to that of true notables, as they are both business and social elites, well represented in government and respected in local communities. The UAE however is a regional outlier in terms of extremely high per capita rents, low levels of political mobilization and an atomized civil society. Even in traditionally quiescent but less rich Oman, the Sultan had to get rid of a number of ministers from established business families when young protestors called for an end to high-level corruption in the Sultanate in 2011. Only Qatar—not represented in this volume—has comparable social and economic structures to the UAE; but there, the ruling family is more dominant in business.

Aside from the small and rich GCC autocracies—and to a lesser extent Morocco—the age of notables is over and attempts to reinsert businessmen into politics as a substitute for an eroding working and middle class constituency have not worked out. The Arab uprisings have shown that the age of mass politics is not congenial to indirect rule by propertied elites, not even in traditional political systems. And even when business elites have social influence, this often remains tied up with sectarian or ethnic identities—both in monarchies like Bahrain and Kuwait and in republics like Syria and Lebanon—undermining the private sector's political role as national bourgeoisie.

Both in business and in their relations with regime elites, Arab capitalists have gained much strength on an individual level. But this has not translated into capacity for independent collective action.[22] The largest and most visible business organizations often serve no purpose and/or do the regime's bidding, and other forms of business-financed civil society activity have either been subdued and kept on a small level, or become part of a regime-orchestrated strategy of façade liberalization. Attempts to integrate business clients into the political elite seem to have weakened rather than strengthened the latter, particularly in the Arab republics.

Why was business absent in Arab political transitions?

It is not surprising that business seems to have played no organized role in the political revolts and transitions across the region.[23] While some brave individual businessmen signed political petitions or joined illegal parties in Arab countries even before the uprisings, they did so on an individual basis, not as the representatives of a broader class constituency. Similarly, the young Egyptian entrepreneurs—often active in the IT sector—who joined the movements in Tahrir Square are perhaps better understood as members of the educated middle class than as capitalists.[24] In Libya, though individual entrepreneurs helped finance the rebellion, its political leadership was in the hands of professionals.[25] To the extent that business was visible, it was so rather as supporters of the ancien regime—most clearly in Bahrain, where large parts of the Sunni business elite allied with the more repressive parts of the Al Khalifa family, as Valeri's chapter shows.

Looking at a variety of developing world case studies including Saudi Arabia and Egypt, Eva Bellin has argued that a tradition of state sponsorship and state dependence of business accounts for the absence of democratizing bourgeoisies in late developers worldwide.[26] There have indeed been "dependent" bourgeoisies in many regions, but in the Middle East the phenomenon is particularly pronounced.

We have seen that MENA business classes are fragmented, lack autonomous organizational space, continue to depend on bureaucratic if not fiscal patronage of an arbitrary state apparatus, and have in important parts been created by the state, the result being closed and collusive networks with regime elites. At least at the higher levels, MENA political economies are a classical case of neo-patrimonialism, a system in which political power determines access to economic resources, not the other way around,[27] be it through state patronage over business, as in most Arab states, or direct control of means of production by different factions of the state elite, as in Iran. While business traditions are deeper in the monarchies and capitalists have more autonomous social standing, the difference is one of degree: true independence from the state is unthinkable.

Research on Latin American cases has shown that business tends to function fine within any political system as long as it has access to decision-making.[28] This is in line with the observations from several cases in this book, where individualized access to the administration of interventionist states has sustained the allegiance of large businesses to local regimes. Smaller players have usually lacked such access, but had no organizational means to protest.

The Arab uprisings might point to a more fundamental reason why business in MENA has not acted as a force for political relaxation: perhaps the whole notion of a democratizing bourgeoisie is problematic in an age of mass politics. Where European bourgeoisies pushed for more political participation in the eighteenth and nineteenth centuries, they did so in the context of a limited franchise and politically demobilized societies.

In the MENA countries, by contrast, important parts of the business classes—including non-cronies—are concerned about the economic policies that mass electoral democracy might bring. In Kuwait, the Sunni merchant elite was the main driver of electoral politics and constitutionalism between the 1920s and the 1960s.[29] But as in most of the Arab world, notables and business elites lost their status as nationalist leaders when middle class political movements became organized and directly mobilized a mass constituency. Nowadays, most Kuwaiti merchants abhor the populist economic politics of the National Assembly, in which they lost most of their seats since the 1970s, and many wish their forebears had never let the democratic genie out of the bottle.[30]

All over the region, business has much to lose from the democratic game of numbers. Given the anti-crony sentiment of the Arab Spring, post-revolutionary populism could lead to a halt to (or reversal of) privatization, increased labour protectionism, and a diversion of state resources away from infrastructure and towards consumer subsidies. These concerns are particularly acute in poor and unequal countries like Egypt or Syria, where a class compromise is harder to reach.

Of course, business in the developing world has not been anti-democratic everywhere. Capitalists in the modern world do not start rebellions, but in several mid-income countries in Asia and Latin America, well organized business elites have tipped the balance, once a regime crisis has set in, by collectively defecting from the regime and providing organized backing for the opposition.[31] Capitalists in these cases have tended to be more coherent, autonomous, socially legitimate, and often export-oriented than MENA business has been to date.

MENA opposition forces seem to have received little organized backing from business in either the quick or the slow transitions that started in 2011. As this chapter is written, the conservative bourgeoisie in Syria still straddles the fence of the protracted domestic conflict, although many old families detest the regime and seem to think in private that Asad's days are numbered.[32] In June 2012, Syrian businessmen set up a Doha-based fund to support the opposition, but this happened more than a year after the start of the uprising and represents capital in exile rather than local business.[33] The most daring collective act inside the country seems to have involved Damascus shopkeepers in some areas closing their shutters to protest against the regime's violence in the summer of 2012.[34]

While the contribution to regime change appears to have been modest, prominent businessmen in Egypt and Tunisia started to back a variety of parties once it became obvious that free elections were under way. New parties created by businessmen have however not fared well in either country, indicating limited social legitimacy.[35] Important members of the business elite appear to hope for a counter-revolution: the presidential candidate of the ancien regime, Ahmed Shafik, was applauded enthusiastically at the elite, regime-sponsored American Chamber of Commerce in Egypt in May 2012 when calling Mubarak a role model.[36]

The middle-sized "Islamic bourgeoisie" that is perceived to back the Muslim Brotherhood in Egypt might be the closest to an autonomous, organized and pro-democratic group of capitalists with wider social backing. In the 2010 edition of *Globalization and the Politics of Development in the Middle East*, Henry and Springborg place much hope on the region's Islamic bourgeoisie as the potential backbone of a conservative, but economically open and politically plural Middle East.[37]

Yet, much of this bourgeoisie still operates on a small scale and often on an informal basis, and the Muslim Brothers in Egypt and elsewhere are led by professionals rather than businessmen. Small scale and informality have often been a stratagem to avoid predation by MENA state elites; under a new political dispensation, there might be more scope for growth in scale, modern corporate structures and political visibility.

The democratic commitment of the Islamic bourgeoisie, however, still has to be put to the test. Hopeful commentators draw analogies with the Turkish AKP and the backing it receives from a conservative Anatolian business class, but Turkey has a much longer history of democratic competition into which its Islamists have been gradually socialized. Khairat al-Shater, a businessman and the Egyptian Muslim Brotherhood's would-be presidential candidate in the spring of 2012, has publicly taken pro-market and pro-free trade positions, but seems to have a distinctly authoritarian take on the Brotherhood's internal politics.[38]

The future direction of MENA business as an organized political player cannot be predicted with any precision. What we do know with more certainty after the first wave of Arab uprisings is that organized business backing was not a major factor in regime change—which is different from what some of the international transitology literature might have made us expect.[39] In line with this, Kurzman and Leahey have argued in their international study of early and late twentieth century democratizations that the role of the educated middle class appears to have been more important.[40]

Future roles

Looking at the non-MENA literature about the developmental and political roles played by bourgeoisies in the developing world, MENA capitalists tend to stand out in terms of what they do not do: with some notable exceptions, they are not export-oriented, do not engage in close policy coordination with the state, along the lines of Peter Evans' "embedded autonomy",[41] generally have limited collective lobbying and self-regulation capacities,[42] and have lacked a coherent political, let alone democratic agenda. Instead, they have been engaged in low-tech production, have been cronyist at the top and marginalized below, and much of their formal politics and civil society involvement has been orchestrated by local regimes.

We now know that in the republics in particular, this orchestration has not been very effective: the more outward-looking business cronies have given regimes in Egypt, Syria, and Tunisia some sheen of modernization, especially vis-à-vis international audiences. But by building crony capitalism, regimes had also thrown in their lot with allies that were small in number and socially discredited. In the face of visible top-level corruption, rising inequality, and the erosion of old lower and middle class constituencies, this seems to have rendered the regimes fragile. While large capitalists are more of an "organic" elite in the monarchies, high-level cronies have come under fire there, too.

The private sector's larger share in the economy and its gradual assumption of previously public functions tell us little about the quality of business activities either economically or politically. Yet, all problematic historical baggage notwithstanding, the need for business capacities is only set to grow across the region and has become all the more acute with civil unrest, which has further strained public resources in old and new regimes.

The new regimes might open a chance for a more even-handed accommodation between state and business, and a more level playing field among businesses themselves. There is much potential for growth of small and particularly middle-sized companies in a less predatory environment, from which a more coherent bourgeois politics could emerge—not only among Islamists, but also among young secular entrepreneurs.

Reporting from the region has raised hopes for startup funding and SME growth, open competition, and social and political pressure for cleaner business, even in the non-revolutionary states. Some MENA capitalists already report less fear of political interference.[43]

A new generation of businesspeople could set up new or increase their influence in existing "independent" business associations, filling them with political life. As Luciani points out in his chapter, it is more useful to speak of several bourgeoisies rather than one. While this is likely to hold true in the foreseeable future, the more independent and dynamic segments might become more prominent after the Arab uprisings.

This is far from a foregone conclusion, however: international experience shows that business conditions and practices do not necessarily improve in poor countries that experience democratic transitions. Cronyism was reconfigured, but did not disappear in low-income democratizers like Mexico, Indonesia and the Philippines, where state-business transactions have remained personalized. In fact, the temporary fragmentation of state power and the temptations of populist politics might make things worse for MENA capitalists in the coming years. Owing to the relationship-based nature of business even among non-cronies in MENA countries, it is unlikely that modern capital markets and corporate governance will qualitatively change regional capitalism any time soon. The shift from cronies to entrepreneurs might be under way, but it still has a long way to go.

2

OLIGARCHY VS. OLIGARCHY

BUSINESS AND POLITICS OF REFORM IN BAHRAIN AND OMAN

Marc Valeri

When called upon to assume the government, [the bourgeoisie] took it up as a trade; it entrenched itself behind its power, and before long, in their egoism, each of its members thought much more of his private business than of public affairs, and of his personal enjoyment than of the greatness of the nation.

Alexis de Tocqueville, 1850.[1]

The last fifteen years have seen unprecedented awareness among Gulf Cooperation Council (GCC) elites of the need to rethink their states' socio-economic structures, in order to address challenges of political and economic sustainability. Thus, while high oil prices arguably reduced the pressure to transform and diversify in the 1970s, the latest period of high oil prices (2004–09) has instead coincided with changes in the role of the state, economic diversification policies, and reforms in labour markets, health, education and the judiciary. This has had major implications for the whole social contract in these states, and more particularly for the relations between the business sector and political authority.

Given their limited oil and gas resources by comparison with their neighbours, Bahrain and Oman are viewed as laboratories of reform policies implemented to address the challenges of sustainability in the post-oil social and economic context. Thus it is not surprising that political debates in Bahrain and Oman over the necessity to rethink their economic model of development are not new. As early as the 1970s, Bahrain was the first oil-rentier state in the Gulf to implement a wide-scale policy of diversification of state revenues, focusing on major industrial projects, such as ALBA (Aluminium Bahrain), the first non-oil industry venture in Bahrain, opened in 1971, which is now the fourth largest smelter in the world and contributes 12% of total GDP; and ASRY (Shipbuilding and Repair Yard Company), which started operations in September 1977. The decline in oil production in the late 1970s coincided with the second phase of diversification in Bahrain and the Al Khalifa ruling family's attempt to position Bahrain as a banking hub for the Persian Gulf. In Oman, the regime's awareness of the need to rethink the model of development based on oil rent happened later, owing to the combination of the economic slowdown and the emergence of endemic unemployment among the younger generations in the 1980s. In April 1990, a British press correspondent noted that "diversification and Omanization are Oman's obsessions,[2] the Muscat 'buzz words.'"[3] As for the labour market, while the Bahraini government initiated a series of employment schemes to favour the recruitment of nationals in the private sector, the first five-year comprehensive Bahrainization plan was formalized in 1989. In Oman, an April 1987 decree by the Minister of Labour announcing that eleven categories of jobs (like those of public relations officer, security officer and bus taxi driver) were reserved to nationals represented the first major step aimed at slowing down the increase in numbers of foreign workers in the Sultanate.

However, the true turning point in economic policies came concomitantly in Bahrain and Oman in the 1990s, when lower oil prices impacted the states' budgets, and forced the authorities to prepare drastic long-term plans to diversify their revenues and curb growing youth unemployment. The argument this chapter develops is that internal power politics within the ruling elite in Bahrain and Oman largely explain the manner in which these reforms have been implemented. In particular, the focus of this chapter, which is based on the results of a series of personal interviews with local political, economic and social actors in Bahrain and Oman between 2005 and 2010, is the business elite conceived as a key actor in the current social and economic reforms. The key hypothesis to be tested is that the independent variable of the degree of proximity/independence of the business elite vis-à-vis the ruling elite decisively shapes the quality of reform. The private sector's varying power of influence has had a major impact on the direction taken by the economic reforms implemented for the last ten years in a country (Bahrain) where the political elite and the economic elite are distinct and another (Oman) where the bourgeoisie has been directly involved in the decision-making sphere since the 1970s. This choice is supported by the political role played by the business elite in the GCC polities even prior to the influx of oil revenues, and their crucial role in supporting the established socio-political order and shaping political legitimacy subsequently.

After a first section focusing on the state-business relationship in Bahrain and Oman in a comparative perspective, this chapter will present both countries' comprehensive plans since the end of the 1990s to diversify state revenue sources and evolve an alternative model of economic development. Then, following a particular emphasis on the labour market reforms implemented in Bahrain and Oman since the beginning of the 2000s, the business community's comparative desired and actual role in affecting the orientations and outcomes of these reforms will be addressed. Finally, in the wake of the 2011 Arab Spring, this chapter reflects on the roles and attitudes of the business elite towards these events, and their implications for the nature of business politics in both countries.

State-business relationship: a different balance

Prior to the influx of major oil revenues, domestic stability in the monarchies of the Arabian Peninsula was ensured by an arrangement linking rulers and local merchant families, who helped provide the rulers' financial needs, in return receiving political influence and protection of their economic interests. The merchants remained key partners until the surge in oil revenue accruing directly to the rulers from the 1950s. The historic alliance between merchants and rulers was disrupted by the unexpected material sufficiency of the rulers, after oil was discovered. The rulers were thus freed from their economic dependence on the merchants. In one of her most famous books,[4] Jill Crystal explained that the development of oil production in Kuwait and Qatar forced the merchants to renounce their historical claim to participate in decision-making; in exchange, the rulers granted them a large share of the oil revenue. Strong similarities with the Kuwaiti and Qatari situations can be detected in Bahrain, contrary to Oman, where, unlike the other Gulf monarchies, the country is not under the rule of a tribe or a family, but under that of a man, who has constantly shown his determination to keep control of all matters in the country.

Qaboos holds concurrently the positions of chief of staff of the armed forces, Minister of Defence, Minister of Foreign Affairs and chairman of the Central Bank. As Sultan Qaboos has never been able—or willing—to rely on his small family, he has allied with the merchant elites, a practice in keeping with the pre-1970 period. He has assured them of the protection of the political authorities, and privileged access to the oil windfall through public contracts. In return, the merchant families have helped the ruler to finance his nation-building endeavours. Moreover, until the late 1990s the Omani merchants were never "forced to choose money over formal political influence" as in states like Kuwait and Qatar.[5] Thus some of the pre-eminent merchant families' members have been given strategic positions to secure public contracts and control over distribution of the oil wealth.

A former chairman (1987–91) of the Chamber of Commerce, Maqbool al-Sultan, whose family acted as representatives in Oman for the British India shipping line and Lloyds in the first half of the twentieth century, held the post of Minister for Commerce and Industry from 1991 to February 2011. His brother Jamil was vice-president of the Omani Chamber of Commerce and Industry until 2011. The leading al-Sultan family company is WJ Towell, which is involved in more than forty sectors (motors, telecommunications, construction, computer engineering, insurance, etc.) and represents brands like Mars, Unilever, and Nestlé in Oman. Another obvious example of direct participation of business families in the decision-making process is the Zawawi family. Yusuf al-Zawawi, who came to Muscat at the end of the nineteenth century to establish a trading company, became one of the unofficial advisers to Sultan Faisal (r. 1888–1913). Qays al-Zawawi, Yusuf's grandson, held the position of Foreign Minister between 1973 and 1982, then became Deputy Prime Minister for Finance and Economy until his death in 1995. His brother 'Umar, possibly the richest man in Oman after the Sultan, currently holds the position of Special Adviser to the ruler for External Affairs. Economically speaking, the Omar Zawawi Establishment (OMZEST) has become one of the leading Omani holding companies. The Zubayr family also owes a lot of its economic success to its old connections with the Sultans of Muscat. Zubayr al-Hutti acted as Governor of Dhofar in the 1930s and Sultan Sa'id entrusted him with running his real estate projects. Muhammad Zubayr, who helped set up the Omani Chamber of Commerce in 1972 and was its first chairman, was appointed in November 1974 to the post of Minister for Commerce and Industry; he left it in 1982 to become Personal Adviser to the Sultan for Economic Affairs, his current position. Muhammad Zubayr's son, Khalid, is currently on the board of the Chamber of Commerce. The nephew of Muhammad Zubayr, Juma'a bin 'Ali, was Minister for Manpower until 2008.

The oil rent has at the same time profoundly changed the boundaries between politics and the economy, as many ministers whose families were not active in the economy before have become personally rich. This process has not been questioned by the ruler, as it has increased both the elites' loyalty to him and the stability of his rule.[6] The symbolic debts owed by Qaboos at the beginning of his rule to those actors who supported him after 1970 has thus gradually turned into a weapon in his hands, forestalling any challenges to his reign by turning them into unfailing allies. On the eve of the 2011 Arab Spring, few members of the Council of Ministers had not personally derived material profit from the oil rent. One of the most illustrative cases of such tribal notables, who have been active in business thanks to politics, is the noble branch of the Khalili family, heirs to a prestigious lineage of Ibadi imams. Sa'ud al-Khalili, the nephew of a former Imam of Oman (Muhammad al-Khalili, 1920–54), became one of the four members of the very first Cabinet appointed in August 1970. In 1973 he founded the powerful Al Taher business group, which is active in construction contracting (Caterpillar), food and drink (Sprite and Coke) and the distribution of Shell products. His nephew Salim bin Hilal, Minister for Agriculture until 2011, was formerly chairman of the Chamber of Commerce, while another of his nephews, 'Abd al-Malik bin 'Abd Allah—who had previously held successively the positions of executive chairman of the Royal Court Pension Fund, chairman of the first Omani banking group, Bank Muscat, and Minister for Tourism (2011–2012)—is currently Minister of Justice.

The situation in Bahrain, where the sovereignty ministries and the most sensitive ones are monopolized by the Al Khalifa,[7] cannot be compared with that in Oman, where only two members of the Cabinet belong to the Al Sa'id royal family but where businessmen hold prominent decision-making positions.[8] Moreover, the Bahraini business elite, which is mainly composed of Sunni families, either of Najdi background or Hawala,[9] and views itself as a minority, has never been powerful enough to force the ruling family to stay out of business. Thus not only has the Al Khalifa family never been forced to grant a substantial number of decision-making positions to the economic elite, in addition the Al Khalifa themselves have always been substantially involved in business, and the first beneficiaries of the oil rent: "the wealth of the state has been the Al Khalifa's to distribute as largesse to grateful citizens ... Most of the land on the island belongs to the Al Khalifa family and there has been no institutional accountability of the family to the public ... since the suspension of the parliament" in 1975.[10] In the 1990s, Sheikh Khalifa, the Prime Minister, "allegedly became the richest person in Bahrain with extensive holdings in land, hotels, commercial property and profits on government contracts",[11] while it was well known that "you can't get permission for any project without giving a percentage to the Al Khalifas".[12] In 2012 only two members of the business elite held positions in the Cabinet. Jawad al-'Urayyid, a former Minister of State for Cabinet affairs (1973–82), who is the grandson of Mansur al-'Urayyid, a leading pearl merchant in the 1930s, has held the position of Deputy Prime Minister without portfolio since December 2006. Hassan Fakhro, who belongs to a wealthy Hawala merchant family, is currently Minister of Industry and Commerce. His brother 'Isam, chairman of the Fakhro Group,[13] succeeded Khalid Kanoo at the head of the Chamber of Commerce in 2005 and was re-elected its chairman in 2009.

In Bahrain and Oman, the Chamber of Commerce has long been a stronghold of the merchant elite. The first Chamber of Commerce on the southern shore of the Persian Gulf was established in Bahrain in 1939 under the name of "Merchants' Association", "to give a platform for the [larger Bahraini merchants'] complaints and to protect their interests".[14] It continued until 1945 when it officially became the "Bahrain Chamber of Commerce".[15] The Omani Chamber (OCCI) was founded much later—by royal decree in 1972, under the impulse of a group of prominent Omani businessmen led by Muhammad Zubayr,

'Ali al-Sultan and Qays al-Zawawi. If the OCCI, like in Bahrain, has been controlled since its foundation by the merchant elite,[16] it has played a much less substantial role in lobbying for business interests, given the direct political influence this elite has had by controlling Cabinet positions.

To gain a comprehensive perspective on business involvement in politics, it is worth mentioning that there are very few prominent businessmen in the elected Bahraini Majlis al-Nuwwab and Omani Majlis al-Shura. As a senior member of one of the leading Bahraini merchant families frankly admits, "Businessmen are not running for elections because they are afraid of losing. And in such a small country, everybody will be aware of this defeat and it will have very bad effects on the image of the company".[17]

Similarly revealing was the relative absence of any members of Oman's leading merchant families among the candidates for the 2003, 2007 and 2011 Majlis al-Shura elections.[18] This situation in Oman and Bahrain is due to the widespread perception of the proximity between the ruling elite and the merchant families: such candidacies face the risk of being over-invested symbolically by voters and observers, their results being interpreted as a referendum on the authorities' general policies. On the contrary, at least ten prominent businessmen (that is, 25% of the assembly) are members of the Bahraini appointed Majlis al-Shura, including its chairman since 2006, 'Ali al-Salih.[19]

The Bahraini private sector is thus heavily dependent both on the balance of power within the royal family and on its good relations with the most influential individuals among the royal family. In Oman, on the contrary, as a legacy of twentieth century history, Sultan Qaboos has been as dependent on the business elite for the stability of the regime as the merchants have been on the ruler for developing their economic assets.

Economic diversification and labour market reform: a shared necessity

In Oman and Bahrain, the end of the 1990s marked a shift in long-term economic policies, following the fall in oil prices and the resulting fiscal crisis in the states. Both countries embarked on wide-scale programmes of diversification and economic liberalization. In Oman, a long-term programme entitled "Oman 2020: Vision for Oman's Economy" was established in June 1995. One of its main objectives had to do with economic diversification: the oil sector's share in GDP had to fall from 41% in 1996 to 9% by 2020, while that of non-oil industries was to increase from 7.5% to 29%. The Sixth (2001–05) and the Seventh (2006–2010) Five-Year Plans of the Sultanate continued to emphasize the scope of economic diversification, by working simultaneously on three main issues: the development of the gas sector, tourism and non-oil industries. To promote use of gas resources, the Sultanate launched several large-scale industrial projects. The most important is the Sohar industrial port, under development since 1998. On the site, various activities, including a 116,400-barrels-per-day oil refinery and a US$2.3 billion aluminium smelter, scheduled to generate more than 8,000 stable jobs and 30,000 other jobs indirectly in the region, were planned for a total investment of US$12 billion. "Selective quality tourism"—that is, tourism aimed at predominantly wealthy and easily controllable Western elites—has been another priority for diversification. A Ministry for Tourism, the first of its kind in any of the GCC states, was created in June 2004. In November 2004, a decree from the Ministry for Housing authorized non-Omanis to own land or homes in special areas devoted to tourism and established by law. A number of major tourism and real estate projects have been set up, such as The Wave, near Muscat, worth US$800 million, along 7 km of sea shore behind Seeb Airport. The state, in partnership with the Dubai-based al-Futtaim group, launched in May 2005 the first phase of this complex hosting 4,000 residential properties, expected to be completed by 2013.

In addition to gas and tourism, six industrial zones benefiting from exemptions from customs duty have been set up. By making Salalah port the leading element in the south's economic development following the opening of a free zone in 2006, the government signalled its intention to compete with Dubai for container shipping. In Muttrah, Sohar and Khasab, lengthy work has commenced to increase port capacities further, while a deep water port at Duqm, on the Indian Ocean coast, is also under construction. In addition, the plan to widen the state's financial resources explains why several taxes—not only customs duties—have been established since the 1990s. Since 1994 all companies, whether Omani or foreign, pay taxes on profits. Moreover various indirect taxes on citizens, like municipal taxes on restaurants in Muscat and Salalah or on real estate transactions, as well as direct taxes, like a tax on crossing the UAE border, have been set up since the early 2000s. Even total exemption from health care payment for nationals was abandoned, with the introduction of an annual family medical card together with a small fee for each medical consultation.

This diversification policy was supported by a strong desire to promote the private sector, aiming both to attract foreign capital and to support the role of local companies in economic diversification. Oman thus chose to focus on the private sector as "the main contributor of growth" and on disinvestment of the state from various sectors.[20] Based on a May 1996 royal decree that had established the practical modalities for implementing privatization, two privatization laws were promulgated in July 2004, one setting out plans for the responsibilities of the Ministry of Electricity and Water to be divided among several entities, before its dissolution. Another important axis of the Oman privatization process is the telecommunications sector. In March 2002, an enabling law established the Telecommunications Regulation Authority, which was put in charge of competition regulation in the sector, privatization of the sole operator Omantel, the granting of licenses and the implementation of tariffs. Since 1996, foreign investors in Oman have enjoyed exemptions from taxes (for the first five years) and from customs duties (for imports for processing in Oman), and finally the possibility of repatriation of profits. The foreign shareholding allowed in Omani companies was extended in 2001 to 70% in all sectors, and even 100% in banking and insurance since 2003 and in telecommunications since 2005. Thus the government has decided to grant investors much greater latitude of action than before, while only retaining the role of facilitator.

In Bahrain, Hamad's accession to the throne in 1999, upon the death of his father Sheikh 'Isa Al Khalifa (r.1961–99), followed years of civil unrest,[21] which had been triggered by the combination of a deteriorated economic situation after the fall of oil prices in the 1980s and growing frustration at the lack of political opening since 1975. In order to assert his own political basis vis-à-vis the irremovable Prime Minister Sheikh Khalifa bin Salman (in office since 1971), widely viewed as the real "power behind the throne for decades",[22] the new ruler implemented a series of political reforms. In February 2002, Sheikh Hamad promulgated a new constitution by decree and replaced his title of Emir with that of King, as part of a formal re-labelling of the country as a constitutional monarchy. In the economic sector, an Economic Development Board (EDB, Majlis al-Tanmia al-Iqtisadiyya), chaired by his son, Crown

Prince Sheikh Salman, was created in 2001 by royal decree. The EDB was initially conceived as a public think tank, whose board of directors had sixteen members including the Crown Prince, six ministers,[23] the Governor of the Central Bank, seven representatives of the private sector and the chairman of the governmental Bahrain Centre for Studies and Research. In 2004, McKinsey, the American consultancy firm, was commissioned by the Crown Prince to draft a comprehensive long-term economic programme for Bahrain. In May 2005, a royal decree expanded the EDB's authority by hiving off the whole "national economy" element of the Ministry of Finance and National Economy to the EDB. The EDB was thus given the overall responsibility for outlining, proposing and managing the economic reforms for Bahrain in a comprehensive manner—including education, labour, tourism, industry and healthcare.

Following McKinsey's recommendations, its extended mission included: the promotion of private sector growth and investment, by enhancing the incentives for businesses and favouring foreign direct investment; the implementation of a comprehensive labour market reform programme "to address the structural imbalance in the existing labour market [between nationals and expatriates]" and to reduce levels of unemployment amongst Bahrainis; and the diversification of economy away from oil.[24] In October 2008, Vision 2030, a comprehensive economic, social and political long-term plan for Bahrain developed by the EDB, was unveiled by the King. The idea was to develop "a productive, globally competitive economy, shaped by the government and driven by a pioneering private sector", diversified away from a dependency on energy.[25] At the top of the EDB are Western-educated expatriate and Sunni national technocrats in their thirties and forties, chosen by the Crown Prince personally, who often have at best only an abstract understanding of the country, but consider that "[they] are here to stay and [they] are committed to build a better Bahrain",[26] to "ensure that every Bahraini has the means to live a secure and fulfilling life and reach their full potential".[27] As an official benchmark for "good governance" and technocratic efficiency, the EDB, under the Crown Prince's leadership, has been a key component of Hamad's legitimation strategies.

In 2011, hydrocarbons still contributed some 25% to GDP, as well as 70–75% to government revenues. The National Oil and Gas Authority announced in May 2009 a US$20 billion twenty-year plan to bolster the energy sector. Additional fields were to be developed as well as advanced extraction technology used to increase output to 100,000 barrels/day within seven years to reposition Bahrain as an oil exporter. Banking accounts for 25% of Bahraini GNP. This lightly regulated and taxed sector, serving the needs of rich Saudis, makes Bahrain the fifth offshore banking centre in the world. The total contribution of tourism to the Kingdom's economy in 2011 was approximately 6% of GDP, the Formula 1 Grand Prix generating half of the sector's revenue.

The role of real estate sector, as part of Bahrain's diversification strategy, was much more important than in Omani plans. Twelve zones have been specifically designed in Bahrain for tourism development, like mega-projects that are currently under-construction, such as Durrat al-Bahrain (in the south), the Amwaj Islands (near Muharraq) and Northern Town. This has led to an uncontrolled real estate boom which has been serving, in a large part, as a diversification policy by itself, with mega real estate projects being erected on reclaimed lands, like Bahrain Bay (in which the King is a partner) and Bahrain Financial Harbour (in which the Prime Minister is involved). More generally, it induced a huge shift of wealth: prices of property have multiplied by ten since the late 1990s. Much of the Bahrain's prime land was locked up by the royal family until 2010, when speculators were paying top prices to acquire properties for development.

As in Oman, non-oil manufacturing is another targeted sector in Bahrain's economy. Salman Industrial City is a manufacturing and trade zone that has already drawn an investment of US$3.5 billion. Bahrain has also put in place measures to attract manufacturers to the Kingdom. New industries setting up in one of Bahrain's free trade zones can benefit from a series of state-backed incentives, including a ten-year tax holiday, exemption from import duties on raw materials and equipment and, in theory, duty-free access to all GCC markets. Last but not least, the construction of the 40 km causeway linking the Kingdom with Qatar, often delayed and still on hold, was supposed to start in 2011. It is currently scheduled to be completed in 2015 for a total cost of US$5 billion.

Thus, the raft of reforms planned since 2000 in both countries to diversify state revenue sources and promote the private sector's role in the economy has been out of proportion to the policies of the 1980s and the 1990s. However, as we will see, these liberalization policies serving business interests have directly conflicted with simultaneous labour market reforms favouring employment of nationals in the private sector. The outcomes of concomitant policies of privatization and economic liberalization (which mainly benefit already leading actors) and nationalization of private sector jobs (which directly damages these interests) are reliable indicators of the nature of relations between the state and the business elite, and especially of the different role that the business elite has played in shaping the reforms' results.

Reform results shaped by the capacity of influence of the private sector: the example of labour market reform

In a paper on the political consequences of labour migration in Bahrain, Laurence Louër states that "Bahrain is a textbook case of the fostering of state/society conflicts resulting from mass labour migration, … caught between the requirements of an economy driven by cheap labour and the need to create jobs for their citizenry outside of the already saturated public sector".[28] In this perspective, the labour market reform issue is revealing of the private sector's capacity to influence recent trends of reform. In Bahrain and Oman, labour market reforms have been decided on and organized at the top of the regime, since they have been considered as a national challenge by both rulers. At the end of the 1990s Bahrain faced endemic unemployment unofficially estimated at 30% of the national population, while in Oman in 2000, 55% of nationals were less than 20 years old and 50,000 young Omanis left school and university (with or without degrees) every year to enter the labour market.

As early as 1995 the Oman 2020 long-term economic roadmap focused on human resources and employment. It was planned to raise the rates of nationals in the public and private sectors from 68 to 95% and from 7.5 to 75% respectively, while the share of expatriates in the whole population would be reduced from 25% in 1995 to 15% by 2020. A Ministry of Manpower was set up in 2001, by amalgamating the Ministry of Labour with the one for Social Affairs and Vocational Training. The Sixth Five-Year Plan (2001–05) estimated that 92% of the 110,000 new jobs available between 2001 and 2005 would be in the private sector. The Plan provided for total Omanization over five years in twenty-four low-skilled occupations. In February 2003, a Five-Year Plan for Omanization (2003–07) was drawn up which defined ambitious Omanization rates to be achieved for each economic sector in

2007. The Labour Law, issued by royal decree in April 2003, illustrates these priorities. According to its rules, the employer gets a permit from the Ministry of Manpower to bring in foreign workers only if there are not enough Omanis available for the post on the job market and if the company has complied with the prescribed percentage of Omanization in its sector (Art. 18).[29] Once the permit is granted, to take up the position, a non-Omani can obtain a labour card delivered by the Ministry (for a duration decided by the Ministry) on condition that the worker has the professional skills or the qualifications needed by the position and the prescribed labour card fees have been paid by the company (Art. 18 and 19). Moreover, nationals enjoy a set of benefits expatriates do not, including a minimum wage (raised by 43% to 200 Omani rials [OR][30] per month in February 2011 for full-time unskilled jobs), a monthly allowance (OR150) for job seekers registered at the Ministry for Manpower (introduced in 2011), and strict protection against dismissal. And an employer can terminate the contract of an Omani only during the three-month probation period or if the employee absents himself or herself from work for more than seven consecutive days, or in case of a major mistake.

As for immigration, the turning point in official policy, which took place in 2000, can be understood in the same perspective. The government set limits to the issuing of Omani documents to Omanis who lived in Africa, as they were thought likely to compete with young home Omani job-seekers. Measures to catch illegal immigrants were also tightened, as demonstrated by strengthened police checks on the coasts to intercept illegal migrants crossing the Gulf of Oman.

Thus, the challenge of employing young Omanis led to a national mobilization driven from above. By comparison with similar policies in neighbouring countries, the Sultanate can be proud of some successes. In December 2010 the civil service sector showed an average Omanization rate of 85.6%, stable for the last three years. Moreover, 91% of employees in the private banking sector were Omani in late 2010. In the private sector in general, the number of active expatriates stabilized progressively while the rate of nationals increased to 19% by the end of 2005.

However, this was not enough to hide structural difficulties experienced by the policy. In 2005, civil servants of the Ministry for Manpower spoke privately of 300,000 job seekers[31]—an unemployment rate around 25%. Moreover many employers compared Omanization to a "tax on business". A former senior state official who had joined the private sector summarized the situation with explicit words: "Never will a government be able to force companies to prefer badly-trained Omanis to experienced Indians, with a salary three to five times lower".[32]

Since 2006, the authorities have decided that Omanization does not boil down any more to a post-for-post substitution of expatriate manpower with Omanis, but is rather a question of comparative skills and added-value of local and expatriate workforces, as a small business owner, who was then a member of the Majlis al-Shura, noted in 2005: "Three or four years ago, the government pushed the private sector to hire Omanis. It looked like forcing. With time, the government analysed that what was done was wrong … Omanization is not a replacement process. It is necessary to ask instead how to appoint more Omanis! We will always need expatriates".[33]

The fact that most cabinet members have been involved directly or indirectly in business explains why the quota-based labour market policy could not be maintained as such in the long term. The major Omani business families, who control the Chamber of Commerce and are represented in the Cabinet, were well positioned to express their disagreement with the previous labour market policy to the ruler—and thus to advocate changes in long-term policy. Since 2005–6, the Omani authorities have focused on economic liberalization, by giving prominence to a stronger role for private (national and foreign) capital, even if it means the emergence of lasting inflation and acceptance of a pause in the Omanization policy in employment. For instance, the new tax system, which came into force in January 2010, cancelled the distinction between local and foreign companies, by establishing a fixed tax rate on profits of 12% for all companies, both foreign and local, after an initial tax-free exemption of OR30,000 of profits.[34] Even if this measure could lead to strengthening of their foreign competitors, Anwar al-Sultan, a director of the WJ Towell Group and the Minister for Commerce's brother, explained his satisfaction with it: "The new corporate tax law … is meant to spur foreign investment into the country. The more foreign investment that comes to the Sultanate, the more advantages it will bring for Omanis in terms of jobs and to the country as a whole".[35]

The effects quickly materialized, with foreign investment flows doubling between 2005 and 2007, from US$1.5 billion in 2005 (5.9% of GDP) to more than US$3.1 billion in 2007, amounting to 25% of gross fixed capital formation in 2007.[36] Moreover, in January 2006 Oman signed a bilateral free trade agreement with the United States which came into force in January 2009; many services are excluded from it, in order to preserve the local network of small and medium-sized enterprises, while the Omanization requirements are still valid, even in the sectors concerned by the agreement.

As a consequence of this 2005–6 strategic U-turn, the Omanization rate in the private sector plummeted from 18.8% at the end of 2005 to 12% in September 2012—by far the worst rate since 2003. This can be explained by the fact that the number of active expatriates has tripled since the end of 2005 (reaching 1,271,120 in September 2012). From this viewpoint, the Omanization "national challenge" goes far beyond the employment issue and calls into question the whole economic structure on which Oman has relied for forty years. Most of the decision-making elite are directly involved in business and must avoid questions being asked about the conflict of interest between the nation's general interests they have been supposed to promote (like the Omanization policy) and the particular interests they have defended as businessmen. The priority granted since 2005 to the private sector and to investment in major projects, like Sohar port and tourism infrastructure, to the detriment of openly claimed objectives like Omanization in employment and control of immigration of workers, clearly indicates on which side the balance has been tilting for several years now.

A further illustration of this shift in priority among the elite has been the growing involvement of royal family members in business. Until recently, while Qaboos himself and some of his closest relatives have played a role in the Omani economy, this was almost solely through indirect participation in other companies. Only a handful of Qaboos' relatives occupied a visible role in the private sector. Historically the most active of the Al Sa'id family directly involved in business has been the ruler's paternal uncle, Sayyid Shabib, who has held the position of Special Adviser to the Sultan for Environmental Affairs since 1991. In 1982 he created the Tawoos Group and set up one of the leading Omani business groups, involved in various sectors ranging from agriculture, telephones and services to leisure, and concluding contracts with Petroleum Development Oman, the Diwan of the Royal Court and the Ministries of Defence and Oil. Another rare example is Qaboos' maternal uncle Sheikh Mustahil al-Ma'ashani, a former Minister of Labour and

Social Affairs in the late 1980s. Since its creation in 1974, he has chaired Muscat Overseas Holding, which is probably the most active business group in Dhofar, especially in agriculture, banking and real estate sectors. One of his sons, Salim, a former chairman of Nawras telecommunications private company, now holds the post of Adviser to the Diwan of the Royal Court with ministerial rank. Another of Mustahil's sons, Khalid, is chairman of the first Omani banking group, Bank Muscat.

For several years now, a series of Qaboos' relatives who were previously not involved in the private sector have built and consolidated positions in business, the most prominent of them being the ruler's first cousin and potential successor, Sayyid Haytham. He is the main shareholder of the National Trading Co., which had remained discreet until recently.[37] The group, which has acquired a disproportionate visibility as a holding company for investment and project development, has been involved in the construction of two major power plants (Manah and Sohar) and is an agent in Oman for several multinational companies including Alstom and Thyssenkrupp. Sayyid Haytham is also involved in a number of other prominent companies (such as OHI, representative in Oman of Alcatel or UPS) and projects, in particular the mega tourism-devoted new venture, Blue City, worth US$20 billion, in which he shares a 30% stake with another investor. Situated between Sohar and Muscat, and covering 35 km^2, this project was supposed to accommodate 200,000 residents in 2020, but suffered heavily from the 2008 regional real estate crisis. His elder brother As'ad, who has held the position of personal representative of the Sultan since 2003, has also been active in business, as head of the board of trustees of Oman's first private university (the University of Nizwa). While he was involved in different aborted projects,[38] his son Taymur, who is married to Mustahil al-Ma'ashani's daughter Salma, was director of the fourth Omani bank, Bank Dhofar.

The new expansion of the ruling family members into business is a further illustration of the choice made by the political elite to privilege economic liberalization and an increasing role of the private sector over the official "national priority" of Omanization—and of their capacity to privilege their direct interests, due to their direct involvement in top decision-making circles.

In Bahrain too, the labour market reform has been thought out at the highest level, as a key element of the new King's strategy of legitimization. In September 2004, the Crown Prince and the EDB held a workshop on labour market issues based on the study carried out by McKinsey. The key idea was that, over the following decade, employment must be found for 100,000 new job market entrants, corresponding to almost 92% of the existing local workforce. Until then, the government's policy was focused, like in Oman, on the nationalization of employment (Bahrainization) by increasing the percentage of nationals to be employed by branch. The philosophy of the reform proposed by McKinsey was to deregulate and liberalize the job market and redress the imbalance between the local and the cheap expatriate workforce in order to address the structural causes of unemployment among nationals.[39] It included the gradual phasing out of existing Bahrainization quotas, allowing easier termination procedures of Bahraini employees and replacing them with a fee-based system under which employers pay a BD75 monthly fee per expatriate worker and a BD600 visa issuance and renewal fee per worker for each two-year period, in order to bring the cost of local and expatriate labour force closer to each other. In order to implement this reform, which came into force on 1 July 2008, the Labour Market Regulation Authority (LMRA) was created by law in May 2006. This government body with a corporate identity, under the authority of a board of directors chaired by the Minister of Labour, was endowed with full financial and administrative independence. Another new body, Tamkeen (Labour Fund), was created in 2007 to collect the fees paid by the companies employing foreign workers, 20% of the proceeds going towards the government budget while 80% is invested in training and qualification programmes for the national workforce and the provision of consultative and financial services to private companies in order to increase Bahrainis' productivity.

In an IT businessman's words, "With this reform, the Crown Prince opened a wide battle front. The Prime Minister moved quickly. While they usually never talk against the government, he encouraged the Chamber of Commerce and the leading contractors to speak up to create cracks in the reform."[40]

The business community, led by the Chamber of Commerce (BCCI), pushed for a cut to the fees; an agreement was finally reached in 2007 on a payment of BD10 per month per expatriate plus a BD200 visa renewing fee for each two-year period. A number of businessmen criticized this reform, as 'Adil Fakhro, from the Fakhro Group, explains:

"There isn't Bahraini labour available, the unemployed have no skills, so if you begin to force labour charges and fees on the private sector to make foreign labour more expensive, then the next question is where is the Bahraini? Even jobs like drivers, you can't get them … Education, training and the labour market reforms must go hand in hand".[41]

The private sector spared no effort to make its voice heard by the EDB and the LMRA—not only through informal channels and lobbying to the King and the Prime Minister, but also by repeated public demonstrations outside the LMRA building and the Parliament to pressure the authorities and attract the support of the representatives. One of the most repeated grievances concerned the use of the money by the Labour Fund, as one small business owner in a forum organized by Tamkeen explains:[42] "All you do is take our money and say you are doing plans and then nothing happens. We don't want anything from you, just stop taking our money and leave us alone".

In March 2009, in a demonstration by small business owners, various placard-drawings represented the LMRA laughing while taking money from families of employers crying tears of blood.[43] Among those most targeted by this lobbying has been the Prime Minister, from whom the private sector rightly expects a sympathetic hearing. In April 2010, the BCCI announced that a letter was to be sent to the Prime Minister to ask for his intervention, while a proposal by the Council of Representatives to the Cabinet demanded an immediate one-year suspension of the LMRA fees.[44]

Contrary to Oman, where the business elite has direct control over a series of decision-making levers, the Bahrain private sector has to adapt and respond to the evolution of the balance of power among the Al Khalifas. In this perspective, the shaping of the labour market reform is a superb illustration of the power struggle within the ruling family, between what a lot of observers labelled as the "old guard", surrounding the Prime Minister and his supporters among the ministers, and the new generation of technocrats led by the Crown Prince and the EDB. This discrepancy of views within the ruling family surfaced in January 2008 in the shape of an open letter the Crown Prince wrote to the King, in which he reckoned that the "persisting disharmony and lack of cooperation between the EDB and certain government bodies are no longer acceptable" and complained that "the EDB's endeavours … have often been thwarted … by the [Cabinet's] status quo".[45] The King arbitrated without ambiguity in favour of consolidating the influence of his son, by issuing a public statement ordering the Cabinet to follow the directives of the EDB, adding that any minister who failed to comply would be dismissed.[46] Also, a new law was introduced that increased the number of ministers on the board of the EDB from six to sixteen—changing the EDB into a second "shadow" Cabinet. As the Crown Prince explained, "Our task is to make sure that the government delivers faster by eliminating bureaucratic steps within the Cabinet. Expanding the board makes this easier. We do not need to discuss things twice. We do it just once and pass it along for approval [by the King]".[47]

After 2008, the EDB was almost granted decisional independence, being accountable neither to the Cabinet nor to the Parliament. The private sector was forced to adapt to this changing balance of power. Members of merchant families founded in 2006 the Bahrain Family Business Association, the first of its kind in the Gulf, to facilitate the resolution of various inherent problems faced by family businesses, but also to create a unified spokesperson for merchant families. It has been chaired since its beginning by Khalid Kanoo. Moreover, the Chamber of Commerce has launched a series of initiatives to increase the role of small and medium companies (SMEs) and take their interests into account. Not only was an SME committee created in 2009 to focus on their particular needs, two service centres were also launched to assist them in promoting their export activities and increasing their international competitiveness.[48] This new trend obviously aimed at changing the widespread perception of the BCCI as the traditional representative of the leading business groups and attracting the SMEs' support for the BCCI, in order to increase its capacity of negotiation and influence vis-à-vis the ruling family (and the Crown Prince in particular).[49] For the 2010 Council of Representatives elections, the BCCI decided to logistically support several candidates either with connections to the private sector and/or ready to defend its interests, in order to have a stronger influence within the Chamber.[50] This has not happened in Oman, where the business elite is powerful enough to protect and assert its interests directly at the executive level, and thus does not need the Consultative Council.

As a further step towards the liberalization of the job market, Bahrain adopted in May 2009 a law (decree 79/2009), which came into effect on 1 August 2009, reforming the sponsorship system for residence and employment in Bahrain. This new system allows foreign workers, except domestic workers, to switch jobs simply by informing their existing employers of their intention to end the contract. Contrary to what was initially proclaimed by the government,[51] the aim was not to abolish the sponsorship (*kefala*) system: the LMRA is now the official sponsor of foreign workers, being responsible for issuing two-year work visas once an employment contract has been signed. Understandably this move raised strong concern among the private sector, and especially the Chamber of Commerce. As well as the General Federation of Trade Unions, it was officially consulted and some of its suggestions accepted, such as the three-month notice by an employee before switching jobs and the possibility for an employer to terminate a member of staff's contract and deport him with a month's notice. The BCCI wanted the period before an employee can leave a company to be extended to six months,[52] but this was rejected. Again this was an illustration of the merchant elite's limited capacity of influence in Bahrain by comparison with its counterpart in Oman, where the business elite hold decisional Cabinet positions.

Furthermore, the established Bahraini business families, who control the Chamber of Commerce, have not been powerful enough to oppose, as in Oman, the emergence of new economic actors. The most prominent of these very influential business actors was 'Isam Jinahi, the chairman of Gulf Finance House (GFH), Bahrain's leading Islamic bank, which has been involved in projects with an aggregate value of over US$20 billion across the Arab world. 'Isam Jinahi, a company clerk in the mid-1990s, was involved in several major real estate and infrastructure projects in Bahrain over ten years, such as Bahrain Financial Harbour, the US$1.5 billion financial city on the Manama Corniche (in partnership with the Prime Minister).[53] Another example of these new Bahraini business actors is Khalid 'Abd al-Rahim, the chairman of the leading Bahraini building and civil engineering company, Cebarco, founded in 1992. During the last ten years, Cebarco has been awarded the completion of some of the most prestigious projects such as the Bahrain Formula 1 racing circuit (with the Crown Prince's support) and the King Hamad Highway.

Until the 2011 Arab Spring, for more than two years after the implementation of the labour fees reform, the private sector's opposition to the LMRA was strong in Bahrain. Such a situation, leading to public demonstrations by businessmen and trade unions, recurrent appeals to members of Parliament and leading figures of the royal family, and tight negotiations on the concrete implementation of the legislation, was not conceivable in Oman. A decisive factor which helps explain this difference relates to the nature of the state-business relationship. In Oman, the Sultan has never been able to prevent the merchant families from taking political positions and actively participating in (not to say determining) decisions on economic policy. At no time has the business elite needed (and wished) to mobilize publicly for their interests, partly because it would have risked drawing public attention to the incestuous relationship between business and politics in Oman. From this point of view, rather than encouraging an economic mobility that would put into question the established authoritarian order and contribute to a renewal, or at least a revitalization, of the socio-economic fabric, economic reforms in Oman have done nothing but to confirm the hierarchy of established social and economic positions. In Bahrain, the elite-driven reform, managed by a technocratic and unaccountable body (EDB), has shown that the latitude of action of the prominent business families and their arm (the Chamber of Commerce) is much more restrained. Not only do the Al Khalifa monopolize decision-making positions, the merchants have never been able to prevent the ruling family from developing their economic assets. Even more, they are not immune to the emergence of competitors, like nouveaux riches who have benefited from new diversifications policies, with the patronage of the Al Khalifas.

The Arab Spring and its aftermath: the revenge of vested interests?

In 2011, Bahrain and Oman experienced their widest popular protests since the 1970s. Obviously a variety of views and demands were represented. In Bahrain, while "the bulk of the protesters belonged to the majority Shi'i population, their demands were not sectarian or religious".[54] The vast majority were calling for the ousting of the incumbent Prime Minister Khalifa, and for the establishment of a constitutional monarchy with a parliament holding legislative power and a government accountable to it. But it is important to stress that social and economic demands were also at the top of the demonstrations' agenda in both countries, revolving around job opportunities, proactive measures to curb rising inequalities, and action against corruption among top officials. Socio-economic reforms implemented by the Bahraini EDB have not had the expected effects. Official figures cannot hide endemic unemployment among the Shi'i youth. The reforms have not stopped widespread discrimination in access to public housing, or addressed the poor quality of infrastructure in Shi'i villages, not to mention structural corruption in awarding public contracts and reclaimed lands, the main beneficiaries of which have been the King, the Prime Minister and the Crown Prince. In Oman, the limited results of the Omanization policies, favouring nationals for private sector jobs, and the slowness of the process of diversifying sources of revenue are illustrated by dramatic social inequalities and endemic unemployment and poverty.[55] Estimates show a persistent unemployment level among nationals between 15 and 20%, and certainly above 25% among 18–24 year olds. These figures leave unacknowledged what is probably a considerable rate of underemployment, particularly in rural areas.

In an attempt to manipulate the movement and to pull the rug from under its feet, the Omani and Bahraini regimes initially implemented arbitrary gestures of goodwill. In Bahrain, two days before the gathering announced by the "February 14 Youth", King Hamad decided to grant 1,000 Bahraini dinars to each family. In Oman, Sultan Qaboos ordered an increase in the minimum salary by 43% in mid-February; this preceded the establishment of a monthly allowance for individuals registered as job seekers, the announcement of the creation of 50,000 new public sector jobs in late February, and two reshuffles of the Cabinet in February and March 2011. These long-practiced techniques of using the oil rent to buy off the opposition proved to be unsuccessful, however. In Manama, tens of thousands of protestors converged upon the Pearl Roundabout on the scheduled day. Crown Prince Salman, who has embodied the reformist side of the royal family under his father's rule, was entrusted by the latter with engaging in a dialogue with representatives of the legal opposition. However, fear changed sides in March 2011 and the regimes began to sense a distinct possibility that they might lose control of the population. After the military intervention of the joint GCC force (Peninsula Shield) on 14 March, it became clear that repression remained the preferred regime strategy to choke off dissenting voices. More than eighty people have died in clashes between protestors and the security forces so far in Bahrain, and the state of emergency law was re-enacted between 15 March and 1 June 2011. As a final crackdown on opposition leaders, the heads of unlicensed societies, who had issued a joint statement on 7 March calling for a "republican system", as well as other non-violent opposition figures were sentenced to life imprisonment for their alleged role in "plotting to topple the regime". In Oman, two protestors died in clashes with the police in the northern town of Sohar in February and April 2011; several hundred protestors were arrested all around the country.

If anything, the 2011 protests in Bahrain and Oman reveal yet again an economic resistance to change, that is, the business elites' inclination to privilege the political status quo over any kind of reform debate, and the extent to which the interests of the main business actors are intrinsically linked to those of authoritarian rule. The business elite, accused of corruption, unwarranted privileges and political and economic opposition to change in both countries, has been one of the main targets of the protestors. From this perspective, it is not insignificant that early attempts by the Omani ruler to show his supposed benevolence towards the protestors led to an extensive reshuffle of the cabinet in March 2011, with the removal of long-serving ministers widely perceived as embodying a conflict of interest between business and politics (such as Ahmed Makki, the Minister for National Economy; and Maqbool al-Sultan, the Minister for Commerce and Industry). The fact that demonstrations were particularly active in the town of Sohar, conceived as the international showcase of the economic liberalization of the country, is highly symbolic too. The transformation of Sohar within a few years from a small sleepy provincial town into the industrial capital of the country led to a disruption of social structures. This badly-digested economic boom benefited above all a handful of local notables, who have taken advantage of the dramatic rise in land prices, as well as the top Omani business groups (OMZEST, National Trading Co., Zubayr, WJ Towell, Bahwan, etc. in partnership with foreign investors) already embedded in the heart of the political-economic decision process—while the majority of the local population had no access to the fruits of economic development, and experienced stagnation or diminution of their living standards, due to inflation. The dismantling of the Ministry of National Economy in March 2011, the announcement of social and economic measures (such as the creation of public sector jobs for nationals and sharp increase in public benefits or salaries in the public and private sectors) that openly contradict the liberalization policies implemented for a decade illustrate the dilemma facing the Omani leadership. The fundamental question regarding the regime's future relates to the political-economic conflict of interest at the top levels in the country: the fact that the business elite is in charge of economic policies, which the 2011 Cabinet reshuffles did not end. While this elite has held the levers of power since 1970 and has predominantly benefited from the oil rent, this oligarchic pact has become unacceptable for a new generation who are calling into question the whole economic structure on which authoritarian Oman has relied under Qaboos.

In Bahrain, except for some isolated cases like Faisal Jawad, who sympathized with the protestors,[56] business actors have constantly reasserted their proximity to the regime and the necessity to preserve the stability of the country—an allusion to the protestors, considered as troublemakers. In a statement on 11 May 2011 referring to the Peninsula Shield Force military intervention, the Chamber of Commerce explained that "due to the timely measures taken by the leadership and the support of neighbouring GCC countries to ensure security and stability in the country, the [national] economy is back on track".[57] A few days earlier, it had called on "all business enterprises and owners in Bahrain" for a complete boycott of trade with Iran to protest against Tehran's alleged fuelling of unrest in Bahrain.[58]

Moreover, the massive crackdown that followed the protests in 2011 has once again changed the balance within the ruling family, and proved successful in marginalizing the less uncompromising component of the Al Khalifas, surrounding the Crown Prince and the EDB, in favour of the Prime Minister and his supporters, first among whom are the Chamber of Commerce and the business elite. In order to reduce the impact of the crisis on the private sector, the Cabinet ordered in April 2011 a six-month freeze on the fees on foreign workers levied by the LMRA, and later extended the suspension until 31 December 2012. This measure, which probably marks the death of the EDB-led technocratic plan by robbing the labour market reform of its substance, was highly praised by the BCCI. On several occasions since April 2011, its chairman reasserted the business elite's support for the Prime Minister's economic decisions. In March 2012, he wished the latter "every success in carrying on the nation-building march" and affirmed that the Prime Minister's "stances in support of the private sector have always been a source of pride for BCCI and the … business community",[59] an implicit reference to the hated policy pursued by the EDB.

Thus, if the Bahraini private sector has turned out to be one of the key beneficiaries of the marginalization of the Crown Prince since March 2011, there is no doubt that its lobbying for the reversal of EDB policies has only had a limited impact on this evolution. Both the EDB-led reforms until 2011 and the new balance of power among the Al Khalifas since then have confirmed that economic decisions are still made by the royal family. Contrary to Oman, where the ruler cannot rely on his small family and has allied with the merchant elite, which has been given political positions to secure public contracts and determine long-term economic policies, the condition for business families to remain the privileged interlocutor of the political elite requires adapting their strategies according to the balance of power among the Al Khalifas, on whom they remain heavily dependent. The Bahraini business sector has to press for its interests by making use of the divisions within the ruling family in a much more tactical and noisier way than is the case in Oman, where the 2011 protests and the widespread social frustration have not yet put an end to the direct interference of the bourgeoisie in the decision-making process.

3

PRIVATE SECTOR ACTORS IN THE UAE AND THEIR ROLE IN THE PROCESS OF ECONOMIC AND POLITICAL REFORM

Khalid Almezaini

This chapter aims to examine the main actors in the private sector in today's United Arab Emirates, their relationship to political elites and their role in the process of economic and political reform. In particular, it seeks to answer the following three questions: (1) how can the structure of the private sector in the UAE be explained?; (2) who are the main actors in the private sector?; and (3) what is their role in the economic and political reform process?

The vast influx of oil revenues since the 1970s has had a significant impact on the political and economic infrastructure of the UAE, as it substantially altered the dynamics between the private sector and the state. Prior to the discovery of oil in the 1960s, the private sector had been the predominant contributor to GDP and had therefore exerted great influence on the politics of the Coast of Oman.[1] Trade, agriculture and the pearling industry were the three main components of the private sector. In contrast, the political authorities at that time played a minimal role, providing security and collecting tax revenue from businesses. However, with the discovery of oil and the formation of the Emirates in

1971, oil revenues fundamentally transformed the structure of the state and its institutions, and as a consequence the private sector was weakened and became greatly dependent on the government.

This paper argues that certain actors in the private sector—merchant elite individuals and families—were able to link their wide-ranging economic, political and social interests with those of members of the ruling families, as well as with general government interests. However, there were relatively few families capable of playing this role. Through their historically close social relations with the political elites, families such as the al-Muhairi, al-Rumaithi, al-Qubaisi, al-Dhaheri, Bin Hamoodah, al-Suwaidi, al-Otaiba, al-Mulla Bin Harib, al-Tayar, al-Habtoor, al-Fahim, al-Futtaim and others managed to gain access to oil revenue in the post-1971 period. By maintaining their historical relations with the political elites, they were favoured by the ruling families over other less prominent tribes and families that had little contact with ruling families.

In addition, the current merchant elites who emerged after 1971, and some from the pre-1971 era, were also able to build up their wealth through their social relations with the ruling families and their ability to reach members of those families. This was done through social connections, or *wasta*, which has been one of the main keys to their wealth. This is similar to the case of Qatar and Kuwait. In analyzing these two cases, Crystal argues that "in time this arrangement was institutionalized through protective nationality and commercial laws which restricted property and business ownership rights to nationals. The primary beneficiaries were the old trading families".[2]

The interrelations between merchant elites and ruling families did not result in any demands for economic or political change. In fact, merchants were more concerned with their own economic interests, and their limited political interests were focused solely on the condition that ruling families should use their "political power" to stop foreign merchants from competing in the private sector. In return, members of the ruling families would be involved by the merchant families in the running and managing of their businesses.

The current structure of the private sector in the UAE is a result of a historical interaction between local merchant elites, foreign merchants, political authorities, and the increase in oil prices during the early 1970s that led to the dominance of the state over the private sector. While local merchant elites in the pre-oil era had been major actors in the economy, foreign merchants had also contributed to the survival of the private sector before 1971.

In the past forty years or so, the UAE has transformed its economy from being dependent on a single commodity to being highly global and diversified. This transformation has resulted from the engagement of different major merchants in the diversification process in the private sector. Following the decline in oil revenue during the 1980s, the UAE embarked on a process of economic diversification and liberalization that facilitated foreign direct investment. Over this period, the share of the private sector in the UAE's GDP increased significantly from around 15% during the 1970s, in nominal terms,[3] to over 50% until the first quarter of 2012.[4] Led by Abu Dhabi and Dubai, the UAE's non-oil sector contributed 71% of total GDP in 2009,[5] and even though oil prices dropped in November 2008 to $50 per barrel, the UAE continued to sustain its economic growth. However, despite these economic changes, the dynamics of the political structure of the UAE have remained authoritarian. This emphasizes how economic development and liberalization have enhanced the survival of the rentier structure.

Rentierism continues to enhance the authorities' legitimacy. The UAE government traditionally offered material rewards to those who supported the ruling families, including merchants' families. Loyal supporters received direct income, land and privileges.[6] At present, as the population continues to increase, the state continues simultaneously to grant privileges to the population by increasing salaries to get further loyalty and avoid any domestic threats. Thus, the formula is simple: the more the state increases people's income, the greater is the legitimacy conferred on it by its people. This legitimacy, gained through economic performance, has enabled the state to gain the confidence of its people. During the so-called Arab Spring in 2011, the UAE government increased public salaries up to 70% and provided further material privileges to citizens. This indicates that buying off loyalty through economic means remains a prominent tool in the relations between the regime and its people. Consequently, most tribes in the UAE declared in the media their strong support for and loyalty to the regime.

The chapter will focus on some of the major Emirati families against this analytical background. It will mainly focus on families from the three main emirates—Abu Dhabi, Dubai and Sharjah—and is divided into three main sections that will elaborate the argument above. First, it will discuss the historical relationships of the merchant and ruling elites, focusing on specific families from each emirate. Second, it will look at the structure of the private sector in order to understand the positions of merchant elites and ruling families within this sector. Third, it will investigate some of the main merchant families in the private sector from each emirate, and analyze the extent to which they have or have not had any role in the process of economic and political reform in the UAE.

Historical relations between merchants and ruling families in the UAE

Well before the discovery of oil, the relationship between merchant elites and ruling families had been fairly strong, the former exerting more power than the latter. This was due to the economic weight of merchants in the UAE before the discovery of oil. Their financial influence originated from their dominance in the pearling industry and trade in general. This gave them political clout, leading ruling families to establish strong relations with them. However, as Abu-Baker argues, "the political power of this class [merchants] though limited, by no means challenged the authority of the ruler".[7] The merchants were local Arabs, Persians and people from the Indian sub-continent.[8]

The pre-oil era is considered pivotal to understanding the existing strong relationships between merchants and ruling families, that have developed from being simply economically focused to a much more complex relationship, that encompasses all aspects of state-society relations. Merchants provided the necessary financial means for rulers, not only because of their duties as members of the society, but also in order to maintain their relations with rulers. Herb explains that before oil, the relationship between the rulers and the merchants had the character of a protection racket: merchants subsidized the rulers, and the rulers in turn protected the merchants' trade.[9] While the merchants had little to do with members of the ruling families in political matters, owing to the independence of economic institutions at that time, members of some of the ruling families, such as Al Maktoum and al-Qasimi, worked as silent business partners with certain merchants.[10] Some of the merchant families of Arab background were already allied to ruling families, such as the al-Otaiba, al-Za'abi, al-Mansouri, and al-Qubaisi (a close ally of Al Nahyan), which furthered the economic interests of both families.

The ruling families had the power to tax these merchants, and taxes collected from pearling businesses constituted a major source of income for the rulers, who relied on it to a great extent. This, according to Abu-Baker, was used as a financial subvention to the tribal elites[11] who provided the political support that enabled the Sheikhs to control their communities, including the merchants and their divers.[12] This is confirmed by Muhammad M. Abdullah who states that the pearl trade enabled merchants to occupy a central political position,[13] due to the taxes paid to rulers. Abu-Baker also comments that "the source of the merchants' political power was their economic power, and over the decades it was routinized in social institutions that highly differentiated between participants in these economic activities".[14]

In addition, members of ruling families paid much attention to merchant families which owned the means of production (mainly trading and fishing boats, as well as all related equipment). Most prominent merchants, among them the al-Otaiba, al-Tajar, al-Mulla, al-Habtoor, al-Ghurair, al-Qumzi, and al-Rumaithi, were involved mainly in trade and pearling, which required only fishing boats. Such boats could be regarded as a means of production since they were the source for generating both income and food. Thus the owners of boats (merchants) were the bourgeoisie of the Trucial States, and they have remained so until the present. They succeeded in involving ruling family members, linking their interests with their own, and developing strong relationships in the process. Even after the decline of the pearling industry, some merchants, such as the al-Otaiba, al-Qubaisi and al-Rumaithi, remained closely connected with members of ruling families, through intermarriage, business cooperation and political support.

There were a number of factors that caused a decline in the role of merchants both in paying taxes and in internal politics. Ragaei El Mallakh identifies three main reasons: first, the Japanese introduced a new "cultured" pearl, which was much cheaper than those produced in the Trucial States; secondly, the worldwide depression during the 1930s resulted in the loss of luxury markets; and thirdly, the demand for Trucial Coast pearls was reduced by the Second World War and the consequent loss of their large American and European markets.[15] All this upset the relationship between merchants and ruling families. Despite the lack of economic resources, some merchants remained closely related to the ruling families through intermarriage. However, some others became involved in the Reform Movement during the 1930s, asking for local elections. As Abu Baker explains, the political reform movements were centred in the most important commercial areas of the Gulf—Kuwait, Dubai and Bahrain. Interestingly, he notes:

> the reform movements occurred in 1938, i.e., after the decline of the pearling industry … and the World Depression in 1929. The figures indicate that the revenue from pearls reached its rock bottom around the time of these Reform Movements. In other words, the movement of the merchants was not an indicator of their historical role, nor their penchant to political reform, nor their political prowess; and if it were all of these, it should have occurred between 1903 and 1913 when they were at their zenith.[16]

This indicates that the demand for political reform did not surface until the merchants had suffered a decline in their income.[17]

In contrast to the above-mentioned Arab merchants, the impact of the decline in the pearling industry on foreign merchants,[18] particularly those of Persian origin, was limited, owing to their experience in trade and their well-established trading businesses in their home countries. Merchant families of Persian background such as the al-Khoori and Abdul-Rahim Bin Ibrahim (known as Galadari) remained relatively strong. These merchants, and many others, were based mainly in Dubai where pearling was only one of their principal trading businesses. Many, such as Abdul-Rahim Bin Ibrahim and his brother Abdul-Latif, were also successful gold merchants. Experience and a good education helped them overcome the economic failures of the 1930s and 1940s. Later, many foreign merchant families, who subsequently became Emirati citizens, were close allies of the ruling families and well-trusted members of the business elites. This is due to their wealth and support of ruling families in the pre-1971 era. These families include the Galadari and al-Khoori of Abu Dhabi, the al-Khoori and al-Ansari of Dubai, and the al-Fardan of Sharjah.[19]

The post-1971 period was a new era in relations between merchants and ruling families, and those who had maintained relations with the ruling families, despite the decline of the pearling industry, were favoured over others. Oil revenue had now begun to flow into the various Emirates, but the distribution and organization of this wealth created major concerns for the ruling families. They therefore sought to employ some of the merchant elites, and those who had historically been allied to the ruling families began to occupy important positions in a variety of government departments (see Table 1) as the oil income flooded into the newly-established state, the UAE.[20] The ruling families of all seven of the Emirates began distributing this wealth, but closely-related (and intermarried) merchants, such as the al-Suwaidi, al-Qubaisi, al-Rumaithi, al-Otaiba and Al-Zaabi, were more favoured than other lesser-known houses. Most of the merchants have held a number of posts with different governmental and quasi-governmental entities. Although it is clear that tribal and Arab merchants profited more from the post-1971 era than non-Arab ones, some selected Persian merchants remained closely connected to rulers, mainly in Dubai, and therefore benefited from this era.

Table 1: Some of the Social/Merchants elites and their current positions in 2009.[21]

Name	*Position*	*Background*
Abdul Aziz Abdullah al-Ghurair	Speaker of the Federal National Council	From merchant family
Amer Abdul Jalili al-Fahim (Persian origins)	Member in the Federal National Council	From merchant family
Mohammed Abdullah al-Gergawi (Persian origins)	Minister of Cabinet Affairs, and Executive Chairman and CEO of Dubai Holding	From merchant family
Sultan bin Nasser al-Suwaidi	Governor of the UAE Central Bank	Social/merchant elites
Mohammed bin Ali al-Abbar	Emaar Chairman and member of Dubai Executive Council	Social/merchant elite
Essa al-Suwaidi	Director, Abu Dhabi Investment Authority	Social/merchant elite
Ahmed Ali al-Sayegh	Vice Chairman, First Gulf Bank, and Chairman, Aldar Real Estate and Masdar	Social/merchant elite
Essa Saleh al-Gurg (Persian origins)	Former UAE Ambassador to the UK and the Republic of Ireland, current Deputy Chairman of National Bank of Fujairah	Social/merchant elite
Sultan bin Said al-Mansouri	Minister of Economy	Social/merchant elite
Obaid Humaid al-Tayer	Minister of State for Financial Affairs	Social merchant elite
Maitha Salem al-Shamsi	Minister of State	Social elite

Those who were closely integrated with and socially related to the ruling families were the local Arab merchants, although this relationship has varied across the individual Emirates. While merchants have been very prominent (mainly in commerce) in Dubai without strong relations with the Al Maktoum, in Abu Dhabi and other northern Emirates merchants were closely linked with the ruling families, at a social and political level. As indicated in Table 1, there are more merchants from non-Arab backgrounds in Dubai than in Abu Dhabi.

More generally, in the social composition of many government departments, three main segments of society are dominant: merchant elite, social elite, and ruling families. However, the leading merchants of Abu Dhabi, Dubai and Sharjah remain in the ascendant with regards to the number of government positions held. Indeed, many of the social elite are businessmen at the same time, such as Ghanim bin Hamdan (a prominent businessman) and Thani bin Abdullah (speaker of the FNC 1972–76), Faraj Bin Hamooda (a prominent businessman and Vice-Chairman of Abu Dhabi Council for Economic Development) and Mohammed Ahmed al-Otaiba (member of the Federal National Council (FNC) and a prominent businessman).

The structure of the private sector

In order to understand the position of merchants and their relation to the government or the ruling families, the structure of the private sector should be clearly examined. However, defining the boundaries between what is private and what is public in the UAE is challenging, owing to a lack of clarity in the state structure. This difficulty arises because of the complex patron-client relationships and the traditions of the ruling tribes. These complex structures are due to the high degree of integration existing between the political elites and the economy, since the former dominate the means of production. There are no clear-cut boundaries defining government ownership in the private sector in the UAE. Oil revenues are controlled by ruling families who have the ability to invest in the private sector by establishing large enterprises. One prominent example is the monopoly in construction and property market activities in Abu Dhabi of the Aldar Company. Its major shareholders are the state wealth fund Mubadala and the Abu Dhabi Commercial Bank, controlled by the Abu Dhabi government through its other state wealth fund, the Abu Dhabi Investment Authority. As a result, it is not clear if this entity is public or private, if the company is owned by the government of Abu Dhabi or a particular member of the Al Nahyan family. Examination of the structure of the private sector in the UAE will underline the blurred boundaries between sectors, and the interdependency of the private sector and the state.

With the discovery of oil the economic structure in the UAE changed dramatically from being solely dominated by merchant families to being state-led. When oil revenue began to flow into the Emirates, this signalled a change in the relationship between the private and public sectors, with the former subordinated to the latter. A relevant concept here is "neopatrimonialism". Christopher Clapham provided one of the most comprehensive definitions of this concept, defining neopatrimonialism as:

> a form of organization in which relationships of a broadly patrimonial type pervade a political and administrative system which is formally constructed on rational-legal lines. Officials hold positions in bureaucratic organizations with powers which are formally defined, but exercise those powers, so far as they can, as a form not of public service but of private property.[22]

It can be argued that the structure of governance in the UAE is characterized by neopatrimonialism, a claim that would be supported by Michael Herb, who describes the ruler in a neopatrimonial state as organising the regime around himself, by maintaining other members of the elite in a relationship of dependence on his personal grace and good favour. Outside the elite, society is kept politically inchoate.[23]

The current shape of the private sector structure in the UAE and the patron-client relationships between regime and business actors are the result of a number of motivating factors including both economic gains and non-economic objectives, such as national security and regime survival. Families that maintained strong relations with the ruling families have gained more economic interests than those that have been politically marginalized. Families whose members have helped ruling families to run their businesses today occupy important ministerial positions, such as the al-Mansouri family and the al-Tayer, where Sultan Bin Said al-Mansouri is the Minister of Economy and Obaid Humaid al-Tayer is a minister of state (see Table 1 for more examples). Marginalized families such as the al-Sa'idi, al-Kalbani, al-Riyami or al-Khatri, have received less support from the government owing to their limited historical and social connections with the ruling families.

There is no federal or local emirate law that sets limits on state ownership and dominance in certain economic sectors. However, the degree of government ownership is not the same in every Emirate; federal law permits local Emirati rulers to draw up their own economic policies. An examination follows of the three main segments of the private sectors, including state-dominated companies; small and medium enterprises (SMEs); and family businesses in the UAE.[24]

State-dominated Companies (SDCs)

This term signifies all those companies that have the characteristics of private companies but are dominated, organized, and managed by the state (the dominant shareholder). The SDCs are often grouped in holding companies, such as Dubai World. Private investors tend to own a limited number of shares and do not play any influential role in policy-making. The state has monopolized certain industries, such as oil, and other highly valuable areas of manufacturing, not because of the limited capacities and capabilities of the private sector, but because of concerns for national security and regime survival.

State-dominated companies are run by the state or by state wealth funds such as Mubadala, Dubai World, Dubai Holding or the Ajman Investment and Development Authority (AIDA).[25] With the state's intensive involvement in some large enterprises, this overlapping creates some confusion in distinguishing large private enterprises from state companies, including entities such as the Abu Dhabi National Oil Company (ADNOC), the Dubai Petroleum Company, the Abu Dhabi Media Company, the Sharjah Liquefied Gas Company (SHALCO), the Emirate Petroleum Products Company (EPPCO), the Dubai Aluminium Company (DUBAL) and the Abu Dhabi National Energy Company (TAQA). However, privatization appears to be shaping some of the state-dominated companies, which are evolving to become semi-private, such as TAQA.

The fact that merchant elites have a strong presence on the boards of directors in many, if not most, SDCs is a clear indication of the trust ruling families accord to merchant elites and the strong relationship between them.

Small and Medium Enterprises (SMEs)

The definition of SMEs varies greatly from one country to another and from one economy to another. The European Commission defines SMEs as "those enterprises that employ fewer than 250 people and have annual sales not exceeding $67 million and/or total assets not exceeding $56 million". Small enterprises are defined as those with fewer than fifty employees and with annual sales or total assets that do not exceed $13 million.[26] In contrast, the Asia Pacific Economic Cooperation (APEC) defines SMEs as enterprises with fewer than one hundred people. A medium sized enterprise is one that employs between twenty and ninety-nine people, whereas a small firm employs between five and nineteen, and a micro firm employs fewer than five employees including self-employed managers. Although the latter definition seems to fit the UAE case, the former could also be applicable to many enterprises in the UAE.

SMEs are considered the cornerstone of Western economies and the main economic driving force. Not only do they contribute to the economy, they are also a vital source of employment opportunities. In this respect, the UAE is no exception, and SMEs in the UAE have evolved since the 1970s to form a significant part of the UAE's economy, particularly in Dubai. There are almost 175,000 SMEs in the UAE, 95,000 of which are in Dubai.[27] They constitute around 90% of the total number of companies, and around 7,000 of them are located in the free zones.[28] Furthermore, according to Abdul Baset Al-Janahi, chief executive of the Sheikh Mohammed Bin Rashid Establishment for Young Business Leaders, "SMEs contribute over 70 per cent of Dubai's GDP".[29]

A large proportion of the SMEs are family businesses. In the UAE the *kafeel* or sponsor plays a major role in the way SMEs are established. Many local sponsors are involved with some foreign investors but only for formal and legal registration; they are not in fact the owners of these types of businesses. SMEs are a significant contributor to the state's economy; however, owing to their small size and capital, they are limited in certain sectors because of the dominance of larger businesses by either ruling or merchant families. The UAE government announced in December 2010 a new law for SMEs and the establishment of a council to support them. According to Sultan bin Said Al-Mansouri, the UAE Minister of Economy, "the new law is on par with similar laws in the European Union, Japan, South Korea and other advanced nations … the incentives for such projects include government purchase of a specific percentage of their products".[30] This is because SMEs are excluded from policy-making process, and well-connected large family businesses always win government contracts.

Large Family Businesses (merchant families/elites)

As noted, large numbers of SMEs are actually family businesses. Many UAE family businesses have become well known and successful large merchant families, such as the al-Futtaim who started with a small trading enterprise in 1930, or the al-Yousef, Juma al-Majed and al-Habtour.

In the UAE, family businesses are not as old as they are in some other Arab states. While some families emerged during the pearling era and from traditional economies, many appeared upon the discovery of oil. According to Abu-Baker they are "the traditional merchant families that have consolidated their holdings in one group of companies with highly differentiated lines of business".[31] Their economic activities range widely from agriculture and extractive industries to commerce, construction, services, import and export of goods, stocks, and finance. They constitute over 90% of the private companies in the UAE. The figures concerning their contribution to the economy are among the most protected in the country; hence neither private nor governmental statistics are available.[32] However, it is estimated that they contribute around 30 to 40% of the state's total GDP.

Family businesses in the UAE vary from one Emirate to another according to their size, relation with ruling families, and their historical development and origins. They are ranked in importance according to their wealth and their relation to the ruling families. Table 2 shows some of the most important and leading family businesses in the UAE.

Most of these families began with construction, trade and some light manufacturing, but now they are highly diversified in their business activities. Since the early 1970s, the leading merchants in most of the Emirates have become strongly connected with their local governments and ruling elites, including, for instance, the al-Fahim (Abu Dhabi and Dubai), Juma al-Majid, al-Habtoor, al-Tayer, and al-Dhaheri (the latter of Abu Dhabi). Because of their wealth, and, to some extent their social relations with the ruling families, they have succeeded in positioning themselves parallel to the state and ruling families. Therefore, many merchant families have been assisted by the state, and those with stronger ties to "leading families" could easily obtain commercial lands and low interest loans. Other families have won government construction contracts and/or benefited from many of the subsidies or free-interest loans offered by the state.

A large number of family businesses across the Emirates accumulated their wealth on the basis of their total dependence on the government, their relations with ruling families, and their trading history during the pearling era. Those who evolved before the 1970s, such as the al-Futtaim, al-Otaiba, Kanoo and al-Fahim, are among the most prominent and respected names in the country, and attribute their successes and their role in the state to what Fareed Mohamedi describes as "a historic compromise made between the royal families and the pre-oil merchant classes, whose original wealth came from pearling and entrepot/caravan trade: the merchants would forego political participation in exchange for wealth beyond their wildest imagination".[33] These families have the advantage of being intermarried with or having strong social relations with ruling families, as well as their long historical relations in the pre-1971 era.

Another way in which the politics of *wasta* (connections) have undoubtedly helped many leading merchants develop has been the state's distribution of lands on an individual basis. Michael Field demonstrates how in all the oil states, when the rulers have wanted to make a particular individual really rich, they have given him land—with the result that in the last thirty years land has become by far the most important source of personal wealth in Arabian society.[34] Rulers grant land to their closely-related connections, to ministers and to anyone else they wish to favour. A number of families have developed from small family businesses to large enterprises—including the al-Jaber, Bin Salem, Bin Hamouda and many others—through their relations with rulers who granted them commercial lands. Those who received free lands have, since the 1970s, established strong companies. Land ownership is a vital source of wealth, and most of the residential and commercial buildings in the UAE, with some exceptions in the case of Dubai, are owned by merchant or ruling families.

Close social links between certain merchants and ruling families have also allowed merchant families to win construction contracts from the government. Many of those who did so during the 1970s have become today's "merchant elite". Many families who were not involved in trade

Table 2: Some of the Leading Merchant Families in the UAE.

Emirate	*Families*	*Company*	*Year of Est.*	*Founder*	*Business Activities*
Abu Dhabi	al-Jaber	al-Jaber Group	1970	Obaid Khalifa Jaber al Murri	Construction, engineering, industrial, trading, real estate etc.
	al-Otaiba	al-Otaiba Group	1946	Mohamed Hareb al-Otaiba	Oil, construction
	al-Fahim	al-Fahim Group	1958	Abdul Jalil al-Fahim	Motors, Tourism, hotels, properties and travel.
	al-Khoori	Mohammed A. H. Y. Khoory	1930	Mohammed A. Khoory (Persian)	Trading, engineering, transport and recycling.
Dubai	al-Futtaim	al-Futtaim Group	1930s	Majid al-Futtaim	Motors, electronics, industries and real estate.
	al-Majid	al-Majid Group	1950	Juma al-Majid	Motors, contracting, trading and travel
	al-Habtoor	al-Habtoor Group	1970	Khalaf al-Habtoor	Engineering, hotels, real estate, and sports
	al-Ghurair	al-Ghurair Group	1930s	Saif al-Ghurair	Real estate, shopping malls, manufacturing and investments.
	al-Nowais	Emirates Holdings	1979	Hussain al-Nowais	Energy, food and industrial services.
	al-Tayer	al-Tayer Group	1979	Humaid Obaid al-Tayer	Motors, engineering, jewellery, publishing, fashion and jewellery.
	Galadari	Galadari Brothers Group	1960	Abdul-Rahim Galadari (Persian origin)	Motors, industrial trading, media, retail, engineering, hospitality, real estate, etc.

	Gergash	Gergash Group	1950	Anwar M. Gergash (Persian origin)	Motors, Insurance, travel, hospitality, real estate
	al-Rostomani	al-Rostomani Group	1954	Abdullah Hassan al-Rostomani (Persian origin)	Real estate, information technology, trade, construction, food, foreign exchange services, etc
Sharjah	al-Fardan	al-Fardan Group	1954	Ibrahim al-Fardan (Persian origin)	Exchange, jewellery and real estate.
R/al-Khaimah	Hamarain	Hamarain Centre	1992	Rashid Saif Hamarain	Contracting, real estate, shopping malls.

Source: Dubai Chamber of Commerce and Industry, www.aljaaber.com, www.alotaibagroup.com, www.mahykhoory.com, www.alfahim.com, www.al-futtaim.ae, www.majedalfuttaim.com; *The International Who's Who of the Arab World* (Edinburgh and London: Morrison & Gibb Ltd, 1978); Abu Dhabi Chamber of Commerce and Industry; Sharjah Chamber of Commerce and Industry; Albadar S.S. Abu Baker, "Political Economy of State Formation: The United Arab Emirates in Comparative Perspective" (PhD thesis, University of Michigan, 1995).

before the 1970s accumulated their wealth in the construction sector. For example, the al-Jaber Group, owned by Obaid Khalifa Jaber al-Murri, began its business in 1970 as a small construction company. Currently, al-Jaber has over 50,000 employees and a total asset base whose value exceeds AED10 billion (around $US3.7 billion).[35]

The leading merchant families have strong business partnerships with ruling families. Either they run businesses for certain members of the ruling families, or the latter enjoy a 70% or higher share in a joint partnership. It is difficult to estimate precisely how much each member of a ruling family or merchant elite contributes to these joint businesses, since the ruling families of the seven Emirates, with the exception of Dubai, tend to avoid reporting their involvement in any economic activities. However, it is clear that top merchants, members of the social elite and individuals from the ruling families dominate the boards of directors of state-dominated companies. The Mubadala Development Company is a Public Joint Stock Company with headquarters in Abu Dhabi. The company appears to be owned by Sheikh Mohammed bin Zayed Al Nahyan, the Crown Prince of Abu Dhabi. The board of directors includes the following individuals: Mohammed Ahmed al-Bowardi, Khaldoon Khalifa al-Mubarak, Nasser Ahmed Khalifa al-Suwaidi, Mohamed Saif al-Mazrouei, Ahmed Ali al-Sayegh and Hamad al-Hurr al-Suwaidi. Quite apart from Abu Dhabi's Crown Prince, the social composition of this company's board consists of top social elites and merchant families.

Most boards of directors of other leading public, semi-private and private companies also include members of ruling families along with leading merchants (often several of the latter).[36] There is strong economic cooperation between merchant families themselves, as in the case of the Emirates Bank, where the Board of Directors includes the al-Tayer, al-Gurg, al-Fardan, Lootah, al-Sayegh, al-Futtaim and al-Mulla families. Abu Baker explains how a wide range of overlapping and interlocking ownership can be detected between and among these institutions and families through their boards of directors, thus demonstrating the relative cohesiveness of the commercial bourgeoisie in the UAE.[37] For example, the Abu Dhabi Commercial Bank includes both members of the Al Nahyan ruling family and merchants such as al-Khoori, al-Mazrouei and al-Fahim. Furthermore, the Board of Directors of Etihad Airways includes Sheikh Hamed bin Zayed Al Nahyan, Sheikh Khaled

Bin Zayed, Ahmed Ali al-Sayegh, Mubarak al-Muhairy, Hamad Abdullah al-Shamsi and Khalifa Sultan al-Suwaidi. The board of directors of First Gulf Bank[38] includes HH Sheikh Hazza Bin Zayed Al Nahyan, HH Sheikh Tahnoon bin Zayed Al Nahyan, Khadem Abdulla al-Qubaisi, Khaldoon Khalifa al-Mubarak, Ahmed Darwish Dagher al-Marar and Ahmed Ali al-Sayegh. Among these are two members of Abu Dhabi's ruling family, two from the social elite (al-Muhairy and al-Marar), and two from merchant families (al-Sayegh and al-Mubarak). There are many other instances, such as banks, telecommunications companies, and property and insurance firms, where the political and economic interests between the ruling families and merchant elites meet.

Looking at most government and other executive and legislative positions, one realizes that leading merchant families are ranked second after members of the ruling families. Most of the twenty appointed members of the Federal National Council (out of a total of forty) are from among the country's leading merchants or social elites. Amongst those are al-Ghurair, al-Dhahiri, al-Hai, al-Qubaisi, al-Mansouri, al-Dhaheri, al-Suwaidi, al-Sha'afar, al-Madfa and al-Zaabi. In addition, Anwar Gergash is a Minister of State for Federal National Council Affairs. The interrelationship between merchant and ruling family goes back to the pre-oil era; there are few who emerged later in the post-oil boom. While merchants provided financial support to the political elite before the 1960s, at present there is political and economic interlocking between them.

The role of "family businesses" in the private sector has been impressive, though with exceptions, like telecommunications and the petroleum industry. They have played a significant role in developing the private sector and the economy of the state from a local to a global competitive environment. In particular, merchants from Abu Dhabi and Dubai have brought major transformations to the economies of their respective Emirates. The following section will examine in more depth some of the merchant elite families in the UAE and how they have emerged both as an important business elite in the private sector and as political elites along with ruling families.

Merchant elites: case studies

Building on the preceding section's analysis of how many family businesses evolved to be strong merchant families, this section will provide a number of illustrative case studies of some of the leading merchant elites. Even though the UAE consists of seven emirates, this section will look only at the three major ones—Abu Dhabi, Dubai and Sharjah. The leading merchant families in these three emirates appear to control a large portion of the UAE economy overall. This is due not only to their historic economic role in the pre-1971 era, but to the oil boom which made a substantial contribution to their emergence as the bourgeoisie of the UAE.

In Abu Dhabi, the al-Otaiba and al-Fahim are among the most significant merchant elites (families). The contemporary Al-Fahim Group was established by Abdul Jalil al-Fahim in 1958. Abdul-Jalil al-Fahim, who came from the island of Sirri, had trading experience and was a well-educated merchant. After arriving in Abu Dhabi, he became a well-known merchant and married a woman from the al-Hawamil[39] tribe in 1905.[40] His marriage was attended by the ruler of Abu Dhabi, Sheikh Zayed Bin Khalifa.[41] Thus, from his arrival al-Fahim began to integrate strongly with the ruling family of Abu Dhabi, eventually creating an influential and well-renowned family himself. Some family members now occupy high government positions or executive and legislative ranks, like Amer Abdul Jalil al-Fahim who is a member of the Federal National Council.

Today, the al-Fahim group, which began as a small company trading in vehicle parts, is a family business led by Abdul-Jalil's eight sons. It has thirteen companies that include activities such as motors, travel and tourism, real estate, hospitality, industrial development, and oil and gas. With their offices in Abu Dhabi, Dubai and Sharjah employing over 1,300 staff, their revenues are estimated at around $US1 billion annually.[42] Even if there are few statistics available for the al-Fahim family, it is possible to realize the dominance of al-Fahim in certain key sectors such as real estate, motors and retailing. The family has been the main investor in many major projects in the UAE. Amongst the most notable are the (now troubled) real estate venture Dubai Pearl, estimated to cost up to $US3 billion and originally due to be completed by 2011. Al Fahim owns the Paris Gallery, Emirates Motor Company (EMC), Western Motors Company, Golden Tulip Dalma Plaza (Hotel Apartments), Hilton Corniche Hotel Apartments and Garden View Hotel Apartments. Al-Fahim also owns Marjan Industrial Development; established in 1978, it is one of the leading local establishments in the UAE for supplying engineering products and technical services related to oil, gas and petrochemicals, as well as water and power utilities.[43]

In contrast to al-Fahim is the al-Otaiba family. Al Otaiba or Otibat (plural) is a well-rooted indigenous Arab family from Abu Dhabi. This particular family is among the most important of the clans related to the Al Nahyan, Abu Dhabi's ruling family, and while this has made it a well-respected clan, parallel to the ruling family, the relationship has also compelled the Al Nahyan to favour the al-Otaiba by granting them more privileges than to others. For example, al-Otaiba Enterprises has succeeded in winning many project contracts with government and semi-government departments (mainly relating to infrastructure, networking, security systems, and software). Amongst its main clients are Abu Dhabi International Airport, Emirates Palace, the Ministry of Culture, the General Headquarters of the Armed Forces, Abu Dhabi Cultural Foundation, Dolphin Energy, Etisalat, Abu Dhabi Educational Council, Paris Sorbonne University (Abu Dhabi), the Ministry of Finance and Industry, and so on.

Prominent Dubai merchant families have similar trajectories to those in Abu Dhabi. Amongst the most important are the al-Tajir and al-Futtaim. Mahdi al-Tajir is one the most prominent merchants in the UAE, particularly in the Emirate of Dubai. Bahraini-born and educated, Mahdi Al Tajir was sent from Bahrain to Dubai as a customs clerk before the oil boom, and subsequently established good relations with residents of Dubai. James Paul points out that al-Tajir became the main confidant of Sheikh Rashid, having negotiated Dubai's oil concessions and acquired a reputation as an indispensable middleman.[44] His relationship with the ruler of Dubai continued to strengthen, and he was eventually appointed by the ruler as UAE Ambassador to the UK, where he still lives. It is clear that his wealth was very much linked with Dubai's ruling family, and that without their support he would not have been as successful today. He is among the wealthiest Arab businessmen and the richest man in Scotland, according to a recent report by BBC.[45]

The al-Futtaim is another highly successful family business in Dubai. Majed Mohammed al-Futtaim was a prominent pearl merchant in the pre-1971 era, having established his group as a small trading enterprise in 1930. He has a relatively long trading history that has placed him amongst the wealthiest merchant families. However, Al-Futtaim's strong relations with the Al-Maktoum since the early 1970s have undoubtedly helped in accumulating this wealth. The group collectively operates over forty companies bearing the al-Futtaim name. It dominates many market segments in the UAE, and has expanded its sphere of operation to include Bahrain, Kuwait, Qatar, Oman and Egypt.[46] The group has over 6,500 employees. This particular family business has strongly contributed to Dubai's service-oriented diversification strategies.

During the 1940s and 1950s the al-Futtaim's relations with the Al Maktoum were fairly negative, and remained so until the 1960s. Al-Futtaim himself had conflicts with Rashid Al Maktoum on many matters. In political terms, he clashed with members of the Al Maktoum family in the Dubai National Front,[47] and Davidson notes that in its early years "the main voices and the permanent 'backbone' of the Dubai National Front ... were the al-Futtaim and al-Ghurair families, supported by Sheikh Rashid bin Said al-Maktoum's...uncle, Sheikh Juma bin Maktoum Al Maktoum..."[48] Although a member of the family (Hamad al-Futtaim) was exiled to Saudi Arabia, he later returned to Dubai.

Al-Futtaim was well educated, and this contributed to his demands for political and economic reform. He was amongst the merchants who asked for the establishment of a proper municipality. Abu Baker comments that:

> Shaikh Rashid in what would seem to be an attempt to cajole the merchants held weekly meetings which included members of the National Front. A member of the latter, Murshid al-Usaimi, declared that 'there will be no opposition party in Dubai if Rashid agrees to a council of merchants to advise on and contribute towards a proper *baladiya* (municipality)'. The Majlis al-Tujar, Merchants Council, when it was founded, was packed by National Front supporters and excluded Persian merchants. Furthermore, Arab merchants schemed to control the Municipal Council which was founded in March 1957.[49]

Sheikh Rashid bin Said Al Maktoum acceded to the throne after his father's death in 1958, and unlike his father, proved to be an important figure for the merchants. Although he had clashed with some merchants before the death of his father, merchants preferred dealing and cooperating with him, as he complied with some of their conditions in order to avoid any further clashes with them that could have endangered his rule. Abu Baker maintains that Rashid, being a merchant himself, institutionalized his relationship with the merchants through his *majlis* or court.[50] He offered them protection and managed to create harmony between Persian and Arab merchants. At that time, too, al-Futtaim, who was a member of the Municipal Council and the Chamber of Commerce, contributed along with other merchants including Galadari, al-Naboodah, al-Tayer, al-Kindi, al-Fardan, al-Ghurair, and Bel Hasa, to Dubai's political status quo. As Abu Baker points out, Dubai's politics revolved around the ruler, his immediate family and sons, and the merchant elites that constituted the patrimonial regime.[51] Al-Futtaim's strong relations with the Al Maktoum since the early 1970s have undoubtedly helped the group become one of the largest and most successful ones in the UAE, while the family members have had little inclination to aspire to political office. The group collectively operates over forty companies bearing the al-Futtaim name.[52] It dominates many market segments in the UAE, and has expanded its sphere of operation to include Bahrain, Kuwait, Qatar, Oman and Egypt. The group has over 6,500 employees. This family business has strongly contributed to Dubai's service-oriented diversification strategies.

One of the prominent merchant families from Sharjah is the al-Midfa. It has a strong history in trade, as well as in the political and cultural life in Sharjah. Al-Midfa migrated from Oman in the eighteenth century, and established himself as a well respected pearl merchant and owner of large number of ships used by traders to travel to Arab countries and India. Amongst the prominent members of this family is Ibrahim Mohammed al-Midfa, who was an adviser to the ruling Al-Qassimi family in the 1930s and started the first newspaper in the Gulf, *Oman*, in 1927. The well educated al-Midfa family has contributed to economic and political reform in Sharjah through their direct involvement in local civil society, establishing several cultural institutions such as the Islamic Forum.

At present, members of this family occupy different positions at both local and federal levels. Amongst those members are Mohammed Ahmed al-Midfa, the chairman of the Sharjah Chamber and Industry; Hamad Abdul Rahman al-Midfa, the Minister of Health until May 2009; Saif Mohammed al-Midfa, chairman of Sharjah Expo Centre. The family is well connected and integrated with the ruling families in the UAE in general and Sharjah in particular. From a business point of view, one of the prominent members of the al-Midfa family, Khalid bin Mohammad, a grandson of Ibrahim Mohammed al-Midfa, who invested greatly in building materials and oil, is the current Chairman of Gulf International Trading Group.

The merchant families discussed above, and many others such as the al-Tayer, al-Dhaheri, al-Kitbi, al-Jaber, al-Mahmoud, al-Darmaki, Al-

Suwaidi and Al-Mansouri, have dominated many parts of the private sector. Their emergence as the "merchant elites or bourgeoisie" was determined by two factors outlined above: first, their family ties and connections with the political elites, contributing to their access to commercial land; second, the social and historical relations between certain merchants and ruling families, which helped many merchant families win construction contracts from the government.

Implications of the Arab Spring

The "Arab Spring" has affected political, economic and social elites all across the MENA region. In Egypt, Libya and Tunisia, it brought about the downfall not only of political leadership but also, to a great extent, of business elites that had benefited from the protection of these regimes. The UAE, however, just like its small and rich neighbour Qatar, has been only weakly affected by the regional unrest. In fact, the UAE underwent an economic leap, as tourism and investment in unstable countries in the region were diverted to its territory. It saw 3.8% economic growth in 2011.[53] At a political level, the country witnessed no unrest or organized demands. The majority of UAE citizens actually showed further loyalty to the regime, not least as they witnessed the political instability in neighbouring countries. In return, the state increased salaries and gave citizens more privileges than before. However, in March 2011 over 100 Emirati intellectuals submitted a petition to the UAE government demanding more legislative power for the elected Federal National Council. It was not surprising to see no business elites signing the petition. These elites sided with the government and, if anything, showed more support for the leadership than before. Politically connected business elites continue to benefit from the status quo, and support the government's economic and political policies. This pattern of state-business relations in the UAE remains a prominent feature today.

Concluding remarks

The interrelation between merchant class and ruling family members has evolved over the years to include political, economic and social aspects. The rulers of the Trucial States, politically powerful but economically weak, were able, through various channels, to establish strong relations with the merchants, both before and after the discovery of oil. At present, it is clear that to a great extent, it is *wasta* (connections) that determines the financial status and class of many members of a society. However, owing to a relative increase in population, the ruling families have maintained their relations only with those social elites and merchant families that are already well-established.

Furthermore, the merchant elites have succeeded in linking their interests with ruling family members across all the Emirates. The ruling families of Abu Dhabi, Dubai and Sharjah preferred educated merchants and social elites as their business partners and political advisers. However, after the decline of the pearl industry, merchants who came from educated and highly-experienced backgrounds became involved with demands for political and economic reform, as in Dubai with the Reform Movement of 1938, where an oppositional member of the Al Maktoum was strongly backed by the merchant elites. In Abu Dhabi, the ruling family has been involved with merchants from Persian backgrounds, as well as experienced indigenous Arab merchants such as the al-Qubaisat and al-Otaibat.

The relationships between merchant elites, social elites and the ruling families of the UAE are and have been based on the patrimonial regime, with a political-economic exchange between the political elites and merchant elites. Although merchant families dominate a large segment of the private sector, they also occupy high government positions, and these connections have further cemented their position in the private sector by allowing them access to various sources of revenue such as land ownership, as well as preventing both ownership by foreign merchants and competition in the private sector. Thus, they seem to put little pressure on the government for political or economic reform, as there is a strong correlation between the economic wealth of the merchant class and their desire for political change.

Therefore, real reform in the UAE will probably begin only with the decline of its economy and the introduction of a tax system, since as long as the state continues to provide welfare, citizens and merchants have no incentive to make any participatory demands on their governments. Merchants appear to play a supportive role for the government's economic policies. The linkage between economic development and political participation, as represented by modernization theory, appears weak; the regime retains a hold on the political structure, and rents from oil accrue to the ruling families. As a result, the nature of the UAE as a rentier state continues to shape its current government.

The "Arab Spring" appears to have done little or no harm to the relationship between state and merchant elites in the UAE, being so politically and economically intertwined. This is reflected in the fact that no new families appear to be joining the core circle of merchants. The structure of the private sector remains the same, and members of ruling families across the Emirates continue to maintain their relationships with the prominent business and merchant elites and families.

4

THE POLITICS OF SHI'I MERCHANTS IN KUWAIT

Rivka Azoulay

Introduction

Over the past two decades, the role of the private sector has expanded and deepened in the political economies of MENA states, republics and monarchies alike. Since the failure of statist development projects in MENA republics, these regimes started to turn away from their populist policies and broad-based corporatist class alliances by adopting, from the 1990s onwards, a series of neo-liberal reforms. This "post-populist" turn in most of the MENA republics marked the political rise of businessmen as clients of state power.

Despite being dethroned in the republics following post-independence revolutions, the old commercial elites in the GCC monarchies maintained their economic position and were instead protected by Gulf regimes. Having always benefited from pro-business policies, these business elites in the GCC have been able to mature gradually. Moreover, oil resources have allowed regimes, to a certain extent, to perpetuate pre-oil alliances and elite links in a path-dependent process, particularly in the small monarchies, in which individualized patronage plays a central role. The early independence of merchant families vis-à-vis the rulers was compromised with the discovery of oil. Whilst the Gulf merchant families formed an important political force in the liberal and nationalist movements of the 1920s and 1930s—like the notables in countries of the Levant at that time—they had to give up their political independence in exchange for a privileged share in oil wealth since its discovery. With the deepening of the rentier state and the onset of mass politics, these formerly independent business elites have turned themselves into the strongest allies of GCC regimes, upon which they depend for lucrative contracts and import licenses.

Although much of the above is reasonably well established, much of the literature on MENA business politics has taken macro or state-centred perspectives. The politics of business elites in the region is analyzed in terms of "crony capitalism" or a "comprador bourgeoisie", referring to the mutual dependency between business and state elites through informal patron-client relations. Studies on state-business relations in GCC monarchies usually with the statist perspective of Rentier State Theory (RST).[1] These studies, whilst convincingly demonstrating the client status of business actors, fail to provide micro-sociological details as to the social embeddedness of these commercial elites, their historical roots and the social mechanisms through which regime-business relations are articulated. Specifically in smaller GCC rentier monarchies, the embeddedness of business elites in wider communities and social networks seems important for understanding the nature of the private sector's social power and social status, as well as its political utility for regimes.

This chapter centres on a case study of the politics of Shi'i merchants in Kuwait, through the lens of their relationship to the state and to social constituencies in both pre-oil and contemporary Kuwait. This analysis might at first sight seem prone to selection bias, since it sets apart the Kuwaiti merchant class a priori on religious lines. Why should we analyze a group of merchants in Kuwait on the basis of religious allegiance rather than on socio-economic or ideological lines? This chapter will demonstrate that Kuwaiti Shi'i merchants historically occupied a particular position both in the Shi'i community and in the political history of the Emirate, and have differed from their Sunni counterparts in both these regards. Moreover, over the course of the twenty-first century, old merchant and notable traditions were revived by the Kuwaiti regime in a policy of divide-and-rule, aimed at rallying the Shi'i minority behind government policies in the face of rising Sunni Islamist and tribal opposition. The chapter will show how new Shi'i merchants have been co-opted by the regime and have emerged as informal intermediaries between the government and wider Shi'i constituencies through the use of the media, politics and heavy investment in community charities.

In order to make sense of the social and political role of these Shi'i merchants, I employ the concept of "notable politics" (popularized in *Middle Eastern Studies* by Albert Hourani) throughout the paper. Although it is rarely used in studies on Arabian Gulf societies,[2] I argue that the concept of the "political notable" applies well to the case of Shi'i elites in Kuwait. In Hourani's definition, political notables are individuals who can play the political role of intermediaries between the government and the community, in which they have some social power of their own.[3] From this definition, we can infer two essential sources of political influence, namely, access to authority and a certain degree of social power. Historically, politics in the Emirate of Kuwait has been dominated by political notables, as various conditions propitious to this form of patrician politics existed.[4] With the onset of mass politics, the independent position of the merchants as political notables waned and a new generation of political entrepreneurs from middle-class backgrounds replaced them as representatives of wider constituencies and as new social elites. However—as demonstrated at various stages in Kuwait's political history—this transition from notable politics to that of political entrepreneurs has not been complete, as political entrepreneurs themselves do not correspond to the ideal-type of the political entrepreneur, as defined by Max Weber.[5] The small size of the Emirate, the absence of formal political parties and the rentier nature of the state might all contribute to the fact that members of Parliament in Kuwait have often been caught up in patron-client games with the regime and tend to act as intermediaries (*wusata*) for services between their voters and the government.[6] Hence, politics in Kuwait is best described as hybrid, in the sense that "traditional" and "modern" modes of political exchange co-exist. The current study places itself in this analytical dialectic of transitional societies.

Finally, it is essential to note that this case study is placed in the broader political context of Kuwait's political history: the various governments of Prime Minister Nasser Mohammed Al-Sabah (2006–11) and the politics of alliance-building by competing princes through the co-optation of forces in parliament, society and through the use of media outlets. Intra-family rivalry between princes of the second generation reached a climax under the governments of Prime Minister Nasser Mohammed. Moreover, rivalry between Sheikh Nasser and the former Deputy Prime Minister Ahmad Al-Fahd was fierce and played out in society in their patronizing opposing factions. As head of government, Nasser Mohammed, in the later years of his regime, solicited the support of the Shi'i minority and some liberal forces, as the government's vote-buying strategies towards the large voting bloc of tribal constituencies appeared to be no longer effective.

These policies of co-optation of societal forces through political financial inducements came to the fore with the discovery of $350 million of deposits in the bank accounts of thirteen former members of parliament. The scandal triggered a broad-based mass movement, instigated by young political activists, seeking the dismissal of Sheikh Nasser in November 2011. The current case study is representative of the social mechanisms at work in these policies of co-optation through the indirect recirculation of rents to society, which have provoked the youth counter-movement in 2011. Whilst this case study points to the capacity of the rentier state to co-opt societal groups, I argue that it is mostly its minority status that explains the Shi'a rallying behind the government since 2009. Traditional patronage politics and divide-and-rule games have become increasingly ineffective among the larger middle classes, to the point of being actively resisted in recent years. Nonetheless, the current case study provides us with an important insight into the concrete social mechanisms through which GCC rentier monarchies strive to manage state-society and state-business relations. Furthermore, it might be representative of a transitional stage in distinct MENA regimes, corresponding to the decline of old intermediary institutions and elites upon which these authoritarian regimes used to rely in order to maintain social control and reach out to constituencies. There might be a deeper phenomenon to be observed in the wider region—republics and rentier monarchies alike—corresponding to the political emancipation of the middle classes, increasingly disengaged from established forms of social inclusion, whether modern functional corporatism in the republics or a sort of primordial corporatism mediated through social elites in the monarchies.

Nonetheless, in their quest for survival, regimes continue their attempts to create new loyal strata of elites through a policy of co-optation and rent transfers. It is this transitional stage of disintegrating social hierarchies, coupled with (often failed) efforts to re-create new ones, that has triggered the grass-roots countervailing forces of the Arab Spring. This needs to be understood in its own right in order to make sense of the unrest that has gripped the region.

Sheikh Mubarak and the birth of a Shi'i-al-Sabah alliance

The Shi'i merchants of al-Sharq: political notables in a fragmented group of Shi'i diasporas

With a view of adding a historical context to our understanding of the current politics of Shi'i merchants, the following section traces the position of Shi'i merchant families until their loss of notable power, due to the advent of mass politics in the 1980s. Crucial, in this respect, is an understanding of the Shi'i-al-Sabah alliance, which crystallized in 1938, and hereafter influenced future political developments within the Shi'i community, notably, the turnaround in Shi'a-government relations following the Mughniey affair on 12 February 2008, which involved members of the Shi'i al-Tahaluf movement (Hizbullah line) meeting to commemorate the assassination of a leading figure of Lebanese Hizbullah, and thus provoking widespread indignation in Kuwaiti society. An overarching theme developed here is the depth of historical memory in rentier states, where initial alliances are perpetuated and reinforced through the gradual growth of state revenue and rent distribution over time.

Before proceeding to the historical background for Shi'i-al-Sabah relations, we should give a general overview of the nature of the Shi'i social fabric, that informs us about the position of the Shi'a in Kuwaiti society at large. It is important to note that before the politicization of Shi'ism in the 1970s, the Shi'a in Kuwait constituted a rather fragmented community, divided into different ethnic sub-communities. In fact, the heterogeneous and diasporic nature of the Shi'a in Kuwait led to diverging processes of community-forming, or *Vergemeinschaftung* in Weberian terms.[7] Although this ethnic diversity also concerns the Sunni population, ethnicity often coincides in the Shi'i case with specific religious belonging. The group formation effect was thus strengthened by the double distinction of ethnic group and of religious affiliation.

Thus we can differentiate three main categories: the 'Ajam (from Iran), the Hasawiyyin (from al-Hasa) and the Baharna (from Bahrain). The majority of the Kuwaiti Shi'a (around 70%) are of Iranian descent and emigrated to the Emirate from the end of the eighteenth century onwards in a migration pattern that continued until the twentieth century. The earliest migration flows consisted mostly of Iranian merchants from the Western provinces who were escaping the harsh fiscal measures of the Qajar regime. Some of the wealthiest Shi'i merchant families, like the Ma'arafi and the Behbahani, arrived in Kuwait in this period. By the beginning of the twentieth century, Iranian migration had become more diversified in its social composition, with the emigration to Kuwait of poor farmers severely hit by the administrative reforms of the new Pahlavi regime (1926).[8] Most of them came from the region of Tarakma in Southern Iran and are generally referred to as Tarakmas by Kuwaiti Shi'a. Their particular strong group identity was reinforced by the fact that, once in Kuwait, they were to constitute a subclass of workers, employed in the shipping industry and, to a lesser extent, in handicrafts.

As for the Shi'a from al-Hasa (around 15%), most of them came to the Emirate in the nineteenth century after the various Saudi conquests sweeping the Eastern Province. These Hasawiyyin have developed a particularly strong group identity in Kuwait due to their common belonging to a minority branch within Twelver Shi'ism—Sheikhism, which follows the teachings of Ahmad al-Ahsa'i (1753–1826).[9] The group coherence of the Kuwaiti Sheikhis has also been strengthened by the fact that an important line of the Sheikhi *maraja'* ("sources of emulation" or senior clergy) had itself settled in Kuwait by the end of the 1950s: the Mirza Al-Ihqaqi family.[10] This strong group identity has led to the development of specific communal relations and distinct processes of socialization. As far as the Baharna Shi'a are concerned (around 5%), they also combine specific ethnic membership with a particular current in Twelver Shi'ism, being descendents of the Gharbi tribe in Western Arabia and belonging to the Akhbari school of thought.[11] Most of the Baharna came to the Emirate during the eighteenth century, fleeing political instability after the settlement of the Al Khalifa in Bahrain.

Within this heterogeneous group of Kuwaiti Shi'a, socialized in distinct community institutions, merchants were the central pillars of community life and crucial intermediaries between the masses and the central power of the Al-Sabah clan. Like their Sunni counterparts, these

Shi'i merchants were typical political notables of the city-state. The concept of political notables, has rarely been applied in Arabian Gulf societies, which are commonly analyzed from a political-anthropological perspective. Yet, the Emirate of Kuwait is exemplary of the importance of notable politics in organizing social and political life in early city-states. In fact, various conditions propitious for the development of notable politics were combined in the Emirate.[12] The small size of the city-state, the historical social pact between the Al-Sabah and a merchant oligarchy, the development of early class relations due to the regional trade system, were all conducive to the crystallization of notable politics in Kuwait.

For the Shi'i merchants, their position as political notables was the consequence of both their social power within their respective communities and their privileged access to the ruler. Within the ethno-religious community, social prestige was mainly linked to charitable giving in the religious field. Since there was no indigenous Shi'i clerical class in Kuwait (as there were hardly any clerics among the Shi'a who came to settle in Kuwait), merchants were the central actors in religious life and, as such, enjoyed strong social prestige.[13] They played an essential role in popular religion, financed the mosques and negotiated with the *mujtaheds* in Najaf or Qom to identify clerics ready to come to Kuwait to act as religious leaders. Because of their social capital within their constituencies and their status as affluent merchants, these families were central interlocutors between the Al-Sabah and the Shi'i minority. As paraphrased by one of our interviewees:

> The merchants were the link between the common Shi'a and the ruling family. In order to reach the people, they would go through the merchants. Even in finding out where people were coming from. This became very helpful in organizing nationality. This minister would ask the merchants if they knew the person. So if you go back to the old files of each Kuwaiti, you will find the signature of my father (Mohammed Qabazard), of Mohammed Rafi Ma'rafi, etc.[14]

Moreover, following the coup d'état by Mubarak the Great (1896) and the breaking of the consultative agreement with the Sunni merchants, Shi'i merchants were co-opted by the ruler in his efforts to counterbalance the nascent mercantile opposition. Since the Shi'i merchants had never been included in the consultative agreement—because of their lack of kinship ties to the Bani Utub tribe—they became crucial allies of the regime. Being a national minority without any kinship ties to the regime, the Shi'a were less problematic allies, as they could not contest the central elite's status.

The coup d'état of Mubarak the Great and the birth of a Shi'i-al-Sabah alliance

When authoritarian rule was introduced in Kuwait by the coup d'état of Mubarak, the state, now separated from its socio-economic basis, had to compensate for its loss of legitimacy with the search for new allies. On an external level, this resulted in the signature of an Exclusive Agreement (1899) with the British that would curtail the autonomous development of Kuwait as a mercantile centre by putting an end to its age-old regional trade system.[15] This agreement not only threatened the vested class interests of the Sunni oligarchy as regional traders, but was also opposed by them on ideological lines, as they were heavily influenced by the Arab nationalism emanating from Iraq. The anti-Iranian stance of the Arab nationalists naturally added to the Shi'i mistrust of the political activities of the Sunni merchants. The co-optation of the Shi'i merchants can only be understood in this context of emergent social antagonism, instrumentalized by the state in order to maintain its hegemony over society. Thus, rulers played on nascent social divisions in order to set themselves up as neutral arbiters over society, establishing a political strategy of co-optation and discrimination. As in other Gulf monarchies, the divide-and-rule game has been a typical government strategy for maintaining social peace.

It is within this context that we should analyze new internal alliances that emerged as a consequence of the new regime. Jacqueline Ismael (1982) demonstrates how petty merchants from the Utbi clan—whose interests were locally defined by the transfer of subsistence products to the desert hinterland—were financially backed by Mubarak in order to counterbalance the Sunni mercantile opposition. In the same logic, the Shi'i merchants became the object of a policy of co-optation by Mubarak and his successors. Although these Shi'i merchants shared class interests with the Sunni oligarchy,[16] they were excluded from the highest political merchant *'asabiyya* on the basis of values of lineage,[17] placing the Sunni families of "pure" Arab descent at the top of the social hierarchy. In existing literature on Kuwait, this preeminence of primordial factors has often been overlooked, instead portraying the group of merchants in

Kuwait as a very cohesive, homogeneous coalition.[18] As the alliance gave Mubarak the societal support he needed to maintain his authoritarian rule, it presented the Shi'i merchants with an opportunity to reinforce their position within the Emirate. Although the alliance between the Shi'a and the al-Sabah during the 1938 crisis (see below) has been acknowledged in scholarly work,[19] in no case has it been analyzed against the historical context in which it started: the breaking of the consultative agreement by Mubarak. Since 1896 the Shi'a and the al-Sabah were already gravitating towards each other, a historical process in which the Shi'i merchants played an active role.

In Arabic sources we can find interesting information that reinforces our interpretation. An example is the work of Saleh al-Ghaz'ali on Shi'i political movements, in which he describes the lobbying of some Shi'i merchants, among them Ali H. Abdal, for a protection agreement with the British.[20] These merchants used their proximity to the Shi'i ruler of Muhammara, Sheikh Ghaz'al, who was already under the British umbrella, to bring the two sides together.[21] Moreover, the Kuwaiti envoy to the meeting where the Protection Agreement was signed was a Shi'i merchant.[22] Because of their economic influence in the port of Muhammara and their religious proximity to its ruler, the Shi'i merchants played an important role in Kuwait's diplomatic relations with Muhammara. This explains the cordial relations between Mubarak and Sheikh Ghaz'al and the influence of the latter in turning the Shi'i population in Kuwait into a pro-Emir constituency. This was done through the appointment by Sheikh Ghaz'al of an Iranian, Molla Salih, as a chief secretary to Mubarak.[23]

The pro-al-Sabah discourse of the Shi'i merchants must be understood in light of this historical process of alliance-formation between the Shi'a and the al-Sabah, which started during the rule of Mubarak. In our interviews, the old Shi'i merchant families, such as the Ma'rafi, Behbahani, Hayaat and Al-Wazzan families, underlined their historical proximity to the al-Sabah, which they generally attribute to their early settlement in the Emirate concomitantly with the al-Sabah family. Moreover, not unlike the Sunnis, they consider themselves to be the true pillars of Kuwait's nationhood, as the merchants enabled the old city to prosper and to develop into an independent political entity. However, whereas the old segments of the Sunni oligarchy tend to be rather critical of the al-Sabah, the Shi'i merchants are particularly in favour of the ruling family, whom they consider the true protectors of Shi'a against hostile societal forces. The historically close relations with the al-Sabah are also reflected in the urban geography of the old city: the Emir's fiefdoms are located in the middle of al-Sharq, a neighbourhood long dominated by the Shi'a.[24] It is interesting to note that the *husayniyyas* of the Ma'rafi and the Behbahani families are located next to the Emir's palace. Furthermore, the pro-al-Sabah stance of these Shi'i merchants is generally blended into an overtly patriotic narrative in which Shi'ism and love for the nation are assimilated. One of our interviewees, belonging to the ancient Shi'i merchant al-Wazzan family, paraphrases this by saying, "We can never give up Kuwait for anything in the world. Loving your country is like loving your Imam".[25] During our interview, the al-Wazzan brothers proudly showed us an article in the *Al-Qabas* newspaper in which the role of the family in protecting Miriam al-Sabah against the Bani Ka'ab tribe during the battle of Al-Riqqa is mentioned.[26] According to the family, because of their role in protecting the Emir's wife during Kuwait's first sea battle, they were granted the exclusive right to weigh products coming into Kuwait—a monopoly granted by the Emir himself.

These families, the Ma'rafi, Behbahani and al-Wazzan, belong to a larger group of ancient Shi'i merchant families who were engaged in two main economic activities: they were either merchants of the old *souq* of Kuwait, such as pearl merchants, or sea-captain families who owned the dhows.[27] Along with the Sunni merchants, they represented the financial class in Kuwait. Yet, next to these old families, who settled in Kuwait by the eighteenth and nineteenth centuries, it is interesting to note that some of the Shi'i merchants who would come to occupy important political positions in the nascent administration of modern Kuwait, were not part of the old mercantile elite but, instead, were of modest background and had only gained their fortunes in the early half of the twentieth century. They represented a group of nouveaux riches who profited from a policy of co-optation by Sheikh Mubarak and his successors. An example is the Qabazard family, whose ancestors started as simple pearl divers, but profited from the integration of Kuwait into the world capitalist system by trading with the British power. The old patriarch of the family, Mohammed Qabazard, developed close relations with the British, thanks to which he was appointed head of the port of Kuwait. After the discovery of oil, the family became one of the biggest state contractors for the building of roads and houses in Kuwait.[28] The same is true for the al-Kadhemi family, from al-Kadhimiyya in Iraq, who settled in Kuwait around 1921. During our interviews, the family underlined the success of their grandfather as a "self-made man" who was able to gain his wealth in the inter-war period and became one of the richest merchants of the Muhammara port. After the discovery of oil, the al-Kadhemi family became the commercial agent of Mercedes. Unlike the Sunni oligarchy, these Shi'i merchants gained their wealth in a period of relative decline in the 1930s and profited from the new economic configuration under British tutelage.[29] We could hypothesize that these nouveaux riches profited from a deliberate policy of co-optation by the ruler in order to weaken the Sunni mercantile opposition.

Hence, it is only within this historical context of alliance-formation that we can understand the nature of the Shi'i-al-Sabah alliance as it crystallized in 1938. During these events, the Shi'a, under the patronage of their merchants, rallied behind the al-Sabah against the Assembly Movement (Harakat al-Majlis), in which Sunni merchant notables formed a National Bloc (al-Kutla al-Wataniyya) and created a legislative assembly to formally protest against the ruler's policy and demand political reforms.[30] The Shi'i merchants, allied to the ruler ever since Mubarak's reign, were excluded from participation in these parliamentary efforts of the Sunni oligarchy. This is illustrated in the account of Habib Hayaat: "The Sunnis only invited my father and Ahmed Ma'rafi. But al-Ghanim told them 'we brought you here only to listen, since you are a minority. You cannot vote.' After this, my father and Ma'rafi decided to organize a movement in Husayniyya Ghaz'aliyya with Sayyid Jawad al-Qazwini".[31] An important ideological factor exacerbating the political rift between the Shi'i and the Sunni merchants was the influence of Arab nationalism on the Sunni oligarchy. The anti-Iranian discourse naturally led the Shi'a to rally behind the ruler, who was considered to be the sole protector of the Shi'a in the midst of a hostile society.

As 1938 structured the dialectic relationship between the Sunni merchants and the al-Sabah, it also marked the collective memory of the Shi'i merchants and future political developments within the Shi'i community. Because of their socio-economic status and prestige within the Shi'i community, they were chosen to represent their constituencies in early parliamentary life, where they would form a coalition of pro-government deputies in a rather vocal parliament. From this essential point of departure, we will focus, in the next section, on the politics of Shi'i merchants after their demise as political notables in the 1980s.

Political Shi'ism, mass politics and the demise of the notables

Until the 1980s, the Shi'i merchants could, on account of their wealth, devote themselves to politics. Moreover, it was thanks to their social prestige within the religious community that they were considered by their constituencies as their legitimate representatives in politics. Hence Shi'i political life was dominated by a group of notables. For these merchants, politics was essentially centred on the preservation of their status, which itself was dependent on their relations with the ruler. With the discovery of oil, the merchants maintained their privileged position in the private sector, but at the cost of a more subservient position as commercial agents or importers in an international capitalist context. Being largely reliant on the goodwill of the sovereign in the granting of lucrative contracts and important licenses, the level political playing field for the merchants was henceforth dependent on acquiescence to government rule. It is only within this macro-structure of the rentier state that we can understand micro-relations between social actors.[32] The demise of the Shi'i merchant notables as a consequence of mass politics is inextricably linked to these macro-micro correlations within rentier state systems. In the coming section, we will analyze the "power" of the Shi'i merchant families after their demise as political notables in the face of a young generation of political entrepreneurs.[33]

It was in the 1970s that the foundations of the contemporary political and religious Shi'i field were laid in Kuwait. As so often in Kuwait's history, external factors triggered a reconstitution of the domestic political field. As demonstrated by Laurence Louër (2008), the politicization of the *marja'iyya* (the supreme religious Shi'i authority)[34] in Iraq since the 1960s reached Kuwait through the arrival of several leading activists of the al-Da'wa movement.[35] Following Ba'thist repression of al-Da'wa, its activists were chased out of Iraq and went into exile in Kuwait, where they arrived through the official networks of the *marja'iyya* of Najaf, as *'ulema* for local Shi'i mosques. Facing a Kuwaiti state that had no policy on granting refuge to political exiles, this dual positioning of the activists (being activists and *'ulema* at the same time) allowed them to establish themselves in Kuwait. They were integrated into existing community institutions, where their aggressive (*haddi*), politicized style of speech galvanized a young generation of educated Shi'a. These "young men" (*shabab*)—as they were called because of their young age and willingness to break away from traditional patterns of politics—called upon the

Shi'i masses to emancipate themselves in the name of political Islam and break away from the patronage of the notables.

At the same time, another movement spread in Kuwait's society, this time through the settlement in Kuwait of the *marja'* himself: Mohammed al-Shirazi. Like the al-Da'wa activists, Mohammed al-Shirazi (1926–2001) sought refuge in Kuwait following Ba'thist repression of the Shi'i clerical establishment. His installation in Kuwait in 1971 was rendered possible because of his good connections with some prominent Shi'i merchant families, whom he had known from their pilgrimage to Karbala. As a self-proclaimed *mujtahed*, al-Shirazi, scion of a prestigious clerical family of Karbala, challenged the *marja'iyya* of Najaf as a source of religious authority.[36] It is within this context of competition that one should place the birth of the Shiraziyyin, following the marginalization of Karbala as a learning centre and its rivalry with Najaf.

The competition between the two movements, Shiraziyyin and al-Da'wa, representing two different *maraja'*, was transposed onto Kuwait's local political scene, as it combined with cleavages that had started to develop within the Shi'i community between the old generation of merchants and the young counter-elite of political Islamists. Whereas the merchants generally disapproved of the politicization of Shi'i identity, for the bulk of the Shi'a the Islamist discourse of al-Da'wa meant a religious awakening and an assertion of their Shi'i identity. These young Shi'a—socialized in the networks of al-Da'wa—adopted the emancipation of the Shi'a on a national level as their primary goal.[37] Contrary to the old notables, they considered politics as a primary vocation to which they were devoted full-time. Their emergence in the political field marked the transition from the politics of notables to the politics of a group of political professionals[38] who radically transformed the political field through the creation of political Shi'i movements. As a consequence, mass politics was introduced, which gradually led to the demise of the power of the merchant notables as they lost their social power in community affairs to a new elite of middle-class Islamist politicians.

In this process towards the horizontal political integration of the community, an interesting mixture between the traditional way of doing politics by the notables and the new strategies of the political entrepreneurs could be observed. In order to acquire social power in the community, the young men appropriated the old local traditions prevalent in society—centred on traditional *'asabiyyat*—as well as the traditional structures of socialization.[39] A first objective of the young men was the takeover of the Jama'iyyat al-Thaqafa al-Ijtima'iyya,[40] a Social Society for Culture established by the merchant notables that essentially served as a means to unify the different Shi'i fractions under one umbrella in order to exercise effective influence over their electorate. The institution was mainly engaged in promoting what its members considered the Shi'i culture (*thaqafat al-Shi'a*) in the sense of an ethnic, inherited identity. The young men, criticizing what they considered to be narrow-minded political interests of the notables, succeeded in 1972 in winning the elections for the board of the Social Society for Culture and transformed it into a front for the al-Da'wa movement in Kuwait. However, since the young men were still dependent on the social capital of the notables to reach the Shi'i masses, they decided to join forces with the notables for the elections of 1975 by supporting candidates from the notability. Profiting from a new electoral law, they succeeded in having ten Shi'i deputies in parliament, which also enabled them to negotiate the appointment of the first Shi'i minister, Abdelmutalib al-Kadhemi, who became Minister of Oil.

The dissolution of the Parliament by the Emir in 1976—in reaction to the vocal opposition of the Arab nationalists and the liberals—brought an abrupt end to the cooperation between the notables and the young men. Whereas the young men fiercely criticized the dissolution and organized themselves to oppose the government's decisions, the notables refrained from any criticism. For these merchants, for whom government procurement had become a major source of their business profits after the oil boom,[41] personal interests in maintaining close ties to the government prevailed over ideological convictions. Following the abstention of the notables, the young men circulated a petition in which they denied the deputies any right to represent the Shi'i community.[42] This episode marked a turning point in the political history of the Shi'a in Kuwait, as a new generation of Shi'i Islamist deputies—expressing an oppositionist discourse—would come to dominate the representation of the Shi'i community in Parliament, a situation that lasted until the elections of 2008.

The advent of the Islamic Revolution in Iran only exacerbated the rift between the merchants and the masses. It triggered great enthusiasm among the majority of Shi'a from middle-class backgrounds and would be the start of the emergence of a pro-Iranian political current in

Kuwait, as an offshoot of the al-Da'wa movement, called the Hizbullah line or Imam line (*Khatt Al-Imam*), in reference to its support for the *wilayat al-faqih* of Ayatollah Khomeini and present-day Ayatollah Khamene'i. In the 1990s, with the re-establishment of Kuwaiti political life, the group was transformed into a formal political movement, the Islamic National Alliance (al-Tahaluf al-Islami al-Watani, referred to as al-Tahaluf throughout this text). Only a minority of former al-Da'wa activists were to stay faithful to the initial al-Da'wa line and follow the *marja'iyya* of Mohammed Hussein Fadlallah, the spiritual mentor of the Lebanese Hizbullah. In 2005, this rump movement would be transformed into al-Mithaq (The Pact), in which the merchant Abdelwahhab al-Wazzan was to play a leading role.[43] Consequently, the initial factionalism between the Shiraziyyin and al-Da'wa was gradually replaced by a new division between pro- and anti-Iranian currents. In Kuwait, the first was represented by the popular al-Tahaluf movement, whilst the second would refer to the Shiraziyyin.

The Shi'i merchant families were generally sceptical about the Iranian revolution, as they used to entertain very close relations to the regime of the Shah, which was related to their commercial interests in Iran. According to Jasem Qabazard:

> We were very shocked by this, my father used to have a very good relation with the old regime, with its ambassadors. For you want to boast about your roots. But when they started to blend politics with religion, we weren't happy. Before the Revolution, being Shi'a in Kuwait was only a religious issue. The older generation never talked in terms of Shi'i-Sunni because that would have been the downfall of our country.[44]

Moreover, the Islamist project was in profound contradiction with the nationalist inclination of the merchants, who considered themselves the pillars of Kuwait's nationhood. Yet, for the Shi'i masses, notably those of Iranian origin, the revolution gave them an important sense of pride in a society where they constituted a minority and had for a long time been dependent on merchants as patrons.

Despite the advent of mass politics, the Shi'i merchants were still favoured by the government in its communication with the masses. Although they had ceased to be the faces (*wujaha*) of their constituencies, they continued to act as intermediaries and behind-the-scenes bargainers. When the cleric Abbas Al-Mohri, who was the imam for the Tarakma community and the representative of Ayatollah Khomeini, together with his sons, started to organize political meetings that gained a wide audience including the Arab nationalists, the patriarchs of the Marafi family intervened to ease the tensions: "He exceeded the red line in criticizing the government. So I went with my two cousins to Sayyid al-Mohri and said to him, 'What your son is doing, to show that you are powerful, isn't a good thing.'"[45] However, since the contestation of the al-Mohris was of a political nature, they did not accept the bargaining attempt, and this led to their expulsion from Kuwait.

The Iran-Iraq war only further aggravated sectarian tensions in Kuwait's society, as the country became a theatre for violent terrorist attacks. The gravest among these attacks took place in the midst of the 1980s with the hijacking of a Kuwaiti aircraft on its way to Karachi and, five months later, the assassination attempt on the Emir Jabir al-Ahmad. Their perpetrators, members of Islamic Jihad (a splinter group of al-Da'wa) wanted to pressure the government into releasing some of their gaoled members who were held responsible for the 1983 attacks on the French and American embassies in Kuwait.[46] Imad Mughniyeh was considered the mastermind behind these attacks. In this extremely tense period for Kuwait, Shi'i citizens suffered from social discrimination because their Shi'ism made them suspect as potential allies of Iran. This feeling of a hostile society would reappear in 2008 with the Mughniyeh affair that tore open the old sores within the Shi'a community.

In this context of increased societal tensions, the government resorted to Parliament as an instrument for moulding societal forces according to its needs. It is the rentier nature of the state in Kuwait—implying a very high level of financial independence—that explains the relative ease with which the government can switch its political alliances, basically by courting the enemies of whatever opposition group it fears most. This explains the election results of 1985, where the government, in an attempt to weaken the influence of Shi'i Islamists, encouraged its old enemies, the Arab nationalists, by allowing them more political space in the public arena.[47] Constituency boundary changes hurt the Shi'a in particular, whose representation fell from ten to three seats, two of which were occupied by pro-government Shi'i deputies belonging to the merchant elite.[48] However, exacerbating regional tensions led to the dissolution of Parliament in 1986. It was also in this period that Kuwait Shi'i citizens were for the first time involved in political violence against the state.[49]

In sum, the official split that took place between the merchants and the Shi'i masses in 1976 was symptomatic of their deep underlying social and political divergence. The ideology of political Shi'ism was discarded by the merchant elite. For them it endangered not only their relations with the rulers but also their privileged position with the Shi'a community. By the end of the 1980s they had lost most of their social power within their constituencies. For the government, the tense interlude of the 1980s brought about the realisation that it needed more effective interlocutors with the Shi'i mass in order to maintain control over this minority.

Sociological recompositions of power of the old merchant families

Having described the demise of the merchants as notables, we can proceed to an analysis of the strategies of power of the Shi'i merchant families since the 1980s, which will allow us to understand the current role of the private sector in politics and state-society relations in Kuwait. This analysis of the politics of Shi'i merchants can only be properly understood in a broader analytical context of literature on modernization and development, in which issues of social stratification and class formation are of central importance. Various scholars have contested the convergence assumption inherent in modernization theory by emphasizing the viability of so-called transitional systems where "traditional" and "modern" modes of production coexist.[50] In these transitional societies, kinship/ethnic and other community-based solidarities impede the full formation of horizontally articulated status groups. Though rentierism is not a necessary condition for such hybrid polities, financial independence from society gives regimes more space for the development of informal, patronage-based modes of governance, such as neo-patrimonial rule, drawing on "traditional" social structures. It is only in this context that we can analyze the influence of the Shi'i merchants in politics and society since the 1980s, and thus understand the mechanisms through which their power is articulated.

Although the Shi'i merchants share a class identity—belonging to the old mercantile elite of Kuwait—these class interests are not translated into coordinated political action. Instead, vertical relations to the state, personified in the sovereign, determine the merchants' political action and undermine the crystallization of class-based politics. This explains the current competition between the old Shi'i families and those they consider to be "newcomers"—those merchants from middle-class background who gained their wealth during the 1980s and 1990s. It also explains the generational decline of the old merchant families, who have ceased to be part of the top elite stratum around the al-Sabah family and the esprit de corps that incorporates the country's major social groupings, such as the affluent merchants and the *shuyukh* from the important clans and tribes.[51] We could argue that it is the rentier-institutional context that impedes cohesive class formation, because entrepreneurial classes become dependent on the state's discretion for access to the rent circuit.[52]

When analyzing the current position of the old Shi'i merchant families, we can quickly conclude that they have become marginalized in politics, when compared to new Shi'i actors. However, the end of the politics of notables has not been accompanied by the fading of the traditional modes of politics, since the political entrepreneurs of the 1980s have, to a certain extent, taken up the role of notables in community affairs. This is especially due to the fact that parliamentarians in Kuwait, instead of representing political platforms, generally function as de facto personal intermediaries between their voters and the government, whom they represent and for whom they facilitate numerous services, ranging from acquiring government permits to providing them with government jobs. Hence, and notwithstanding their legislative power in Kuwait's parliament, members tend to act as intermediaries (*wusata*) and brokers for state resources.[53]

The political movements they represent are typical "parties of cadres" rather than broad-based mass parties, especially as political parties are still illegal in Kuwait.[54] The legitimacy of these deputies generally depends on their *personal* social capital to mobilize financial and material resources. In this regard, the electorate is not actively engaged in the political process of the party and its elite. An example is the popular pro-Iranian al-Tahaluf movement that does not divulge its executive structure: a very small group of deputies supporting it has been successively elected to Parliament without any formal role in the movement.[55] Moreover, like other members of the new middle class that came onto the political scene in the 1980s, the Shi'i political entrepreneurs have reappropriated local social traditions to acquire political visibility. An example is the creation of personal *diwaniyya*s, the merchants' traditional semi-private loci of socialization, which have gained a wide audience and currently play a pivotal role in politics, notably during elections.

Finally, although these political entrepreneurs often represent political movements, their electoral success does not seem to derive from ideologically driven interests of the masses but rather from traditional *'asabiyyat*. One example is the fact that each Shi'i sub-community tends to favour deputies from its own group of belonging, despite their political differences.[56] It is with this logic that one should appreciate the long-lasting political visibility of those deputies belonging to the "Tarakma",[57] as the bulk of their electorate consists of the Tarakma Shi'a who represent the demographic majority of the Ajam and have come to play a more pronounced role in the electoral process with the advent of mass politics. Another important factor explaining the deputies' electoral success is the fact that the *sayyid*s (descendants of the Prophet Mohammed) are particularly successful in Parliament.[58] In sum, the emergence of the political entrepreneurs did not follow a process of political modernization but seems rather to be a perpetuation of personalized *'asabiyyat* dominated by loosely organized groups of notables who determine the nature of political action. One of the reasons for the merchants' political decline is their low-profile stance in the Shi'i political field, which has been dominated since the 1980s by the pro-Khomeini opposition movement al-Tahaluf. Yet although the old merchants do not play an overt role in politics, it became clear from our interviews that they do support some of the Shi'i Islamist movements, namely those which maintain a nationalist political discourse, such as Tajammu'a al-Adala Wa-Salam (Assembly for Justice and Peace) and al-Mithaq (the Pact).

One of the Shi'i political movements that particularly counts on the moral and financial support of the old merchant families in Kuwait is Al-Adala Wa-Salam, the political branch of the Shiraziyyin movement. Upon his arrival in Kuwait, the *marja'* Mohammed al-Shirazi had already succeeded in developing very close ties with the Shi'i merchants, through whom he was also introduced to the royal family. It is this historical legacy that explains the merchants' current support for al-Adala Wa-Salam. The movement's narrative is centred on the religious rather than political emancipation of the Shi'a in Kuwait, on Islamic unity; it rejects Khomeini's *wilayat al-faqih* principle and profoundly supports the ruling house.[59] The considerable financial resources of the Shiraziyyin stem from the support of the affluent old Shi'i merchant families, for whom its nationalist bent not only corresponds with their political convictions as an old elite historically loyal to the al-Sabah, but also has become their only access to public politics as merchants in the rentier-state context, as they have lost their own notable status. The movement has transcended ethnic affiliations, since the Sheikhi-Hasawi community—whose members are particularly affluent in Kuwait—seems to be particularly committed to the Shiraziyyin. This has been so especially after the death of the late Mirza al-Ihqaqi, which led to a split within this community, as some do not recognize his son as their *marja'* and instead switched to the *marja'* of Sayyid al-Shirazi.[60] This support from Kuwaiti Sheikhis for the Shiraziyyin is due to the fact that, during his stay in Kuwait, Mohammed al-Shirazi explicitly developed close ties to the al-Ihqaqi *marja'*, forming like the Shiraziyyin a minority branch within Shi'ism.

Hence, it is the merchants' support that explains the prominence of the Shiraziyyin movement in the religious field. The Shiraziyyin have the largest number of mosques in Kuwait, as well as numerous charitable institutions in and outside Kuwait.[61] This stands in stark contrast to the politically strong al-Tahaluf movement, which is only marginally represented in the religious Shi'i field in Kuwait. It possesses only two mosques (of which one has been built only recently in 2006, named after its deputy, Adnan Abdelsamad) and one library in Kuwait. Moreover, the Shiraziyyin are known to have heavily invested in modern means of communication. It was the first to create an explicitly Shi'i satellite channel emanating from a *marja'*, al-Anwar (2003).[62] However, despite their strong visibility in the religious field, the Shiraziyyin are marginalized in the political field where they could not compete with al-Tahaluf, the movement supported by the Shi'i masses.

Like the Shiraziyyin, al-Mithaq (founded in 2005) presents itself as a nationalist and pro-al-Sabah movement. Although referring to the *marja'iyya* of Mohammed Hussein Fadlallah (the spiritual mentor of the Lebanese Hizbullah), its political discourse is centred on the spirit of the nation (*ruh al-watani*) and on Islamic unity. Especially since the merchant Abdelwahhab al-Wazzan has joined the movement and has become its de facto leader, al-Mithaq presents itself as a nationalist movement whose members "are not influenced by any outside forces and are not thinking in terms of their sect, but work in the interests of Kuwait".[63] However, I argue that al-Mithaq, by contrast to the Shiraziyyin who can count on the support of Shi'i civil society actors, is a top-down created movement which fits in the new government's policy aimed at unifying the Shi'a community behind its flag, following the new regional context post-2003 (the American invasion of Iraq) and the rise of political opposition from tribal-Islamist constituencies.

All of Al Mithaq's leading members are former ministers and so represent, in some way, the interests of the government.[64] Moreover, the merchant who heads the movement, Abdelwahhab al-Wazzan, has very close ties to the ruling family, and has profited from government appointments in the various positions he holds.[65] The family, which arrived in Kuwait by the mid-eighteenth century from the north of Iran, is particularly known for its patriotism and defence of Kuwait. It protected Miriam al-Sabah against the Bani Ka'ab tribe during the battle of Riqqa (1783). Moreover, Abdelwahhab al-Wazzan played a key role in distributing food to Kuwaitis during the 1990–91 Iraqi invasion and occupation, and together with the Sunni Islamist activist Ahmed al-Baqir took the lead of the popular government in Kuwait which coordinated with the government in exile in Ta'if during the occupation.[66]

I consider the overt engagement of Abdelwahhab—as a merchant—in the field of Shi'i Islamist movements, and his efforts at unifying the different Shi'i currents, to be a manifestation of a new government policy. This implicit policy of co-optation is revealed by the presence of several members related to the "group" around the person of al-Wazzan in high government positions.[67] The primacy of kinship links is important in explaining the political affiliation of Shi'i merchants. An example is the old generation of the al-Wazzan family, which criticizes the Islamist ideology of al-Mithaq, but is associated with the movement because of kinship ties to Abdelwahhab.[68] The same is true for the al-Kadhemi family, which has been linked by matrimonial alliances to the al-Zilzalla family. Although most of the al-Kadhemi are not actively involved in Shi'a politics, they are somehow associated with and represented by Sayyid Youssef al-Zilzalla, an al-Mithaq deputy and former Minister of Commerce and Industry. Hence, it is the patriarch who indirectly channels the interests of the extended family he represents.

However, like the Shiraziyyin, al-Mithaq is marginalized in parliament, as it has not been able to win the support of the Shi'i masses. In sum, the merchant families have lost their social prestige in community affairs and have not been able to regain their political influence over the

Shi'i masses, since they do not support the Islamist ideology as propagated by the al-Tahaluf movement. For them, Shi'ism is essentially an inherited religious identity which should be practiced on religious grounds, without any political ramifications that transcend the borders of the nation state. They support those Shi'i movements that display a nationalist, pro-government discourse, but even that only tacitly. The allegiance of al-Tahaluf to the Islamic Republic and its principles is fiercely criticized by these old merchant families who—because of their historical legacy as an old (*asli*) elite and current position as merchants in the rentier state—claim true patriotism. Consequently, they do not want to play any *overt* role in the field of Shi'i movements, whose partisan Islamist nature runs counter to their convictions.

I argue that it is in light of this loss of community power that we should interpret the creation of a new Shi'i mercantile clientele by the state in its efforts to regain effective control over the Shi'i population. This new generation of Shi'i merchants differs from the old one in its overt implication in the field of Islamist movements. As they are in some way top-down created, and thus representing the interests of influential members of the ruling elite, in particular PM Nasser Mohammed, we could argue that they have got no autonomy in their political action.

The emergence of new Shi'i merchants as notable intermediaries between the Al Sabah and the Shi'i masses

Since 9/11, but especially since the American intervention in Iraq, starting in 2003, Kuwaiti society has become polarized into two major blocs, comprised of those in favour of a liberal pro-American policy (liberals, Shi'a and the government), and of those criticizing the government's support for the Americans, notably the radical Islamists and the Arab nationalists. This polarization coincides with another major social division, the historical one between the nomadic (*badu*) and the sedentarized (*hadhar*) population of the Emirate. At this moment, the major debates in society concern the growing tensions between the radical Sunni Islamists and the rest of the Kuwaiti population, mostly *hadhar*. The latter consider the *badu* to be "primitive" people who have introduced tribalism and Islamist radicalism into Kuwait's political system.

The Sunni Islamist and tribal forces (there is an important overlap between the two) have become increasingly oppositional towards the various Kuwaiti governments. This is due to several developments in Kuwaiti politics over the past decade. First of all, the tribal constituencies have become increasingly assertive politically. This is largely the consequence of the socio-political emancipation of a new generation of highly educated tribesmen, who have come to demand a greater and more just inclusion in the state's political and redistributive order. Tribal members of Parliament have become true political icons in Kuwait, as they do not refrain from voicing opposition to the government, using a political discourse centred on citizenship, transparent governance and other cross-cutting issues of politics.[69] In addition to this social emancipation of the tribal constituencies, Sunni Islamist forces, attracting considerable support from tribal constituencies, have also become increasingly vocal opponents of the government's pro-American policies. It is in this context of the failure of the government's vote-buying strategies towards tribal and Islamist forces, and growing societal polarization, that one should place the rapprochement between the government and Shi'i forces in society.

Finally, since the death of Emir Jaber in 2006, policies of co-optation by members of the ruling elite have become increasingly overt and are being played out in public. Until then, elite division had remained largely confined to indoor struggles, resolved within the family without influencing the open political game. However, the succession struggle which broke out after the death of Emir Jaber differed from earlier such struggles, as it was to break the conventions on possible succession lines. His natural successor, Sa'ad al-Abdullah al-Salem, was "impeached" by the parliament after only nine days of rule, considered to be physically too weak to rule. He was replaced by Sheikh Sabah al-Ahmed al-Jaber, then Prime Minister (2003–2006) and third in the line of succession. The rise to the throne of Sheikh Sabah IV introduced a new dynamic to the traditional competition between the al-Salem and al-Jaber branches. Given the new Emir's violation of established customs of succession and his talent for forging political alliances in society, other members of the ruling family became hopeful that they too could aspire to the throne.[70] These princes and their fathers have started to play out their differences by creating alliances and acting through competing segments of society. It is also from this perspective of intra-family competition and the growing visibility of "political money" that one should understand the politics of alliance-building with Shi'i constituencies by Nasser Mohammed al-Sabah as head of government. Consequently, one should bear in mind, references to government in this text very much forefront the person of Sheikh Nasser Mohammed, who was a key figure in forging these alliances with the Shi'i minority.

In order to reach Kuwait's Shi'i masses, the regime relied upon a limited group of "new" Shi'i merchants, who have been incorporated into the highest political *'asabiyya* around the House of al-Sabah. These Shi'i merchants currently belong to the wealthiest families in the Emirate and differ from the old families in the sense that their wealth has only been created since the early 1990s. I argue that it is the rentier nature of the state that has enabled it to revive with relative ease a form of notable politics through a policy of political patronage in the private sector. The capacity of the rentier state to create classes has been suggested by a number of authors and has also been revealed in other rentier state contexts. An example is Saudi Arabia, where the rent has enabled the state to create a Najdi bourgeoisie at the expense of the established commercial elite from the Hijaz region.[71]

One of the newly prominent Shi'i merchants is Jawaad Bukhamseen, who belongs to the Sheikhi community. Coming from an old clerical family from al-Hasa, the Bukhamseen family only settled in the Emirate at the start of the twentieth century. With no prior social capital as a merchant, Jawaad Bukhamseen started as a small broker on the Kuwaiti stock market and benefited in the 1980s from state incentives to invest in the then booming real-estate sector, a sector which has profited from a policy of state patronage aimed at weakening mercantile opposition. Currently, Bukhamseen Holding represents a conglomerate of economic activities, with a concentration on real estate and contracting. Moreover, the merchant is on the executive board of the International Bank of Kuwait, which, being presided over by Abdelwahhab al-Wazzan, is often referred to as a Shi'i bank. The charitable activities of Jawaad Bukhamseen are considerable and differ from the old merchant families in the sense that they exceed the Sheikhi community and include all political Shi'i movements, including al-Tahaluf.[72] We could argue that his exorbitant charitable activities are a means for this "new" merchant to buy social prestige in the Shi'i community, which will also enhance his position as a political notable among the various Shi'i movements and the central power. Furthermore, by contrast to the old elite, the Bukhamseen family has been actively involved in Shi'i politics. An example is the alliance between his son, Anouar Bukhamseen, and Saleh Ashour during the 2008 elections when they decided to work together for al-Adala wa-Salam.[73] However, al-Adala wa-Salam only succeeded in gaining one representative in Parliament, the leading political figure of the movement, Saleh Achour. As a merchant, Anouar Bukhamseen, despite massive financing for his campaign, could not mobilize enough popular support and lost against the al-Tahaluf deputies in the first district, leading the Bukhamseen family to criticize Saleh Ashour, accusing him of having used the family's money to get into Parliament.

In the elections of May 2009, Jawaad Bukhamseen, as with the other new merchants, publicly insisted on the need to unify the Shi'a, and actively supported the unification efforts by the representatives of the main Shi'i political currents,[74] namely al-Tahaluf, al-Mithaq and Tajamu'a al-Risalat al-Insaniyya (the latter, "Assembly of the Human Message", was created in 2006 and emanates from the Sheikhi community). I argue that this position reflects the regime's strategy towards the Shi'i minority. It is also by this logic that we should understand the creation in 2007 of his personal daily newspaper, *Al-Nahar*, characterized by its pro al-Sabah stance and which—although not officially presented as a Shi'i newspaper—serves a largely Shi'i audience.

On the regional level, Jawaad Bukhamseen has played an important role in Kuwait's soft-power diplomacy towards its new Shi'i neighbour, Iraq. He is particularly known in Shi'i society for his economic alliances with business families in Iraq. Moreover, Jawaad Bukhamseen was the first to use the direct flight to Najaf airport, built in 2008 by the al-Aqeelah group—a Kuwaiti company that specifically invests in the Shi'i shrine cities in Iraq and Syria, and is essentially financed by the Shi'i merchants in Kuwait.[76] His economic investments in Iraq have gained him prominence in top political and religious circles, through which he can play an indirect role in the reinforcement of Kuwait's diplomatic ties to its neighbour. The following statement by Nouri al-Maliki is telling in this context: "We will never forget what Bukhamseen has done for Iraq through his investments and his dialogue with important Iraqi personalities".[77]

Another merchant who has gained prominence recently is Ali al-Matruk, belonging to the Baharna Shi'a. One of our interviewees has described him as follows:

> Ali Al-Matruk and Mahmud Haider, they aren't from the old merchant families, they are really new. There is a very rich old Al-Matruk family, but Ali Al-

Matruk he is not from the same family. He didn't have any money, but the government supported him and wanted to give him the image of an old family. So that is why most of the Shi'a think he is an old merchant.[78]

Being from a modest family, Ali al-Matruk started his career as a bureaucrat with the Ministry of Finance and gained his riches in the 1980s through a policy of land allocation by the state. Instead of investing in commercial activities, Ali al-Matruk is a rich landlord and has profited from government patronage through land distribution.[79] As a poet and columnist for the *Al-Watan* newspaper (owned by Sheikh Ali Al Khalifa), Ali al-Matruk presents himself as an enlightened person and as neutral amidst what he considers to be a fragmented Shi'i landscape in Kuwait.[80] It is interesting to note that Ali al-Matruk, like other new Shi'i merchants, has since 2004 been on the board of the International Bank of Kuwait. As is the case with Jawaad Bukhamseen, al-Matruk portrays himself as a merchant who transcends the ethnic Shi'i *'asabiyyat* and supports all sections of the Shi'a community.[81] Moreover, since the Mugniyeh affair, in which he played a crucial role as mediator, al-Matruk has supported the pro-Iranian al-Tahaluf movement, which is remarkable if we consider that he had fiercely criticized this movement in his past columns. Like the other new merchants, Ali al-Matruk is considered in Shi'i society as a very close friend of the Emir himself, Sheikh Sabah al-Ahmed. Furthermore—although it is beyond the time scope of this study—it is interesting to note that at the start of the uprising in Bahrain, Ali al-Matruk played a key role in the Kuwaiti delegation to mediate between the opposition group al-Wefaq and the Bahraini government.[82] Finally, there is another "new" merchant who has become one of the wealthiest persons of Kuwait: the Iranian merchant Mahmud Haider, who has gained his wealth since the 1990 invasion. The companies Mahmoud H. Haider presides over, among these Mahmoud H. Haider and Sons Trading Company and the Al Zumorrodah Holding Co., represent a capital of approximately two billion dollars each. Telecommunications and real estate constitute the bulk of the family's activities.[83] It is important to note the hatred existing among the group of old merchant families towards those whom they consider to be newcomers, as reflected in the following statement: "Mahmud Haider is very young. He is not a merchant and he was never a merchant".[84] This illustrates the general rivalry within the group of Shi'i merchants, the strength of ascriptive identities, as well as the weakness of class-articulated relations in Kuwait's rentier institutional context.

Even more than the other new merchants, Mahmud Haider embodies the will of the government to unify the Shi'i population behind its rule. As such, he owns a daily newspaper, *Al-Dar* (2007), which is explicitly presented as a Shi'i newspaper and which also includes the Shiraziyyin movement, as the latter's secretary-general is currently editor-in-chief of *Al-Dar*.[85] During my fieldwork, I noticed the omnipresence of *Al-Dar* stickers, as well as Bukhamseen's *Al-Nahar*, in neighbourhoods with a high concentration of Shi'a, such as al-Da'iyya and al-Dasma. In terms of charity work towards the Shi'a community, Mahmud Haider supports all Shi'i branches and has enhanced his visibility in the public space by the establishments of medical centres in his name. It is important to note that the merchant has good relations with Sayyid Mohammad Baqer al-Mohri, a politicized Shi'i cleric who regularly publishes fierce statements against the Salafists and maintains close ties with prominent pro-government personalities, such as the Speaker of Parliament, Jasem al-Khorafi. Although Mohammed Baqer al-Mohri presents himself as the official spokesmen of Shi'i *ulema*, he is not considered as such by most of those *ulema*.

Vergemeinschaftung of the Shia by the neo-patrimonial state and the return of the merchant notables

I argue that these new merchants have been able, through their important charitable activities for all segments within the Shi'a community and through their closeness to the al-Sabah, to play the role of intermediaries between the Shi'i masses and the government. Although they are not the ones who literally give visibility to those they represent (*wujaha*)—a role that has been taken up by the Shi'i deputies—these merchants resemble new political patrons who "protect" and who can "intercede" at crucial moments. Their political action is top-down driven, as they have come to constitute a new Shi'i client stratum of the al-Sabah and, as such, represent the interests of their patron. I will illustrate my reasoning through the analysis of concrete examples of government policy aimed at unifying Kuwait's Shi'i minority.

One of the top-down measures with regard to the Shi'a has been the creation of a Shi'i Awqaf Department at the Ministry of Religious

Endowments in 2004. Despite various previous attempts to regularize the *husayniyyas* and to control the financing of religious affairs, it was only in the post-2003 context that the project was finally implemented. As in other Gulf Cooperation Council countries with Shi'i minorities, the Shi'i accession to power in Baghdad was accompanied by state-led anti-discriminatory policies in the religious sphere in those countries, which also served as a means to better control their minorities.[86] In this context, the initiative to establish an Awqaf Department came from the Emir of Kuwait himself, without prior parliamentary approval, which explains the opposition of the al-Tahaluf movement to the project.[87] However, the pro-government Shi'i movements such as al-Mithaq and the Shiraziyyin, supported by the old merchant families, were in favour of the project, which they saw as a means to control the flow of Islamic funds that could potentially be used for non-nationalist causes. During our interviews, the resentment of Shi'i *ulema*—both independent and those of the al-Tahaluf movement—towards the Awqaf Department was particularly pronounced, considering it a violation of the principle of financial independence from the state.[88] They emphasized that most of the *ulema* have not accepted to receive a government salary. Hence, instead of representing a policy of religious recognition responding to grass-roots demands, the creation of the Shi'i Awqaf should be understood as a top-down measure by the state, aimed at better controlling its religious minority.

Various attempts have also been made to unify the Shi'i branches in the political domain. The merchant Abdelwahhab al-Wazzan has played an important role in this process, notably since 2003. The alliances in 2003 and 2006 ('Itilaf al-Tajammu'at al-Watani) comprised all the Shi'i political movements except the oppositional al-Tahaluf movement. However, because of their weak social base, these unions did not succeed in vanquishing the al-Tahaluf deputies in parliament. Hence al-Tahaluf presented an obstacle to the new government's policy aimed at rallying the Shi'a behind its rule.

It is in this context that we should understand the reaction to the events of 12 February 2008, when members of al-Tahaluf came together to commemorate the assassination of Imad Mughniyeh, one of the leading figures of Hizbullah in Lebanon. This gathering (*ta'bin*) provoked widespread indignation in Kuwaiti society, since Mughniyeh was considered to be the mastermind behind the terrorist attacks of the 1980s, including the assassination attempt on the Emir. Vocal accusations in the media—notably from radical Sunni Islamists—against the deputies revived sectarian tensions. Shi'a generally refer to this episode as a period of societal hostility towards them, comparing it to the tense interlude of the 1980s. This context of sectarian tensions has enabled the state, through the intermediation of the new Shi'i merchants, to draw closer to its minority. As in 1938, the context of a society considered to be hostile towards the Shi'a was a crucial factor in explaining the reshaping of Shi'i politics after the Mughniyeh incident. One of our interviewees put it as follows: "For the Shi'a, it is not the government which is the problem, it is society".[89]

Following the incident, the government and high personalities close to the Emir tacitly supported the Shi'a. The Speaker of Parliament, Jasem al-Khorafi, appeased tensions by saying that no final proof existed regarding the implication of Mughniyeh in the attacks. However, the merchants Ali al-Matruk and Mahmud Haider were the ones who presented themselves as crucial mediators in the conflict by organizing meetings between al-Tahaluf and government representatives in their *diwaniyyas*.[90] It is here that a tacit agreement was made: the government approved the Jama'iyyat al-Thaqafa Wa al-Ijtima'iyya—the old bastion of al-Da'wa activists, most of whom had adhered to the Imam Line after 1979—in exchange for political compliance with the government. Furthermore, the government appointed Fadhal al-Safar, from al-Tahaluf, as a Minister of Public Works and Municipal Affairs. This was the first time that an al-Tahaluf deputy had ever been appointed minister. It is interesting to note that most of the "new" merchant elites have been active players in the unification of the Shi'i movements. Abdelwahhab al-Wazzan was, for example, the driving force behind the merger (following the Mughniyeh affair) between al-Tahaluf and al-Mithaq, to form the new movement al-I'tilaf al-Islami al-Watani (The National Islamic Coalition).

How should we interpret this mediation role of these Shi'i merchants? Have they become new notables? Although the merchants present their mediation as a means to "defend the Shi'a", it seems that the government itself conferred upon them the role of political notables. Even though the Shi'i deputies of al-Tahaluf have continued to represent their constituencies, they have become de facto dependent on the patronage of the merchants and, indirectly, the government. An example is the recent declaration in *Al-Dar* that "the members of the Society for Culture are grateful for the charitable giving of Hajji Haider and for his positions in favor of Kuwait's society in all its components".[91] Moreover, the following statement by the secretary-general of al-Tahaluf, Hussein al-Ma'atuq, reveals the new position of the movement: "We represent Khamenei and Khomeini, but also Sistani and Fadlallah. The most important for us, the Shi'a is to be united at this moment. Although we are close to Khomeini, we try to be united".[92]

Finally, a last word on the election results of May 2009, which give credit to our argument, identifying a policy of *Vergemeinschaftung* by the regime towards the Shi'a, as the latter almost doubled their representation in Parliament, whereas the Islamist groups (Ikhwan and Salafists) lost one third of their deputies.[93] These results reflected the state's policy of segmentation aimed at marginalizing the Sunni Islamist radicals, implemented by favouring their opponents, notably the Shi'a and, to a lesser extent, the liberals.[94] Hence, whereas the Sunni Islamists were heavily criticized in pro-government media, women, the Shi'a and the liberals benefited from government support.[95]

Henceforth, for the first time since 1976 with the birth of a Shi'i opposition in Kuwait, the Shi'a were represented in the Parliament by pro-government members and constituted a pillar of support for the government. Yet, whilst this case study points to the capacity of the rentier state to co-opt societal forces, I argue that it is mostly their minority status that explains the Shi'a' rallying behind the rulers since 2009. It was the fear of an increasingly hostile society that had led them to seek state protection, as in 1938. However, even in a rich rentier state such as Kuwait, the large salaried middle class has become increasingly dissatisfied with the overt co-optation policies of the former government of PM Nasser Mohammed and the widespread use of political money.

These policies of co-optation of societal forces through political money came to the fore with the discovery of $350 million in deposits in the bank accounts of thirteen former members of Parliament. As early as 2009, money laundering scandals were discovered and led to a parliamentary grilling of the Prime Minister. It triggered a broad-based movement, instigated by the youth, pleading for the dismissal of Nasser Mohammed in November 2011, following the storming of the Parliament. As with the youth in Tunis and Cairo, their chief complaint was corruption, whilst they also advocated a more civic order, grounded in constitutional rights. As a result of this widespread popular anger towards corruption, and in conjunction with the Arab Spring, the 2012 elections gave power to a tribal-Islamist opposition (34 seats out of 50) at the expense of the pro-government forces of earlier cabinets—the Shi'a and the liberals. With the removal of PM Nasser Mohammed from the government, the social forces loyal to him have seen their political role decline. Being in a certain way created by a policy of co-optation in the private sector, the new Shi'i merchants owe their position completely to the state. This is also their weakness, as a change in government policy or in backing from a *sheikh* is likely to lead to the decline in their power, as has happened recently following the 2012 elections.

Conclusion

By focusing on the Shi'i merchants in Kuwait, this paper has sought to add value to the academic debate on the changing role of the private sector in Arab politics and state-society relations. Following an analysis of the sociological recompositions of the Shi'i merchant families and the evolution of their power in politics and in society, we have gained a better understanding of the sociology of power in rentier states, a field which remains largely unexplored. The macro-structure of the rentier state is a determining factor in understanding the politics of private sector players. Notwithstanding the economic diversification policy and increased intra-Arab levels of investment since the 1980s, this research lead us to conclude that the private sector still serves as a primary tool for political patronage in the rentier state of Kuwait. Because of the rentier state's financial independence from society, the rich rentier is not dependent on a thriving business class to effectively govern and will instead use the private sector as a playing field for the creation of strata of loyal state clienteles.

The old Shi'i merchants of al-Sharq, favoured by the al-Sabah family in order to weaken the Sunni mercantile opposition, maintained their privileged position after the discovery of oil, but in a much more subservient way, being henceforth dependent on the goodwill of the ruler in the award of lucrative state contracts. Hence, their nationalism in favour of the House of al-Sabah not only corresponds to their historical memory as an old elite traditionally allied to the ruler, but has also become their sole means to play a social and economic role as merchants in the rentier state context. This explains not only their resentment towards the pro-Iranian Islamist discourse of al-Tahaluf as a mass movement, but also their deep support for the Shiraziyyin, whom they consider to be essentially "religious" and in favour of the al-Sabah. It is because of their continuous loyalty to the ruler—even during the tense interlude of the 1980s—that those families finally lost all their credibility to represent the Shi'i masses, who would hereafter favour the oppositional pro-Iranian deputies.

It is also in this context that the state, having lost its crucial channels to reach its minority, started to favour new private sector Shi'i elites—through specific public policies such as economic subsidies and land allocation—in order to regain its influence over the Shi'a community. Like the Bedouin and Sunni Islamist groups in the same period, these Shi'i merchants benefited from an implicit policy of co-optation in the construction and real estate sectors during the 1980s.

These "new" merchants, such as Jawaad Boukhamseen, Ali al-Matruk and Mahmud Haider, have come to prominence particularly in the new post-9/11 political context. Their preeminence in the private sector reflects the reorientation of the government's policy towards its Shi'a population. Indeed, as so often in its political history, the government played on social antagonisms to erect itself as a neutral arbiter for maintaining its hegemony over society. Facing growing opposition from the radical Sunni Islamists, notably since the American intervention in Iraq, the government moved closer to the Shi'a, the radical Sunni Islamists' opponents. In this, it relied upon the new merchants as informal intermediaries in its efforts to unify the fragmented Shi'a community behind its rule. Because of its command of externally provided financial resources, the modern rentier state can continue to exercise its authority in a neo-patrimonial way as it acts as a benevolent patriarch in distributing the rent to society. As such, the state continues to favour informal (mediated) forms of rule over rational, bureaucratized modes.

The political and social action of these new Shi'i merchants must be interpreted in this light. As we have seen, these actors are heavily invested in real estate and have often benefited from the government's land allocation policies. Through the support of all major Shi'i branches and through investment in Shi'i media, they have become active players in the process of unifying the Shi'a of Kuwait behind the al-Sabah. This enabled them to play a crucial role as mediators between the government and the Shi'i masses, notably during the Mughniyeh affair in 2008, which resulted in the co-optation of the oppositional al-Tahaluf movement. It is the rentier nature of the state that explains the relative flexibility with which the government can change its political allegiances, which is achieved through instrumentalization of the private sector.

Thus, the renewed participation of Shi'i businessmen in politics is an illustration of their dependence on the government rather than a manifestation of independent class interests. Under rentier conditions, loyalty to the system still seems to be the most rational choice for the entrepreneurial class, which is also the main obstacle to the maturation of independent, class-based business politics.

5

BREAKING LOOSE

REDUCED PRIVATE SECTOR DEPENDENCE ON GOVERNMENTS IN GCC ECONOMIES[1]

Nathan Hodson

Introduction

Governments in GCC states have long played a central role as the prime mover of economic activity, particularly after the first oil boom in the early 1970s. With the influx of wealth, they adopted generous welfare systems, established massive public investment programmes in infrastructure, and provided fiscal incentives to develop the industrial sector. The massive distribution of wealth meant that nearly all economic activity was linked to, and conditioned by, the active presence of the state. Giacomo Luciani describes five main channels through which oil rents were transformed into private wealth: local representation of foreign companies; land distribution and real estate speculation; government procurement; government support to industry; and the promotion of extensive agriculture.[2] In addition to transferring large amounts of wealth through practices such as land speculation, the government has also served as the major employer in the economy, with those not working directly for the state often performing government services. In a number of ways, this reality and the nature of the sources of state income influenced the basic rules of political life.[3]

To a large extent, the private sector remains predominantly dependent on government contracts and other business opportunities that are highly influenced by government decisions and initiatives.[4] However, the private sector has made great strides since the 1970s, developing a number of new capabilities and capitalizing on state-directed development and infrastructure investment. Many genuinely private business groups have greatly increased their financial capabilities through international investment in addition to public spending, and they are increasingly engaging in lines of business that cater to open and fairly competitive markets.

Since the mid-1990s, GCC governments have attempted to limit some of the impact of abrupt declines of government spending on economic development by expanding the role of the private sector. To this end, most GCC states have taken steps to privatize major state-run enterprises such as telecommunications and utilities, ease rules on foreign investment, reduce bureaucratic hurdles, and strengthen financial systems and markets. The manufacturing sectors in Bahrain, Saudi Arabia and the UAE have been growing and are increasingly diversified, and governments are using the massive proceeds from recent oil revenues to lay the foundation for a host of future non-oil industries.

This paper will examine macroeconomic shifts over time in order to explore ways in which the private sector has grown more independent of the public sector in GCC economies. It begins with a brief examination of the role of hydrocarbons, before detailing changes in government revenue and expenditure with a focus on capital and current spending. The paper then investigates shifts in public and private sector consumption and capital formation. It also takes a closer look at the composition of non-oil GDP in Saudi Arabia and briefly illustrates other indicators of increasing private sector independence, including the expansion of regional stock markets, Gulf investment in the broader Middle East, and low tariff rates, which require local business to be more competitive.

Both easily discernible and more subtle changes in all of these areas point to a more independent private sector. Hydrocarbons remain important, but at least up to 2010, there was less oil wealth per capita than there was throughout much of the 1970s. The ratio of government capital to current expenditure has declined and remained relatively low, which means that business has had to turn to private clients rather than rely almost exclusively on the government. And government capital spending has declined not only as a share of total government spending but also as a share of total fixed capital investment, the difference being made up by the private sector. As oil prices have remained high in recent years, both of these ratios have begun to creep up, particularly in Oman and Saudi Arabia.[5] However, they remain far from the levels of the 1970s. While state spending has been increased in the wake of the Arab Spring, a large share of this is accounted for by current spending in the form of higher salaries and consumer subsidies, from which business profit only indirectly through consumer markets.

While one should not exaggerate private sector independence, the general trend does appear to be towards growing autonomy, the effects of which could be vast. It has the potential to change not only the nature and composition of economies in GCC states but also political and social structures. Such a shift may be a long way off and may take many forms, but a more autonomous private sector could take steps to redefine its relationship to the state, which would have important consequences for political systems as well as theories about rentier states.

Continued dependence on hydrocarbons

Oil and gas continue to dominate GCC economies. This is evident in GDP figures, in the composition of exports, and in oil's contribution to government revenue. The hydrocarbons sector constituted over 40% of aggregate nominal GDP in the GCC in 2010, while mineral exports make up the vast majority of total exports in all GCC states except the UAE. Only in Qatar did hydrocarbon revenue account for less than three quarters of total government revenue in the 2005–09 period.

However, these figures mask several important differences across time and between individual states. For the GCC as a whole, the contribution of the oil sector to GDP dropped from a high of 75% in 1974 to a low of 26% in 1986. It has since risen, displaying a rough U-shaped pattern that coincides with the boom and bust cycle of oil markets (see Graph 1). Yet while real oil prices in the recent boom in the 2000s surpassed those in the first boom, oil sector contributions to GCC economies have not reached similar highs. This could be indicative of the

Graph 1: Value Added of Mining and Utilities[6] as a Percentage of Nominal GDP, Three Year Moving Average (1970–2010).

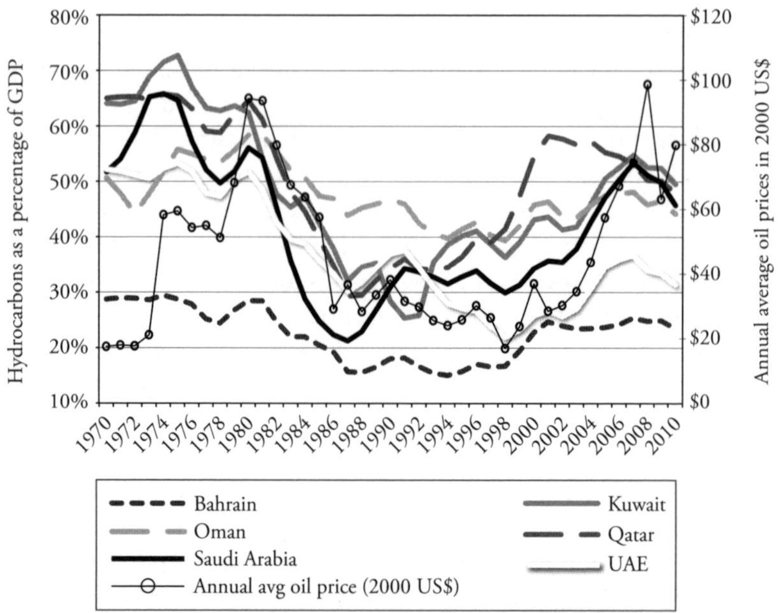

Source: United Nations National Accounts Main Aggregates; oil prices are crude oil refiner acquisition costs from the US Department of Energy's Energy Information Administration.

growing importance of the non-oil sector in GCC economies, but it is also due to a smaller share of oil money being spent than in the 1970s and early 1980s. A deeper statistical analysis would be required to more fully explain this shift.

At the same time, there is also important variation across countries. In 2006–10, hydrocarbons accounted for roughly a quarter of Bahrain's GDP, whereas they constituted over half of GDP in Saudi Arabia, Kuwait and Qatar. Several countries, most notably Kuwait and Qatar, have supplemented government revenue with investment income, which has reduced government dependence on oil and gas income to a certain extent. According to the IMF, hydrocarbon revenue made up 76% of revenue in Kuwait and 60% in Qatar in 2005–09. However, oil revenue

Graph 2: GCC Hydrocarbon Dependence (2005–09 Average).

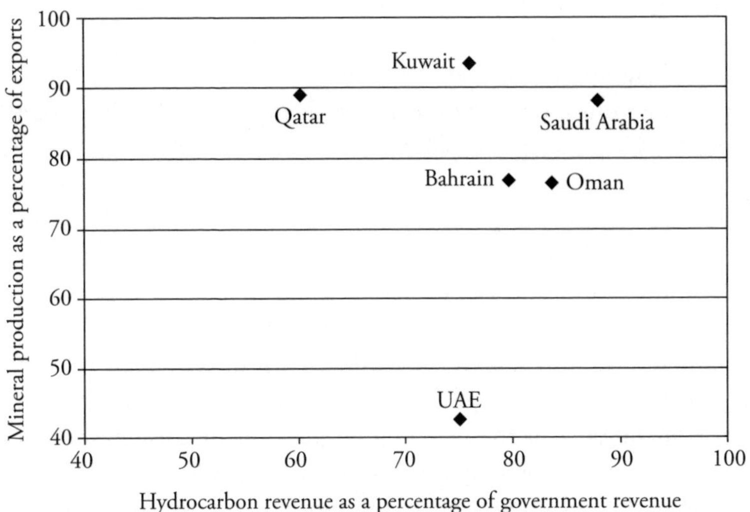

Source: Various national reporting data; IMF Article IV Reports and Statistical Appendices.

as a percentage of the total has remained above 75% in all of the GCC states except Qatar (see Graph 2).

Similarly, mineral products continue to make up the vast majority of total exports in all GCC countries except the UAE, where re-exports have probably surpassed the total value of oil and gas exports.[7] During the 2005–09 period, oil and gas constituted around 75% of Bahrain's and Oman's exports, roughly 90% of Qatar's and Saudi Arabia's, and an incredible 94% of Kuwait's. These figures indicate that oil dependence in GCC economies remains high, with the lowest rates of dependence in Bahrain, Oman and the UAE. In terms of oil's contribution to GDP, these states have also been the least affected by the recent oil boom.

These findings are not surprising. Oman's oil resources are relatively limited, although the fall in oil output since 2001 has coincided with a switch to natural gas. Bahrain's oil production and reserves are far smaller than those of the other GCC states. In part for this reason, Bahrain has long been ahead of the other regional states in terms of economic diversification. It invested heavily in industrial infrastructure in the 1970s and early 1980s, and services surpassed oil and gas as the single largest contributor to real GDP in 2003.[8] The story of Dubai's economic liberalization is well known, although Abu Dhabi remains highly reliant on natural resource wealth.[9]

Hydrocarbons are likely to maintain their high level of importance in most GCC countries—Bahrain and Oman excepted—given sustained high levels of production and large proven reserves. In 2010, the GCC supplied 21% of global crude oil production and 9% of global gas production. However, according to BP, GCC countries hold roughly 36% of the world's proven oil reserves and over 23% of proven gas reserves.[10] Despite persistent efforts to diversify away from oil, hydrocarbons still dominate GCC economies both directly and indirectly. The indirect contribution of the oil and gas sector to the overall economies is manifested in the recycling of government consumption and capital expenditure, as well as subsidized energy, water, and feedstock supplies to the industrial sector. With this in mind, the total contribution of hydrocarbons is even larger than official statistics or traditional measures indicate.

For most GCC states, oil revenue appears sufficient to cover most public expenditure on infrastructure, education, health, and other social services. However, with oil revenue continuing to account for such a large portion of government revenue, fluctuations in crude oil and gas prices have led to volatile swings in revenue and public spending. Demographic realities have made it all the more important for oil-producing countries to transform natural resources into other forms of capital and diversify government revenue. High population growth rates have meant there is less oil revenue per capita than there once was. In at least several cases real oil revenue per capita still lags behind numbers from the 1970s. This is best demonstrated in the cases of Saudi Arabia and Kuwait (see Graphs 3 and 4). In both countries, per capita oil revenue has been climbing dramatically since 2003, but much less dramatically in real terms and nowhere near earlier highs.

The same general phenomenon has been witnessed in Qatar and the UAE. However, the numbers portend a less drastic situation in these two countries, given the extremely large proportions of expatriates and the growing importance of sovereign wealth funds as alternative sources of income. In the case of Qatar, the relatively slow growth of oil and gas

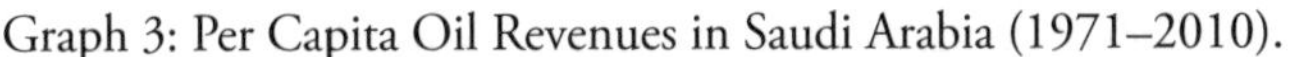

Graph 3: Per Capita Oil Revenues in Saudi Arabia (1971–2010).

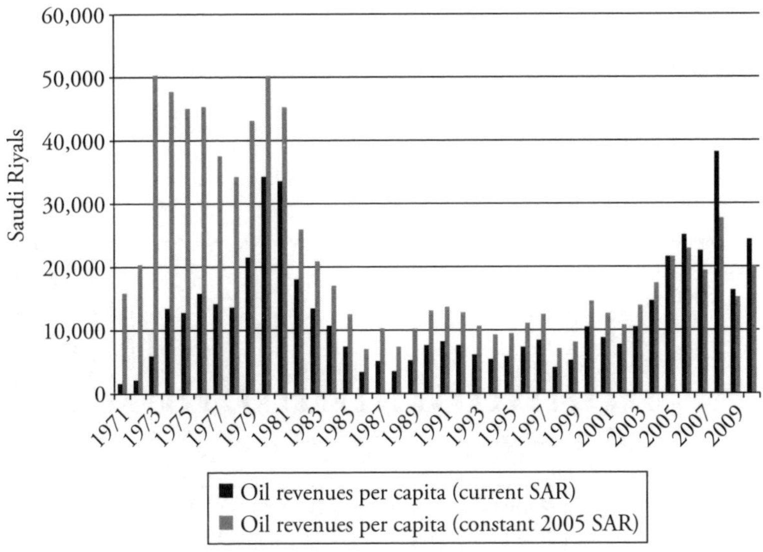

Source: Population statistics and annual implicit price deflators are both from the UN; oil revenues are from Saudi Arabian Monetary Agency, *Annual Report* (2011).

revenue per capita is due at least in part to staggering population growth in recent years.

While oil revenue will continue to be central to GCC economies, it is important to look at patterns of general government revenue and expenditure to examine similarities and differences between the two boom periods and explore what shifts in these areas imply about changes in private sector roles and capabilities.

Government accounts, expenditure breakdowns, and employment

Despite recent increases in government revenue, GCC states have not increased expenditure proportionally, which indicates that non-state spending is playing a larger role in their economies, at least in the short term. In particular, the shift from capital to current spending implies that business has had to turn to private customers rather than rely on

Graph 4: Per Capita Oil Revenues in Kuwait (1977–2010).

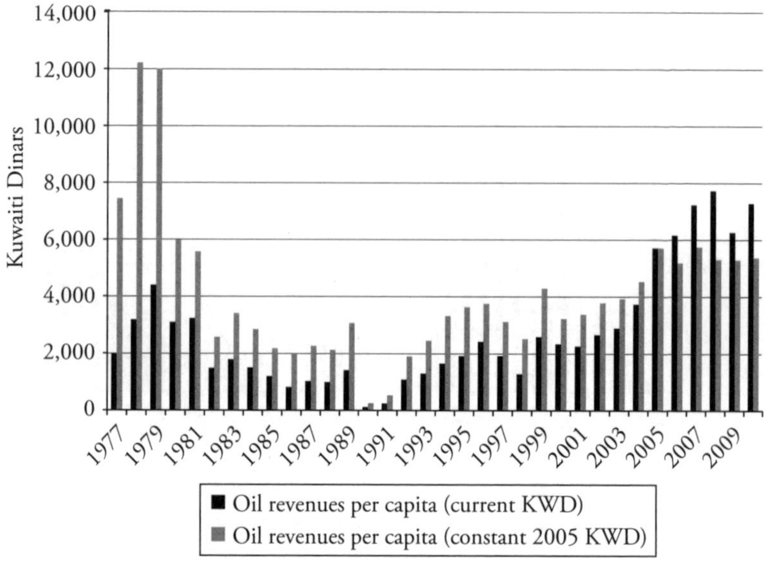

Source: Population statistics and annual implicit price deflators are both from the UN; oil revenues are from Kuwait Central Bank and from the United Nations *Statistical Abstract of the ESCWA Region*.

government spending. Although the state remains the main employer of GCC nationals, the private sector contributes the vast majority of total employment in GCC economies. In this section, government accounts, expenditure breakdowns, and employment figures will be examined in turn, and their effects on private sector autonomy will be highlighted.

Government revenue and expenditure

GCC governments have generally followed procyclical fiscal policies coinciding with changes in oil revenue (see Graph 5). During the boom in the 1970s and early 1980s, government spending rose as oil income increased. This took the form of fiscal incentives to develop the industrial sector, a massive public investment programme in infrastructure, and the adoption of generous welfare systems. Such programmes contributed to an initial growth in non-oil activities. At the same time, fiscal surpluses

Graph 5: Government Revenues and Expenditures as a Percentage of GDP (Averages Over Five-Year Periods).

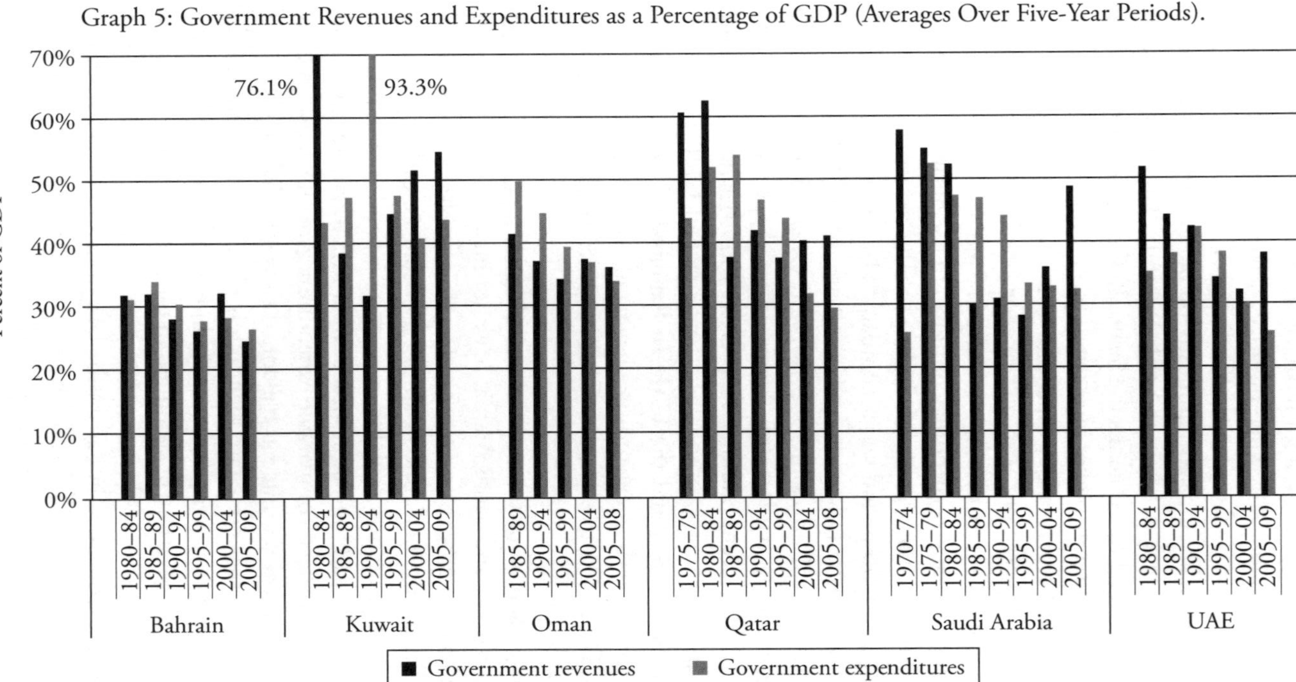

Source: United Nations *Statistical Abstract of the ESCWA Region*; various national reporting data; IMF Article IV Reports and Statistical Appendices.

were recorded, which allowed for relatively little adjustment in spending in the early and mid-1980s when oil prices declined. Spending was cut by half of the fall in total revenue in Saudi Arabia, 20% in the UAE, and 10% in Qatar.[11] The cutbacks fell mostly on outlays for projects, while current expenditure rose, except in Saudi Arabia. In Bahrain and Kuwait, spending continued to rise across the board. In Oman, lower oil revenue was more than offset by higher investment income and fees and charges, leading to a further increase in expenditures in the period.[12]

After the 1990–91 Gulf War, oil prices declined and more attention was given to fiscal adjustment, particularly in Saudi Arabia and Bahrain. In the other GCC states, spending continued to rise during the first half of the 1990s even though revenue declined.[13] The recovery of oil prices during the 1994–96 period was accompanied by an increase in spending, notably in Qatar (related to LNG projects) and the UAE. However, after the collapse of prices in 1998, Kuwait, Oman and the UAE cut spending modestly, while Saudi Arabia adjusted spending most dramatically. In the recent boom, several GCC countries have seen sharp increases in government revenue as a percentage of GDP, particularly Kuwait, Saudi Arabia, and the UAE. In Bahrain and Oman, government revenue as well as expenditure has remained fairly constant as a share of GDP. In Qatar, expenditure has remained steady while revenue has increased.

Strikingly, several of those countries with recent gains in revenue, including Kuwait and Saudi Arabia, have not increased expenditure in line with revenue growth (see Graphs 6 and 7). In 2009, Saudi Arabia ran a deficit for the first time in almost a decade. In earlier periods of growth, expenditure rose quickly as revenue expanded, although this was seen more clearly in Saudi Arabia than in Kuwait. Yet in neither country has there been comparable expenditure growth relative to GDP even as government revenue has ballooned to around half of GDP.

This indicates that non-state spending is playing a larger role in the economy. However, it is too early to conclude that such spending might be pushing aside government spending. In the previous boom, there was a time lag of several years before government spending caught up with government revenue, due in part to the lack of institutional capacity to spend the influx of wealth. While this is less of an obstacle today, large capital projects still take time to get off the ground. In Kuwait, the general downward trend in state spending as a share of GDP that had

Graph 6: Saudi Government Revenues and Expenditures as a Percentage of GDP (1969–2010).

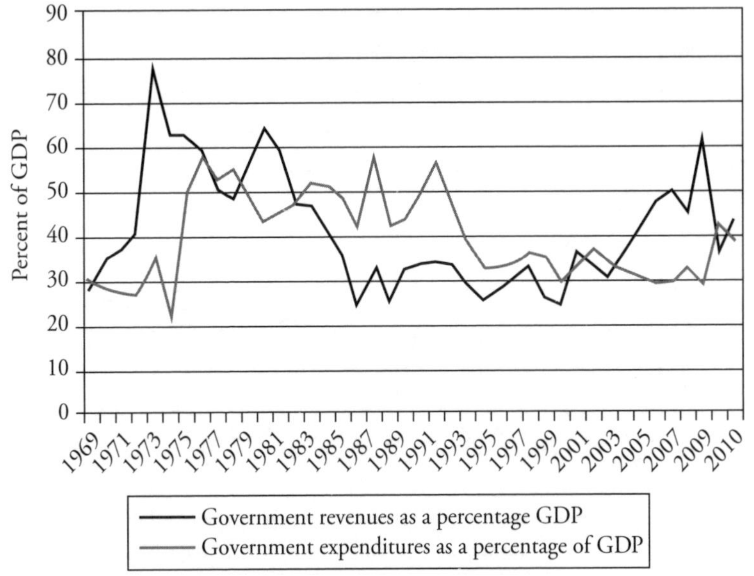

Source: Saudi Arabian Monetary Agency, *Annual Report* (2011).

been apparent since 1999 reversed in 2008, and spending may increase even further with the February 2010 passage of a major development plan. So what initially looks like a greater propensity for saving and the smoothing of consumption and capital formation could in fact only reflect a time lag as governments determine how they will spend oil revenue and establish the necessary capacity to do so.

Government capital and current spending

Another important shift that has implications for the private sector's role is increased government emphasis on current spending. This trend is clearest in Bahrain, Kuwait and Saudi Arabia, although it is also evident in Qatar and the UAE. For example, in 1980–84, current expenditure accounted for 66% and 49% of total government expenditure in Kuwait and Saudi Arabia respectively. By 2000–04, these figures had risen to 89

Graph 7: Kuwaiti Government Revenues and Expenditures as a Percentage of GDP (1977–2010).

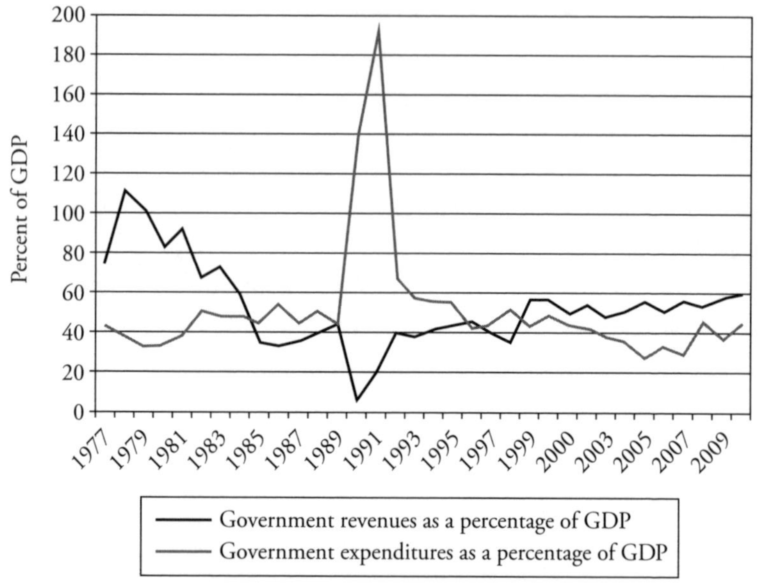

Source: Kuwaiti Central Bank Quarterly Reports; United Nations *Statistical Abstract of the ESCWA Region.*

and 88%. The share of current expenditure in total government spending was 85 and 58% respectively for Egypt and Syria during this period.[14]

Generally, there was a decline in this ratio of government capital to current expenditures in all countries in the 1980s, general stagnation in the 1990s, and an increase since the early part of the 2000s (see Graph 8). While the downward trend has reversed in recent years, with more government money being spent on capital projects—in Bahrain, Oman, Qatar, and Saudi Arabia—the ratio of capital to current expenditure has not come close to reaching the same levels as during the boom in the 1970s.

In the past, when confronted with the need to cut spending, GCC governments have often chosen to reduce capital rather than current spending. The spending trends are particularly striking in Saudi Arabia (see Graph 9). While real aggregate spending has in fact surpassed spending levels during the first boom, current spending accounts for a

Graph 8: Ratio of Government Capital to Current Expenditure (1972–2010).

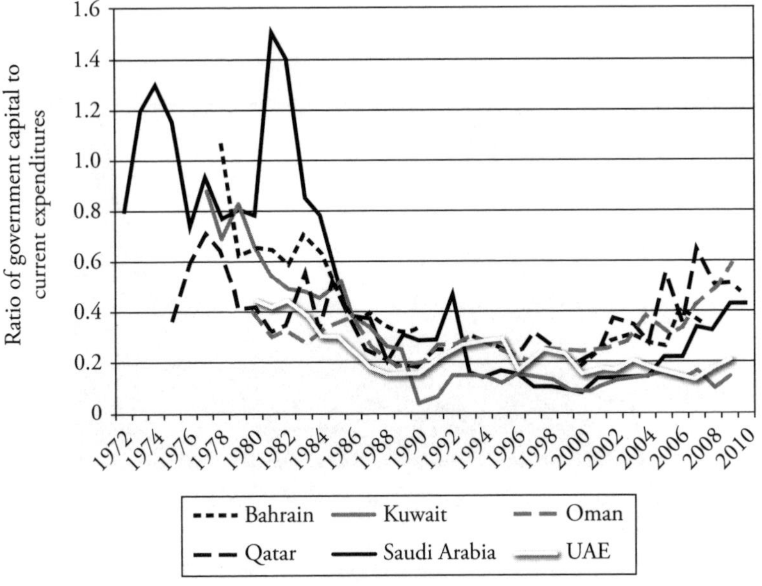

Source: United Nations *Statistical Abstract of the ESCWA Region*; various national reporting data; IMF Article IV Reports and Statistical Appendices.

much greater percentage of the total. The public sector budget has undergone considerable change since 1980, with increases in human resource development and health and social development and simultaneous declines in transport and communications, economic resources development, and infrastructure. This entails a broadening of public services for a growing general population.

As a result of declines in government project spending, business had to look to private clients rather than to the government. This stands in contrast to the 1970s when much of the business growth was driven by public spending on large projects. Private capital has tended to pick up the slack for lagging government capital investment. Even if this is largely made possible by state salaries and high public sector wages, it represents an important shift in how much control the state has over the effects of its spending. In addition to the private accumulation of capital, other developments during the recessions of the late 1980s and early

Graph 9: Real Saudi Government Current and Capital Expenditure and Oil Prices (1969–2010).

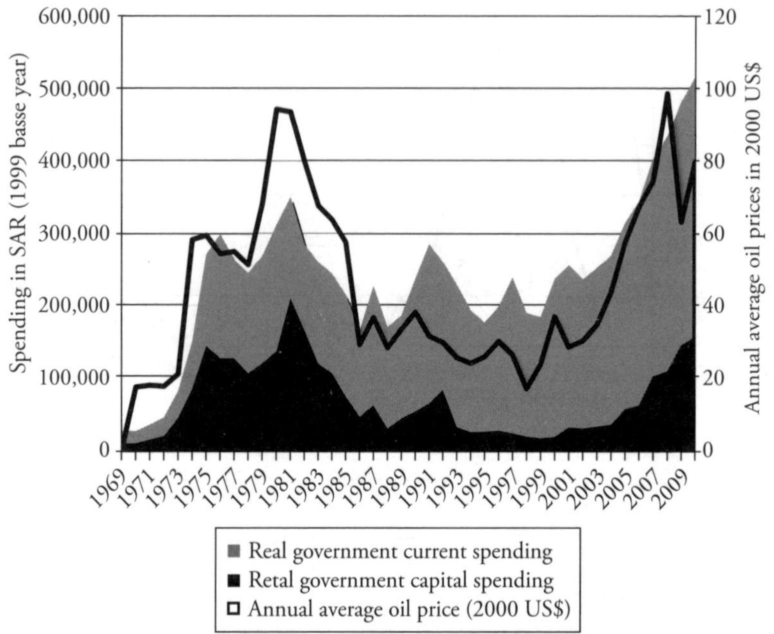

Source: Saudi Arabian Monetary Agency, *Annual Report* (2011); oil prices are crude oil refiner acquisition costs from the US Department of Energy's Energy Information Administration.

1990s contributed to a stronger private sector. Businessmen in Saudi Arabia have pointed to the emergence of new leadership, a reduced dependence on subsidies, and the elimination of the least efficient companies during this period.[15]

The trend of increasing current expenditure will be extremely difficult to turn around, especially since such a large percentage of current spending goes on wages, salaries, and pensions (see Graph 10). In 2009, government spending on wages and salaries as a share of GDP ranged from 3% in the UAE to 10.3% in Saudi Arabia. As a percentage of total government spending, compensation was approximately 28% in Kuwait, 40% in Bahrain, and 44% in Saudi Arabia.[16] If one were to examine only nationals, the share of government compensation would be consid-

Graph 10: Government Spending on Wages and Salaries (2008).

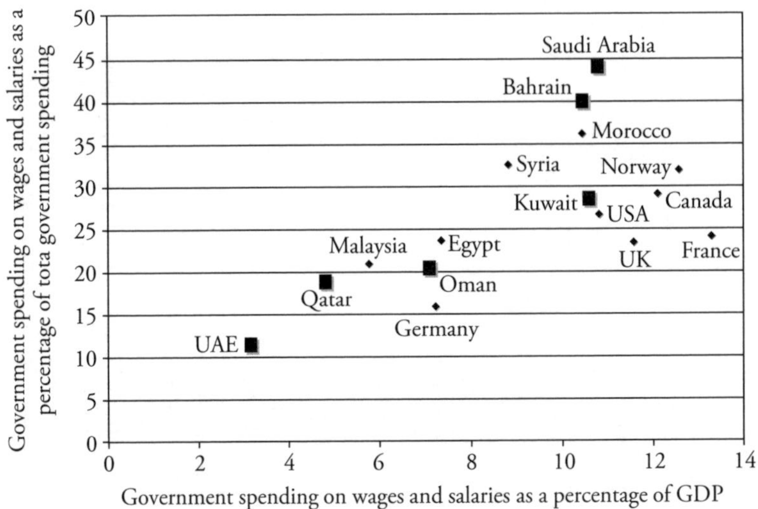

Source: National reporting data (Bahrain, Kuwait, Oman, Saudi Arabia); IMF Article IV Reports and Statistical Appendices (Egypt, Malaysia, Morocco, Qatar, Syria, UAE); OECD Statistics (Canada, France, Germany, Norway, UK, US).

Notes: UAE figures explicitly exclude military wages and salaries; Syria data are from 2007.

erably higher, since public sector salaries tend to be higher than those in the private sector and more nationals tend to be employed by the government.[17] In part for this reason, government salaries or salaries from government projects make up the greater part of private purchasing power in the GCC. There has not been much change in the share of public spending on salaries and wages in recent years, except a slight downward trend as a percentage of current government and total government spending. But the Arab Spring and GCC government reactions to it have likely changed the overall shape of current spending.

Employment and labour

As has been mentioned, governments are the primary employers of GCC citizens. However, there are important differences across countries

Chart 1: Public and Private Sector Employment in the GCC by Nationality.

	Public Sector (Number and Percent of Total)			*Private Sector (Number and Percent of Total)*			*Totals (Number and Percent of Total)*		
	Number of Nationals	*Number of Expats*	*Total Public Sector*	*Number of Nationals*	*Number of Expats*	*Total Private Sector*	*Total Nationals*	*Total Expats*	*Total Labour Force*
Bahrain (2009)	47,059 (7.9%)	12,232 (2.0%)	59,291 (9.9%)	91,605 (15.3%)	448,120 (74.8%)	539,7251 (90.1%)	138,665 (23.1%)	460,352 (76.9%)	599,017 (100%)
Kuwait (2009)	271,240 (13.2%)	120,529 (5.9%)	391,769 (19.0%)	67,510 (3.3%)	1,599,573 (77.7%)	1,667,083 (81.0%)	338,750 (16.5%)	1,720,102 (83.5%)	2,058,852 (100%)
Oman (2008)	131,209 (12.0%)	22,319 (2.0%)	153,528 (14.0%)	147,194 (13.4%)	794,806 (72.6%)	942,000 (86.0%)	278,403 (25.4%)	817,125 (74.6%)	1,095,528 (100%)
Qatar (2009)	61,452 (4.9%)	88,614 (7.0%)	150,066 (11.9%)	9,387 (0.7%)	1,100,786 (87.3%)	1,110,173 (88.1%)	70,839 (5.6%)	1,189,400 (94.4%)	1,260,239 (100%)
Saudi Arabia (2008)	827,846 (11.6%)	71,865 (1.0%)	899,711 (12.6%)	829,057 (11.6%)	5,392,890 (75.7%)	6,221,947 (87.4%)	1,656,903 (23.3%)	5,464,755 (76.7%)	7,121,658 (100%)
UAE (2005)	192,000 (6.4%)	200,000 (6.7%)	392,000 (13.1%)	70,000 (2.3%)	2,538,000 (84.6%)	2,608,000 (86.9%)	262,000 (8.7%)	2,738,000 (91.3%)	3,000,000 (100%)

Sources: Bahrain Labour Market Regulatory Authority, *Bahrain Labour Market Indicators* (2009); Kuwait Public Authority for Civil Information (2009); *Oman Annual Statistical Yearbook* (2009); *Qatar Labor Force Sample Survey* (2009); Saudi Arabian Monetary Agency *Annual Report* (2009; Tables 18.8 and 18.10); UAE Tanmia *Human Resource Report* (2005).

Note: In Saudi Arabia, the number of nationals working in the public sector would probably be much higher were the security and religious sectors included. For simplicity's sake, data have been combined in certain instances. In Bahrain and Kuwait, the private sector includes domestic workers. In Oman, the public sector includes the Civil Service, Diwan, Public Corporations, and Royal Court. In Qatar, the private sector includes the Mixed Sector and domestic workers. The Mixed Sector includes firms that are partially owned by the government. This is also likely true in the UAE.

Graph 11: Labor Breakdowns by Sector and Nationality.

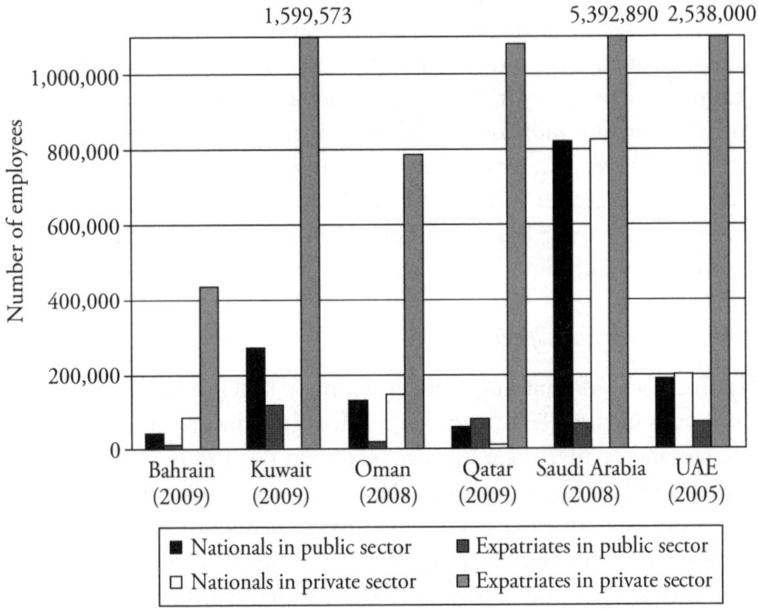

Source: National reporting data (See Chart 1).

Note: In Oman, the public sector includes the Civil Service, Diwan, Public Corporations, and Royal Court. In Qatar, the private sector includes the Mixed Sector and domestic workers.

(See Chart 1 and Graph 11). Bahrain and Oman are the only countries in which nationals working in the private sector significantly outnumber those working for the government. The number of nationals in the public sector in Saudi Arabia is roughly equal to the number in the private sector. In the UAE, Kuwait, and Qatar, nationals working for the government vastly outnumber those in the private sector.

Expatriates make up at least three quarters of the labour force in every GCC country. In the UAE, the figure is 91%, in Qatar it is 94%. In terms of the share of total employment, the public sector is largest in Kuwait, employing 19% of the labour force, 69% of whom are nationals. In Saudi Arabia, the public sector employs 13% of the total workforce, 92% of whom are nationals. While the private sector now constitutes the vast majority of total employment, the benefits of this are not usually felt by nationals.

High levels of spending on salaries and wages and large public employment schemes indicate that the state has less control over how oil wealth is distributed within the economy. Decision-making power has shifted to private individuals and consumers. Although this is not the case everywhere, as capital expenditure remains relatively high in Qatar and certain Emirates in the UAE, it does denote a general trend with governments having less direct control over who in the private sector receives oil wealth.

Public versus private spending

Massive state-led spending and development schemes dominated GCC economies in the 1970s, and this resulted in a limited role for the private sector. Yet after the oil price collapse in the 1980s, business began to play a larger role. Over time, the private sector accumulated capital that could be reinvested. As opposed to governments, which are under considerable demographic and political pressure to continuously spend their income, private actors have been more able to save and delay investment and capital spending.[18] As a result, at least in part, business has not been pushed aside to the same degree in the most recent boom as it was in the 1970s.

(1) Consumption: Private final consumption makes up about two-thirds of total final consumption in GCC economies, ranging from 58% in Saudi Arabia to 87% in the UAE in recent years (see Graph 12). Yet on the whole, this lags behind private spending in several other regional states. Egypt, Syria, Malaysia and Morocco all have private consumption rates above 75%, with private consumption accounting for 87% of Egypt's total consumption. And once again, much private sector consumption in the GCC is the result of government salaries and wages.

The share of government consumption in GCC states has changed little over time (see Graph 13). With the exception of the UAE, there does not appear to be any clear pattern of a reduced government role in consumption. In Bahrain, there has actually been an increase since the mid-1970s. Government consumption spiked in Oman in the early 1970s and in Kuwait after the Gulf War in 1990–91. However, for most GCC states, it has been fairly stagnant. The same cannot be said for capital spending.

Graph 12: Consumption Expenditure Breakdown (2006–10 Average).

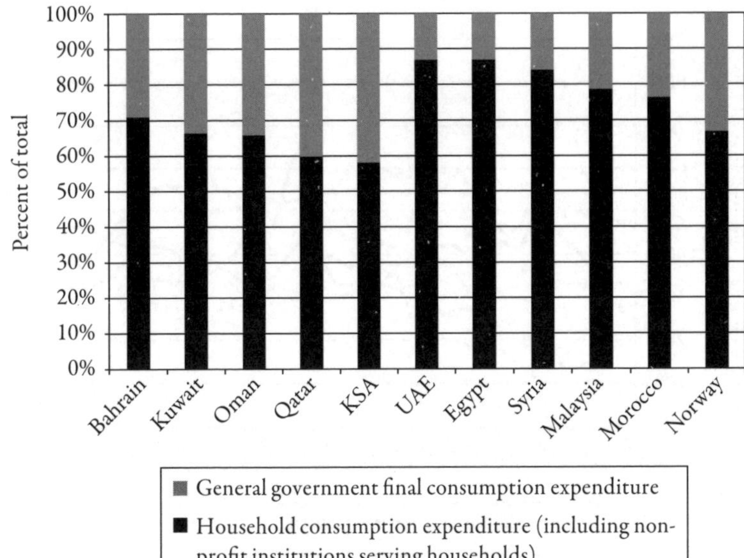

Source: United Nations National Accounts Statistics.

(2) Fixed capital formation: Private contributions to national fixed capital formation make up the majority in every GCC country except Oman, where recent oil sector spending has crowded out private sector capital investment (see Graph 14). Private sector capital formation is highest in Bahrain (at 72%) and Kuwait (at 77%). It should be noted that figures for Oman and Saudi Arabia include oil sector fixed capital formation, the majority of which would be public.

As opposed to consumption trends, there has been a clear downward shift in governments' share of capital expenditure since the 1970s (see Graph 15). This is evident throughout the GCC, with the possible exceptions of Oman and the UAE, in which the government contributed relatively low levels of capital formation as early as 1980. For the other four GCC states, there was a general decline in government capital expenditure as a percentage of gross fixed capital formation until the mid-1990s, at which point rates have more or less remained between 20 and 40%. It should be noted that Saudi Arabia saw significant increases in the government's share of capital spending in 2009 and 2010 in the

Graph 13: Government Final Consumption as a Percentage of Total Consumption, 1970–2010.

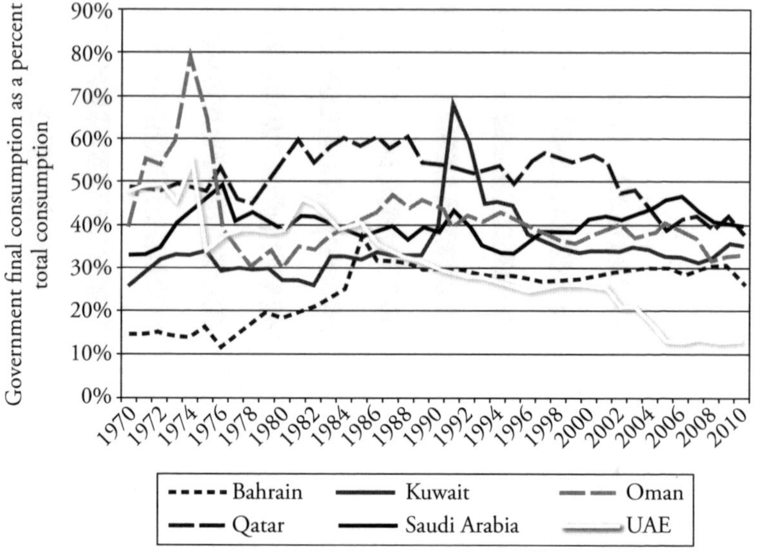

Source: United Nations National Accounts Statistics.

wake of large-scale public infrastructure investment at a time when business remained credit-constrained.

Viewed together with the previously cited data indicating a decline of government capital spending as a share of total government expenditure, this indicates that private sector capital is becoming more important. During the bust period in the 1980s, the private sector was able to accumulate capital while governments continued to spend their rent income. A lot of this capital spending has been in real estate, but private capital investment is increasingly channelled towards heavy industry, health, education, and utilities.[19] This general trend has continued in the recent boom. Governments are pursuing large national infrastructure and petrochemical projects in cooperation with local business families like the Zamil Group in Saudi Arabia and Habtoor in the UAE, which means that local business has an increased role in shaping policy in sectors that had previously been dominated by the state.[20]

Graph 14: Fixed Capital Formation Breakdown (2006–10 Average).

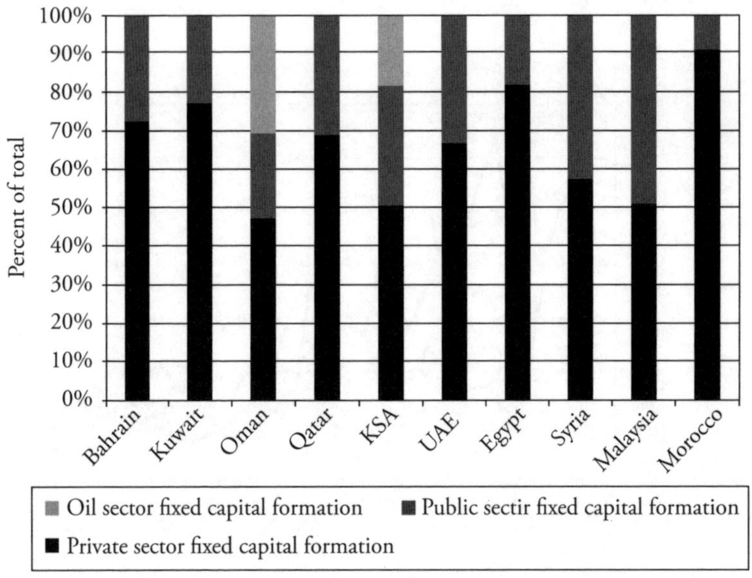

Source: National reporting data and IMF Article IV Reports for sector contributions.

Notes: Qatar figures are for 2006–07; Egypt, Morocco and Syria figures are for 2006–08; UAE figures are for 2006–09. Oil sector capital formation is only broken down for Oman and Saudi Arabia, where private sector capital formation is specifically non-oil.

Public and private spending in Saudi Arabia

Comparing total public and private spending in Saudi Arabia, where good data are available for public/private breakdowns, yields several interesting results. While public and private contributions to GDP shadowed each other closely in the 1970s and early 1980s, this has generally not been the case since the mid-1980s (see Graph 16). Only since 2007 do private sector expenditures again appear to move in line with government disbursements. However, the gap between public and private contributions, although it has narrowed in recent years, remains substantial. High oil prices have not marginalized the private sector as much as in the 1970s. This serves as another indication of the growing strength of the private sector in the Saudi economy.

Graph 15: Government Capital Expenditure as a Percentage of Gross Fixed Capital Formation.[21]

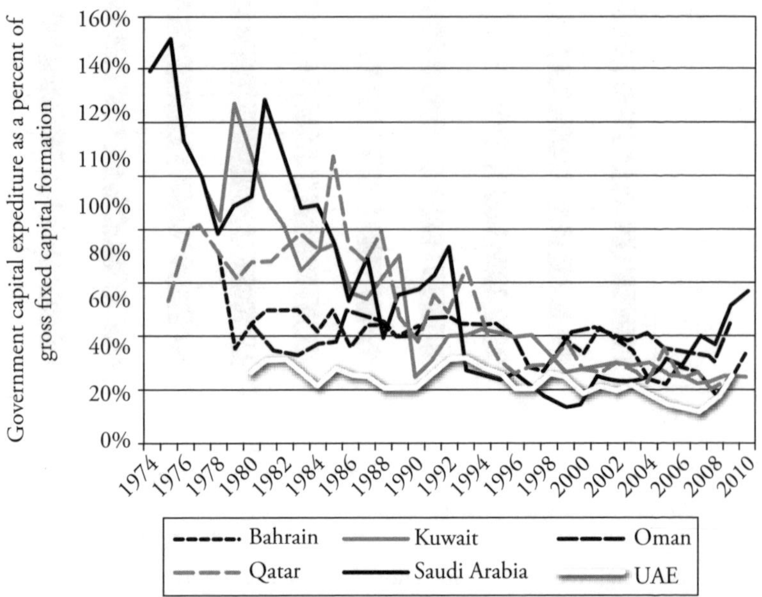

Source: United Nations National Accounts Statistics for total fixed capital formation; national reporting data and IMF Article IV Reports for sector contributions to fixed capital formation.

Greater independence from state spending has also been demonstrated in econometric time series tests run by Steffen Hertog on Saudi and Kuwaiti data. He finds that in both cases, the short-term impact of government spending on business growth has been much stronger through the mid-1980s than afterwards. This is the case for the private sector in general as well as for sub-sectors. The coefficients measuring the impact of state spending on business growth are halved in the Kuwaiti case and decline even more strongly in the Saudi case. He concludes that business is on a more autonomous growth trajectory that is less affected by fluctuations in government spending.[22]

It remains clear that for some private companies, government procurement remains a fundamentally important source of business and profit. But for many others, business is conducted primarily with private

Graph 16: Public and Private Contributions to Saudi Non-Oil GDP (1970–2010).

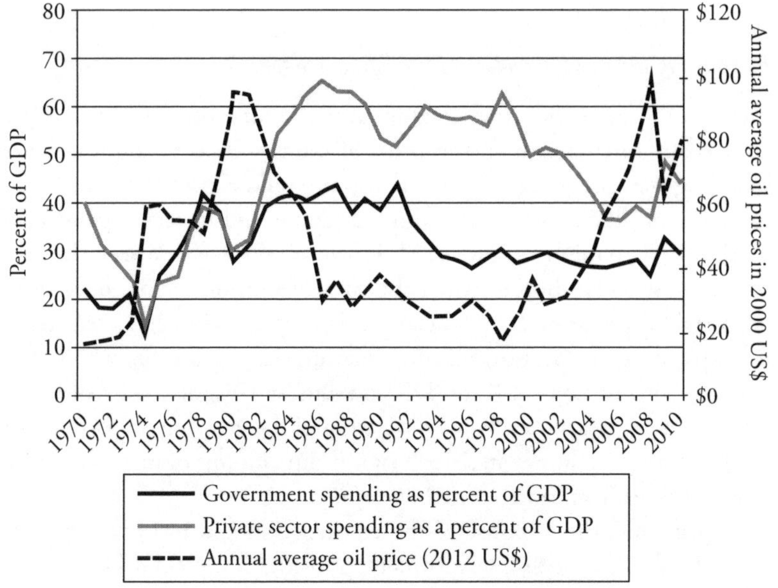

Source: Saudi Arabian Monetary Agency, *Annual Report* (2011); oil prices are crude oil refiner acquisition costs from the US Department of Energy's Energy Information Administration.

Note: Contributions represent aggregates of capital formation and consumption spending.

customers, be they final consumers or other business enterprises. Of course, the purchasing power of final consumers will be influenced by government spending, and in this respect the wellbeing of the GCC economies remains substantially influenced by government expenditure. However, the significance and implications of a private sector directly dependent on government business are different from the implications of a private sector that caters to a market whose overall purchasing power is influenced by government expenditure but where individual purchase decisions are made privately and without government interference. The government lacks monopsony power in such an environment and cannot dictate terms as the only purchaser of goods or services.

Moreover, the private sector must respond to the needs and demands of discerning customers, which makes markets more competitive and demands a higher level of competence.

Examining the non-oil sectors of the Saudi economy

Through the late 1980s, the structure of the Saudi economy was strongly affected by fluctuations in the price of oil as well as changes in state spending (see Graph 17). Sectors that one would expect to expand during a boom, like construction and real estate, did in fact expand dramatically when oil prices increased. However, this has not been the case in the most recent boom, when the sizes of non-oil sectors have been fairly stable. The only sector whose share in the economy has been steadily expanding is the non-refining manufacturing sector, which has reached 13% of non-oil real GDP and almost 10% of gross real GDP. This is not necessarily a reliable indication of the growing importance of the private sector, however, since a significant amount of manufacturing output comes from state-owned enterprises.

In principle, the response of the construction and real estate sectors could be due to shifting government priorities away from large infrastructure projects. However, following higher oil prices in recent years, government capital expenditure has expanded. This would typically be channelled through construction, be it infrastructure, schools or hospitals. However, the overall construction boom has been muted, indicating that considerable construction must have already taken place previously based on private demand.[23] Although time series are too short to come to a statistically significant conclusion, it would appear that recent government spending has not created an artificially inflated construction sector as it did in the 1970s and early 1980s.

Moreover, comparing real growth rates of various sectors in the Saudi case with government current and capital spending indicates less volatile reactions in these sectors to changes in public spending (see Graph 18). Growth rates in several major sectors (construction, manufacturing, and trade, restaurants and hotels are included in the graph) appear to have followed changes in government spending up to the end of the 1980s. Yet in the most recent boom, growth rates of major sectors have remained fairly constant despite increases in public spending. Once again, this implies that these sectors are less reliant on public spending and that the private sector more generally has gained at least some level of autonomy.

Graph 17: Real Saudi Non-Oil GDP Composition and Oil Prices (1968–2010).

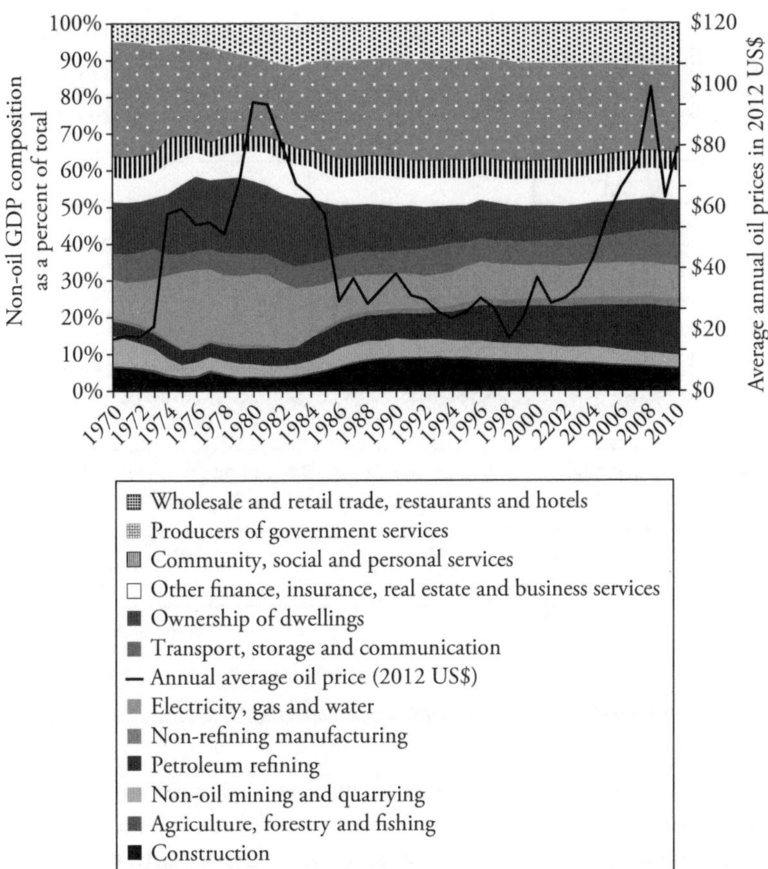

Source: United Nations, National Accounts Main Aggregates; oil prices are crude oil refiner acquisition costs from the US Department of Energy's Energy Information Administration.

Previous studies: the influence of government spending on growth

It is beyond the scope of this paper to examine the relationship between public and private spending in other GCC countries in detail, but several previous studies on Saudi Arabia and other GCC states have reached similar conclusions. Although cause and effect mechanisms are often

Graph 18: Real Growth Rates of Various Sectors and Government Spending in Saudi Arabia (1970–2010).

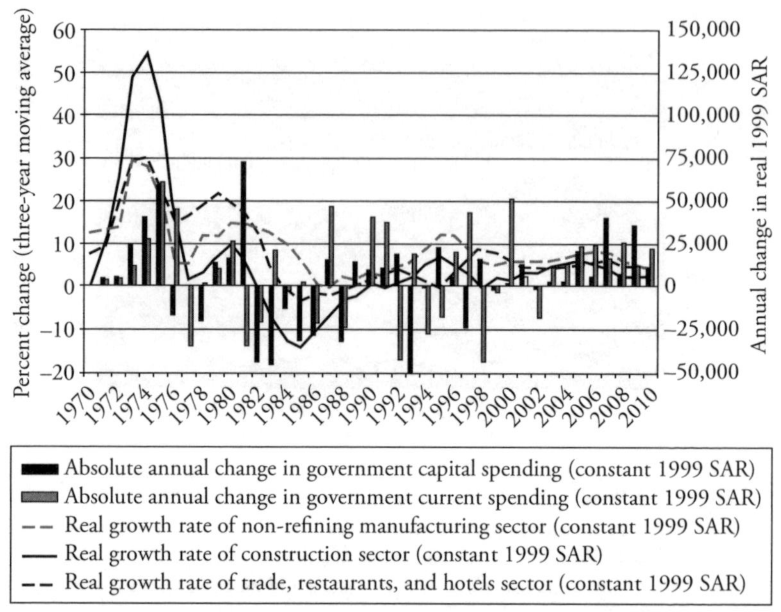

Source: Saudi Arabian Monetary Agency, *Annual Report* (2011).

blurred with regard to the interaction between various economic activities, a number of attempts have been made to determine the impact of government spending on economic growth, particularly that of the private sector.

Robert Looney has examined the impact that various types of public expenditure (investment, consumption, defence, and total budgetary allocations) have on private sector GDP in Saudi Arabia.[24] He found that, although patterns varied over time, there was a general weakening of private sector links to public expenditures. He pointed to four phases: (1) beginning stages when weak or non-existent long-term links with public and private expenditures affect non-oil output; (2) a partial integration stage when the development of longer-term links with public expenditure (and possibly short-term links with private expenditure) further affect non-oil output; (3) an integrated stage when strong links are established with private expenditure; and (4) a mature stage which weakens long-term government linkages and maintains long-term linkages with private sector production.[25]

A 1998 study on Saudi Arabia by Alexei Kireyev found that real non-oil private GDP was strongly and positively correlated with government expenditure from 1969 to 1997, concluding that a 1% increase in total government expenditure generated around a 0.5% increase in private sector GDP growth.[26] However, when the period was divided into two (1969–82 and 1983–97), the relationship between the two variables was statistically insignificant in the second period, suggesting the increasing autonomy of the non-oil economy.

Volker Treichel used cointegration analysis to study the link between the growth rate of total real expenditure and non-oil real GDP growth in Oman from 1981 to 1997.[27] He found that an increase of 1% in current government expenditure was responsible for about a 0.6% increase in non-oil GDP growth, and a 1% increase in capital expenditure resulted in a 0.2% increase in non-oil GDP growth. In the 1990s, this relationship appears to have weakened. However, as Fasano and Wang point out, Treichel assumed rather than tested the direction of the causal relationship.[28] Ghali and Al-Shamsi tested the relationship between current government spending and GDP growth in the UAE from 1973 to 1995.[29] They observed that government investment had a positive and significant effect on economic growth, while government consumption had a negative and insignificant one.

Writing in 2001, Fasano and Wang found that, in the short run, current expenditure has a negative effect on non-oil economic growth in GCC countries and capital expenditure has a positive one, although both effects are weak. In the long run, they determined that sample non-oil real GDP was negatively related to capital spending and positively related to current spending.[30]

While several of these studies have found historical linkages between government spending and private sector growth, taken together they suggest a declining relationship between the two, which hints at the growing independence of the private sector.

Other indicators of an increasingly independent private sector

In addition to the changing nature of state spending in the Gulf and weakening ties between private sector expenditures and government spending, several other indicators point to increased private sector autonomy. These include the expansion of stock markets in GCC states, low tariffs compared with those of other important regional economies, large private Gulf investments in the broader Middle East and beyond, and a process (albeit a slow one) of diversification and privatization.

Expanding stock markets

The growth of stock markets in the Gulf points to the establishment of a local private sector that consists of more than a few big families. Each GCC country now has at least one formal exchange, while most had none in the 1980s; stocks existed, but they were often traded informally over the counter. The Dubai Financial Market was founded in March 2000, and the Abu Dhabi Security Exchange was established in November 2000. From 2000 to 2010, market capitalization grew roughly 300% in Bahrain, over 500% in Kuwait and Saudi Arabia, and 800% in Oman (see Chart 2). Most markets demonstrated strong recovery after the global recession.

Before drawing too many conclusions from these changes, however, several caveats are in order. First, significant shares of many of the largest listed companies are government-owned. Second, many other shares are not actively traded, but held passively by large families. Third, the "free float" of many companies is fairly small. Still, the overall point about diversification and the spread of private assets holds.

Low MFN tariffs

GCC states also have very low applied tariffs, particularly in comparison with other regional states (see Chart 3). Essentially all non-agricultural products and the overwhelming majority of agricultural products have tariff rates less than 5%. This is not the case in Egypt, Iran, Jordan and Morocco, where many products have tariff rates above 5%, often significantly so. The rather low tariffs on manufactured goods in the GCC expose local industrialists to competition and demand greater professionalism and performance, at least to the extent that private business is not subsidized and does not benefit from cheap inputs that non-national competitors do not have access to.

Chart 2: Arab Stock Market Comparisons.

	Market Capitalization (Billions of USD at end of year)			*Number of Listed Companies (end of year)*			*Average Company Size (Millions of USD)*			*Share Market Depth (Percentage)**			*Share turnover (Percentage)***		
	2000	*2008*	*2010*	*2000*	*2008*	*2010*	*2000*	*2008*	*2010*	*2000*	*2008*	*2010*	*2000*	*2008*	*2010*
Saudi Arabia	68	247	353	75	127	146	905	1941	2421	39	53	81	26	212	57
Qatar	–	77	124	–	43	43	–	1782	2875	–	80	97	–	63	15
Kuwait	20	70	114	86	204	214	231	344	532	49	47	92	21	190	38
Abu Dhabi	–	69	77	–	65	64	–	1059	1204	–	29	26	–	92	12
Dubai	–	63	55	–	65	65	–	971	841	–	26	18	–	132	29
Oman	4	15	28	131	122	119	27	124	238	18	33	49	16	57	12
Bahrain	7	20	20	41	51	49	162	391	409	91	107	87	4	11	1
Egypt	31	86	84	1071	373	212	29	230	397	33	54	39	38	102	68
Morocco	11	66	69	54	77	75	201	854	925	32	76	76	11	21	20
Jordan	5	36	31	163	262	277	30	137	112	60	178	112	8	80	31
Lebanon	2	10	13	13	13	11	122	739	1152	9	34	32	8	18	15
Tunisia	3	6	11	44	50	56	64	126	190	14	16	24	24	27	18

Source: Arab Monetary Fund, Arab Capital Markets, Quarterly Bulletins; United Nations National Accounts Statistics for GDP.

* Share market depth is market capitalization divided by GDP.

** Share turnover is the value of shares traded divided by market capitalization.

Chart 3: MFN Applied Tariffs, Frequency Distribution for Non-Agricultural Products (2009).

	Duty-free	*0≤5*	*5≤10*	*10≤15*	*15≤25*	*25≤50*	*50≤100*	*>100*
Bahrain	6.8	93.0	0	0	0	0	0	0
Kuwait	6.8	93.0	0	0	0	0	0	0
Oman	6.9	92.9	0	0	0	0	0	0
Qatar	7.8	91.9	0	0	0	0	0	0
Saudi Arabia	6.8	92.9	0	0	0	0	0	0
UAE	6.8	93.0	0	0	0	0	0	0
Egypt	7.1	54.1	20.5	0	3.1	15.1	0	0.1
Iran (2008)	0	37.5	11.1	7.4	11.4	15.8	15.9	0.5
Jordan	57.4	3.4	7.7	0.9	13.6	17.0	0	0
Morocco	0	23.3	43.3	0	7.1	26.4	0	0

Source: World Trade Organization, *Tariff Profiles.*

Gulf investments in the broader Middle East

Some larger Gulf businesses have begun investing widely within the GCC, in the broader Middle East, and beyond. The more this is done, the more a given company can be considered to be operating independently of its home government. Although this is partly attributable to sovereign wealth fund investments, in the eight-year period from 2003 to 2010 the UAE, Saudi Arabia and Kuwait were among the largest sources of foreign investment in North Africa and the Levant, rivalled only by the United States, France and the UK.[31] In 2008, the UAE announced projects whose cumulative gross worth totalled 16.8 billion euros. Kuwaitis invested in thirty-four projects primarily in Egypt and Jordan, and Saudis invested in twenty-two projects principally in Egypt and Algeria.[32] Gulf businesses have largely invested in the banking sector and in real estate, although companies such as Al Marai, Savola, Saudi Al Rajhi Group, and the Kuwait Food Company have invested widely in agriculture and agribusiness.[33] Other major companies that have been involved in projects outside the Gulf include transport and logistics giants like Aramex and Agility.

Diversification and privatization

There have been three main approaches to diversification in the GCC: (1) creating a parallel economy to overcome existing rigid structures and burdensome regulations, as in Saudi Arabia; (2) promoting the competitive position of sectors like finance, tourism and education, as in the UAE, Bahrain, and Qatar; (3) and general economic reform, which has been pursued to varying degrees in all GCC states.[34] The restructuring and privatization of utilities and related services have been placed at the top of the agenda in many GCC countries.

Oman, Qatar and the United Arab Emirates are currently relying on the private sector and foreign direct investment to fund and manage infrastructure projects in the energy and water sectors.[35] Oman passed a new tax law in September 2003 and a privatization law in July 2004, which is meant to help open key economic sectors to private sector participation. Al Maha, a petroleum products company, was privatized in 2005, and the government sold a 30% stake in Oman Telecommunications Company (OmanTel) the same year. The seventh development plan (2006–10) called for the private sector to contribute 46% of total investment planned for the period.

Like other GCC countries, Qatar has also implemented a privatization programme. In 1998, power plants were slowly transferred to the majority private-owned Qatar Electricity and Water Company (QEWC), and the government sold 45% of its shares in Qatar Telecom (Q-Tel). In 2003, a 30% stake in Industries Qatar was floated on the Doha Securities Market, and in 2005, 60% of the Qatar Gas Transport Company was floated. The 2000 investment law allows foreign companies to hold up to 49% of equity in all projects and a 100% stake in some sectors, including education, tourism and healthcare.

Saudi Arabia has also made strides toward privatization, having divested 30% of the Saudi Telecom Company (STC) in 2002. Another recent privatization was the IPO of Saudi Kayan Petrochemicals in 2007. Approximately US$ 800 billion worth of assets are slated to be privatized in the coming decade.[36] Saudi Arabia has also been pursuing the development of economic cities in order to encourage foreign and domestic investment. Typically, however, there has not been much direct privatization in the form of sell-offs of government assets. Instead, local and international business has been licensed to operate in many areas that have been state-dominated since the 1970s, such as health, education, utilities, transport, and telecommunications.

In general, private manufacturing is particularly developed in Saudi Arabia, the Kuwaiti private sector is powerful but hamstrung by a divided government, and Qatari and Emirati business classes are still eclipsed by state-owned enterprises. Bahrain and Oman are the two states that have demonstrated the most movement away from public sector dominance, largely because the governments in these states must rely less on natural resource wealth.

Conclusion

Despite the continued dominance of the government in GCC economies, the private sector has grown more competitive and independent. As a result of many years of public employment schemes, large subsidies, and growing populations, GCC governments are spending a far greater percentage of income on current rather than capital expenditures than they did during the first oil boom in the 1970s. Higher government spending on salaries and wages means that GCC states have less control over how oil wealth is recycled and distributed. Moreover, the expansion of regional stock markets, Gulf investment in the broader Middle East, and low tariff rates all point to an increasingly competitive and capable private sector.

At the same time, the private sector has largely supplemented and reduced government spending on capital formation and investment. Ibrahim Saif writes, "The private sector evolved from a merely rentier private sector into a sector run by competent entrepreneurs who find themselves forced to compete more aggressively in order to win contracts and ensure business access".[37] GCC economies remain highly dependent on oil, but many have built up competitive manufacturing, service, and banking sectors. Although government spending will continue to be an important engine for growth both directly and indirectly, non-oil private sector activity will likely expand further because of governments' continued implementation of structural reforms and various budgetary constraints.[38] In Saudi Arabia, the business leadership is slowly pressing for a more transparent and less corrupt economic system. Indeed, an increase in the importance of the business class could have noticeable effects on the formation and continuation of relationships that influence decision-making. While these changes will not come rapidly, budgets dominated by current expenditure combined with the growing economic capacity of the private sector could lead to a new role for business in politics.

6

CSR AND REPUTATION BUILDING IN SYRIA

CONTEXTUALIZING "THE BUSINESS CASE"

Kjetil Selvik

Introduction

Interest in Corporate Social Responsibility (CSR) is on the rise in the Arab world. The concept was largely unheard of as late as the 1990s, but it has rapidly gained prominence and is now an integral part of the development discourse in most countries in the region. The fundamental cause of this spread is the international campaign for CSR to contain the negative effects of globalization. International organizations, such as the United Nations, the World Bank and the Organization for Economic Cooperation and Development (OECD), actively promote CSR as a way to fill the gap between global markets and national regulations.[1] But there are also local driving forces and dispositions for the CSR wave in Arab countries. In a context where state funds have been stretched by population growth and public sector inefficiencies, Middle East governments are looking for alternatives to state-led growth and welfare. Reformers turn their eyes to the economically thriving private sector in the hope that it can play a more active social role.

The combination of global trends and local adaptations creates new spaces and opportunities for the private sector. This paper provides a case study of this development by focusing on the introduction of CSR in Syria, a typical transition economy. From a state-socialist starting point where the private sector was seen as irrelevant at best, an "enemy sector" at worst, the Syrian government has recently taken steps to increase private contributions to social and economic development. The Tenth Five-Year Development Plan (2005–10) identified the private sector as a pillar of growth and also introduced CSR in Syrian development thinking. In 2008 the Syrian government, represented by the State Planning Commission, and the UNDP Country Office Syria launched the UN Global Compact in Syria as a practical step to follow up on the development plan's ambition. The Compact works to spread awareness of and encourage CSR activities in the Syrian business community.

However, the government's and the UNDP's ambition of developing CSR in Syria is not an easy task. Owing to the turbulent history of state-business relations in the Ba'thist republic, trust is in short supply. The Syrian regime has difficulties linking up with society's trust networks which feed on opposition to the state.[2] Scepticism towards government initiatives runs deep in the private sector and in particular among the religious-oriented parts of the Sunni business class. As one industrial manager put it: "the government wants to rid itself of all kinds of responsibilities and push it on the private sector … it will apply the new rules of the social market economy to force the private sector to pay even more".[3]

Appealingly, from the authorities' viewpoint, the international CSR discourse comes with an argument that can help bypass the lack of trust in the private sector. In what is usually referred to as "the business case for CSR" the claim is made that companies should adopt socially responsible practices out of self-interest.[4] The argument rests on a number of sub-arguments that link CSR with long-term sustainability and profits for the corporation. One is the idea that CSR contributes to a company's cost and risk reduction by warding off potential attacks from society, governments, and the media. A second is the claim that CSR helps gain competitive advantage by attracting higher-potential human resources, improving the company's perception among its employees, and branding its products to consumers. A third is CSR's assumed positive impact in terms of reputation and legitimacy, which enable the firm to operate in society. The importance for performance and profits of appreciation and recognition of a company's activities among its stakeholders, be they regulators, partners, or consumers, is beyond doubt.[5]

CSR promoters in Syria have adopted the business case as a cornerstone of their branding activities. Reproducing phraseologies from the international CSR discourse, the Global Compact Network Syria's promotion folder promises benefits like "increased legitimacy and licenses to operate", "improved reputation and increasing brand value" and "increased employee morale and productivity" for those who implement CSR practices.[6]

But is there a business case for CSR in Syria? This article argues that the direct reproduction of the business case argument is problematic, or at least needs qualification, in the Syrian context. I focus on the Global Compact's contribution to "reputation-building", which is the quintessential promise of the business case. As the Global Compact Syria Network states on its website, "the Global Compact is first and foremost concerned with exhibiting and building the social legitimacy of business and markets".[7] However, the recipe for social legitimacy is not a "one size fits all" affair regardless of a country's history, politics and culture. Legitimacy, Suchman's definition reminds us, is "a generalized perception or assumption that the actions of an entity are desirable, proper, or appropriate within some socially constructed system of norms, values, beliefs, and definitions".[8] This article attempts to shed light on the socially constructed system that affects Syrian businessmen's reputation and approach to social responsibility.

Let us start by acknowledging that there is a pre-existing normative framework for socially responsible behaviour in the Syrian private sector. For members of the Sunni Muslim community, which is the concern of this article, I call this framework the Zakat model as it is grounded in religious beliefs and practices and lays down that all able Muslims must return a portion of their working capital, usually 2.5%, to needy parts of the community. This almsgiving is one of Islam's five "pillars" and goes hand-in-hand with other dimensions of being a believer like fasting, praying, and accomplishing the pilgrimage.

Depending on one's viewpoint CSR can be seen either as related to the philosophy and functions of Zakat or as fundamentally different from it. Some CSR promoters are concerned to distinguish CSR from what they see as Islamic "charity" whereas others, of which we will see examples later, downplay the differences between the concepts. This article's basic assumption is that we need to distinguish between philosophy and function in this matter. At their origins the Zakat and the CSR models are two different normative systems—one is rooted in religion and the other in global norms building. Zakat starts with the principle that businessmen, as believers, have a God-given obligation to return parts of their profits to the community.[9] The Global Compact, on the other hand, is an attempt to contain the negative effects of globalization by building support for a set of ethical norms among businesses across the globe.

In their contributions to businessmen's reputation, on the other hand, Zakat and CSR have more similarities. Although proponents of the Zakat model are not as forthright as CSR in their concern with reputation building, and in fact actively reject claims that their actions are driven by this-worldly considerations, Zakat is also an important source of community recognition. I will draw on Bourdieu's theories of capital to substantiate this claim in the article. As we shall see the Zakat and CSR models imply very different strategies for reputation building, which again have consequences for their use by Syrian businessmen.

From its creation in 2008 until the outbreak of the Syrian uprising in March 2011 the Global Compact Syria network recruited fifty members, thirty-eight of which were private companies.[10] The network growth was so fast that Syria was referred to as a Global Compact "leadership case",[11] but the membership list also revealed that the initiative appealed to certain kinds of companies. For one, most of the subscribers were big firms by Syrian standards and many of them internationally oriented. Moreover, businessmen with a crony reputation figured prominently on the list. By contrast, the broader private sector had not been responsive to the CSR campaign.

To explain this uneven response from the Syrian business community the article distinguishes between different registers of symbolic capital. It draws on qualitative interviews with thirty businessmen between 2007 and 2010 and in particular sixteen who were selected on the basis of having a reputation for social responsibility. Aiming to explore the ways in which these actors conceptualize "social responsibility", I intentionally leave room for relatively long quotations from interviews and observations to give the reader first-hand impressions of the Syrian context.

Background: a changing Syrian context

State-business relations in the Arab world are undergoing steady, if incremental, change. The days of state-led development are over in most countries, while the private sector's capabilities increase. Shifts in economic power put strains on political and social arrangements and force the state and private actors to renegotiate the distribution of rights and responsibilities. One of the most contentious issues in this process is the pressure on welfare arrangements and the extent to which the private sector is able and willing to play a more prominent social role. The question is delicate because it touches on the political foundations of the region's regimes. In both its rentier and socialist versions, the Arab state has drawn a significant part of its identity, support, and even legitimacy from the services it distributes to the population. It cannot be seen to fail in its social responsibilities. Moreover, having the private sector play a more active social role means strengthening civil society, which carries its own political risks. Arab leaders are not prepared to give free rein to social initiatives out of fear that they might evolve into political counter-powers.

The private sector's newfound status as "development partner" for the Syrian state is a remarkable shift from the original line of the Ba'thist regime that took power in 1963. The socialist and anti-imperialist Ba'th party had no faith in the private sector's ability to bring about social and economic development, and installed a populist-authoritarian regime bent on liberating the Arab people from the dominance of colonialists and the upper classes. It coercively subdued all landowners, capitalists and religious leaders in the name of modernity and progress. Among other things, the state expropriated and redistributed farmland, banned the organization of the Muslim Brothers, and nationalized all big industrial ventures in the country. In February-April 1964, business groups and Islamists launched a nationwide series of protests, strikes and riots that was ruthlessly repressed by the state.[12]

In this process of "revolution from above",[13] the creation of a welfare state was an important goal and strategic component. The Ba'th regime sought to reduce community dependence on pre-existing "feudal arrangements" where notables provided services to the inhabitants in exchange for political support. It developed state welfare institutions as an alternative and used them to win the support of peasants and workers who were mobilized in the fight against Western powers and the old upper classes. Until the mid-1980s development aid from the Arab Gulf states and the Soviet Union allowed for constantly expanding public sector services. Although Hafiz al-Asad's 1970 "corrective movement" (*al-haraka al-tashihiyya*) downplayed the goal of social revolution and eased relations with the clerics and the private sector a little, the latter was still considered irrelevant for social and economic progress.

A financial collapse in 1986 reversed the expansion of the public sector and increased the private sector's relative importance. The government responded to the crisis by introducing an economic reform programme along two main axes. On the one hand, it targeted public expenditure to curtail the budget deficit; the state embarked on a course of austerity by cutting wages, reducing subsidies and downscaling public investments. On the other hand, it delegated an increasing part of its developmental responsibilities to the private sector. Through what is usually referred to as the Syrian *infitah*, the legal business framework was liberalized to give room for private investments. The 1991 investment law opened most fields of the economy, including manufacturing industry, to local as well as foreign investors.[14]

After a halt in the 1990s when fresh windfall revenue reduced pressures on economic arrangements and Hafiz al-Asad concentrated his political capital on peace negotiations with Israel, the process of restructuring the economy resumed under Bashar al-Asad. In 2005 the tenth Ba'th Party Congress declared that Syria was heading towards a "social market economy" (*iqtisad al-suq al-ijtima'i*). In this new phase of market adjustment, the private sector made its appearance in services like banking and insurance which since the 1963 takeover had been the exclusive prerogative of the state.[15] Damascus also witnessed the opening of a stock exchange in 2009.

Beyond the streamlining of rules and regulations for the private sector, however, more deep-reaching reforms like administrative downscaling and subsidy cuts were slowed down by concerns over the social repercussions of such moves. The International Monetary Fund pointed to "the quasi-absence of social safety nets" as one of two principal obstacles to achieving the goals of the Tenth Five-Year Development Plan (2006–2010) in Syria: "The lack of an efficient social safety net system stands in the way of most reforms if it is not addressed as a matter of priority … As long as there are no adequate social safety nets, the government will shy away from introducing any reforms whose impact on the poor could not be mitigated by targeted support".[16]

This is the context in which the Plan's introduction of CSR in Syrian development thinking should be seen. According to Chapter One of the Tenth Five-Year Development Plan the private sector shall be "partially involved" in "the social responsibility concerned with local community development ... as well as contributing to the projects concerned with the development of remote and backward regions".[17] As mentioned in the introduction, the achievement of this goal was delegated to the UNDP and the UN Global Compact framework. The Compact is conceived as a public-private partnership where business works side-by-side with governments in promoting social development.[18]

However, when the Ba'th regime decided to renew its relations with the private sector and draw on the latter's contributions to social development there were few pre-existing practices to start from. Having been treated with suspicion throughout forty years of socialist rhetoric, the capitalists had learned to stay away from public display and avoid entering non-economic domains where the state claimed ideological control in the building of a new social order. The only precedents for business engagement in society that existed were in fact religiously grounded. Centred on the Islamic institution of *zakat*, these practices linked the pious business class to religious associations that held different views on community order from the secular-oriented and 'Alawite-dominated regime.

Starting in the mid 1990s the regime initiated a liberalization of the associative sector that led to a rapid increase in the number and scale of faith-based welfare initiatives. The pious business class responded favourably to the opening and seemed especially inclined to contribute financially when the religious leaders in charge of a project could demonstrate a degree of independence from the state. The expansion of community welfare benefited the independent-minded and critically oriented Zayd movement that was able to extend its reach over Damascus' biggest associative projects. The rise of Zayd to the status of a potential counter-power alarmed the Syrian security officials who reacted by curtailing the autonomy of religious associations in 2008.[19]

Mindful of this experience, the Syrian government, which has put a socially responsible private sector on the agenda, prefers this social responsibility to take other forms than the traditional religious model. The concept of CSR as brought to Syria by the winds of globalization might seem an appealing alternative from the regime's perspective in the sense that it provides a non-religious justification for social engagement and invites the private sector to partner with the state. However, winning acceptance for the CSR framework in the Syrian private sector is easier said than done. In the following sections I shall compare the Zakat and CSR models, explain how the latter has been adapted to fit the local context, and discuss both models' usefulness for building reputation for Syrian business.

Social responsibility—the Zakat model

My life philosophy starts with belief in God. God honoured man, and made him his vicegerent on earth. Man has two responsibilities: i) to believe in God, and ii) to build the world through interaction with other people.

The interaction has its rules. God taught Adam, and all the other prophets, how to relate to others. Interaction should be based on love (*amana*), generosity (*ithar*), truthfulness (*sudq*), and affection (*mahabba*). Of these, affection is the most important. Love between man and God, on the one hand, and between man and man on the other. My love to God leads me to love other people, to wish for them what I wish for myself. ... By pleasing my brother I gain acceptance and love from God.[20]

The reflections above are the words of Said Hafez, a philanthropist and one of Syria's most accomplished industrialists. As the head of the Concord and Hafez refrigerator producing plants in Beirut and Damascus, he manages a family firm with 2,900 employees and is the dominating actor in the Levant's refrigerator market.[21] Besides being a seasoned industrialist Said Hafez is, as the quotation suggests, a highly conscious and pious individual. He represents a segment of the Syrian business segment which puts Islamic doctrine centre stage in its life and takes on certain social responsibilities on this basis. Said Hafez is for instance known to provide financial assistance to a host of charity associations. He also administers the association that finances the Sheikh Badr al-Din al-Hassani religious institute in Syria.

The example of Said Hafez is emblematic of the traditional approach to social responsibility in a Sunni Muslim context that I call the Zakat model. Businessmen who refer to this model see themselves as perpetuating a proud tradition of community welfare that goes back to the very first years of Islam. The Prophet Muhammad introduced *zakat* in the state of Medina and the religious tax was further institutionalized under the Caliphs. *Zakat* is a pillar of Islamic faith and practice and is often juxtaposed to prayer (*salat*), the most obvious external sign of adherence to Islam.[22] It is a question of debate whether wealth or property is a condition for giving, as some Qur'anic *suras* seem to indicate that "kind gestures" can be given as *zakat* by anyone. For Said Hafez, however, there is a clear understanding that Islam wants believers to be financially independent in order to be able to help the community. Because of their wealth the merchants have always been an important source of religious taxation, and Syrian religious scholars frequently underscore their fundamental role.[23]

It should be clear from the above that the basis of social responsibility in the Zakat model is a religious commandment. According to Said Hafez, the money paid in *zakat* does not in fact belong to the individual but is considered *haqqun ma'lum*—a share that is due to God. Failure to pay this share is considered a grave sin, and to deny the obligatory nature of *zakat* amounts to unbelief.[24] The Qur'an makes clear that the prayers of those who do not pay *zakat* will not be accepted. Such people will instead suffer painful chastisement in the fires and torture chambers of Hell.[25]

In the absence of the Caliphate or an Islamic state that collects *zakat* in Syria, the tax is usually paid to a religious institution. The *sheikh* or the board in charge of the association then redistribute the funds to members of the eight categories that according to the Qur'an are entitled to receive *zakat*.[26] Businessmen can also manage the distribution of alms themselves, and many keep parts of the money for personally chosen beneficiaries instead of delivering all to a religious charity. Said Hafez is one of those who have established a section of his company administration that works with charitable projects. If an organization asks for services he sends someone from the section to check the needs and activities of the association before making a donation.[27]

In choosing the recipients of *zakat* money, the benefactor is supposed to follow a principle of proximity where he or she starts with the needy in his/her immediate surroundings and then gradually moves outwards within the limits of the available resources. Although *zakat* is meant to extend beyond familial obligations to the wider community, several businessmen explain that they pay special attention to their extended family members.

There is also a special "etiquette" associated with the Islam-based social responsibility model. According to Hafez, "the poor shall not ask for money from the rich; the rich is responsible to give him his needs without anyone asking".[28] In other words both begging and miserliness are condemned. The believer is supposed to show enthusiasm in paying his taxes, without in any ways bragging about it. It is in fact both common and expected to express gratitude, when paying, to the religious *sheikh*.

Members of the "pious business segment" in Syria express strong faith in the utility of the *zakat* institution and deplore the negative effects when society forgets its religious roots. For Said Hafez, if everyone (including Christians and Jews) had followed the orders of God and the Prophets, "We would no longer have any problems on earth". Conversely, he explains, "When the rich fails to respect his obligation, society turns sick and the poor who cannot find food begin to take it by force".[29] This being said, Hafez also warns that charity is not a long-term solution; social responsibility must also have a "deeper base" where other requirements of Islam, and first and foremost the imperative of education (as in the Qur'anic injunction *iqra!*), are taken care of. The hungry and the sick must gain the autonomy that make them able to help other people. Along this line of reasoning Hafez says, "I consider that my most important charitable work is our factory because it teaches workers skills and give them money for a decent life".[30]

Social responsibility—the CSR model

Compared with the Zakat model, the Global Compact has a more pragmatic and mundane rationale. It was originally developed for the office of the UN Secretary General as a way to address the growing international imbalance between the market and society entailed by the process of globalization. Recognizing the lack of a government to act on behalf of the common good at the global level, it seeks to instil in the global market "shared social values and institutional practices" and to provide a platform for negotiation between business and social norms.[31] The Global Compact's prime objective is in other words global norms building, which it perceives as both a theoretical and practical endeavour. It organizes global policy dialogues on the challenges of globalization and encourages local learning forums in various countries, but also engages in multi-stakeholder collaborative development projects to further the Millennium Development Goals.

The philosophy behind the Global Compact is that governments need the cooperation of business, but that regulations only turn business off. Hence, rather than threatening with sanctions, the strategy should be to convince the private sector that it has a vested interest in promoting sustainable development.[32] This means that the CSR model of social responsibility rests on a principle of voluntary compliance, contrary to *zakat*. The agent is also different in the two cases. Whereas *zakat* is primarily (if not solely) an individual responsibility, CSR is—as the name tells—about a corporation's social impact. The Global Compact is promoting certain norms that should regulate a company's behaviour, but is not concerned with individual employees.

The crucial question with regard to norms building in a place like Syria is, of course, which social norms shall lay the ground for corporate behaviour. The norms promoted by the Global Compact are not—nominally at least—the norms of Islam, but rather the social norms of internationally agreed human rights, labour rights, environmental protection and anti-corruption. These are concretized in a list of ten principles:

1) Businesses should support and respect the protection of internationally proclaimed human rights;
2) They should make sure that they are not complicit in human rights abuses;
3) Businesses should uphold the freedom of association and the effective recognition of the right to collective bargaining;
4) Elimination of all forms of forced and compulsory labour;
5) Effective abolition of child labour;
6) Elimination of discrimination in employment and occupation;
7) Businesses are asked to support a precautionary approach to environmental challenges;
8) They should undertake initiatives to promote greater environmental responsibility; and
9) They should encourage the development and diffusion of environmentally friendly technologies;
10) Businesses should work against corruption in all its forms, including extortion and bribery.[33]

Responsibility in the Global Compact is in other words defined in relation to a broad set of values that concerns society—or the world—as a whole. This contrasts with the Zakat model's stress on "priority to the closest". In some formulations the Global Compact explicitly asks private enterprises to help "find solutions to global problems".[34] The argument is also made that companies' responsibilities in the global economy know no borders: when brand names, company offices and production structures leave the confines of the nation state, "people hold firms responsible for actions far beyond their boundaries".[35] The precise meaning of responsibility in such a wide approach is however in question. The Global Compact's initiator, John Ruggie, has recently taken an important step to clarify the distribution of responsibilities between the state and business.[36]

Last but not least, there are some fundamental differences between the Zakat and CSR models with regard to publicity and etiquette in the carrying of social responsibility. Companies that adhere to the Global Compact are supposed to report on their CSR activities and entitled to reap publicity benefits from it. Marketing of CSR is believed to have a positive knock-on effect on other companies which may be encouraged to similar endeavours. The Zakat model, on the other hand, is more critical of public display of generosity because it sheds doubt on the benefactor's intention (*niyya*). The Qur'an warns that God is "all-knowing" and can see when a giver falls into bragging and private self-satisfaction.[37] Anonymous giving is believed to have the additional advantage of protecting the identity of the recipient to avoid reproach and doubt about the latter's need and reduce the feeling of shame.

Local adaptations

Between October 2008 and January 2009, the enterprise Stars produced, printed, and distributed 50,000 colouring books to children in twenty-seven schools in Aleppo and six in surrounding suburbs. The books, which included pages for kids to fill in and create their own drawings employing images of Stars biscuits, were given to children around nine or ten, along with some simple colouring supplies. They were told that if they drew in them and returned them to their teachers, they would be given a small prize.

> The response was overwhelming. Expecting only a small return, they were thrilled to receive nearly 9,000 books. … Reflecting on the campaign, [the company entrepreneur] Kalioundji adds that it has transformed his conception of the relationship of business and social responsibility. For him, the campaign has made it clear that the two are not contradictory objectives but produce

impressive marketing results as a pair. … 'You don't need a budget for being social responsible. It's pushing kids to do something good and at the same time people are buying more of the product in the stores.[38]

This is an example of how the English-language magazine *Forward*, run by the Syrian entrepreneur Abdulsalam Haykal, describes and introduces CSR in Syria. Haykal is a member of the Global Compact Syria Network and was in 2009 honoured by the World Economic Forum as one of ten "distinguished young Arab leaders" who, as a press report put it, had been "active in advancing new concepts in the business and society in Syria, including CSR".[39] But Haykal is not only a Syrian CSR promoter; he also gives the concept his personal twist. When I consulted him during interviews for this paper in May 2010, he showed me outlines of an advertisement campaign he intended to run in the form of smiling faces accompanied by various positive messages. For Haykal this was a way of exercising CSR by sharing traits of his corporate culture with the wider Syrian society:

My understanding of CSR is that you have to feel that you have responsibility for something and then find out how to do it. Syrian companies that are known to have CSR usually operate by responding to proposals from the public. But in Transtek I would like to approach the issue differently by reflecting to the outside world the company's internal culture. What I have in mind is an advertisement campaign that carries the message of our vision. We want to promote slogans like 'positive thinking,' 'talk,' 'smile,' 'create your own environment,' and 'be the change.' When I first introduced the idea to a friend he said 'are you crazy, do you want to call for a revolution here?' But we'll go to the universities with this message and we'll create a computer game with it. This is a time for change in Syria. We need change agents here. It is not necessary to spend a lot of money; some can exercise social responsibility by saying things, lobbying for something, or spreading an idea. CSR cannot be limited to anything as long as you are making an impact. Start by defining what you want to achieve, how to get there, and follow your heart.[40]

Haykal's publicity campaign is not easily fitted into the Global Compact's focus areas of human rights, labour rights, environmental protection and anti-corruption. In fact, by a stringent definition, it may not even qualify as CSR. However, it illustrates how the theme CSR is subject to local adaptations. The concrete ways in which the internationally crafted concept finds its way into Syrian ideals and practices are not the simple fruits of standardized formulations in the UN Global Compact. Actors who adopt the CSR discourse also have their own interpretations and interests and often adjust their retransmission of the concept accordingly. For someone like Haykal who is supportive of Bashar al-Asad's development line and enjoys the personal trust of the first lady, CSR is the way of the future and a tool of progress. But his conceptualization is also strongly marked by his passion for "entrepreneurship" as the president of the Syrian Young Entrepreneurs Association. In fact, in the quotation above, CSR has for all practical reasons become a synonym for entrepreneurship, as Haykal calls for "change agents" to create a better Syria. And in this synonym of entrepreneurship, entrepreneurs are no longer limited to economic transactions, but can and should exploit their creativity in society as a whole.[41]

Beyond such discursive twists to the CSR concept, Haykal also gave proof of CSR adaptation on an organizational level. Speaking of his discussions with the Global Compact Syria coordinator Muhammad Agha when the latter introduced the idea of promoting CSR through the UN in Syria, Haykal explained that he did not give the project much chance to succeed since, in his view, there is a general negative feeling about the UN in Syria.[42] As a businessman concerned with his company's brand value he recalled having told his friend Muhammad Agha, "I don't care whether the UN will put a stamp on my projects or not, you need something else to make the project attractive". From there on, Haykal recalls, the idea came up for a handpicked advisory council that would give local credibility to the Global Compact.

The council Haykal refers to is the Syria National Advisory Council to the Global Compact, which is composed of prominent representatives of the private sector, civil society organizations, the UNDP, and the Syrian government, media, and education sectors. The first category has the strongest presence by far and includes top rank Syrian businessmen like Abdulrahman al-Attar, Rateb al-Shallah, Imad Ghreiwati, Firas Tlass, and Haytham Joud.[43] The council's formal responsibilities are "overall endorsement and guidance on the implementation of the UN Global Compact ten principles", "representation in domestic and global forums" and "lobbying, advocacy and resource mobilization for development projects".[44] In addition, the presence of private sector "heavyweights" in the council provides valuable social capital to businessmen who adhere to the Global Compact Syria Network. In Abdulsalam Haykal's words, "We meet every month, eat together, lobby together, and so on, it is an interesting network".[45] The promise of networking with prominent businessmen was in other words the CSR promoters' device to offset reticence towards the UN in Syria.

The paradox is that the UN Global Compact holds human rights as its core value while some of the businessmen in the National Advisory Council are close historical allies or associates of the Syrian regime. The latter has a long record of human rights abuses and is also very critical of the international human rights discourse which it sees as an attempt to undermine Syrian sovereignty. Interestingly, however, this has not prevented these businessmen from signing up with the Global Compact. One reason for this may be that the Global Compact Syria Network has chosen not to emphasize human rights as much as the UN internationally. The thematic areas for its partnership projects are education, capacity development and human resources, the environment, health, social development and safety, and enhancing the business environment—the latter is hardly a conventional CSR theme.[46] Reports of CSR initiatives and projects that emanate from the Global Compact Syria Network seldom refer to human rights specifically.

According to Nader Kabbani who represents the Syria Trust for Development in the National Advisory Council, the level of institutionalization in the Global Compact Syria programme is low. There are no clear guidelines for how the council should operate and capacity building in the Syrian private sector is therefore ad hoc.[47] Few Syrian companies have their own CSR departments or coherent strategies in this regard.[48] Most companies that have subscribed to the Global Compact instead respond to government or civil society initiatives for fund-raising. To mention a few examples of the achievements put forward by the Global Compact Syria, one is the funding for a cancer research centre by the telecommunication company MTN, in cooperation with the UNDP and the Ministry of Higher Education, which made the request.[49] Another example is donations from the Byblos Bank Syria to the NGO Basma, affiliated to the first lady, to help children with cancer.[50] A third Global Compact member, the construction company Emaar Syria, is providing support for the Syrian organization for the disabled, Aamal.[51]

Reputation building

The money for the above-mentioned CSR projects is taken from the companies' marketing budgets, according to Global Compact Syria coordinator Muhammad Agha. As he puts it, "They hope to get some publicity in return for it, which is fair".[52] As alluded to in the introduction, the stated aim of the Global Compact is to exhibit and build the social legitimacy of business and markets. From this perspective, spending a part of the corporations' financial resources makes economic sense.

However, as Bourdieu reminds us, the sources of community recognition are complex and social legitimacy cannot be bought in a straightforward manner. When considering Zakat and CSR contributions to reputation building in Syria, some lessons from the French sociologist and philosopher's theory of the "forms of capital" are useful. For Bourdieu, capital, in the sense of resources that can be used to appropriate social energy within a system of exchange, should not be reduced to a question of money (economic capital), but also takes the form of networks (social capital), educational and intellectual background (cultural capital), and honour, prestige or recognition (symbolic capital).[53] It is the uneven distribution of these resources that produces and reproduces inequalities within a particular social formation. The ability to generate symbolic capital is the closest connected to this article's concern with reputation building. Indeed, we started out by noting that both CSR and Zakat can be means to obtain community recognition. The former model's challenge is however that its language has been crafted outside the Syrian system of norms, values, beliefs, and institutions. Not being attuned to local sensibilities, it fails to strike the symbolic chords that create prestige and recognition in the Syrian society.

The pre-existing normative framework for social responsibility in Sunni Muslim Syria, the Zakat model, is associated with a particular code of reputation. As alluded to earlier, it is not simply the fact of paying that is important, but first and foremost how you do it. In particular, Bourdieu stresses the role of personal sacrifice in the conversion of economic capital into cultural or symbolic resources. Honour, prestige and recognition can only be acquired through time and work. Merely giving away money runs the risk of being seen as a bribe, but when accompanied by the additional commitment of personal resources—which is seen as more precious in the sense that one is "paying with one's person"—it signals devotion and thereby inspires community recognition. In Bourdieu's words, "The wasting of money, energy, time, ingenuity, is the very principle of the efficiency of the social alchemy through which the interested relation transmutes to disinterested relation".[54]

An interesting illustration of this point in the Syrian business community is the industrialist Muhammad al-Sha'ir who runs a detergent producing plant with 250 employees with a capital of $20 million. A dedicated Muslim, al-Sha'ir divides his time between economic and social work and is an active member of no less than seven associations. As he told me during one of my interviews, "At 15.30 we close the doors of the factory, even if we have more demand. Then I engage in social activities".[55] These activities are varied and include lecturing in the Social Awareness Association, which "strives to strengthen the consciousness of fundamental social values" about Islamic views on topics such as health and marriage. In the Association for Young Syrians he works to provide housing for young people who are getting married and lack a place to stay. And in the Association for Protecting Syrians he, among other things, helps students gain access to free education. The philosophy behind this work, according to al-Sha'ir, is from Islam: "Islam does not want you to help yourself more than helping others. If you wish for wealth, health, nice clothes and a car, then you should wish so for everyone. If you want for others what you seek for yourself, then you are a believer (*mu'min*)".[56] His social engagement has gained al-Sha'ir a special recognition in Damascene business circles. During the preparations for the Tenth Five-Year Development Plan in 2006, he was chosen from among the members of the Chamber of Industry to represent the manufacturing industry in a national deliberation committee.

Not many businessmen can match the level of active community engagement of Muhammad al-Sha'ir. But reverence for Islamic principles and attention paid to social responsibility in the form of *zakat* have a similar effect on symbolic capital in the wider business community. The sacred provides a space where businessmen can rid themselves of the weight of conflicts, animosity and exploitation, and appear disinterested in worldly affairs. Performing one's religious duties by giving away money is sending a signal that personal ambitions are subordinated to the love of God. As the industrialist and philanthropist Mounzer al-Bizreh expressed while talking about social responsibility in Syria, "The social solidarity is a sign that we believe in God". He continued, "Religion is conduct (*mu'amala*). Our Prophet used to say, 'God gave me insight to teach you noble characteristics.' But unfortunately, morals in the region today are in a very poor shape. The world has become material only. People say, 'Give me money,' and forget that He who gives us money is God".[57]

The insistence on "love of God" as motivation for taking on social responsibility stands in contrast to the way in which CSR is promoted to companies as a way to generate profit. But the attraction of *zakat* for many Syrian businessmen is precisely that it is dissociated from the logic of profit and is therefore seen as transgressing self-interest. The halo of piety which covers the ritualized renunciation of money makes possible the "social alchemy" that Bourdieu describes.

The word *zakat* is derived from the Arabic verb *zakā*, which among other things means "to increase" and "to be pure". It is commonly seen to have a purifying function, both for those who pay and for the property itself.[58] Echoes of this theological interpretation are frequent in Syrian business circles. In Amin Hafez's words, "Zakat is considered as a form of cleansing for small mistakes you might have made with your customers during business activities or transactions".[59]

Last but not least, *zakat* offers businessmen the additional advantage of association with religious *shaykh*s who are a source of prestige in Syrian society. Merchants who give financial support to religious associations receive privileges and special attention from the religious dignitaries in return. To give some examples, benefactors can be included in the boards of directors of charitable associations, have their names attached to buildings or projects, get private lessons from leading religious authorities, have the *shaykh*s visit their personal parties, or sit next to the *ulema* during public ceremonies. Privileges such as these are unmistakable symbols of status that add to businessmen's symbolic resources.

By way of illustration, consider the following example. In a luxurious private residence in the outskirts of Damascus, a *mawlid* (celebration of the Prophet's birthday) took place in June 2007. The feast was given by the Damascene industrialist 'Adnan Abu Chaar who had gathered some 250 people, predominantly from the business community, along with prominent persons like ambassadors, parliamentarians and religious dignitaries. The guests were seated in a beautiful garden where a group of musicians played religious hymns. In front of the tables stood a stage-like gazebo, which the host had reserved for the VIPs. As the prominent persons entered the garden, a film crew followed their movements and projected the images onto a live-transmitted screen. The *ulema* received the greatest attention, and for a privately organized party, their attendance was impressive. One after another, top religious leaders like Sa'id Ramadan al-Buti, Syria's most renowned Muslim scholar, Husam al-Din al-Farfur, director of the al-Fath Islamic Institute, Abu al-Khayr Shukri, director of the Sheikh Badr al-Din al-Hassani Islamic Institute, Salah Kaftaru, son of the former General Mufti Ahmad Kaftaru and director of the Islamic high school that was named after him, Sariya al-Rifa'i, the preacher of the Zayd bin Thabit mosque, the Second Mufti of Aleppo Mahmud 'Akkam, and the General Mufti of Syria Ahmad Badr al-Din Hassun made their appearance. The host then entered the scene to give a welcoming speech to the audience. He introduced the four main social categories present—*ulema*, members of parliament, industrialists and traders—in the following manner:

> When I invited you, I intended to invite the makers of this nation [*umma*]—those who make the minds and hearts and shape them in the Prophet's manner, as wanted by God for humans. You my teachers and masters: The honorable Ulema ...
>
> I also addressed my invitation to those who hold the reins of power and have taken upon themselves to be the guardians of the pact that ties us to our state and our laws, be they civil or religious. I mean our brothers in the parliament who have devoted themselves to work for the public interest and influence the historical movement of the development of this country—the people of this country—and first of all for us.
>
> Then there are those skilful industrialists who produce for the consumers and every person in this nation to allow them to be connected with the technologies and products of the material culture, which let us live a comfortable life.
>
> And finally I invited my brothers the merchants who strive their life to reach the threshold of God, lay their foreheads in front of it and say O Lord, this is the world we live in, and this is the society we live in, and this is the one-eyed material culture that only sees half of your elevated creation. ...

The host was dressed in a dignified white coat which the General Mufti had bestowed on him on arrival. Solemnly thanking him for the gesture, he described its colour as a reflection of the purity of heart of the Mufti and expressed hope that it would nourish and protect his own heart. He then invited Hassun to give a speech in remembrance of the Prophet. The General Mufti seized the opportunity to turn back the praise to industrialists and merchants:

> My brothers, you whom God has placed to shape this nation, you know that industry was started by our blessed prophets. Our master Noah was the first industrialist as he built the first ship ... I tell you gentlemen, you have been trusted to carry out a mission.

As for the merchants, what more could be said in their honour than that our Prophet visited our land as a merchant. At the age of twenty-five he came to Busra in Syria [*Sham*] and engaged in trading.

The wider theme of Hassun's speech was the life and love of the Prophet as an ideal for present-day believers. He solemnly praised the host for building communal ties through the social gathering. Hassun also drew a line from piety to prosperity and success. "When the hearts are lightened with faith", he told the audience, "then the minds are filled with thought, the money is purified in our pockets, the earth sprouts from its cleanness and heaven gives us prosperity and grace".

The evening's second religious speaker dwelt further on the theme of community and cooperation. Having been introduced as a great Islamic philosopher—"the Ghazali of his time"—Sa'id Ramadan al-Buti made the following statement:

Honourable people, I would like to summarize the essence of our meeting in a few words: religion is planning, industry and investment are building, and commerce is selling. Together, these aspects contribute to the creation of a society. When I look at this gathering I see those who are planning, or rather pass on the plan that has been drawn by God; I see those who tie this *sharia* to the nation in the People's Assembly; I see those who devote themselves to industry and those who engage in commerce. And I return to say that verily, I'm standing before a reservoir of the ideal Islamic society. Religion is planning, industry is providing and completing, commerce is selling and our Lord, praise Him, is watching …

I'll end my words by stressing the magnificent presence I see in this gathering. By magnificent presence I mean the signs of cooperation; the coming together of all the indispensable pillars of the Islamic society that God has told us to create …

For Sa'id Ramadan al-Buti, there was thus a religious purpose for strengthening elite networks within the Sunnite community: businessmen, parliamentarians and *ulema* were the bearers of Islamic society. The listeners seemed to appreciate the task—and sense of agency—that they were given: each eloquent formulation from the scholar provoked approving sounds from the audience. When Buti ended his speech, the time had come for invocation of God (*du'a*). The host called on Sheikh Sariya al-Rifa'i, head of the Zayd movement, to lead the faithful. It was by far the evening's most captivating moment. The crowd collectively echoed the calls of the *sheikh*, filling the air with a feeling of spirituality and belonging.

Following this, the host invited his guests for dinner. The formal part of the programme was over, but the social gathering was still in its beginning. The food was served as a standing buffet where the guests would pick from numerous delicious dishes. While circulating around the tables, those present could have a chat with elite members of the Sunni community. For those with worldly affairs to settle, it was an excellent opportunity.

Reputation and business

The argument in the foregoing has been that there is a distinct code of conduct associated with the Zakat model which is the key to symbolic capital in the pious business segment. The internationally crafted CSR model largely fails to buy into these symbolic resources because it makes the unspoken explicit and uses the business case as a marketing tool. One can therefore question the usefulness of CSR for reputation building in the Syrian context. Before drawing too sweeping conclusions, however, one should keep in mind that there are different registers of reputation that a businessman can draw on. The kind of community recognition that springs from pious behaviour is not the only game in town, and recognition from the UN Global Compact can under certain circumstances be an asset. I will elaborate on this point below, but first it is necessary to clarify what is really the importance of reputation for business.

David Vogel has critically examined the merits of the business case in a Western, late-capitalist context. He finds no clear causal link between CSR and profitability for corporations except for certain niche markets. The reason, Vogel explains, is that socially responsible standards tend to make products more expensive whereas the majority of consumers let price determine their shopping behaviour. Some brands like Fair Trade and GoodWeave have obtained success by targeting consumers who are prepared to pay for ethically produced products. But this market remains relatively small and is not yet a driving force in global capitalism. Another category of companies that may have a business case for CSR consists of those that rely upon widely known international brands such as Nestlé and Nike and therefore are vulnerable to consumer boycott or NGO campaigns of "naming and shaming". But in the majority of cases, Vogel concludes, company managers may not see compelling evidence that socially responsible behaviour is good for their bottom line.[60]

There are few available data about the preferences and behaviour of Syrian consumers, but anecdotal evidence suggests a similar situation to what Vogel describes for the global economy. On the one hand, there *is* a niche market for "moral goods" where products seem to sell more the more they appear religious. On the other hand, Syrian consumers struggle to make their ends meet and shop on the basis of price (and quality) as in any other market. When I asked the above-mentioned industrialist 'Adnan Abu Chaar about the importance of religious reputation for business he made an elucidating point and gave two amusing examples:

> A man can be known as *fasik* (straying from proper Islamic conduct) without it affecting his sales. Take the example of the mobile provider Syriatel which is associated with a man who is infamous for his personal conduct, yet most Syrians choose to subscribe with Syriatel because their services are better.
>
> In other cases, however, religious conduct can in fact make a difference. Let me tell you the story of the Wattar company and its washing machines. The al-Wattar sons are known for their good Islamic conduct. One of them, Khalid al-Wattar, had the idea that he would provide a washing machine that would purify (*tatahhar*) according to the requirements of the Shafi'i school which predominates in Syria. He went to Shaykh Sa'id Ramadan al-Buti and asked whether he could write a religious certificate for his washing machines. But the Shafi'i school has very strict rules for purification. If there is urine on your pants, for instance, the water you wash your pants with must fall to the ground and not touch any other part of the clothes. So when al-Buti saw the washing machine which spread the dirty water all over the pants he was horrified and said that it was the very opposite of a religiously sanctioned tool. So Khalid al-Wattar had to invent a device to overcome this challenge. He took one of the European-technology machines they're using and installed an additional programme—*tatahhur*—which purified the clothes with water that was washed away *before* the regular washing programme started. He showed it to al-Buti and had him write a *fatwa* stating that some washing machines were washing in accordance with the Shafi'i school requirements. Although Buti refrained from mentioning brand names, Khalid al-Wattar used the religious certificate in his marketing campaign. The result was a huge commercial success and the Wattar machine captured the market.
>
> The prime competitor, Joud, who is not a practicing Muslim, tried to respond by a marketing stunt claiming that his machines were 'purifying more' (*yutahhir akthar*), but there is no such thing as 'more purifying' in Islam, so he was made a laughing stock.[61]

The example of religiously purifying washing machines shows that there is a market for Islamic virtue in Syria. But the industrialist's response reminds us first and foremost that products are sold on the basis of their quality and price, regardless of religion or ethics. A businessman's personal reputation is not the same as the reputation of his goods and cannot compensate if the products are lousy. Likewise, consumers will seldom ask where a service comes from as long as they are satisfied with the product.

The direct economic gain of any reputation, personal or corporate, CSR or Zakat, is therefore limited. But the primary importance of reputation for business is elsewhere—in the social legitimacy of market actors. The status of capitalism in Syria is still a potentially vulnerable position. For one, socialist ideals are not dead and gone and many inside and outside the Ba'th party are still sceptical about the country's new economic orientation. Secondly, Syria's business class has thrived in the shade of an authoritarian state that is associated with corruption, and is popularly seen as opportunistic. Thirdly, property rights are not duly enforced and actors without support from above, from below, or in the wider business community can fall victim to predatory behaviour.

For all these reasons, reputation building in Syria makes economic sense, and piety is the most effective way of obtaining community recognition. CSR, again, is largely ineffectual in filling the mentioned need for social legitimacy. 'Adnan Abu Chaar put it plainly, "We have a deep scepticism in this country about foreign institutions and don't trust that their intentions are benign. The historical reasons for this are obvious. Syria has been manipulated and exploited by outside powers since the time of the Crusades. When a foreign entity tells us it's a welfare organization, ordinary people don't believe in it. They wonder who is pulling the strings".[62]

Nevertheless, as alluded to earlier, there may still be a niche for CSR-based reputation. After all, as many as thirty-eight firms signed up to the Global Compact Syria network over a three-year period.[63] As mentioned in the introduction, the subscribing companies tended to be big, by Syrian standards, and internationally oriented. Another characterizing feature was the strong presence of crony capitalists. Starting with the National Advisory Council members Rateb al-Shallah, Abdulrahman al-Attar, and Firas Tlass, several participants were known to have enjoyed close ties to the Syrian regime.[64] Among the regular Global Compact members Syriatel and Gulfsands Petroleum were controlled by Bashar al-Asad's cousin Rami Makhlouf, whose estimated personal wealth is some $6 billion, according to *Le Monde*, and whose name is synonymous in Syria with the excesses of crony capitalism.[65] Other members with a strong crony reputation were the United Group, Alfadel Group, MTN Syria, and the MAS Group.

On the basis of these observations, we could put forward the hypothesis that the reputation of the UN Global Compact label is of interest for Syrian companies that deal with foreign partners, or for companies that would like to be seen as answering favourably to an initiative that is supported by the regime. While CSR and the UN logo are not particularly cherished in the local business community, international companies are accustomed to both. Labels like CSR and the UN Global Compact are recognizable internationally and signal connectedness with the global business community. For the few big Syrian companies that have international partners or aspirations, that can be a valuable asset.

To take one example, consider the case of the Madar industrial group which runs a double digit number of factories and is the number one actor in the Syrian aluminium industry. Madar joined the Global Compact in 2009 after the Compact coordinator Muhammad Agha made a personal request to the company manager Hassan Da'bul,[66] who describes Muhammad Agha as his friend. In Hassan Da'bul's words:

> I had a look at their policies; environment, anti-corruption, social responsibility and stuff like that, and I thought that we are doing these things anyways. We consider ourselves an ethical organization and already care about the environment and all the stuff that is required by the Global compact. It did not look like something that was very hard to achieve as we already have the beliefs. It is more like a PR issue for us. We have done a couple of projects that go along with their profile...
>
> The Global Compact was not involved in the implementation, but they provided us with good encouragement and support. They clearly showed us how happy they were about it. And having someone from the UNDP at the inauguration ceremony was a very good support for us. We see it as a PR, marketing, image-developing tool. Mentioning them, having their logo on our activities, etc. is a good image-enhancer for our group.[67]

Interestingly in the context of this paper, the Da'bul family is also a proud defender of *zakat* and its utility for social development. In a previous interview I conducted with Hassan's brother and business partner

Muhab Da'bul, the latter explained that Madar gives money to some 300 charity organizations in addition to poor employees in the company and orphans, widows and elderly who ask for help. He estimated that Madar with a turnover of some $155 million pays in the range of $1.5 million in *zakat*.[68] It shows that CSR and *zakat* are not necessarily at odds with each other although their rationales are fundamentally different and businessmen may pursue them for very different reasons. What we face, at the end of the day, are different registers of reputation that can be used for different purposes.

Conclusion

This article has introduced a development that is relatively new in Syria and largely unaccounted for in the academic literature, which is the promotion of CSR in the Middle East through programmes like the UN Global Compact. It has followed a fieldwork-based approach, investigating ideals and practices of social engagement in the Sunni Muslim business community, and argued that the CSR discourse runs parallel to a pre-existing and religiously grounded framework of social responsibility that I call the Zakat model. It differs from the CSR model in that it builds on an Islamic commandment, involves cooperation with religious associations, and encourages believers to be modest and avoid publicity about their social deeds.

Regardless of differences in the ethical foundations of the CSR and Zakat models, the article has suggested comparing the two, sociologically, as resources with potential for generating symbolic capital for businessmen in Syria. I have argued that the so-called "business case" may frequently not apply because the CSR model's approach is foreign to local sensibilities. This is not only because of CSR's Western origins or negative perceptions of the UN in Syria, but also because it lacks the ability to produce the "social alchemy" that is encouraged by piety. The Zakat model provides businessmen with the means to transgress self-interest and escape the worldly conflicts that otherwise may tarnish their reputation. In the absence of mediation through a belief system such as Islam, which is emotionally experienced at an individual level, the CSR model fails to hit the essential triggers.

This does not mean that CSR is stillborn in Syria or that the business case has no merit. But it limits the scope of where and how CSR will have the assumed positive impact in terms of reputation and legitimacy. First, we need to take into account whether a business actor is dealing with an international or a domestic audience; the Global Compact label may well generate symbolic capital in the West, but *zakat* remains the preferred currency in a local Muslim context. Second, we should consider whether the aim is to accumulate goodwill with the regime or at the social level. For actors targeting political support, the embrace of CSR can be a good reputation investment. It sends a positive signal of heeding the President's call for social responsibility and doing so in a non-Islamic, "modern" manner. Zakat, by contrast, is a greater source of prestige in society. Partly this is due to the independent political language of Islam, but many simply cherish the value of piety.

In light of the remarkable presence of crony capitalists among the Global Compact membership, we should finally keep in mind that the UN label provides a certain potential for "blue-washing". For businessmen who have made their wealth in association with a stigmatized and authoritarian regime, partnering with the UN in the name of human rights and anti-corruption can be part of their process of reinvention as respectable business actors. The Syrian uprising that broke out in March 2011 has however demonstrated the fragility of this legitimatization strategy. The Assad regime has resorted to open repression to quell the uprising and thereby cut itself off from the majority Sunnin segment and the international community. Many of the businessmen who maintained political connections in the past, including several who had joined the Global Compact, have reacted by dissociating themselves from the regime.

Armed conflict put an abrupt end to the first experience of CSR promotion in Syria. The lessons learned are however of relevance for similar processes across the Arab region. Syria is not the only place where a globalized vision of social responsibility is introduced with the help of the state against the backdrop of a pre-existing, Islam-based, ethical framework. Those seeking to understand the impacts, potentials, and problems of CSR as it gains prominence in the Middle East development agenda will need to be aware of this overarching context.

7

SYRIA'S REFORMS UNDER BASHAR AL-ASAD

AN OPPORTUNITY FOR FOREIGN-EDUCATED ENTREPRENEURS TO MOVE INTO DECISION-MAKING?

Tina Zintl

When Bashar al-Asad became Syrian President in 2000, he tried to build a hands-on and reform-oriented image for himself and his government. This image suffered severely during the crackdown on the "Damascus Spring" in 2001/02 and imploded after the violent repression against Arab-Spring-inspired protesters ten years later.[1] Yet, in 2011, the international community seemed reluctant and slow to acknowledge the scale of the suppression: a young and tech-savvy London-trained ophthalmologist with a progressive British-born wife at his side, al-Asad seemed to be more amenable than obstinate autocrats like Hosni al-Mubarak or Muammar al-Qaddafi. Until then, al-Asad's modernization and liberalization of authoritarian rule had appeared exceptionally successful in the eyes of foreign governments and scholars alike.

This "authoritarian upgrading" drew,[2] to some extent, on the Syrian President's own foreign-trained background and, sure enough, he appointed technocrats with Western degrees or working experience to cabinet positions. Scholarly research has occasionally suggested higher education abroad as a common trait shared by post-2000 Arab rulers,[3] or listed individual foreign-educated politicians with an almost exclusive focus on the highest levels of government.[4] But the educational background of broader economic or social elites has not been investigated, nor has foreign-educated persons' influence on reforms or their ambiguous position in the authoritarian balance of power been scrutinized systematically.[5] Likewise, literature on highly-skilled return migrants has either concentrated on their economic investment rather than their political impact or, as in Spilimbergo's research, taken a macro-level perspective that does not allow an explanation of why some foreign-educated returnees play a political role while others do not.[6]

This chapter seeks to investigate the role of foreign-educated businessmen in Syria's reform process between 2000 and 2011 in terms of the scope and channels of their influence as well as the reasons for their political inclusion. Particularly close attention will be paid to *who* made this happen—that is, whether foreign-educated businessmen themselves pushed for more influence or else were summoned by a regime in need of consultancy by economic experts.

It will show that, in Syria, being foreign-educated helped to gain influence but was not independent from other, more "traditional" credentials—that is, it did not have the power to overrule older sets of privileged strata but overlapped with them. At the same time this chapter illustrates how foreign-educated entrepreneurs have gained a new status and "modern" self-image as well as new channels of influence, overriding other actors, while their initiatives fell into fields that were welcomed, closely monitored or even solicited by the leadership. The chapter will thus provide a close-up picture of the mechanisms of authoritarian rule.

As a first step, theoretical considerations on foreign-educated entrepreneurs' specific characteristics, which turn them into potential agents of change, will be discussed and visualized in two diagrams. The priorities and state of reforms in authoritarian Syria will then be summarized with specific focus on the gradual inclusion of the private sector. The main part will be devoted to foreign-educated businessmen and their relations with other Syrian agents, as well as their activities and positions in reform policies. A short conclusion will summarize the findings and their significance for the pace and content of reforms. Since written sources on this topic are very scarce, especially in terms of figures and statistics, this chapter is mainly based on qualitative interviews which were conducted during a two-month fieldwork in spring 2010.[7]

Theoretical considerations about the modernizing potential of foreign-educated entrepreneurs

Foreign-educated entrepreneurs fit into more than one analytical category. Their socialization and area of activity stretches domestically and internationally: their significance for developments in a country can, on the one hand, be attributed to the fact that they, after returning to their country of origin, often form part of a modernizing local bourgeoisie, but on the other hand, it can be attributed to the capital and knowledge transfer from abroad which, in the ideal case, is a permanent flow maintained by close transnational personal contacts.

In the following, a framework will be suggested for investigating foreign-educated entrepreneurs' relations to other players in a country's political game and their specific traits favouring their political involvement in modernizing reforms.

Bourgeoisie, middle class and modernization

In terms of social stratification, foreign-educated nationals are mostly to be found within the middle and the upper middle class, sometimes in the upper class. Some are also part of the bourgeoisie. The existence of at least one of these groups, the middle class or the bourgeoisie, is often seen as the precondition for the modernization and political liberalization of a country.[8] Yet, it is important neither to establish a too simplistic causal link between "middle class" and "modernization" nor to lump together "middle class" and "bourgeoisie" in the same analytical category.[9]

"Modernization" is a rather ill-defined and bulky term which seems to encompass everything that happens on the path to prosperity and progress, emphasizing economic, political, social or cultural aspects, or any combination of these. This complexity of societal change causes analytical problems. Most important, the link between economic and political liberalization is problematic: the experiences of other countries—like China or the Gulf states—has blatantly illustrated that there is no specific threshold at which economic development triggers democratization. In order to investigate the more complex interaction between economic and political liberalization, an analysis of foreign-educated persons' involvement in liberalization is particularly interesting in view of the hopes and expectations that they are a driving force in both economic and political reforms.

In a similar way, an imprecise definition and usage of the terms "middle class" and "bourgeoisie" has become widespread. While "middle class" usually points to the middle band of income levels in a specific society—that is, it is defined in relative terms—"bourgeoisie" applies to the owners of means of production and therefore relates to a specific way in which income is generated. Thus, entrepreneurs are part of the bourgeoisie but not necessarily members of the middle class—they may, for example, generate enough income to belong to the upper class. The middle class, conversely, comprises all kinds of salaried employees and white-collar workers, as well as freelancers, and therefore includes several groups which are not part of the bourgeoisie as defined above.

While this distinction has to be borne in mind, it is equally important to realize that, in reality, people move between different groups. Incentive structures (such as financial or reputational gain) lead to shifts between self-employment and public sector employment, with repercussions on who might be considered part of the bourgeoisie. A particularly interesting category in formerly socialist systems is the state bourgeoisie—state employees who do not own but merely control means of production.[10] Although they are not a real bourgeoisie in the literal sense they often have ample opportunities to benefit from the state-owned resources they control, and try to bequeath these privileges to their children. Many of them later enter private businesses themselves or by proxy, thus becoming *embourgeoisés*.[11]

In terms of modernizing reforms, entrepreneurs and bureaucrats often have opposing interests: the first group is frequently in favour of reforms while the latter mostly wishes to protect the status quo.[12] However, if entrepreneurs are privileged by the existing system and cannot see any business gains to be had from reforms, they will not become leading modernizing agents either.[13]

Foreign-educated entrepreneurs are a subset of two groups: the bourgeoisie and foreign-educated returnees. Categorizing them (see Diagram 1) will help to understand how they position themselves in these groups, and whether they feel solidarity within either of them. The diagram also includes a measure of their relations with the existing order, from loyal to antagonistic ("crony bourgeoisie" to "independent bourgeoisie") since, as explained in the preceding paragraph, this is indispensable to allow conclusions about their willingness for and influence on political and economic reforms. Crucially, in an authoritarian setting such as the Syrian one, it also shows the nature and direction of the reforms they advocate: either in line with reforms the regime itself advocates—supporting authoritarian upgrading—or in opposition to the regime.[14]

Diagram 1: Foreign-educated businessmen and potential links to other agent groups.

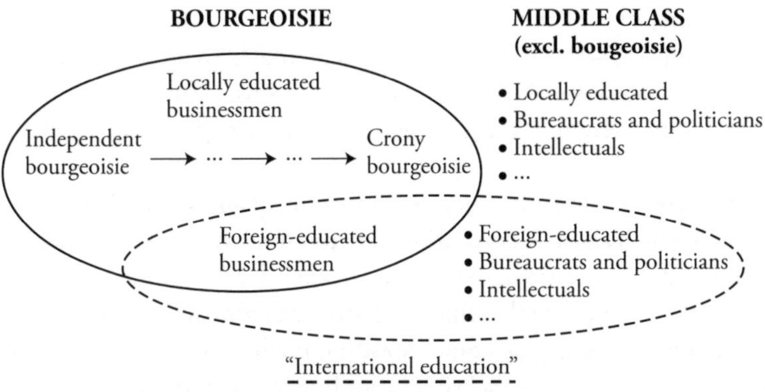

Interestingly, the distinction between foreign-educated bourgeoisie and other foreign-educated persons coincides with different ways of funding studies abroad: in Syria, as in many other countries, foreign-educated middle class employees were often sponsored by the government, while self-funded persons are more often part of the bourgeoisie (for more details, see below). A third and smaller group, former holders of scholarships from private and mostly foreign institutions, also tends to join the bourgeoisie.

Owing to guaranteed permanent employment in the public sector—either at a state university or at a ministry, depending on the kind of scholarship—most former state-sponsored students are civil servants who will enter the private sector only if incentives are high and secure enough. In contrast to this, those who funded their studies abroad themselves or were financed by a foreign institution are more often to be found in the private sector, provided they did not decide to stay abroad permanently.[15]

Highly-skilled return migrants and modernization

For a long time, research on highly-skilled migration has been preoccupied with negative outcomes for the sending countries, in particular brain drain. Meanwhile, positive impacts have moved into the centre of interest, initially in terms of financial gains in the form of remittances and, finally, regarding the return of these migrants to their native countries and the skill and technology transfer this involves. The discussion about the so-called "migration development nexus" is still ongoing.[16] So far, the majority of these research activities has focused on purely economic impacts—the returnees' entrepreneurial activities—and has not attempted to trace influences on policy decisions. Often the findings of these studies were sobering in regard to entrepreneurial and innovative activities.[17]

One remarkable exception is Spilimbergo's quantitative cross-country research which shows a correlation between migrants' international education and democratic developments in their home countries. He concludes that "[the] total number of students abroad … has no clear impact on democracy at home; however, quality of democracy in host countries has a strong a [*sic*] significant impact on domestic democracy; moreover, this positive effect increases with the number of students abroad".[18]

However, Spilimbergo himself admits that his approach cannot trace returnees' exact channels of influence and suggests this as starting point for future research.[19] To achieve this, a qualitative approach was chosen for this chapter, since studying these processes requires understanding of individual persons' backgrounds, like exposure to foreign values and knowhow, and how it affects their political opinions and goals; their decisions to return to their home country and to become politically involved there; how they fare in pushing through their vision in negotiation with, or in resistance to, other local forces, that is, with other private actors (see Diagram 1) and with the government. Thereby, in contrast to Spilimbergo's research, the nature of this vision—democratizing, economic liberalizing or merely streamlining technical solutions—must be part of the investigation.[20]

Recently, another promising and more qualitative approach has become more widespread in migration literature: the assessment of migrants' and re-migrants' social capital.[21] This captures the importance of expatriates' and returnees' transnational contacts, thus helping to shed light on migration's effects on political change. Although the political impact of diasporas and of sending countries' new interest in rallying expatriate citizens has slowly moved in the interest of scholarly research,[22] the effects of return migration on power relations in countries of origin and its repercussions on society's social stratification have rarely been investigated.

Using social capital as a stepping stone, this paper further systematizes return migrants' assets, categorizing them into (1) specialized knowledge; (2) financial resources from home or abroad; (3) transnational contacts and, as a controlling variable; (4) local contacts.[23] These assets—as distinguished in the following list—will help to investigate which characteristics, if any, help returning persons to become involved with economic or political reforms.

(1) Foreign-educated persons' knowledge and professionalism add to their clout. However, there are two follow-up questions concerning its origin: first, does it really matter that they were educated abroad and have not attained a degree at a Syrian university?[24] Second, does it make a difference that they were educated abroad, or is working experience gained in the West or in the Gulf states as significant or even more significant?
(2) Monetary gains—remittances and investments by foreign-educated Syrians—constitute a possible reason for their increasing influence. Here, in contrast to educational attainments, the origin of the asset—local or international—does not change the nature of the resource; therefore it is even more important to introduce a control group of locally educated Syrians using their wealth to become politically active.
(3) International business and personal contacts of foreign-educated persons are supposed to be very valuable for the internationally isolated country. Hence, networking with colleagues abroad—foreigners or Syrian expatriates—might have been the actual reason for these persons' advancement.
(4) Clientele contacts and intra-elite networks within Syria could also be the reason behind these persons' recruitment into political

posts—not least because this is their comparative advantage vis-à-vis foreign experts. Although this explanation would be the least exciting and innovative—Syrian politics have often been described as based on primordial, anti-meritocratic personal ties—the continuing significance of this variable has to be assessed.

These four assets are illustrated in Diagram 2. The matrix depicts six ideal-typical groups of agents who are considered to be especially well-equipped for positions of influence in Syria's political economy: technocrats, cosmopolitans, globally oriented entrepreneurs, crony capitalists, networkers, and the (educationally and financially) privileged. Most persons have all assets at their disposal but if, for instance, a person's educational background and his international contacts are comparatively dominant and strong he might most appropriately be called a cosmopolitan.[25]

Diagram 2: Typology of foreign-educated entrepreneurs' asset combinations.[26]

	Local contacts	International contacts	Financial resources	Education/ skills
Education/ skills	Technocrats	Cosmopolitans	"The privileged"	
Financial resources	Crony capitalists	Globally oriented entrepreneurs		
Interna-tional contacts	Networkers			
Local contacts				

Syria: reforms in a post-populist authoritarian setting[27]

Even before its crackdown on anti-government protesters since 2011, Syria's prerequisites for successful integration into the global economy were extremely unfavourable, owing not only to the country's poor economic conditions, but also—and strikingly so when compared with other developing countries—to its problematic political conditions. Lasting tensions with Israel, the support or at least tacit approval of Islamic fundamentalist groups like Hamas and Hizbullah, and being on good terms with the region's "bad boy" Iran seriously damaged the regime's international standing in the West.

During the 2000s, Bashar al-Asad responded to this high level of pressure with domestic reforms, especially in the economic field, but also in education, administration and the media, and through the promotion of a (loyal) civil society. However, as in other authoritarian systems, Syria's politics of modernization were selective and cautious.

Economic reforms accelerated after 2004, most notably in the financial sector where, for instance, private banks and insurance companies were permitted, the highly-restricted foreign exchange regime was opened up, and a stock exchange was established in 2009.[28]

However, areas of reform which would have been imperative from an economic point of view but unfavourable in terms of political considerations were omitted, even if this undermined already implemented reform policies: major reforms concerning the public sector, cuts in subsidies and institutional reforms ensuring transparency were repeatedly postponed in order to spare the privileges of bureaucrats, workers, and crony capitalists.[29] The slogan "social market economy", which was put forward in the Tenth Five-Year Plan (FYP) of 2005, is a good example for this post-populist authoritarian tightrope walk. With its eloquent formulations the FYP engaged in a rhetoric which accommodated international observers and local modernizers without alarming the domestic social base. Yet, the exact meaning and content of a social market economy has not been defined and workers and peasants, the former prime constituency of the socialist Ba'th regime, were not even mentioned, let alone mobilized by the FYP.

During the 2000s, the private sector's visibility and its approval by the Syrian regime—and vice versa—had been growing.[30] Businessmen in the Syrian Parliament became a common sight: they provided up to 90% of "independent" MPs, parliamentarians who were not associated with the Ba'th or aligned parties and who constituted roughly a third of all members. Their actual influence on political outcomes seemed to be rather weak, corresponding with their often self-interested political motivation and lack of a political programme.[31] While the effectiveness of the Chambers of Commerce and Industry as mouthpieces for private sector interests has been questioned by the business community (mainly because of the regime's prerogative to appoint a certain share of loyal board members),[32] new election rules for board members were introduced in December 2009 and so-called bi-national business councils with,[33] so far, sixty countries worldwide were set up to boost trade relations and investment. Both changes were, however, reported to have been top-down decisions and were not the result of private sector lobbying.[34]

Besides economic reforms, other notable milestones in Bashar al-Asad's early years in power were the permissions to establish private universities (decree 36, 2001) and private newspapers and journals (decree 50, 2001), breaking the state monopolies on higher education and the print media respectively. Arguably the most revolutionary change was the Syrian government's rallying for "civil society" participation in social development. Namely, the Syria Trust for Development (STD), a government-organized non-governmental organization (GONGO) founded in 2007 under the patronage of the Syrian First Lady,[35] took the lead, demonstrating that the regime wanted to take on board an explicitly loyal civil society and wished to establish—through the prototype of the STD—ostensibly "modern" NGOs following the pattern of international institutions.[36] All these sectors under reform—economics/finance, media, and civil society—seem particularly well-suited to attract foreign-educated businessmen and thus were used as a criterion for selecting interviewees and starting points for the analysis.

While the privatization of state-owned companies remained a taboo, it is striking how the Syrian regime started to "privatize" by advertising a "public-private-civil society-partnership" with loyal segments of the private sector and civil society.[37] This "outsourcing" to private partners was born out of the need to gradually cut back state expenditure on economic and social policies.[38]

Meanwhile, the growing role of the private sector in this carefully instructed process of modernization was problematic for historical reasons. The Syrian regime, originating in an "authoritarianism from the left",[39] has traditionally been allied with (or has at least paid lip service to) workers and peasants, and antagonistic towards capitalism and the bourgeoisie. When the political inclusion of the bourgeoisie became inevitable for economic reasons, it was not institutionalized but brought about informally in deals with individual businessmen. This offered the opportunity to differentiate between the "good capitalists" working for the prosperity of their socialist home country and the "parasite capitalists" who were still seen as class enemies.[40] While the first deals between senior officials and entrepreneurs willing to collude were closed in the 1970s, this became more common during the 1980s, especially in the aftermath of the foreign exchange crisis of 1986. In the 1990s, economic pluralism (*ta'addudiya*) and economic opening (*infitah*) were promoted as new economic mantras. However, conditions for private enterprises did not improve substantially. Isolated and inconsistent policies achieved little more than giving rise to more and closer informal state-business networks.[41]

The Syrian bourgeoisie is therefore highly heterogeneous in its relations to the state and, consequently, its potential political influence. While Haddad distinguishes five types of bourgeoisie in Syria,[42] for the purposes of this paper, the crony bourgeoisie and the independent bourgeoisie were chosen as the poles of a continuum from close partnership with the regime to a hostile and critical attitude towards it (see Diagram). The first pole, crony capitalists, is embodied by Rami Makhlouf, a cousin of Bashar al-Asad who owned, until the Syrian uprising, the biggest Syrian mobile phone company and innumerable other business ventures. Riad Saif, one of the most outspoken critics of the regime during the Damascus Spring, is an example of the small group of politically active businessmen within the second pole, the independent bourgeoisie.[43]

Foreign-educated entrepreneurs: a bid for power?

> In all likelihood, persons with "foreign" degrees will continue to have better chances of being recruited into the technocratic segments of the (politically relevant) elite, and incumbent elites will continue to send their sons and daughters to universities abroad or to universities with Western curricula within their countries as a means of reproducing themselves—that is, passing on their elite status to their offspring.[44]

As elucidated above, Syria has been in dire need of, first, a viable strategy for economic integration and cooperation and second, of suitable personnel to put this into practice. Since foreign experts come at a price—both literally and in terms of political conditionality—the recruitment of foreign-educated nationals into influential positions seemed to be the least costly approach for modernizing Syrian authoritarianism. Actions and the rhetoric of the Syrian regime during recent years have indeed shown an increasing interest in this group of people: for example, several ministers in Bashar al-Asad's cabinets were foreign-educated or brought immense international working experience.[45] In 2009, almost half of the cabinet ministers (fifteen of thirty-one persons) had studied abroad, mostly in Western countries (eleven) and/or mostly for a PhD (thirteen).[46] Also, the new-founded Ministry of Expatriates was, until 2008, headed by one of the most publicly known foreign-educated Syrians, Boutheina Shabaan, a UK graduate. Abdallah al-Dardari, Deputy Prime Minister for Economic Affairs until March 2011 and driving force behind the Tenth Five-Year Plan, also has an immense international working experience. Despite all modern credentials, there were hardly any "businesspeople or politicians in the Weberian sense"[47] in Bashar al-Asad's cabinets.[48] Instead, Bashar focused on the recruitment of foreign-educated technocrats.

In the following sections, the significance of this presumed strategy will be explored on the basis of interviews with foreign-educated businessmen. Before that, a quick overview on international education in Syria will be given.

Foreign-educated Syrians: a co-opted state-funded middle class or a self-funded bourgeoisie?

Unfortunately, there are no reliable statistics on the number of Syrian migrants, let alone returning migrants. However, as indicated above, the different ways of financing studies abroad are a useful starting point for investigating the likelihood of foreign-educated persons' return and their involvement in reform politics.

The large scholarship programmes created by the Syrian state are an interesting example of Hafiz al-Asad's populist authoritarian policies. While these programmes date back to the 1920s,[49] they were largely expanded during the 1980s: between 1975 and 1995, more than 3,600 *mu'aidin* (teaching assistants at universities) were sent abroad for further academic training—mostly PhD studies—on scholarships provided by the Syrian state. The overwhelming majority of them were sent abroad between 1984 and 1989, predominantly to Eastern Bloc countries and the former mandatory power France.[50] An additional 1,600 state scholarships were distributed in so-called *ba'that 'ilmiyah* (scientific delegations), that is, to employees of ministries and other government institutions, for postgraduate studies abroad.[51] After the collapse of the Soviet Union fewer scholarships were given out in a period of reorientation. Since 2001 numbers have been rising again and the programme was restructured towards postgraduate studies in Western countries. Owing to higher tuition fees at British and American universities "France and Germany are … focal countries for the foreseeable future".[52]

Because every Syrian who funded his studies abroad by himself has, since 1971, been obliged by law "to put himself under the supervision of the Ministry of Higher Education", some statistics about these persons exist as well.[53] These figures are, however, incomplete because usually the only students registered were those who otherwise were to be conscripted into the army.[54] Snapshots of four years (between the mid-70s and the mid-90s) show that, at one time, between 3,000 and 8,000 postgraduate students and between 7,000 and 16,000 undergraduate self-funded students studied in non-Arab foreign countries. While these figures are certainly too low for the above reasons, they show self-funded students' preference for Western destinations, especially the US. This, as well as such recent changes in the main destinations for scholarship holders, already implies that Western degrees are held in higher esteem than those from the former Eastern Bloc. In fact, the large delegations to former Communist countries have been extremely controversial in terms of the quality of education received.[55]

Since secure long-term employment awaited returning scholarship holders, and since they had to pay back a multiple of the scholarship received if they did not resume their position in Syria for an agreed-on time span, the rate of return from abroad was considerably higher amongst state-sponsored persons than amongst self-funded ones. At state universities, which particularly gained from the large delegations in the 1980s, foreign-educated Syrians account for a staggering majority of staff.[56]

Thus, because of the large scholarship programmes and the differing probability of return, the majority of foreign-educated Syrian returnees graduated from universities in the socialist Eastern Bloc and then were employed in the public sector. However, the number of those who took up a second or even third job, either another public sector position or employment in the private sector, is high. Since Syrian companies employ comparatively few people—the overwhelming majority of companies are still small family-run businesses—those who can afford it and are prepared to take the risk start up their own companies and, thus, join the bourgeoisie.[57]

After 2000, the Syrian regime changed its policies and rhetoric towards Syrian expatriates, thus trying to strengthen relations with those Syrians who financed their studies abroad themselves. However, it is questionable how much impact the Ministry of Expatriates had during its short lifespan and, especially,[58] whether incentives were high enough to attract this hoped-for new bourgeoisie back and make them stay. Since the Syrian leadership's perspective and intentions cannot be directly investigated, the following focuses on foreign-educated returnees' views.

The assets of foreign-educated entrepreneurs in the modernizing process

Respondents were asked to compare between different potential reasons (as introduced in Diagram 2) for them to become involved in Syrian economic and political decision-making.[59] To do so, they were invited to play a "card game", placing in order five possible job recruitment criteria—education, local contacts, international contacts, material resources, and "other"—according to their significance.[60] Thus, this part of the analysis mainly refers to how they see the regime's and private employers' willingness to enlist foreign-educated returnees.[61]

Almost all interviewees considered education and skills as important criteria; many, especially of the younger generation, believed meritocratic recruitment was on the rise. International education provides specialized knowledge, which often is not readily available in Syria: "The mentality of old[-style] businessmen is [to] use price as a weapon while, for foreign-educated, [they also use other] marketing techniques, price is not the only issue [...but also] ways of distribution, product qualifications...".[62]

Furthermore, education abroad—particularly if it is in English-speaking Western countries—is associated with an extremely high social status, thus providing "a winning card from the beginning".[63] According to one interviewee, "In the US you are a nobody, here you can do something … you are special".[64] While all respondents stressed the added value of attaining education abroad, they also addressed the difficulties and the "reverse culture shock",[65] encountered when trying to re-adapt to the Syrian way of life: "If you take fish outside the water, they die. But we don't want these brains to die".[66] At the same time, some criticized the "arrogance" exhibited by foreign-educated people towards their colleagues or society at large.[67]

Respondents were divided on whether foreign-educated persons were more reform-oriented than their locally educated peers. While some interviewees considered those educated abroad as generally more innovative and creative, others stressed that they quickly re-adapt or merely "import" successful business ideas from abroad (like, for example, a grocery home delivery service):[68] "[For persons who studied or worked abroad] the benchmark is not what you have here. The[ir] benchmark is something that they saw or experienced somewhere else. And this is … definitely very necessary for … developing countries. If you have your benchmark locally, you're doomed, gone!"[69]

In general, answers to this question on foreign-educated persons' eagerness for reforms mostly focused on technical aspects of reforms. This could be taken as a sign that highly skilled returnees are more likely to exert an influence on reforms on a purely technocratic rather than a political level.

International contacts—a resource the foreign-educated have at their disposal to a higher degree than their peers—was seen in a rather ambiguous way: several interviewees stressed that international contacts were more a burden than an asset—alluding to the authoritarian regime's fear of influence by foreign powers it cannot control.[70] Other interviewees stated that international contacts were useful but come automatically with the other assets (local contacts, education, and financial resources) and thus could not be considered as an asset by and in itself. For example, non-foreign-educated but locally well-connected businessmen with large companies explained that establishing international contacts for trade relations had not been difficult.[71] Thus, members of the loyal business elite will avail themselves of international contacts easily, and can establish them without having studied abroad. Furthermore, foreign-educated persons who are employed in well-known international organizations with cooperation agreements with the Syrian government can benefit from international networking.[72] All this illustrates that international contacts first have to be "accredited" with the regime or influential parts of society. These contacts are an advantage as long as the regime does not consider them as potentially subversive and challenging.

The remaining two assets, material resources and local contacts, also figured highly: while respondents were less explicit on how material resources help in gaining influence,[73] almost all of them stressed local contacts as important recruitment criterion. As already implied, without *wasta* it is more difficult to capitalize on good skills, international connections and the high social status associated with a Western degree, which points to the ongoing importance of business networks and cronyism.[74] Thus, foreign education joins and complements older recruitment criteria: a locally well-connected person without a university degree will have less opportunity to exert influence on reforms, but the same lack of influence applies to a well-educated person without reliable local contacts. Political decisions thus seem to remain in the firm grip of a well-established elite. As one consultant put it, "Education, skills [he moves this card aside] … But this is not about decision-making, it's about using them to *allow* some success".[75] It is probable that the upholding of old recruitment criteria favours certain religious minorities like, for example, Alawites who have been overrepresented in the Syrian elite since Hafiz al-Asad came to power in 1970.[76]

In this reading—and this was frequently confirmed by interviewees—education from abroad becomes a mere question of etiquette for children of the elite. This interpretation is also corroborated by the fact that foreign-educated entrepreneurs and businessmen do not widely and deliberately play on their international education to define and distinguish themselves.[77] Many of the respondents considered it merely as a part of their biography just like their secondary education at a French- or English-speaking private school.[78] Family and personal contacts remain the predominant criteria for a successful career and frequently overlap with a shared experience of international education. The strongest ties seem to be those formed at private schools in Syria or at the American University of Beirut, which attracts a high number of Syrians who can afford it.

In summary, while the majority of respondents stressed that education and skills became a more important reason for recruitment into influential positions, most also pointed out that this does not mean that older criteria like belonging to a well-connected and wealthy family became less crucial.

Foreign-educated entrepreneurs' activities and their influence on reforms

Foreign-educated businessmen have been active and engaged in the most dynamic fields in Syria, most notably economic reforms and establishing business-related NGOs, but also in the media.

A plenitude of new business-related NGOs was established in the second half of the 2000s, including the Syrian Business Council (SBC, in 2007), the Syrian Young Entrepreneurs Association (SYEA, in 2004), and, as a local offshoot of an international NGO, the Junior Chamber International Damascus (JCI, in 2004). While foreign degrees seem to have played no major role in the appointment of chairmen for the above-mentioned bi-national business councils,[79] the involvement of foreign-educated businessmen in the SBC, JCI and SYEA has been extremely large: a majority of the respective founding and board members hold a degree from abroad.[80] This is particularly remarkable taking into account that foreign education is the exception, not the rule for Syrian entrepreneurs.[81] However, each of them was started by a circle of friends or business partners, showing that local contacts and belonging to the business elite played a large role.[82] Still, foreign-educated respondents at NGOs and GONGOs stressed that their experience of foreign societies had had an impact on their involvement, "having understood what an NGO does, what philanthropic work is".[83]

While the SBC can be understood as an elitist club with well-established links and further outreach to top political staff, both domestically (for example, to ministers) and internationally (for example, to ambassadors and experts),[84] the JCI and SYEA are mostly philanthropic in outlook, organizing social and training events and fostering entrepreneurial spirit through start-up competitions. The latter two organizations have a way of operating and vision similar to the Syria Trust for Development's project SHABAB, which suggests that these initiatives have been approved by the regime and, indeed, form part of its outsourcing of social welfare responsibilities to private agents. It is worth mentioning that SHABAB, other projects by the STD, and the Syria Enterprise and Business Centre (SEBC), which were established as EU-projects in 1996 and have been in full Syrian state ownership since 2006, all employ many foreign-educated Syrians and foreign experts.[85]

Likewise, there have been major contributions by foreign-educated businessmen to the establishment and running of private media ventures, most notably to the English monthlies *Syria Today* (by the Canadian-educated magnate Abdulghani Attar) and *Forward Magazine* (by the Lebanese-educated Abdulsalam Haykal). This is not the case for Syria's biggest private publishing house, United Group, which is owned by the Syrian-educated Majd Suleiman. He instead employed a UK-educated chief editor for his English daily *Baladna English*, which started in October 2009.[86] Yet, the influence of these new publications on reforms or discussions about reforms is rather limited: since English is not understood by a wide audience in Syria, it is clear that they rather aim at transmitting a positive image of Syria to foreign observers and diplomats. Furthermore, the common feature uniting the media tycoons mentioned above is that they all stem from influential and/or wealthy families.[87]

A myriad private consulting firms were established by foreign-educated persons, of which the US-educated Nabil Sukkar's SCB is the oldest and probably the best known. These consultants, as well as some foreign-educated lawyers, exerted noticeable influence on reform policies, for example by preparing feasibility studies, drawing up and commenting on draft laws, or providing consultancy and drafts for several chapters of the Tenth Five-Year Plan.[88] However, the FYP illustrates that their influence was confined to some areas and had to be invited by high officials: it was prepared by a mostly non-foreign-educated team under the supervision of the foreign-trained Abdallah al-Dardari, who sought close cooperation with World Bank and IMF staff and some foreign-educated Syrian consultants.[89]

What all these channels of influence have in common is that foreign-educated persons exerted influence on reforms in a rather indirect manner, since they worked for new institutions or business ventures or acted as advisers on an ad hoc basis. While their engagement was publicly known and open, especially in the later part of the reform process, early examples suggest that their involvement was often concealed: "At that time, I was advising, but I wasn't in the position to say that I was advising the government, so it was meetings being held at night … [The government] sought the opinion of experts and it wasn't disclosed which experts".[90]

Nonetheless, some of these unnamed consultants had considerable influence on draft laws: "If you ask me: was it a good law? I would say: It was a lousy law! There was so much more that needed to be done, but … Is it good compared to the first version I saw? It's like the difference between, you know, the earth and the moon!"[91]

Existing institutionalized channels, like the Parliament and the Chambers of Commerce and Industry, remained rather "old-school", that is, bound by the old clientelist and bureaucratic rules, and seemed to be less involved in the reforms. Here, the influence of foreign-educated persons was less obvious and more anecdotal. While Rateb al-Shallah, longstanding president of the Federation of the Syrian Chambers of Commerce, with degrees from Oxford University and the University of California, has been very active and involved and has definitely had an enormous impact on the Chambers, he inherited his position from his father rather than acquiring it by virtue of his academic and analytical skills.[92] Moreover, other businesspeople involved with the Chambers stressed that foreign education is rather the exception than the rule.[93] Those board members who are foreign-educated or speak a foreign language are reported to have been appointed by President al-Asad,[94] thus arguably serving as living proof of the regime's international opening. For example, one businesswoman says: "There are a lot of other women [active in the Chambers] but maybe, maybe because I'm educated abroad, because I have much more occidental opening, I travel a lot, I … [pause] They consider me as representative. I would say that it's an honour".[95]

In general, most foreign-educated persons prefer either to be employed in newly established institutions (e.g. GONGOs, private banks, private universities) and international organizations, or to run their own companies. Working in the bloated public sector is not an option for most of the Syrians who funded their own foreign education: that work is infamous for low incomes, strict hierarchies, routine work without clear area of responsibility, and, maybe worst of all, a low standing in society. Only the highest political level, the cabinet, is able to attract some of them. But, generally speaking, there are more promising career options, especially for those from old business families.

Agency: in search of foreign-educated entrepreneurs' bargaining power

As has been shown, foreign-educated businessmen possess assets that are particularly valuable in the reform process, and they have exerted some influence on several areas of reform. Now the question remains whether they became active and pushed for reforms themselves (and if so, whether this is because of their education abroad) or whether it was the Syrian regime's call for their help that triggered their involvement.

Referring to Diagram 1 and the fact that reforms are always negotiated with other political and social forces, three kinds of relationships between foreign-educated businessmen and other groups of actors will be looked at: (1) their position in and relations with the highly fragmented business community; (2) their relations with other foreign-educated Syrians; and (3) their relations with the Syrian regime.

(1) Within the business community, it is mainly the *awlad al-sulta* (children of the power[ful]), the younger generation of the rentier bourgeoisie or state bourgeoisie, who hold foreign degrees: other parts of the bourgeoisie either cannot spare the manpower and thus do not send their offspring to study abroad, or consider that their business prospects are too poor for the offspring to return from abroad. For the *awlad al-sulta*, this is not only part of the etiquette, to a certain extent it also constitutes a way of getting a "clean slate"—that is, an image of performance-based success (even if others know or realize that the initial capital for one's own business was paid out of the family's pocket). Non-foreign-educated businessmen of the same stratum who were interviewed—they had not gone abroad for their studies because they were the only sons of their families and were supposed to help in the family business—stressed that their local education did not have a negative impact on their business relations, since they had been abroad for shorter travels and thus establishing business contacts.[96] This was corroborated by several interviewees' assessment that international contacts can be gained through the smart use of other assets as well (see above).[97] Still, it seems that foreign-educated persons were more involved with philanthropic activities—and more encouraged by the regime to become involved (see below)—than their locally-educated peers, who were also very active but more in their respective business sectors. This reflects the feeling that many foreign-educated respondents have of a certain "duty" towards their country of origin and towards "less privileged" peers. As one respondent put it: "I have the platform to transfer knowledge to younger people who are not as privileged as I was in studying at a top-notch school like AUB".[98]

The move of mostly foreign-educated businessmen to found the SBC represents a certain cleavage between them and more traditional, locally-educated persons who try to be active in the Chambers: the first SBC-linked "modern" group is more involved in real estate, tourism or construction, while the chamber-organized "traditional" group is more active in the textiles, manufacturing and agriculture sectors.[99] While, as mentioned above, the SBC tried to establish lobbying events, first and foremost, it was seen as a club for the biggest and richest private businesses in Syria. Asked about their relations with the Chambers, an SBC spokesperson emphasized that they see themselves as "an alternative" to the chambers because "competition is good".[100] At the same time the SBC aspired to be less "slow, bureaucratic and unreliable" and "more independent" because the government does not have the prerogative to appoint a fixed share of board members.[101] Thus, the SBC was not established in direct opposition to the Chambers but certainly out of frustration over their lacking effectiveness; or as one SBC member stated: "both [groups of businessmen] are important but the traditional ones have to modernize".[102] The above-mentioned bi-national business councils are a link between both organizations since they are part of the chamber system but the majority of their appointed chairpersons are also members of the SBC.[103]

(2) Syrian entrepreneurs often sneer at bureaucrats as well as workers for their "laziness" and "incompetence". Interestingly, this perceived lack of competence is occasionally linked to bureaucrats' education in the Soviet Union.[104] The image of the overstaffed and ineffective public sector is pervasive throughout the Syrian public; at the same time, rumours about university degrees obtained from Eastern Bloc universities are widespread. So it is hardly surprising that businessmen, who regularly have to deal with the Syrian "red tape" mentality, adopt this perspective and see civil servants also as less reform-oriented.[105] Apart from that, foreign-educated businessmen did not comment on foreign-educated persons, implying that there are hardly any foreign-educated but not Eastern (ex-Communist Bloc)-educated personnel in the public sector. Thus, these findings seem to corroborate the impression that Western-educated bourgeois businessmen are more reform-oriented—or, maybe, more in favour of the government's announced economic liberalization—than

Eastern-educated bureaucrats. However, while this seems plausible at first glance, a large part of it is due to the lack of incentives for reformist persons to work in the public sector, and thus is only correlated but not causally linked to the place of study. Furthermore, it has to be kept in mind that Western education helps to cultivate a "neoliberal" reformist discourse.[106]

(3) Contrary to expectations, foreign-educated persons whose studies were self-financed (or family-financed) are not generally more independent from the regime than former scholarship-holders with foreign degrees, who are perceived to be more loyal. This is because wealthy business families, who attach particular importance to their children's international education (see above), often have good relations with the regime. Since market entry is difficult in the Syrian economy and even more difficult after a prolonged time abroad, those self-financed foreign-educated Syrians who are not from well-off families often decide to stay abroad or, if they return (often for family reasons), seek employment with international organizations.[107] For all these reasons—that is, largely because of self-selection, and independently of co-optation offers by the regime—foreign-educated businessmen are most often found closer to the "crony capitalist" pole of Diagram 1 above and less frequently in the "independent" category.

Foreign-educated businesspersons' progressive activities largely remained in the areas of reform that were set by the authoritarian state. Foreign-educated modernizers inside the regime—most visibly the First Lady and Deputy Prime Minister Abdallah al-Dardari—led by example and "commissioned" reforms in desired policy areas. This has left the impression that those who studied abroad were called upon by the regime and did not primarily push for influence by themselves,[108] or else they dared to push for specific changes only when they knew that the regime would support these initiatives and that it would not have negative repercussions on their business networks: their above-mentioned commitment in business-related NGOs, or their consultancy for the Tenth Five-Year Plan, banking and insurance laws and the establishment of a stock exchange, are cases in point.

Furthermore, the respondents strongly denied that foreign-educated Syrians have a shared attitude towards the reform process, stressing that they are much too diverse (as regards background, place of study, duration of stay abroad, etc.). For the same reasons, the vast majority of them rejected the idea that foreign-educated Syrians have a group consciousness which stretches beyond personal friendships or normal business cooperation. Although there has been some coordination in alumni associations, and although foreign-educated businessmen took the lead in institutionalizing some of the informal business relations, for example through the SBC and SYEA,[109] they have not understood themselves as a distinct "foreign-educated" political power. Their activities remained within the accepted limits imposed from above, so that, at least until the beginning of the Syrian uprising in March 2011, all factors pointed towards a high degree of co-optation, that is, of foreign-educated individuals, especially foreign-educated businessmen, and not of foreign-educated persons as a group.

Conclusion

The Syrian regime increasingly welcomed the private sector's contributions to economic growth and developmentally oriented NGOs, and used them to widen co-optation. It also recognized the added value foreign-educated businessmen can provide. At the same time, though the pace of economic reforms increased, the distribution of (economic) power in Syria hardly changed—especially in the business sector, international education provided less social mobility than is often assumed.

Foreign-educated individuals were a unique opportunity for the regime to convey a modern image—and sons of the established crony bourgeoisie, as opposed to public sector employees, did so in a particularly cost-saving way. International education thus not only helped by contributing specialized knowledge, experiences, and—in some cases—international contacts, it was also particularly well suited to be incorporated into a successful PR campaign for the Syrian reform process. Furthermore, foreign-educated returnees were, or displayed themselves to be, secular actors—a fact that resonated strongly and positively with Western partners and international organizations reluctant to side with Islamic forces. Thus, they were ideal partners for authoritarian upgrading.

Many foreign-educated businessmen readily seized this opportunity and were remarkably active, not only in situating themselves favourably for safeguarding their business opportunities but also by initiating programmes and NGOs for the good of a wider circle of Syrians. These programmes, however, concentrated on building specific entrepreneurial skills and technical capabilities; they thus left little political impact and fell short of what would be expected by "agents of change". On the other hand their inherited elite status helped to add considerable authority to planned reforms, pushing them through against hardliners in the ruling elite. However, similarly to the STD and other government-approved NGOs, this increased growth and performance while further cutting back on representativeness.

It has been shown that in Syria—as in other resilient authoritarian settings[110]—Western-educated returnees helped in modernizing reforms while further reinforcing the privileged status of the existing elite; the pace and direction of change remained under the close surveillance of the authoritarian state. Thus, the Syrian regime transnationalized its co-optation and, by conveying an image of professionalism, enhanced its credibility and legitimacy.

While this strategy was successful in the short run, over the years, the elitist and exclusionary nature of co-optation undermined the very domestic legitimacy it sought to create: this was one of the factors contributing to the protests in 2011. On top of that, the regime's ruthless repression of the protest movement also dismantled its hard-won international legitimacy. The future will show whether those foreign-educated entrepreneurs who benefited from and, in most cases, believed in the regime's piecemeal reforms will eventually jump ship and join the opposition.

8

THE POLITICS OF "GOOD GOVERNANCE" IN MUBARAK'S EGYPT

WESTERN DONORS AND SME POLITICS UNDER AUTHORITARIAN RULE

Diane Zovighian

Western donors' support for social and economic reforms during the last two decades of Mubarak's rule was paralleled by an emphasis on "good governance",[1] including the need to foster the participation of civil society in the making of reforms, in education, health or private sector development for example. But the promotion by Western donors of civil society organizations' participation in policy-making processes in the pre-Arab Spring Egyptian authoritarian regime raised a number of questions, relating to the potential of foreign-supported actors to promote reforms and to the quality and venues of foreign-induced political participation. In a context where most interest groups, apart from large business associations, had weak advocacy capacities and limited access or none at all to governmental policy-making processes, how and to what extent could foreign donors increase the capacities of civil society organizations to advocate for reform? How did their support affect the access of interest groups to the policy-making process and the regime's top-down approach to the making of reforms? When participation in the policy-making process did occur, what form did it take and what traits did it display?

Reflecting on such questions in the aftermath of the Arab Spring and Mubarak's fall has two main purposes. The first purpose is to provide a better understanding of the dynamics and functioning of the Egyptian authoritarian regime under Mubarak, in particular in its approach to the making of Western-supported reforms, and to look into some of the underlying causes of the regime's resilience and then its fall. The second purpose is to provide some insights into the nature and relationship to the regime of some segments of civil society in the years prior to Mubarak's fall, and to illustrate the biases of and constraints to civil society's engagement.

This chapter builds on a specific case study: the making of micro, small and medium enterprises (SME) development policies in Egypt from the late 1990s to the late 2000s.[2] It examines the effects of foreign donors' "good governance" discourse on the participation of civil society organizations in the SME policy-making process engineered by the Egyptian government. It investigates the capacity of foreign-supported SME advocacy groups to promote reform in Egypt and looks into the venues, strengths and weaknesses of their participation in the making of SME policies. It argues that the combined effects of donors' assistance to SME advocacy groups and their insistence on the design of participatory mechanisms by the Egyptian government allowed for an increase in SME stakeholders' capacity to advocate reform and facilitated their access to governmental institutions, thus enhancing their political participation in the SME policy-making process. This participation was, however, flawed. It was indeed quasi-monopolized by one advocacy non-governmental organization (NGO) whose representativeness of the SME sector was limited. Two main sets of explanations for this quasi-monopoly over political participation are explored. The first set of explanations relates to the concentration of foreign donors' technical and financial support on this one advocacy NGO; the notion of *civil society entrepreneurship* is introduced to account for the ability of this NGO to secure privileged access to donors' resources. A second, and complementary, set of explanations for its quasi-monopoly over political participation relates to the corporatization strategies developed by the state, in a biased response to donors' demands to integrate advocacy groups in the policy process.

In addition to shedding light on the advocacy and political capacities of selected civil society actors, the analysis of the potential role of foreign-supported SME stakeholders in promoting economic reforms and participating in their making provides insights into the political transformations in state-society relations induced by foreign donors' involvement in the making of social and economic reforms in Mubarak's Egypt. Indeed, much of the phenomena and transformations observed in the present case study seem to find an echo in the framework of other foreign-supported economic and social reforms, including, for example, reforms in the field of education or health. It can in fact be argued that the emergence of civil society entrepreneurship and the state's corporatization strategies towards foreign-supported interest groups were common effects of donors' emphasis on "good governance" during the last two decades of Mubarak's rule.

SME policy-making in Egypt: a case study of donor-supported reform

SMEs in Egypt: a key economic development issue

One of the main structural constraints to industrial competitiveness and economic development in Egypt is the weak capacity of SMEs.[3] SMEs account for more than 90% of private sector companies and generate around 75% of the country's employment and 80% of its gross domestic product (GDP). Their development is however hampered by a number of economic, administrative, legislative, and financial obstacles, including a lack of access to finance, a heavy tax burden, cumbersome administrative procedures for registering and licensing and weak business support services.

The establishment in 1997 of a SME Development Unit,[4] in charge of the development of a general policy for micro, small and medium enterprises and active from 1997 to 2008, was one of the main initiatives taken by the Egyptian government under Mubarak's rule to respond to the need for economic, administrative and regulatory reforms to facilitate the development of SMEs.[5] The SME Development Unit's main achievement was the publication of a 2004 report entitled *Enhancing Competitiveness for SMEs, General Framework and Action Plan*.[6] The report aimed to highlight the main obstacles facing SME development and provide the SME development community with an action plan to enhance the competitiveness of SMEs.[7]

The "good governance" of SME reforms in an authoritarian context: questions and issues raised

Foreign donors operating in Egypt have been actively supporting SME development in the past two decades. In line with their assistance to economic liberalization and private sector development, and with the view that SMEs are a key avenue for economic development, poverty alleviation and employment, they funded, under Mubarak's rule, a vast array of projects relating to SME development. Traditionally, most of these projects were focused on service provision to micro, small and medium businesses. However, from the late 1990s onwards, there was a partial shift from service-provision to SME policy reform: foreign donors increasingly assisted economic, administrative and regulatory reforms and the development of advocacy groups promoting reforms. In particular, from 2000 to 2008, the Canadian International Development Agency (CIDA) and the International Development Research Center (IDRC) provided technical and financial support to the SME Development Unit in its efforts to develop the 2004 report and other policy documents. This aid for reform was accompanied by an emphasis on "good governance", especially on the need to design an inclusive and participatory policy-process in order for reforms to be efficient and fair. In parallel, other development agencies and foundations, including the Friedrich Ebert Stiftung (FES) and the Center for International Private Enterprise (CIPE), aided non-governmental organizations (NGOs) representing SMEs and advocating economic, administrative and regulatory reforms. Thus, on the one hand, foreign donors provided the Egyptian government with the technical and financial capacity to engineer a SME policy reform process, and on the other hand, they assisted, through different channels, the participation of SME representatives in such a policy process.

Foreign donors' emphasis on the participation of SME representatives in the making of reforms faced two main constraints in Mubarak's Egypt. First of all, it conflicted with the Egyptian regime's traditional top-down and non-participatory approach to the development of social and economic policies: SME stakeholders, like most social and economic non-state actors, were usually excluded from the making of reforms. Secondly, it stood in sharp contrast with the capacities of SMEs. Indeed, in contrast with big businesses, the advocacy capacities and political access to decision-makers of SMEs were extremely weak.

Under Mubarak's rule, business associations such as the Egyptian Businessmen Association, the Alexandria Businessmen Association or the Egyptian Junior Businessmen Association had considerable leverage over the government's decisions because of their economic weight and also because of their members' direct access to the government. More generally, members of the business elite had the capacity to influence economic policy reforms and capture the benefits of reform and privatization through their direct and personalized access to decision-making institutions and the development of "networks of privilege".[8] Businessmen's influence on economic policy-making further increased from 2004 onwards, with the appointment of businessmen to government positions. The advocacy capacities and access to decision-makers of SME stakeholders were drastically different from those of large businesses; they rather resembled those of other advocacy groups promoting reform in the health, education or environment sectors. As Tamer El Meehy argued (in 2002), "the institutional framework that is supposed to represent SMEs is no different from that governing other aspects of civil society in Egypt. M/SMEs suffer from the absence of effective representative and transparent institutions to represent and promote their interests".[9] In addition, most SME associations were service-providing NGOs,[10] and the number of SME associations involved in advocacy was restricted: in 2009, at the time of field research on this case study, only two associations operating at the national level—a prerequisite to lobby the government—were identified. The most active SME advocacy association was a federation of NGOs, the Federation of Economic Development Associations (FEDA), which benefited substantially from foreign donors' help. Much less active was the Cooperative Society for Small Businesses (CSSB), a branch of the Cooperative Productive Union, a corporatist entity of industrial cooperatives operating under the supervision of the Ministry of Local Development.

Given these constraints, donors' emphasis on good governance and on participation of SME stakeholders in the making of reforms by the SME Development Unit raised a number of issues and questions. First, to what extent could foreign donors facilitate promotion of reforms by SME representatives—in other words, to what extent were donors able to increase their advocacy capacities? Second, to what extent could they increase their access to the policy-making process and the level of their participation in the making of these reforms? Third, if and when foreign donors' discourse on "good governance" had an impact in SME stakeholders' advocacy capacities and access to the policy-making process, how did this foreign-supported political participation operate? It must be noted that this chapter does not focus on the content of political participation but rather on its extent, actors and venues.[11] With these questions in mind, understanding the capacity of foreign donors to transform the political participation of SME stakeholders in the making of reforms under Mubarak's authoritarian regime amounts to examining 1) how both state actors and social actors' political activities and attitudes to political participation were transformed by the involvement of foreign donors (this is, by the opportunities and constraints foreign donors introduced) and 2) how these transformations affected the relation between state and social actors and the general participatory framework. Political participation being a key element of state-society relations, answering these questions provides us with a number of hints on the political effects of foreign donors' "good governance" discourse and measures on state-society relations in Mubarak's Egypt.

Argument and structure of the chapter

The first and second sections of this chapter examine the effects of foreign donors' aid to SME advocacy groups on the latter's advocacy capacities and participation in the SME policy-making process. The first argues that foreign donors demonstrated their ability to enhance the capacity of SME stakeholders to promote reform and opened some space for their participation in the making of reforms by the SME Development Unit. The second section takes a closer look at the characteristics of such participation and shows that foreign donors' financial and technical assistance was monopolized by one unrepresentative NGO (FEDA) and examines why and how an unrepresentative NGO managed to monopolize foreign aid and, subsequently, SME representation and participation in the making of reforms. It introduces the concept of civil society entrepreneurship to account for this bias. A final section turns to the state, and examines state strategies towards the foreign-induced political participation of SME stakeholders: it examines how the SME Development Unit endogenized the CIDA's and IDRC's requirement for a participatory process. It argues that the regime developed a strategy of corporatization towards the FEDA and examines how the resulting corporatist set-up affected the potential of SMEs to promote economic reforms in Egypt.

Foreign donors and SME advocacy groups: doing and undoing civil society activism

The survival of Egyptian advocacy groups and their potential participation in policy processes in Mubarak's Egypt were highly dependent on aid from foreign donors.[12] As an official from a donor agency put it, "participation in policy processes depends on your [the associations'] agenda and on meeting the right donor who has the same agenda".[13] As the case of SME advocacy groups illustrates, donors had the financial and technical capacity (1) to enhance the advocacy capacities of associations and (2) facilitate their access to policy processes: the SME advocacy NGO that benefited most from foreign donor support (the Federation of Economic Development Associations, FEDA) fared much better in terms of visibility and participation in the policy-making process than its corporatist counterpart (the Cooperative Society for Small Businesses, CSSB) which did not manage to secure help from foreign donors.

Western foundations or non-profit organizations (NPOs) are the main providers of assistance to associations advocating economic, social, or civic reforms in developing countries.[14] In this case study, two organizations played a key role in fostering the advocacy capacities of SME representatives and, subsequently, their participation in the making of SME policies: the Friedrich Ebert Stiftung (FES), a German foundation, and the Center for International Private Enterprise (CIPE), an American NPO. Other foundations and organizations were also involved, but to a lesser extent. The FES' and CIPE's approaches to advocacy, their discourses and the activities they have been assisting reflect the general trends in advocacy promotion in Mubarak's Egypt.[15]

Foreign donors are often involved at the very early stages of the establishment or the development of NGOs in developing countries. In Egypt, donor-driven projects or NGOs have been, and remain, commonplace. In the FEDA's case, its history clearly reveals that it could not have emerged without the backing of external actors, notably the FES. From 1996 onwards, the FES indeed played a critical role in encouraging the creation, throughout Egypt, of eleven economic development NGOs in eleven different governorates. These NGOs later gathered under the umbrella of the FEDA whose establishment was also greatly assisted by the FES.

The FES provided the regional economic development associations and the FEDA with different kinds of services to "help them function as civil society organizations".[16] From the viewpoint of foreign donors, functioning "as civil society organizations" equates to being able to raise issues of public concern and discuss them with local or national authorities. This in turn implies having the organizational capacities and the required know-how to formulate concerns and demands and channel them to the relevant authorities. The FES thus provided the regional economic associations and, later, the FEDA with this know-how. For example, it provided the latter with experts who could help it produce quality documents and argumentations. More importantly, it provided the Federation with the tools and resources to gain visibility and access policy-makers. As a FES official put it, "the government really reacts to two things: media coverage and involving sometimes a governor [or any other state actor] in your activities".[17] This requires developing contacts with media and politicians. The FES thus extensively funded networking activities (including meetings, workshops, lunches), including activities within the framework of the debates on the SME Law passed in Parliament in 2004. Such activities involved the FEDA, media (both independent and state media), and parliamentarians, as well as officials from the Social Fund for Development and bureaucrats from the SME Development Unit.[18] This provided the Federation, and its president, with a visibility, network and access to policy-makers that it would not have had otherwise.[19] As a FES official underlined, it made the government "aware" that the FEDA "has the capacity to organize events, conferences, etc".[20] The FES claims not to have intervened in the content of the FEDA's work and to have restricted its contribution to easing the organizational aspects of their work, thus simply setting the stage for the Federation to mobilize and engage. Yet, arguably, its influence was much more pervasive. As the FEDA's publications indicate, the FES's liberal discourse on advocacy and on the role of civil society organizations permeated that of the FEDA.[21] From 2004 onwards, another donor, the CIPE, also developed projects aimed at enhancing FEDA's capacities. The CIPE organized training that addressed issues relating to advocacy: the development of an agenda, the prioritization of policies, the evaluation of policies, etc. It has also financed a number of research projects developed by the FEDA.

Comparing the FEDA with the CSSB (the latter now being completely inactive) hints at the fact that foreign donors' support was vital for advocacy associations willing to participate in the SME policy processes. Indeed, the absence of foreign donors' financial and technical support hindered the CSSB's participation in the SME policy process and led to its slow death. The CSSB was part of the system of industrial cooperatives, the Cooperative Productive Union. The CSSB's president did contact and meet foreign donors, but his attempts to get funds from them were unsuccessful. Foreign donors have traditionally avoided channelling funds to corporatist organizations.[22] This holds true for the CSSB despite the fact that its claims and ambitions were close to the FEDA's, and its modus operandi in many ways similar. The CSSB's inability to secure donors' financial, technical and political support is crucial to understand the decrease of its participation in the SME policy process, from 2004 onwards. An illustration of the gap between the FEDA's and the CSSB's capacity to mobilize can be found in the contrasted level and quality of their participation in the SME Development Unit's policy committees: state officials emphasize that the FEDA was present more often, and was much more prepared, vocal and implicated during the committees' sessions.[23]

This overview of the FEDA's history and activities, and the brief comparison with the CSSB, point to foreign donors' capacity, in Mubarak's Egypt, to foster the advocacy capacities of selected private sector actors and to facilitate their access to and participation in the making of reforms. Yet, foreign donors' involvement had crucial limitations: the participation they fostered was neither pluralistic nor representative.

The FEDA's representativeness of the SME sector in Egypt, at the time of its engagement with the SME Development Unit, was highly questionable. Indeed, although it claimed membership of 32,000 businessmen, most of these individuals were in fact clients of the service-providing NGOs gathered under the FEDA's umbrella. The Federation's declared objectives were to:

> support the participation of its member associations in discussing issues, laws and regulations that regulate SMEs; ensure more participation in taking decisions pertinent of SMEs in order to assume greater roles in economic and social development; and enhance dialogue between decision makers and SMEs representatives to ensure adopting laws and regulations to the advantages of the Egyptian SMEs.[24]

Yet the associations gathered under the FEDA's umbrella were, more often than not, economic development NGOs that provided SMEs with a number of services and participated in development projects in their governorate. These associations were thus service-providing NGOs that have come together at the national level and expanded their activities to advocacy.

Despite this lack of representativeness, the FEDA managed to monopolize access to foreign funding and, subsequently, political participation in the SME policy-making process. The question that arises is why and how foreign donors' assistance to advocacy and participation translated into monopolization of their resources and, subsequently, of SME representation by an unrepresentative NGO. Introducing the concept of civil society entrepreneurship allows for a more thorough understanding of why and how FEDA succeeded in monopolizing foreign donors' support and access to the SME policy-making process. I argue that the FEDA's president is a civil society entrepreneur: having identified the opportunities (such as political participation) and benefits (such as an increase in social and economic capital) foreign donors can provide, he developed networks of privilege within the donors' system that allowed him to secure a privileged access to these opportunities and benefits.[25] In the development of these networks of privilege, he benefited from the specific patronage of one donor, the FES.

Arguably, the relevance of the concept of civil society entrepreneurship goes beyond the case of SME advocacy. Indeed, the emergence of civil society entrepreneurs appears to be one of the main effects of foreign donors' assistance to the participation of advocacy groups in the making of socio-economic reforms in Mubarak's Egypt, and in other developing countries.[26]

Civil society entrepreneurship and the monopolozation of foreign donors' aid to SME advocacy associations

Opportunities and benefits as incentives for the emergence of civil society entrepreneurs

Civil society entrepreneurs can be defined as leaders of civil society organizations, including non-governmental organizations, which, much like business or political entrepreneurs, identify an opportunity and exploit it to gain economic, political or social benefits. Understanding why foreign involvement in Mubarak's Egypt allowed for some NGO leaders to become "civil society entrepreneurs" therefore requires highlighting the opportunities created by foreign donors and the benefits civil society entrepreneurs could extract from exploitation of these opportunities.

Foreign donors supporting social and economic reforms in Mubarak's Egypt needed to face and reconcile two contradictory trends. On the one hand, their aid for good governance required the participation of civil society organizations (that is, advocacy associations such as SME advocacy NGOs). On the other hand, these organizations were weak or non-existent. The issue of the missing constituency for reform is a recurrent one in authoritarian regimes.[27] The combination of the availability of foreign donors' funds and their need for a SME constituency with the absence of this constituency created a unique opportunity for the FEDA and its leader to enter and exploit the "niche" of SME representation.

A series of benefits could be extracted from exploitation of this niche opportunity created by foreign donors. The example of the FEDA's president illustrates the rapid increase in social capital resulting from collaboration with foreign donors.[28] Indeed, through the increased access to media, parliamentarians and government officials facilitated by foreign donors, the FEDA's president gained increased visibility at national level and reinforced his legitimacy as a SME representative. The president established regular relations with the media, which referred to him as a representative of the SME sector, recalled his activities and quoted him in a number of articles, thus granting him visibility and legitimacy.[29] Moreover, his privileged access to Parliament—which was made possible by the FES—and participation in parliamentary commissions also played in reinforcing this legitimacy. By then gaining access to government structures through the SME Development Unit, and personally participating in the policy-making process, he became, in about four or five years, a recognized public figure, including in the mind of government officials.

The "actual or potential resources" linked to this increased visibility and legitimacy are difficult to evaluate at national level.[30] Looking at the evolution of the FEDA president's socio-economic position at the governorate level allows for a better understanding of the effects of donors' support on a NGO leader's social capital. The FEDA president is from Port Said. His position as a NGO leader benefited his social status in two different ways. First of all, he channelled an important amount of donors' funds to the local population, providing, for example, economic opportunities for young people. Some of these projects allowed for the establishment of micro and small enterprises by young entrepreneurs, others facilitated the access of some small and medium entrepreneurs to the Industrial Modernization Center's subsidized industrial upgrading programme. The financial resources and visibility provided by foreign donors therefore helped increase his social status at the governorate level and transform him into a local public figure. This demonstrates, as a foreign donor argued, that "foreign funds are a way up for notability for skilful NGO figures". As he ironically added, "esteem for these people grows with the amount of foreign money".[31] This statement is not only true for the recipients of foreign funds that are channelled through NGOs, but is also valid for local authorities. Indeed, in the last twenty years of Mubarak's rule, local authorities, whose resources were constrained, increasingly tended to rely on NGOs operating at governorate level with foreign funds to provide some services to the population. Getting associated with NGO projects became a classical strategy for local authorities. In the case of the FEDA's president, local authorities also tapped into his organizational and financial capacities to organize meetings or workshops on issues relating to SME development, regulations, or taxes. This clearly played a part in the enhancement of his networks of social relationships at the governorate level and the enhancement of his social capital.

The translation of social capital into economic capital is difficult to evaluate and will not be examined here. Suffice to note that potential direct economic benefits can be gained by civil society entrepreneurs through the exploitation of the opportunities arising from foreign donors' involvement. Through the FEDA president's case, different sources of economic benefits can be identified. The most obvious relates to the grants provided by foreign donors to the FEDA.[32] More generally, foreign donors' support goes hand in hand with travel, conferences in four-star hotels, etc.

Highlighting the opportunities and benefits extracted by the FEDA's president, and more generally by civil society entrepreneurs, thus explains why civil society entrepreneurs come into being. However, understanding how civil society entrepreneurship is fostered requires an examination of the building of interpersonal relations between foreign donors and civil society figures. In this case study, the building of a network of exclusive interpersonal relations with a number of foreign donors allowed the FEDA' president to monopolize foreign funds and support, and, subsequently, to obtain privileged access to the SME policy process. In this sense, these networks of interpersonal relations can be described as "networks of privilege".

Characteristics of donors' patronage

The first step in the building of a network of privilege was the development of a specific type of patron-client relationship between the FES official and FEDA's president. The nature of the relations between these two actors, and the resources exchanged, indeed point to the fact that FEDA benefited from a form of patronage.[33]

The FEDA's president and the FES official insisted on the close and personal nature of their relationship, describing each other as "friends". Friendship is one of the "social institutions" that formalize trust and the sharing of common values,[34] and certainly one aspect of the relationship between these two actors. Their relationship was, however, built on entrenched "discrepancies in status, power and influence",[35] with the NGO being clearly dependent on its donor for its survival. In addition, their relationship was also built on and nurtured by an exchange of financial and social resources: while the FES official has provided the FEDA with financial and technical resources that have allowed for its survival and empowerment, the Federation's president has been promoting the values and message of the donor's foundation (economic liberalization, "civil society empowerment", etc.). This asymmetry and the exchange of resources show that the relationship between the FEDA's president and the FES is a variant of patron-client relations. Arguably, it is close to what Eisenstadt and Roniger would identify as "lopsided friendship".[36] "Lopsided friendship"—one of the multiple types of patron-client relationship—reconciles, on the one hand, the affective and personalized character of the relationship and, on the other hand, its asymmetry. Although lopsided friendship may be based on less inequality than other types of patron-client relations, it remains asymmetrical.

Many elements, it should be noted, indicate that the relationship between donors and NGO or other recipients of foreign aid is often one close to "lopsided friendship". Indeed it frequently displays the traits of a friendship: the sharing of common values (including a liberal approach to politics, for example) and long-term interactions tend to nurture trust. This friendship between actors with different levels of resources and power provides the basis for the resilience of the exchange of social and financial resources and donors' support.

Developing a "network of privilege" within the donors' system

The FEDA case points to the fact that donors' patronage can facilitate access to other donors and the development of a "network of privilege" within the donors' system, thus allowing for the empowerment of civil society entrepreneurs.

The ability of a civil society entrepreneur to elaborate a "network of privilege" within the donors' system results from the combination of (1) relatively strong barriers to the entry in donors' networks and (2) the capacity of this civil society entrepreneur to establish strong and multiple ties with donors.

Under Mubarak's rule, the entry of SME advocacy NGOs, and more generally of civil society organizations, into the donors' system and their access to donors' assistance were subject to a number of restrictions related to the limitations of the Egyptian political system as well as the traditional limitations of the donors' system.[37] Regarding the latter, different elements (which are not necessarily specific to Mubarak's Egypt) converged to exclude a large number of civil society organizations from accessing the donors' system and, subsequently, allow for the concentration of funds on a limited number of these organizations.[38]

Western donors' lack of knowledge of the local environment is one of the main constraints they face in supporting civil society organizations, whether in authoritarian or democratic countries: more often than not, their understanding of the political context and of the actors involved, whether at the governmental or the non-governmental level, is incomplete and their capacity to identify the relevant and legitimate actors in need of help to sustain their advocacy activities is limited. Under Mubarak (and arguably up till now), donors' weak understanding of the civil society scene in Egypt was coupled with an inadequate conception of civil society that contributed to restricting the access of NGOs to donors' funds and support. Indeed, donors' definition of what civil society should be (in particular with regard to ideological or religious orientation) and should look like in order to receive their help has traditionally tended to be extremely restrictive and not necessarily adapted to the local context.[39] A number of actors, for instance, have tended to be excluded from access to donors' funds because of their nature. In this case study, the most obvious example of exclusion from donors' support was that of the Cooperative Society for Small Businesses (CSSB).

Donors' limited time and financial resources are additional constraints, which are not specific to Mubarak's Egypt and reinforce their tendency to assist the same NGOs over long periods of time. In addition, even when looking for "new" NGO partners, donors tend to rely on information provided by other foreign donors.[40]

All these barriers hinder the access of most civil society organizations to foreign aid and facilitate the strengthening of the position of NGOs which have entered foreign donors' closed circle. In this context, civil society entrepreneurship comes to be essentially about having the ability to enter this closed circle and ensure the predominance of one's position in this circle through the building of relationships with different donors.

The FEDA's leader had that ability. The patronage of a FES official allowed him to enter the foreign donors' closed world. On this basis, he then managed to build a network of relations with different donors. By providing him with the tools, knowledge and appropriate vocabulary, the FES facilitated the formatting of his client and created a product that fit donors' requirements in terms of discourse, organization and administrative capacities. The FEDA's leader used these capacities to apply for grants, from USAID, for example, with which he worked on projects relating to the development of technology and communication skills for SMEs. As important as these capacities was the visibility the FES provided for the FEDA president. Through the networking and lobbying activities it assisted, it allowed the president to build relations not only with members of the legislative and the executive, but with other foreign donors, such as the Center for International Private Enterprise (CIPE) and the International Labour Organization (ILO), which later funded some of its projects.

The outstanding capacity of the FEDA's president to develop a network of interpersonal relations with foreign donors aiding SME advocacy allowed for a concentration of donors' funds on the Federation. Given that political participation in the policy process required funds and visibility, the FEDA's quasi-monopolization of donors' assistance for

SME advocacy groups allowed it privileged access to political participation in the SME policy-making process. As a result, rather than fostering pluralistic representation, foreign donors facilitated the monopolization of representation.

The FEDA president's experience is not unique. Donors engaged in supporting social and economic reforms under Mubarak's rule agreed that some civil society figures, generally presidents of NGOs, managed to attract the bulk of foreign donors' funds and to become quasi-exclusive partners in reform processes, or at least visible figures who had privileged access to the media and could occasionally be consulted by the government. These figures tended to be active in areas such as the environment, education, social development, or health. Much like SME development, these areas were perceived by the regime as non-political in that they did not address directly the way power was exercised in the country (as opposed, for example, to human rights organizations).

The spread of civil society entrepreneurship (and its constitutive elements, that is, donors' patronage and the building of "networks of privilege" within the donors' system) in the past two decades in Egypt can be partly explained by the fact that its root causes were widespread. Indeed, most of the "ingredients" that allowed the FEDA's leader to gain a prominent role as a representative of SMEs are not specific to this case study. First of all, personalization has traditionally been a common characteristic of most NGOs in Egypt. This is a prime condition for the development of interpersonal relations and networks. Second, donors' situation and limitations under Mubarak's rule were the same in all the areas in which they intended to assist reforms. Indeed, in most cases, the issue of the missing constituency for reform was a critical one and donors had a limited understanding of the local environment and a restricted knowledge of who the actors supporting reform were. Moreover, the reluctance to work with some groups because of their nature or their ideological orientation was also shared by most donors. This translated mechanically into the creation of opportunities for actors who were not necessarily representative, but who were available and had already been formatted by other donors through training and technical support for specific sets of activities (including networking or budget management).

All in all, the situation appeared to be similar in many areas in which donors assisted reforms. As a consequence, in most fields donors entered, rent-seeking behaviour by civil society entrepreneurs was triggered and the creation of networks of privilege between them and donors was facilitated.

This chapter has so far looked into the effects of donors' good governance discourse on the mobilization of civil society organizations and their capacity to advocate reform in Mubarak's Egypt. However, foreign donors were also directly involved with governmental actors. The Canadian International Development Agency (CIDA) and the International Development Research Center (IDRC) indeed supported technically and financially the development of a SME policy by the SME Development Unit, putting special emphasis on the requirement to design a participatory and inclusive policy-making process. The next section analyzes how this requirement was endogenized by the SME Development Unit and sheds light on the peculiarities and limitations of the foreign-supported participation of SME stakeholders in the making of reforms.

State strategies towards the participation of SME stakeholders: corporatizing foreign-aided advocacy NGOs

The CIDA's and IDRC's "good governance" approach clearly permeated the discourse of Egyptian bureaucrats: the documents published by the SME Development Unit referred to "stakeholders' mapping and involvement" and stressed the need to take into account actors outside the realm of governmental organizations, including advocacy organizations and private sector organizations.[41] This recognition of the need to foster dialogue with key external stakeholders and interest groups is worth mentioning since it contrasted with the traditional approach to policy making of Egypt's authoritarian regime. More importantly, this discursive shift was accompanied by the development of participatory mechanisms at the level of policy practice: the FEDA was invited to participate in the policy committees which were established in 2005 by the SME Development Unit to develop specific reform measures to facilitate the implementation of the General Strategy and Action Plan. In other words, space was created within the SME Development Unit for the political participation of civil society organizations in the policy reform process. Yet, a closer look at the political participation occurring in these policy committees reveals that it had a number of features that point to its corporatist nature.[42]

According to Schmitter, the prime purpose of traditional corporatist arrangements (such as trade unions) is to link the "associationally organized interests of civil society with the decisional structures of the state". His seminal work defines corporatism as:

> a system of interest representation in which the constituent units are organized into a limited number of singular, compulsory, noncompetitive, hierarchically ordered and functionally differentiated categories, recognized or licensed (if not created) by the state and granted a deliberate representational monopoly within their respective categories in exchange for observing certain controls on their selection of leaders and articulation of demands and supports.[43]

While theories of corporatism, including Schmitter's, traditionally referred to the relationship between the state and representational associations such as trade unions, this case study point to their relevance for the study of the relationship between the state and newer forms of associability, such as NGOs.

Indeed, within the framework of this case study, the characteristics of the institutional set-up in which SME stakeholders' participation occurred indicate that it was neither pluralistic nor completely independent from the state. Rather, the FEDA was granted an official monopoly of SME representation and was formally associated with, and to some extent controlled by, state structures. It can thus be argued that the main response of Egyptian bureaucrats to the foreign-induced requirement for political participation of advocacy NGOs in the making of SME policies was to develop a corporatization strategy. The arrangement that emerged from this process was, however, distinct from traditional corporatist arrangements in Egypt (such as trade unions, professional associations) in a number of ways. It was, first of all, highly dependent on foreign donors' involvement and relatively detached from the SME constituency. Secondly, it was, to a large extent, incomplete and more fragile than other forms of corporatist arrangements.

Before turning to the quality and peculiarities of the FEDA's corporatization, it should be noted that some scholars have been introducing theories of corporatism into the study of state-NGO relations in other world regions. The work of these scholars generally addresses newly democratized, semi-authoritarian and authoritarian regimes. It suffers, however, from a serious flaw: these theories of "corporatism" have indeed tended to be applied to state-NGO relations in a non-rigorous manner, and "corporatism" has often been used as an analytically vague category or simply equated to "control" or "co-optation".[44]

In order to avoid these pitfalls and to understand the type of corporatist arrangements that emerged from the corporatization of a foreign-aided advocacy NGO such as the FEDA, the actors and processes involved will be identified and examined. The nature of this corporatism and its political implications will then be discussed.

Questioning the boundaries between "old" and "new" associative actors

The above-mentioned literature incorporating corporatism into the study of civil society in newly democratized, semi-authoritarian and authoritarian regimes is based on the premise that the regimes have to deal with both "old" and "new" forms of associability—that is, traditional corporatist arrangements such as trade unions or professional associations on the one hand and non-governmental organizations on the other. This dichotomy between old and new forms of associability implies that the actors involved in corporatist or semi-corporatist arrangements and those involved in NGOs are different. Such a dichotomy must, however, be rethought. Indeed, a glance at the actors involved in both kinds of structures reveals that old and new forms of associability frequently overlap in newly democratized, semi-authoritarian and authoritarian regimes, and that the boundary between them can be blurred and easily crossed, in both ways. The case of FEDA is instructive: at the time of its involvement with the SME Development Unit, its most active members indeed combined positions in old and new types of associations. The FEDA's president, for example, was also the vice-president of the Cooperative Productive Union, and had been active in this corporatist structure since the mid-1980s. Moreover, he was also a member of the Chamber for Civil Industry of the Federation of Egyptian Industries (FEI).

It can be argued that the corporatist background of some of the actors involved in advocacy NGOs smoothed their interactions with government officials. Indeed, as the FEDA president put it, "we know how to present things".[45] In other words, these actors had some knowledge on how state institutions work and what state actors can expect and accept. This suggests that the background of the FEDA's members, including its president's background, probably facilitated the corporatization of their NGO.[46]

Identifying the steps of the corporatization process: granting a monopoly over, and institutionalizing, participation

The process of the FEDA's corporatization began in 2005. Previously, its president's relations with the SME Development Unit were largely informal. He was indeed in contact with state bureaucrats from the SME Development Unit (as well as with other ministries and agencies) through the networking activities that he organized with the FES' support and the workshops, conferences and seminars he was invited to. This informal relation was formalized from 2005 onwards.

Some of the basic elements of the corporatization process relate to the hierarchical structure of the Federation and the control exerted by the state over its leadership, under law 84 of 2002 regulating NGOs under Mubarak's rule (and which remains in place more than a year after Mubarak's fall). These basic elements of the corporatization process cover a number of the characteristics of "typical corporatist arrangements" identified by Bianchi.[47] State control over NGOs has been exerted through the requirement for registration as well as through control over the composition of their boards of directors. Registration being mandatory in Egypt, the FEDA was registered at the Ministry of Social Affairs (MOSA) in 2001. In accordance with the law, it was initially formed of eleven associations, each one from a different governorate. The first board of the Federation included eleven elected members and five members appointed by the MOSA.[48] The MOSA also exerted control over the Federation's funds: the FEDA—like all other NGOs—needed the MOSA's approval before receiving foreign funding. Moreover, the Federation has been organized in a centralized and hierarchical way. Three levels can be identified: local, regional and national. In 2009, the Federation counted 130 NGOs working at a local level. In each governorate, these NGOs are grouped under a regional association, which itself is organically related to the national Federation, FEDA, which has its headquarters in Cairo.

The FEDA's organization and leadership structure thus comply with the legislation imposed on federations of NGOs in Egypt. In this sense, the legislation in force was responsible for part of the corporatization process. However, corporatism means more than organizing units or controlling their finances. It is indeed above all a system of interest representation. In this regard, the monopoly of representation granted to FEDA as well as the formalization of its participation through its incorporation in intergovernmental SME policy committees both point to the corporatist nature of the institutional arrangement set up to accommodate FEDA's participation.

The granting of a monopoly over representation to the FEDA must be examined in the light of its restricted constituency and its limited representativeness. Officials from the SME Development Unit knew the FEDA president personally. He was perceived as a "good guy" who "has the energy" and "wants to do something".[49] These officials considered the FEDA as a "huge", "well known" and "very active" organization.[50] The fact that it is "nationwide" was also regularly emphasized.[51] For all these reasons, they considered it to be a "representative of SMEs"[52] and other "business people".[53] It should be recalled at this point that although it claims to represent the SME community and gathered more than 130 associations working on SME development in 2009, the FEDA could not be considered a business association representing the whole Egyptian SME community, which comprises millions of individuals who, in their vast majority, have no knowledge of or relation with the FEDA.

Despite this imperfect representativeness, the Federation was granted a formal monopoly over SME representation by the SME Development Unit. The granting of this monopoly was formalized in the Protocol of Cooperation signed between the Ministry of Finance and the FEDA in January 2005.[54] This Protocol marked the official recognition by the government of the FEDA's role as a representative of the SME community. It was signed by the Federation's president and the head of the SME Development Unit and aimed to organize cooperation between the Federation and the Ministry "in the framework of micro, small, medium enterprises' development". This document endowed the FEDA with a high degree of legitimacy. After stating that NGOs play an important role in social development, it recalled the FEDA's membership basis and its role in SME development in Egypt.

The monopoly of representation granted to the FEDA is a key aspect of its corporatization. Its incorporation in policy committees is a second key aspect: it allowed for the institutionalization of its participation.

The Protocol of Cooperation between the FEDA and the Ministry of Finance underlined, in its first article, that the cooperation between the two entities included debating the policies and legislative proposals relating to regulatory, financing, organizational obstacles facing SMEs. The second article provided for participation by the FEDA in policy committees set up by the Ministry of Finance. The objective was to enhance the Federation's role in setting forth the problems encountered by small and medium entrepreneurs. Thus, all in all, the FEDA was granted a central role in the representation of SMEs' interests within governmental institutions.

The institutionalization of the FEDA's role took a number of other forms. The second article of the Protocol also added, for example, that the Federation's members would be given the opportunity to participate in the training, conferences and workshops organized by the Ministry of Finance. The eighth point of the Protocol also declared that some FEDA members would be invited to join the Egyptian delegations in international meetings and events. For example, the FEDA participated in a study tour to Canada with the SME Development Unit and other government agencies.

Examining the corporatization process thus provides us with additional information on the quality of political participation in the SME policy-making process: it was institutionalized and monopolized. Channels of participation were indeed established by the SME Development Unit, which provided the FEDA with quasi-exclusive access to political participation. The extent of the FEDA's influence on the output of the policy process is hard to assess. However, assessing its exact influence is somehow of secondary importance: what is important is that officials from the SME Development Unit turned to the FEDA, included it and listened to its opinions. The FEDA's president, in fact, expressed satisfaction concerning the policy committees, and officials from the SME Development Unit considered its presence important to them.[55]

Peculiarities and limitations of the corporatization process

The corporatist arrangement between the FEDA and the state has a number of specific features and limitations that differentiate it from traditional corporatist arrangements. These features and limitations relate to the process of corporatization itself as well as to the role of foreign donors. They have specific political implications for the participation of SMEs in the making of reforms in Mubarak's Egypt.

Although different steps were taken to corporatize the FEDA, its corporatization was incomplete. This was, first of all, due partly to the FEDA's nature: it indeed remained a federation of NGOs. Hence membership in the Federation could not be compulsory as in traditional corporatist structures. The fact is that its membership remained limited, especially when compared to the size of the Egyptian SME community. Secondly, the FEDA's corporatization depended heavily on one agency, the SME Development Unit. The closing of this Unit inevitably halted the corporatization process. The limited sustainability of the corporatization endeavour was thus a clear limitation to the transformation of the FEDA into a corporatist organization. Thirdly, the arrangement between the FEDA and the SME Development Unit was not as constraining as other corporatist arrangements. For example, the Protocol did not include any kind of restrictions on FEDA activities, and the Unit did not exert any kind of control over these activities. The FEDA indeed developed, in parallel to its work in the policy committees, a range of other activities and SME development projects in collaboration with other actors—essentially donors. This could certainly not be the case for a traditional corporatist group.

Thus, while the FEDA did manage to monopolize representation and participation and get quasi-exclusive access to the policy process, its corporatization was incomplete and its privileged position not as secure as that of other corporatist groups. The incomplete character of the FEDA's corporatization and its relative lack of formality illustrate the weakness of this corporatist arrangement compared with more traditional corporatist arrangements and, consequently, the weak durability of this institutionalized political participation.

Beyond state and societal corporatism: incorporating foreign donors in the theory of corporatism

Another key difference between traditional corporatist arrangements in Mubarak's Egypt and the corporatist arrangement involving the FEDA was the central role played by foreign donors. Corporatist arrangements typically involve state and social actors. However, our case study indicates that a third category of actors, foreign donors, might get involved in the building of corporatist arrangements (at least indirectly) through the development of aid programmes for political participation by advocacy groups. Understanding the peculiarities of the FEDA's corporatization thus requires shedding light on the role foreign donors played in fostering corporatist arrangements between the Egyptian regime and foreign-backed advocacy NGOs under Mubarak's rule.

The previous paragraphs emphasized the strategies developed by the Egyptian state to corporatize the FEDA. In this sense, it is possible to consider that this corporatism had some traits of "state corporatism". However, many features distinguished it from state corporatism. Indeed, the FEDA was not created by the state, nor was its development supported by the state. Moreover, its recognition by the state was, to a certain extent, "granted as a matter of political necessity".[56] According to Schmitter, when this political necessity is imposed from "below" corporatism may be qualified as "societal".[57] In our case, it might be argued that state recognition was granted as a matter of political necessity (a clear difference from state corporatism); however, it was imposed from outside rather than from below (a clear difference from societal corporatism). Indeed, the FEDA did not rely on a powerful broad-based constituency, which would have forced the government to grant it recognition. Rather, external actors created this political necessity: foreign donors fostered the necessity for the state to recognize advocacy NGOs and allow for their participation.

This clearly raises the issue of the FEDA's lack of accountability towards SMEs, which it claimed to represent, and that of the legitimacy of its participation. Arguably, instead of enhancing the quality of the FEDA's representativeness, external support was a substitute for bottom-up support and for the Federation's limited outreach. All these elements cast doubts on the quality of its participation.

Moving beyond the case study explored in this paper, it can be argued that the concept of corporatism has a broader relevance for the study of the relation between the state and advocacy groups in authoritarian regimes: it can provide conceptual tools to account for the strategies developed by authoritarian governments in response to Western donors' and foreign-supported advocacy groups' demands for political participation. Many of the constitutive elements of the corporatization process observed in this case study are widespread. Indeed, donors' aid for the establishment of administrative units, committees or commissions in charge of the development of reforms in specific socio-economic sectors—such as education or health—has become commonplace. It has almost automatically been accompanied by an emphasis on good governance and the development of participatory mechanisms. Cases studies conducted in the pre-Arab Spring Middle East indicate that government response was generally to bring into these units, committees or commissions members of opposition parties as well as representatives of civil society organizations or of the private sector, and to institutionalize their participation. In their analysis of state strategies towards non-state actors' participation in foreign-aided commissions and committees addressing reforms in health, education, or decentralized government in Egypt, Morocco and Tunisia, Allal and Kohstall underlined the effects of the regimes' logics of "selection" of and "negotiation" with non-state actors.[58] While these authors do not refer to corporatization, their conclusions echo to some extent those of this case study: the participation institutionalized in these commissions and committees appears to have been of limited plurality, the space of interaction "temporally limited", and potential opponents turned into "partners in development".

Concluding remarks

Reflecting on the political transformations in state-society relations resulting from Western donors' assistance for "good governance" in Mubarak's Egypt provides food for thought on the realities of Western donors' actual capacities to instill more transparent and participatory reforms in authoritarian regimes. It also provides insights into the dynamic and adaptive nature of the Egyptian authoritarian regime under Mubarak, as well as the strengths, biases and constraints of civil society organizations.

With regard to Western donors' capacities, this case study illustrates their ability to create space for the participation of civil society actors in the making of reforms. Donors indeed facilitated the political participation of civil society organizations both by empowering a SME advocacy NGO (the FEDA) and by encouraging the government to develop participatory mechanisms. Yet, this case study also illustrates the many limitations of this foreign-induced participation, including the low representativeness of the civil society actors involved and their monopoly over participation. Some of these limitations result from the way donors' financial and technical assistance tends to be distributed to advocacy NGOs in developing countries. Indeed, donors can play a key role in the emergence and empowerment of advocacy groups and can thus facilitate the development of actors promoting economic or social reforms. Yet, the numerous weaknesses of the donors' system can also lead to the monopolization of donor funds and support by a limited number of civil society entrepreneurs. The example of the FEDA in this case study provides an illustration of such phenomena, but donors agree in saying that civil society entrepreneurship is widely spread—and encouraged by foreign donors' practices. The dependency of the FEDA, and more generally of advocacy NGOs promoting socio-economic reforms, on foreign funds points to their vulnerability. In addition, the concentration of foreign aid on one advocacy NGO clearly raises the issue of weak representativeness and highlights the risk of empowering certain reform sectors over others.

The limitations of foreign-induced participation by civil society organizations in policy reforms also result from the adaptation strategies developed by the Mubarak regime. The SME Development Unit's response to Western donors' demand for better governance illustrates the adaptive and dynamic nature of the Egyptian authoritarian regime under Mubarak. Indeed, the corporatization of the FEDA reflected the regime's capacity to creatively endogenize donors' "good governance" approach: the government did respond to donors and SME stakeholders' demand for participatory processes, yet this response was framed through channels that closely resembled traditional corporatist channels of interest representation. In other words, the institutional arrangement set up to accommodate participation by civil society organizations in this case study, and arguably in a number of other reform processes, had a number of corporatist traits and did not lead to pluralistic representation. This can become particularly problematic when, like the FEDA, an advocacy group lacks representativeness.

In addition to providing insights into the nature of the Mubarak regime, this case study also reveals some of the recurrent complexities and limitations of civil society organizations in Mubarak's Egypt, which often mirrored the complexities and limitations of the regime itself. It illustrates, for example, the highly personalized nature of civil society organizations, their limited representativeness, their low levels of accountability to their supposed constituency (rather than to donors or to the regime) and their high levels of dependency on donor funding. Arguably, such traits were not specific to civil society under Mubarak's Egypt, but can be found in a number of authoritarian settings. In the post-Mubarak Egypt, as the regime, civil society and state-society relations are reshaping, it is still unclear how the nature of civil society organizations will evolve. It is, however, interesting to note that the Revolution did create space for civil society organizations to modify some aspects of their modus operandi and attitude towards the regime. This seems to hold true even for civil society organizations which had been associated to the regime's reforms. The FEDA's discourse during the 2011 protests provides an illustration of such an evolution and of the adaptive nature of foreign-supported civil society organizations. In a statement issued on 3 February 2011, it expressed demands for political change, including the abolition of emergency laws and investigation of members of the fallen ruling party for corruption.[59]

Overall, the conclusions of this work constitute hypotheses on the effects of foreign donors' "good governance" discourse on the participation of civil society in economic and social reform processes in authoritarian regimes. Further research is needed to assess whether and how these conclusions could apply to other Middle Eastern or developing world authoritarian regimes in which foreign donors assist reforms. This further research could allow for a better understanding of the nature of authoritarian regimes and the political changes occurring in them as a result of external pressure. It might also have useful practical implications for international development agencies, NGOs and foundations involved in aid to socio-economic policy reforms in authoritarian regimes.

9

VECTORS OF IRANIAN CAPITALISM

PRIVATIZATION POLITICS IN THE ISLAMIC REPUBLIC

Kevan Harris

Nearly all politicians in Iran today, no matter where they lie on the political spectrum, noisily declare the need for privatization of state-owned enterprises (SOEs). Indeed, privatization is presented as the main panacea to the country's disappointing record in employment creation and economic growth. Even the Leader and Supreme Jurist of the Islamic Republic, Ali Khamenei, called in 2006 for 80% of Iran's large public sector to be privatized, declaring the effort to be "a kind of jihad".[1] At first glance, it appeared the state was implementing the Leader's forceful recommendation. In 2011, a glossy report for foreign investors entitled *The Business Year: Iran* announced that the country had "conducted one of the most effective and wide-ranging privatization efforts seen in the region in recent years".[2] In the previous year, it asserted, more than three hundred SOEs, including petrochemical plants, banks, fuel refineries, airlines, insurance companies, vehicle manufacturers, and agricultural conglomerates had been transferred out of the public sector by the Iranian Privatization Organization (IPO), a state body established in 2001 during the administration of former President Mohammad Khatami.

At the same time, however, several SOE privatization scandals hit the front pages of Iran's newspapers. Most notable were the transfers in 2009 of Tehran's International Exhibition Center and the Telecommunication Company of Iran to large investment companies attached to, respectively, the Armed Forces Pension Fund and the Islamic Revolutionary Guard Corps (IRGC) Cooperative Fund. Neither of these recipients looked much like the private sector. In fact, in December 2010, a special commission on privatization in Iran's Parliament reported that only 13.5% of the US$70 billion worth of assets of state-owned enterprises, transferred out of the public sector since 2006, had gone to the private sector. The remainder went to what critics label as the pseudo-state or parastatal sector: public banks, military firms, state-linked investment and holding companies, foundations, pension funds, and President Ahmadinejad's dividend programme of "Justice Shares".[3]

The Parliament's report outlined the extent of this "pseudo-privatization" and prompted howls of derision by opponents of President Mahmoud Ahmadinejad, including notable conservatives within the political elite. Supporters of the Ahmadinejad administration countered not only that this privatization was "real" since it shrank the size of the public sector, but also that the transfer of SOEs to pension funds and other large institutional investors was common in wealthier countries. By 2011–12, the debate over privatization entirely concerned its implementation and not its aim. All sides, which by this time meant the many cliques and subdivisions of Iran's conservative political elite, spoke of privatization as the solution. This recent debate, however, begs a larger set of questions. How did the Islamic Republic of Iran, born in revolution and steeled in war and geopolitical strife, reach the point where the discourse of privatization became universal among its political elite? Furthermore, this being the case, why has the transfer of economic power to the private sector been so limited? Instead of state assets being sold to the highest bidder, or handed over to a single monolithic actor, the privatization process in Iran illustrates the complex ways in which intra-elite conflict from above intertwined with social demands from below.

In this chapter, I examine the politics of privatization in the Islamic Republic over the previous three decades. I first highlight the impact of revolutionary turmoil and the Iran-Iraq war (1980–88) in shaping the role of the public sector. Second, I detail three successive presidential administrations and their political battles over privatization: the thwarted liberalization of Hashemi Rafsanjani (1989–97), the growth of the private sector without privatization under Mohammad Khatami (1997–2005), and the growth of the parastatal sector through "pseudo-privatization" under Mahmoud Ahmadinejad (2005–). Third, I discuss three different social actors that hold large stakes in parastatal organizations which received SOE assets: professional middle and formal working classes whose pensions are managed by the Social Security Organization (SSO), poorer strata and special status groups that hold dividends in the Justice Shares Programme, and military officers and cadres whose subcontractor firms and holding companies lay claim to a growing portion of investment and economic activity allocated by the state. Lastly, I use three ideal-types of capitalist development in middle-income countries in Eastern Europe and East Asia—capitalism from without, from below, and from above—to situate Iran's post-revolutionary economic transformations in a broader historical and comparative context.

Privatization paradoxes

Much commentary in Iran, as elsewhere, tends to blame the distortions, failures, and unintended consequences of economic liberalization in low- and middle-income countries on the persistence of state intervention in the market. Yet a central paradox of economic liberalization in the late twentieth century was that the reduction or elimination of state ownership involved the intervention of the state, especially when such reforms were perceived to have succeeded.[4] The "myth of the market" is that economies operate outside state institutions. In reality, processes of commodification and marketization demand a more robust state with a higher regulatory capacity, what Michael Mann identifies as "infrastructural power".[5] Scholars such as Kiren Aziz Chaudhry argue that competitive markets are not simply created by "smashing" the state, but rather, "the instruments of the state must be redeployed to perform the much more difficult task of indirect regulation and administration".[6] In other words, successful privatization of SOEs, often built up during decades of import-substitution industrialization conducted in tandem with state formation itself, requires the state to be able to initiate and carry through such a major transformation. This paradox of privatization reveals that, as Haggard and Kaufman contend, "for governments to reduce their role in the economy and expand the play of market forces, the state itself must be strengthened".[7]

Successful privatization needs high state capacity, then. But perceptibly "strong" states do not always privatize, even if that is desired, since strong state elites can block policy changes from within or without the government. Scholars of economic policy have identified the presence or absence of relatively "autonomous" technocratic organizations within the state, or "insulated change teams", as a key variable for success.[8] The concept of relative state autonomy, though, has travelled a long theoretical distance. Originating in Marxian debates over whether states could be independent of capitalist elites, later usage of the "autonomy" concept shifted towards a Weberian framework within development studies to analyze whether states could be independent from any social pressure in order to carry out structural transformations in the economy.[9] For example, SOE privatization usually requires state autonomy from public sector groups such as workers, often through dismantling or overcoming former corporatist linkages with labour.[10] The varying responses by domestic business to state efforts at liberalization can also depend on how state-business relations have been previously structured during eras of high tariffs, infant industries, and other protectionist policies.[11] The internal configuration and cohesiveness of state elites can be another crucial determinant of the privatization process. During the rapid collapse of the post-Soviet economy, public officials "actively pulled apart" economic institutions by "seeking to extract assets that were in any way fungible", effectively "stealing the state" under a label of privatization.[12] In sum, to act autonomously from powerful social actors that could lay claim to public assets, including state and business elites, governments need to carve institutions out of the state apparatus which are unconstrained by such linkages. For scholars, explaining well-managed privatization via such autonomous state organizations therefore entails an examination of the social and political context in which opportunities to transfer public goods into private hands may emerge.[13]

Yet the social and political functions of state-owned enterprises can widely vary. As Ha-Joon Chang and Ilene Grabel write, "often SOEs are charged with serving too many objectives (e.g. social goals, industrialization, and the provision of basic services), and the relative importance of each goal is unclear".[14] One might expect such overloaded

SOEs in states that heavily depend on natural resource commodity exports for government revenue, especially when tradeoffs between capital accumulation and social distribution may not be sharply demarcated. However, as Steffen Hertog has detailed, Gulf states have produced profitable SOEs in lieu of substantial privatization. In the United Arab Emirates, Saudi Arabia and Qatar, this outcome stemmed from "decades of nonpolitics"—an absence of social pressure from below which allowed for extensive state autonomy in economic policy-making. Populist measures, in these cases, were not required in state-building efforts, and SOEs were relieved both from pressures of bureaucratic predation and from expectations of redistribution. Firms' management could be directed and incentivized towards rationalized market calculations, forming small "islands of efficiency".[15] As a result of historically contingent political and social formations, therefore, certain Gulf states developed "embedded autonomy" in relation to themselves. The "resource curse" of state capture and patrimonial linkage, often attributed to easy access to natural resources, is likely due more to politics than to petroleum.

In Iran, politics also conditioned how, to whom, and over what networks economic resources flowed during the process of restructuring domestic firms and markets. Post-revolutionary state formation after 1979 was highly embedded in, and constrained by, numerous social actors. To understand why, we first need to place Iran's seemingly haphazard economic policies within the political drama of elite intrigue during revolution, war, and post-war reconstruction. Throughout the entire post-revolutionary period, a factionalized and fractious state elite prevented the coalescing of a unified apparatus that could fully apply the technocratic blade to the public sector. The flux of competition among political entrepreneurs—electoral and otherwise—relied upon popular mobilizations of a variety of social bases and status groups. At times, however, intra-elite conflict provided opportunities for activity by domestic private business, as in the banking industry in the early 2000s. In subsequent years, though, state transfer of public sector companies was mostly channelled towards organizations whose member constituencies had been produced alongside the state itself: large pension funds for the formal labour force, "Justice Share" cooperatives for "revolutionary" status groups, or war veterans who sought upward status mobility within the military and its growing network of subcontractors. While states that construct autonomy from protected elites and other powerful social actors are best poised to carry out "real" privatization, Iran's post-revolutionary trajectory embedded the state deeply into the domestic social arena. The result, conversely, has been the pseudo-privatization of the public sector over the last several years.

Nationalization by necessity

Article 44 of the Iranian Constitution, currently the legal basis for SOE privatization after being amended in 2004, has a remarkable history. According to the late Ezzatollah Sahabi, a member of Ayatollah Khomeini's 1979 Revolutionary Council, it was placed into the second draft of the constitution by Ayatollahs Beheshti, Alviri and Hojatolislam Bahonar, and approved by popular referendum in October of that year.[16] In its original form, Article 44 stated

> The state sector is to include all large-scale and mother industries, foreign trade, major minerals, banking, insurance, power generation, dams and large-scale irrigation networks, radio and television, post, telegraph and telephone services, aviation, shipping, roads, railroads and the like; all these will be publicly owned and administered by the state. The cooperative sector is to include cooperative companies and enterprises concerned with production and distribution, in urban and rural areas, in accordance with Islamic criteria. The private sector consists of those activities concerned with agriculture, animal husbandry, industry, trade, and services that supplement the economic activities of the state and cooperative sectors.

As Khomeini's "lieutenant", Beheshti was the scourge of secular left groups in the 1979 revolutionary coalition, such as the Marxist Fedayan-e Khalq, which were also calling for nationalization of major industry. Yet Beheshti was also a political genius in the mould of Trotsky. In 1979, the Islamic liberals surrounding the provisional head of government Mehdi Bazargan were content with keeping a large private sector intact in order to ensure continued domestic investment. Beheshti, more concerned with the success of Khomeinist forces, tried to outmanoeuvre leftist groups' calls for socialist transformation, since at the time they possessed formidable social bases that competed with Khomeini loyalists.

Most of the revolutionaries' antipathy towards the private sector remained directed at those elite families connected with the ancien regime as well as Western-linked capital. The new state did not expropriate all factory owners and landholders but ended up in control of the economy mostly by exigency rather than plan. Banks were nationalized, but because they were bankrupt. Foreign investment was limited and cross-border trade nationalized, but this was to stem ongoing capital flight. At its inception, the Islamic Republic hardly possessed a blueprint for nationalized production. Rather, the spirit of Article 44 was partly a move to bolster the left-leading credentials of the Khomeini-led state, and partly recognition of the circumstantial nationalization that had already taken place amidst revolutionary collapse.[17]

Once war with Iraq began in late 1980, state control over production and distribution was strengthened, but again, more out of need than ideology. The actual maintenance of the economy relied on middle-ranking Pahlavi-era planners to a large degree. Many of these technocrats remained at the Plan and Budget Organization (PBO), churning out reports while the revolution swept through government bureaucracies and brought in new cadres who challenged the planners' expertise as suspect. In most state ministries, low-ranking staff allied with manual labourers such as janitors, gardeners, and kitchen workers to agitate for a levelling of the bureaucratic status order and pay scales. This process was even facilitated by the state—in fact, by Beheshti himself—which sponsored the creation of an official "Islamic Association" in each ministry to steer these bottom-up mobilizations away from the secular left and towards support for those new bureaucrats and managers inclined to follow Khomeinist directives.[18] In other words, the revolution did not fully replace the bureaucracy, but the state machinery was unsettled enough to remain unable to move beyond emergency response.

Bazargan's original intentions for boosting the private sector were therefore sidelined after 1980. By the autumn of 1981, Khomeini loyalists had occupied the state's commanding heights, and a new five-year plan was drafted to commence in 1983. The plan stressed common Third-Worldist pieties such as self-sufficiency in production and unshackling the Iranian economy from the "dependent development" of the Shah's rule. In reality, the document was merely a codification of the war economy, its lofty goals never implemented owing to the country's ad hoc governance. As the war against Iraq dragged on, a crisis plan was drawn up to prepare for worst-case scenarios, including Iraqi chemical weapon attacks and a US ground invasion.[19] While the public sector expanded in the war economy, parastatal organizations formed as

Khomeinist auxiliaries during the initial post-revolutionary struggle—the Islamic Revolutionary Guard Corps (IRGC), the volunteer militia of the mobilized (*basij*), the rural development agency Construction Jihad, and the welfare organization Imam Khomeini Relief Committee (IKRC)—became crucial in operations both on and away from the front lines.[20] As Kaveh Ehsani wrote, "public-sector employment more than doubled after the revolution, from 1.7 million in 1976 to 3.5 million in 1986. According to one estimate, within three years of the revolution, one in six Iranians above the age of fifteen belonged to one state and revolutionary body or another".[21]

Meanwhile, latent ideological differences were emerging within the new political elite. A self-described "radical" faction, with members such as Prime Minister Mir-Hossein Mousavi, Behzad Nabavi and Ayatollah Mohammad Mousavi Khoiniha, consistently pushed for statist intervention on issues of taxes, labour laws, land redistribution, import substitution, and confiscation of private property.[22] Their measures, passed in the Parliament, were doggedly rejected by a conservative faction based in the Guardian Council—a de facto House of (clerical) Lords endowed in the 1979 constitution with veto power. Khomeini frequently sided with the populist radicals until his death in 1989, though little coherent economic policy emerged from the intra-elite strife during his tenure as Leader and Supreme Jurist.

Even during these years, however, the private sector employed the majority of the labour force in agriculture, services, and petty manufacturing. New loans offered by the government financed thousands of small workshops.[23] Such private sector activities often competed with state-sponsored cooperatives and revolutionary organizations. For instance, the Construction Jihad and the Imam Khomeini Relief Committee both created their own carpet weaving workshops and distribution networks, which undercut prices at the same time as US economic sanctions led to a 70% decline in carpet exports.[24] The Chamber of Commerce, Industry, and Mines, an organization dating back to the 1920s, lobbied the government as well as notable clerics during this period over issues of taxation and regulation. Actually, the post-revolutionary economic debate between prominent elites in the 1980s never questioned the sanctity of private property, but rather concerned the right balance of state and market. After an oil slump-induced recession in 1986, the government gradually shifted some activities in trade and commerce to private hands, especially non-oil exports, making effective use of the robust existing black market in order to facilitate consumption needs during the crisis years of the war. During this decade, foreign exchange rates had been broken into numerous tiers by the government. Depending on the activity or the applicant, the exchange rates could be quite generous, guaranteeing large profit margins for importers. Consequently, as Arang Keshavarzian has detailed, the emergent business-state relations under the Islamic Republic did not give rise—as is mistakenly assumed—to the indiscriminate empowerment of a *bazari* merchant class. Rather, the state selectively awarded preferential access to credit, licenses, and protected markets to a chosen few capitalist merchants. This integrative patronage, as much as the nationalization of large industry, broke up the power of the domestic bourgeoisie to act collectively.[25] Capitalists outside such preferential networks invested in the most available and inflation-protected asset around: real estate and construction. Again, however, this process was facilitated by the state, as urban land was freed up for use by the government and housing loans with low fixed interest rates were easily procurable. As the economist Kamal Athari noted, the housing sector has always been the backbone of private sector development in Iran. From 1980 to 1986, even as war and political uncertainty disrupted other economic sectors, there was a housing boom in urban areas.[26]

The limits of liberalization

Once the war ended in 1988, a "third way" political faction coalesced under President Hashemi Rafsanjani (1989–97) which identified itself as pragmatists or "constructionists". It was this faction that first broached the issue of SOE privatization in the public sphere. Politically, Rafsanjani saw himself as an updated version of the modernizing nineteenth century Qajar bureaucrat Amir Kabir, whose biography he had written as a young cleric in the 1960s. The technocrats Rafsanjani brought into his government publicly ridiculed the lack of scientific knowledge and economic expertise visible during the war years. Masoud Nili, an economist at the PBO during the late 1980s and a main author of the First Five Year Plan (1989/90–1993/4), boasted that during this period Islamic leftists and radicals believed in a dirigiste economy, Islamic conservatives believed in a "traditional" market economy (commerce and trade through mercantile networks with a night-watchman state), while a new self-described "expert" faction under Rafsanjani recognized that a "modern" and competitive market economy was the correct path for the country.[27] Technocratic expertise was to supplant revolutionary fervour.

Rafsanjani's First Five-Year Plan aimed to reduce state control in the economy, marketize the distribution of consumer goods, borrow capital on international financial markets, and reform the country's multi-tiered currency exchange rates. It was bitterly attacked by the radicals—solidly entrenched in Parliament in the late 1980s with Mehdi Karroubi as Speaker—in print media such as *Salam* and *Bayan*. They accused the government of capitulating to Western capitalism, favouring industry over agriculture, and relying on foreign debt. Stung by his critics, Rafsanjani repudiated the claims, asserting that his plan was for a "mixed, Islamic economy".[28] Yet, in response, Rafsanjani and his aides strategically allied with conservatives in the Guardian Council to disqualify members of the radical faction from running for the 1992 parliamentary elections. The Khomeinist "left" was effectively purged from the political field, and Rafsanjani was compared to Gorbachev and de Klerk in the international media. However, while GDP and consumption jumped upwards from 1989 to 1992, Iran's *perestroika* was short-lived. Owing to an oil price collapse in 1993–94, a balance of payments crisis ensued. Given that the Iranian Central Bank's international borrowing capacity was severely limited—partly by US strictures on the IMF and World Bank—short-term foreign loans recently acquired could not be rolled over. As had happened in the 1980s, the Central Bank resorted to currency creation to make up for arrears. Unemployment and inflation soon reached untenable levels, triggering austerity riots in major Iranian cities. Rafsanjani reluctantly backed off his reforms.

The political infighting of the early 1990s affected the SOE privatization process. Out of 770 public companies, the government identified 391 that it assessed could be privatized according to the terms of Article 44 of the Constitution. Thousands of mines and quarries were also readied for auction. Officially, the Rafsanjani administration invited both domestic and diaspora Iranian capital to take part. Informally, many SOEs that were offered for sale to the private sector were well known to be loss-making, which decreased the interest of skittish investors who preferred to plough their capital back into the lucrative construction sector. In practice, SOE sales became protracted, and mostly occurred through direct negotiations with interested buyers instead of public auctions. As privatization proceeded, critics in both left and right factions claimed it was riddled with corruption, in effect handing over the state to a new and undeserving *aghazadeh*—the "sons of the elite". In 1994, Parliament, controlled by the conservative faction, prohibited government sale of SOEs through negotiated transfers. Instead, transaction houses were created to preferentially sell companies' shares to large foundations (*bonyad*) whose beneficiaries included war veterans, families of martyrs, *basij* members, and other "devotees" of the revolution.[29] The measure blocked the transfer of SOEs to private hands and established an early precedent of "pseudo-privatization" to these and other parastatal entities.[30] By one calculation, of the 331 companies that were fully or partially transferred in the name of privatization during 1989–94, half of the shares went to parastatal organizations.[31] The remaining SOEs were told to become self-sufficient in their operation costs, but hard budgets were rarely enforced by the state, because of these companies' social function as large employers and easy access to preferential foreign exchange rates.

As the Rafsanjani administration grappled with the conservative-controlled fourth Parliament (1992–96), radicals such as Khoiniha, Mousavi and Karroubi slowly moderated their views and declared themselves as "reformist" politicians. The conversion of most of the Khomeinist left to political liberalism is given much attention by scholars, but their gradual acceptance of economic liberalism is less noticed. Reformist elites and their intelligentsia—indeed, many of these politicians considered themselves intellectuals, and vice versa—publicly rethought their precepts of the revolution. But this explicit challenge to earlier dogma occurred mainly in the realm of politics, while economics was discussed with technocratic, apolitical jargon. Stressing concepts of civil society and a de-ideologization of the public sphere, the reformist movement found a popular champion in Mohammad Khatami, who seemed to promise an Islamic Republic with a human face. By the late 1990s, as post-war sociocultural openings intertwined with a more educated and younger population, the symbol of Khatami generated more excitement than the relatively unknown politician himself. Just before the 1997 elections, amidst fears of poll rigging, Rafsanjani publicly declared that the vote should be honest, signalling that he had sympathies with the new reformist faction and freeing the path for Khatami's landslide victory. Reformists subsequently accepted Rafsanjani's project of economic modernization but reversed Rafsanjani's technocratic top-down approach, arguing that it could only come to pass once political modernization had begun. This factional alliance was a practical marriage of convenience, however, rather than a necessary outcome of Iran's post-revolutionary trajectory.

In part, the reformist shift in economic orientation was not clearly observed because Khatami, who had been Iran's Minister of Culture from 1982 to 1992, did not offer much of an economic plan during his 1997 presidential campaign. Once elected, he proposed an Economic Reorganization Plan in 1998, and then the Third Five-Year Development Plan (2000–05), with the key economic sections penned by former Rafsanjani men. While also emphasizing the goal of a universal social welfare system, these plans continued earlier efforts at economic liberalization. As Masoud Nili recalled in 2002, "the [plan] managers that had statist economic orientations [in the 1980s] are today implementing plans oriented towards a modern competitive economy and support of the private sector".[32] The Khomeinist left had shifted towards economic liberalism, while Rafsanjani's economic liberals began supporting political reforms. The most significant economic success achieved in Khatami's administration, after years of foot-dragging from the conservative-controlled Guardian Council, was the 2002 unification of tiered exchange rates and a floating peg of the Iranian rial to the dollar. Yet economists close to Rafsanjani had first suggested this reform in the late 1980s—an indication of how slowly the state machinery of the Islamic Republic operated when it came to pushes for economic liberalization.

Private sector growth without privatization

In the late 1990s, a curious process began which the economist and former MP Ahmad Meydari called "private sector growth without privatization". As discussed above, private capital never fully disappeared in post-revolutionary Iran. Some Pahlavi-era industrialists and merchants, looking for new opportunities, returned a portion of their capital back to the country. Others, such as middle-level bureaucrats and provincial figures, amassed small fortunes during the 1980s via land grabs in an unsettled legal environment.[33] Beginning in the early 1990s, Gholamhossein Karbaschi, mayor of Tehran (1989–98), encouraged speculative capital to further move into housing and commercial construction projects, extracting "fees and taxes from merchants and developers in exchange for exemption from zoning laws and protection from political pressure". As a consequence of this Iranian "growth machine", $6 billion was collected by the municipality, three quarters of which came from the sale of residential permits that violated zoning codes. Private investment in the city's construction sector from 1987 to 1997 increased by a factor of fifteen, funding urban renewal, thus, Tehran's high-rise skyline and ringed highways took the shape recognized today.[34]

Private capital soon found another outlet. Facing a staunchly conservative Guardian Council which eagerly vetoed any reform too far-reaching, Khatami's administration was well aware of the political limitations to privatization, Rafsanjani-style. As an alternative, the government began to grant private licenses where justifiable under Article 44's wording. As announced in the Third Five-Year Plan, public sectors would be opened up to competition by licensing new entrants into the market except where "the government has a natural monopoly". First issued in banking and insurance, licenses were later extended to the subsidiary oil sector, power plant, construction, airlines, telecommunications, and postal sectors. As a result, new enterprises flowered in sectors formerly dominated by quasi-monopolies. For example, in the 1990s, only a few SOEs produced all industrial dairy products in Iran, but by the late 2000s, over twenty private companies were active in the field along with the original SOEs.[35] Instead of transferring public monopolies to private hands, Khatami's government allowed the private sector to compete with public and parastatal firms for market share. In fields such as banking, this competition generated consumer-friendly innovations like electronic accounts, internet banking, and ATMs, all of which state banks eventually adopted.

Banking exemplified Iran's rising private sector during this period. Three of Tehran's housing construction magnates formed the Housing Credit Institution in 1999, authorized to provide housing and vehicle loans only. To lure in middle class household savings, it paid higher interest than state banks, advertising with the slogan "two percent more". A former Tehran stock market manager, a Central Bank official, and several Pahlavi-era textile and plastics industrialists founded the

Saman Credit Institution in 1999 with start-up capital of 1.1 billion tomans. In 2001, it became Saman Bank with a capital stock of twenty billion tomans. By the late 2000s, Saman was valued at 300 billion tomans ($300 million), with large public pension funds in the steel and copper sectors as major shareholders.[36] One of Saman's founders stated that two changes made their growth possible: consumer credit for goods such as vehicles, appliances, computers, etc., and innovations in electronic banking services. A former industrialist with good relations with the Ministry of Industry founded Karafarin Bank, whose other investors included top members of SOE conglomerates. Parsian Bank, whose advert campaigns lavishly recalled ancient Persepolis friezes, grew out of the investment arm of the vehicle SOE Iran Khodro. Parsian soon became the country's third largest bank and the largest listed on the Tehran stock exchange. As a final example, the major shareholders of Eqtesad-e Novin Bank, advertising itself as "Iran's first private bank", originated in light industry and construction.[37]

By 2009, with only 4.7% of nationwide bank branches, Iran's private banks held 34% of the country's total long-term deposits and 25% of the short-term deposits.[38] As the stories of these banks illustrated, private sector growth without privatization during the Khatami era did not arise from a vacuum. Instead, a particular form of capitalist development, where private entities coexisted with public ones, emerged out of organizational networks linked to previous state-building efforts in the industrial sector as well as networks of diaspora and domestic capital. This would not have been possible if the private sector had been completely wiped out after the revolution. Furthermore, just as nationalization during the war years was a mostly *ad hoc* response to political exigencies and elite factional competition, so too did this new growth in the private sector emerge out of a makeshift solution to constraints brought about by intra-elite political strife during the 1990s.

Khatami's administration attempted to push ahead on SOE privatization without breaching Article 44. Already by 1999, a government commission indicated that only 128 out of 724 firms needed to remain state-owned; in addition, more than 1,000 parastatal companies should be privatized, including those controlled by foundations and related institutions.[39] But the Guardian Council loudly attacked Khatami's plan as antithetical to Article 44's nationalist spirit, partly echoing (without crediting them) the former radicals' earlier critique of Rafsanjani's liberalization agenda.[40] The stalemate was sent to the Expediency Council, a body formed in the late 1980s to adjudicate conflicts between the Parliament and the Guardian Council, and chaired by Rafsanjani himself. In 2004, it released a new and binding interpretation of Article 44 that clearly supported the Khatami administration.[41] The ruling disallowed further protest by the Guardian Council, and amended Article 44 to oblige the government to divest from majority control in heavy industry, downstream oil and gas refineries, mining, power generation, banking, aviation, shipping, insurance, infrastructure, and telecommunications. By then, however, Khatami's second term was nearing its end, and conservative intransigence in other state branches limited implementation of his administration's privatization goals.

Though it is mentioned far less than the shifting debate over democratic pluralism in an Islamic Republic, much of Iran's political elite also underwent an ideological transformation during the 1990s on economic matters. Yet the shift in thought was not unique. As in other middle-income countries in the 1980s and 1990s, privatizing the assets of an ossified, semi-authoritarian state was perceived in Iran as a radical position. It was not surprising, then, that most of the left-leaning Khomeinist elites found themselves, twenty years after the 1979 revolution, extolling the state-tempering properties of market discipline. Only one faction remained outside the consensus on privatization: the conservatives. While during the 1980s they took a relatively laissez-faire position on private ownership, conservatives had never presented private sector growth as the main pathway for developmental success. Furthermore, conservatives stood to lose if SOE privatization reordered the elite and brought in newcomers as potential challengers. They were unwilling to cede the commanding heights of the Iranian economy in an uncertain political climate where new and unknown owners were feared. As Mohammad-Reza Bahonar, a high ranking conservative member of Parliament, bluntly stated, "Article 44 of the Constitution was the place for the disputes between left and right groups within the country's political system that had began during the government of the Sacred Defense [The Iran-Iraq War] and continued for twenty years".[42] After the election of Mahmoud Ahmadinejad, however, the conservatives' stance on the issue shifted significantly.

Parastatal growth through pseudo-privatization

As neither a septuagenarian nor a member of the clergy, Ahmadinejad was not your average Iranian conservative. With a campaign platform of pious competence, his image as an educated, technocratic engineer was strategically cultivated to resonate with Iranians tired of the seemingly useless state apparatus of the Islamic Republic.[43] To his advantage was the presence of an apathetic Brezhnevian air surrounding the reformist movement, which had descended into infighting once conservative obstruction stalled Khatami's sociopolitical agenda. Ahmadinejad's allies deftly took advantage of the stalemate between reformists and the old conservative faction, calling themselves first "developers" and then also "principle-ists". The latter term signified they were the only true adherents to revolutionary principles diluted during the 1990s. Campaign slogans cleverly injected symbols of Iranian nationalism into the visage of a proletarian cum statesman. Ahmadinejad and his circle countered the reformists' faded discourse of civil society and political pluralism with a rehashed critique of perceived corruption on the part of Rafsanjani—who was running for president yet again—and a vague promise of income redistribution to the mass of the population. Old guard conservatives looked on warily. Yet they also envied Ahmadinejad's plebiscitary success, and so hitched their wagon to his rising political clout.

After the second round electoral victory against Rafsanjani in 2005, President Ahmadinejad did what most good politicians do: steal the opponents' ideas. SOE privatization was to move forward, he announced, but with the benefits brought to the people via a programme entitled "Justice Shares". This plan sounded oddly similar to the 2005 presidential campaign manifesto of Rafsanjani, which proposed that every Iranian family would receive stock shares of divested companies. Private sector boosters—including the Iranian Chamber of Commerce, Industry and Mines as well as the Tehran Stock Exchange—had imagined that "popular" share divestment would dilute and diversify stock ownership, thereby increasing the demand for further privatization.[44] The Supreme Jurist Ali Khamenei's intervention and public support on the privatization issue, in his May 2005 announcement and a July 2006 executive order, provided a legitimating push against conservative holdouts. With the Leader's blessing, no one could claim that privatization belonged solely to a reformist agenda. Ahmadinejad, however, soon put his own spin on the plan after his 2005 victory. The revision of Article 44 on President Khatami's watch mandated the state to divest majority ownership to all non-governmental sectors, defined as "private, cooperative and non-government public sectors". The latter category, often called "NGOs" in Iran, is the legal definition of most of the parastatal sector, and includes public pension funds, military contractors, and foundations.

Ahmadinejad followed the article's new language to the letter. The Justice Shares programme created a system of provincial committees that oversaw the formation and administration of investment cooperatives for these shares. By using cooperatives, another institutional layer was added between private and public sectors. Originally, it was announced that the lowest two income deciles of the population—about thirteen to fourteen million people—would be given Justice Shares, at half the share's face value, payable over ten years. The third to sixth income deciles would be allowed to purchase Justice Shares over ten years at full price. Justice Share dividend payments would allow individuals to eventually pay back their share ownership costs. Investment cooperatives could exercise their new power as minority shareholders in divested companies, but government bodies were barred from appointing new company and cooperative managers. During implementation of the programme, however, various status groups received shares in addition to income clusters: low income villagers and nomads (17 million were given shares), public sector retirees (13 million), beneficiaries of the Imam Khomeini Relief Committee and other welfare organizations (8.5 million), families with martyr status (1.3 million), seminary students and clergy (178,000), and, curiously, over 15,000 journalists. Other eligible groups are carpet weavers, Qur'anic scholars, young addicts in treatment, construction workers without labour contracts, and bus and taxi drivers.

These status groups were not chosen randomly. They represent already existing categories of beneficiaries within the fragmented yet broad Iranian welfare system that developed after the 1979 revolution.[45] By 2009, the government stated that forty-one million people—roughly half of the population—had applied for income or status eligibility and received Justice Shares. The Central Board of Justice Shares Distribution includes the President and several key ministers, but also the head of the Martyrs and Veterans Foundation (a welfare *bonyad*), the Commander of *basij* forces, and the head of the Imam Khomeini Relief Committee.

In other words, agents of the parastatal sector, not the private sector, were placed in charge of the Justice Share Programme.[46] As discussed below, although the effects of this programme are still unclear, the fusion of privatization discourse with these "revolutionary" status groups suggests that conservative political entrepreneurs in the Islamic Republic not only have come around to the reformists' economic position, but also are utilizing such a discourse to reshape the political landscape and legitimate their own rule.

Tactically, Ahmadinejad's push for privatization from 2006 onwards allowed his administration to brand its efforts as "performance execution" of the sort earlier administrations failed to enact. Privatization was hardly a secret; rather, it formed a strategic component of the President's public relations campaign against his critics. In late 2009, the Iranian Privatization Organization (IPO) head Gholamreza Haydari Kord-Zanganeh announced that the government had divested 800,000 billion rials (around US$80 billion) and more than 370 companies. Kord-Zanganeh claimed the state's contribution to GDP over the previous four years had accordingly shrunk from 60% to nearly 40%.[47] This huge divestment, far larger (in real terms) than the amounts divested in the Rafsanjani and Khatami administrations combined, took three main forms. First, SOEs were sold through the Tehran Stock Market, public auction, or negotiation. Private sector firms, including private banks and investment companies, as well as the "NGO" parastatal sector, have been active in this type of SOE privatization. Second, SOE shares were transferred out of the public sector under the category of Justice Shares, which placed those assets in the cooperative sector. Third, owing to the 2006 changes in Article 44, government debt owed to parastatal pension funds and other "non-governmental" organizations could be settled, in lieu of cash payments, via direct cash-to-equity divestment of SOE ownership to these NGOs.

During previous administrations, SOE divestment had generated its share of notorious scandals. In the late 1990s, for instance, an upstream management company named Petropars was created to act as the main supervisor for subcontractors in Iran's natural gas sector. Registered in England, Petropars was majority-owned by the National Iranian Oil Company's pension fund. Conservatives in the Parliament accused President Khatami's Oil Minister, Bizhan Namdar Zanganeh, of favouritism and covert deals, especially with Behzad Nabavi, by then an outspoken reformist parliamentarian who also held a position in Petropars. Nabavi eventually resigned the post amidst factional wrangling, but technocrats defended the overall privatization process.[48]

Yet in 2009, amidst post-election street demonstrations and international media attention, far larger SOE divestment scandals made the front pages of Iran's newspapers. Tehran's spacious International Exhibition Center, where the popular Annual Book Fair is held, was transferred in July to the Armed Forces Social Security Organization as payment for government debt owed. In September, 51% of the Telecommunications Company of Iran (TCI) was sold to a conglomerate linked to the IRGC Cooperative Foundation, a large investment company and service contractor. The conglomerate, Etemad-e Mobin, denied that the IRGC's military command would have any role in managing the newly privatized TCI. Yet the opaque auction of over US$8 billion in shares had been limited to two bidders, with the other reportedly linked to a *basij* investment cooperative.[49] In essence, two military parastatals were competing against each other for a major share in the lucrative domestic telecom market. Of course, all of these transfers, whether debt cancellations or block share sales, are included in the IPO's definition of privatization. When criticized by members of the Parliament who were IRGC veterans themselves, the IPO head Kord-Zanganeh and others pointed out that pension funds invest in similar types of holdings in countries around the world, and are legally allowed to do so in Iran under Article 44.[50]

In July 2009 one of these parliamentarians, Hamid Reza Fuladgar, head of a special commission on privatization, candidly spoke to *Etemad* newspaper. When asked about the possibility of SOEs crowding out private sector investment, he stated:

> This is not the only problem. There are many quasi-governmental companies: companies the banks created, the Social Security Investment Company (SHASTA), investment companies formed by Ministries, retirement funds … all of these have assigned duties. Of course, the officials in these organizations say they are working within the law. And they are right—these companies are established according to the commerce law but they now stand as a barrier against the private sector. Article 44's aim is not only to transfer companies. … Shares are only being shifted, and it is not happening in the private sector and new investment is not taking place. *The capital that is circulating is the government's itself.* Was it not our goal to add new capital to the country's production sector? Was not this the [new] vision for Article 44?[51]

Fuladgar is no reformist. The Isfahan-based Parliament member and former Construction Jihad member is allied with elite politicians such as Tehran mayor Mohammad-Baqir Qalibaf and the Speaker of the Parliament, Ali Larijani, both former IRGC members. *Alef*, a news website published by the conservative parliamentarian and former Labour Minister Ahmad Tavakoli, protested in similar terms: "The honourable government has limited the implementation of the general policies of Article 44 and related laws to the transfer of large government corporations to semi-governmental institutions … [therefore] it is difficult to find a company in the private sector that can expand in a logical way based on its work, innovation, and entrepreneurship".[52] These criticisms are notable in light of the widespread assumption by many Iran scholars and Western-based journalists that the IRGC has been "taking over" the Iranian economy.[53] On the contrary, rather than quietly fostering centralization of economic activities under IRGC control, important members of the conservative political elite who shared the IRGC's worldview were vociferously attacking the pseudo-privatization process in which IRGC-spawned contractors and public sector pension funds were participating. Full divestment, not centralization, was their demand.

Criticisms from within the political elite mounted. In November 2009, the Parliament Research Centre—headed by Ahmad Tavakoli—issued the report *Transition from the State to the Pseudo-State Economy*. The report calculated that 264 SOEs valued at US$54 billion had been divested between 2004 and 2009. Of this total, 68.5% went to Justice Shares, 12.5% to debt cancellations, and only 19% was sold or negotiated through the stock market. Yet even SOEs sold on the stock market did not all go to the private sector. From 2007 to 2009, eighty-two firms sold on the TSE, worth $3.7 billion, went to the "NGO" sector. Two NGOs, the Social Security Investment Company (SHASTA) and Iranian Mehr Eqtesad, obtained 46% of these shares. Other major NGOs that acquired SOE assets were IRI Shipping Lines and several public industrial joint-stock companies.[54]

Fuladgar's special parliamentary commission released four short reports on privatization. These stated that $70 billion in over 300 companies had been transferred since Ahmadinejad's first term, including shares in the vehicle manufacturers Iran Khodro and Saipa, Saderat and Tejarat Banks, Asia Insurance, and the aforementioned TCI. After deducting Justice Shares, debt cancellations, and transfers to parastatal or non-governmental organizations and cooperatives, only 13.5% was sold to the private sector.[55] Critics argued that SOEs underwent "a kind of relocation", but not to the private sector.[56] In sum, conservative elites who had long stymied earlier administrations' attempts at SOE privatization were forcefully attacking the Ahmadinejad government for not privatizing the public sector far enough.

This intra-elite struggle over the structure of the economy in Iran is difficult to understand if we assume a priori that the elite operates as a military junta or centralized praetorian ruling apparatus. Instead, the post-revolutionary dynamics of elite conflict need to be embedded in the broader processes of state formation that reshaped the elites themselves. Iran's political field narrowed considerably between 2003 and 2009, as reformist politicians in parliamentary and presidential elections were disqualified, harassed, and sidelined. Concurrently, state ministries underwent a major bureaucratic reshuffling, as older government staff retired and new loyal cadres rose up the ranks. As Mehrzad Boroujerdi has shown, these new individuals were predominantly not clerics. Instead, they were educated in technical fields that had sprung up within domestic higher education organizations founded to populate revolutionary institutions with trustworthy staff. Most of them have engineering backgrounds, possessing forms of cultural capital different than those gained in seminary training. Few of these individuals were active before the revolution. Instead, they rose up through the bureaucracies, akin to the "Red Engineers" of post-revolutionary Russia or China.[57] As with the first generation of post-1979 cadres, who used new revolutionary credentials to overthrow hardened networks of local elites left over from the Pahlavi era, this second "new class" also came from the provincial peripheries of Iran, not the seat of power in Tehran. They are indebted to the state for social prestige garnered in participation both in the 1980s Iran-Iraq war and in post-war administration of provincial bureaucracies in the 1990s.[58]

Ahmadinejad himself governed a northern province before he became Tehran's mayor in 2003. He and his close aides emerged from peripheral circumstances, but were able to transform bureaucratic loyalty into a usable set of credentials. Reformists, older conservatives, and Iranian urbanites may lampoon these credentials—educational as well as cultural—as sub-par, but they are not useless. Men with provincial biographies, stationed outside Tehran for years, now populate the IRGC's top ranks. This enables the many sub-contracting companies today staffed with retired IRGC personnel in the private sector, for example, to adeptly navigate the provincial waters teeming with homegrown urban elites. Older conservatives fear ceding any more political ground to this "new class" of people who can convert their local knowledge and stored accumulation of favours into economic capital. Mimicking the reformists, these now self-described "moderate" conservatives hoped that "real" SOE privatization could empower countervailing forces outside of the state's rising cadres.

Ahmadinejad loyalists, however, do not dominate the IRGC, *basij*, and other high-prestige bureaucratic organizations. Instead, this "new class" has mostly internalized and reproduced the self-dividing tendencies of the first post-revolutionary generation, albeit with one key difference. In the first decades of the Islamic Republic, prestige and status could best be garnered by manoeuvring within the state. Once the entire political elite fell behind an ideological consensus of shrinking the state through privatization, a host of new opportunities opened up. So far, this chapter has mostly focused on the elite level, but the contours of this pseudo-privatization process have been shaped by significant non-elite actors within Iranian society: pensioners, the "deserving" poor, military cadres and retirees, civil service workers and bureaucrats, villagers, and occupational categories. These overlooked status groups all laid claim to a complex and entrenched post-revolutionary social compact, one that the state could not easily jettison. Pseudo-privatization was not simply a top-down elite-driven project, but rather a process that had also been structured by claims from below that were borne out of the country's post-revolutionary formation of a new and broader welfare system. In any country, welfare and social policies do not simply reflect pre-existing social cleavages such as class, but also create templates for "values, attitudes, and interests among citizens in ways that are of relevance for patterns of collective action". These templates can emphasize certain lines of cleavage while "downplaying others".[59] In the Islamic Republic, intra-elite conflict prevented the state from extracting itself out of many sets of social linkages which state organizations had not only fostered, but relied upon during the post-revolutionary decades in order to generate basic capacities for governance. As the state subcontracted out a wider degree of its social welfare and economic functions, pseudo-privatization became the method of least resistance.

A hundred parastatals bloom

Rather than a single connected entity, Iran's parastatal sector contains numerous organizations which do not make up a single distributional coalition. Tension and conflict of interests is the norm. The reason is that the post-revolutionary state has been embedded in a diverse set of non-elite status groups and social actors at different historical junctures. This intertwining of state and society occurred not only because of intra-elite conflict that forced political factions to cultivate strong social bases, but also because of revolutionary mobilization and recurring contention from below, institutions of war mobilization and their organizational legacies, and nationalist projects of economic development amidst geo-political isolation. In this section of the chapter, I discuss how pseudo-privatization responded to and enlarged particular constituencies via three different pathways: the Social Security Organization's (SSO) investment company SHASTA, the Justice Shares Programme, and the IRGC's economic contracting activities.

Pension Funds

SHASTA is one of the largest pension fund investment companies in the country and a major recipient of divested SOE shares. Iran's main social insurance funds cover health insurance as well as pensions, varying from occupational funds where employees contribute a share of monthly premiums to funds for low-income households and special status or occupational categories where the state fully pays enrolment and coverage costs. In Table 1, these large funds and their estimated coverage levels are compiled.

The table's reported coverage levels are undoubtedly misleading, since households can be enrolled in multiple funds. Other households remain inadequately covered owing to the incomplete implementation of universal insurance. Estimates of the uninsured in Iran range between five and nine per cent of the population.[60] Nevertheless, as the table shows, two organizations are responsible for the vast majority of health insurance coverage. The Medical Service Insurance Organization (MSIO) operates under the supervision of the Ministry of Health and Medical Education, while the Social Security Organization (SSO) is under the Ministry of Cooperatives, Labour, and Social Welfare. The SSO's beneficiaries are mostly located in the formal labour force—that is, middle and working class occupations in the public and private sectors with formalized wage and benefit contracts. SHASTA, as the SSO's investment arm, is mandated with expanding and maintaining the asset pools that pay for health and pension costs of these beneficiaries. SHASTA is also, however, designated by the government as part of the NGO sector.

Table 1: Main health insurance funds and coverage in Iran (2008).

Fund name	*Estimated percent of population covered*
Social Security Organization (SSO)	38.50
Medical Service Insurance Organization (MSIO)[a]	50.49
Army Medical Insurance Organization	6.22
Imam Khomeini Relief Committee (IKRC)[b]	2.77
Other funds[c]	0.69

Source: Ibrahimipour et al, 2011: 486.

Notes: a. Oversees funds for civil servants, rural households and smaller funds for particular occupational/status categories such as university and seminary students; b. Foundation which covers eligible low-income households and other status groups defined as vulnerable; c. Specialized public insurance funds for banking, oil, petrochemical, electricity, municipal, airlines, TV and radio, auto, rail, and steel sectors.

Like pension funds worldwide over recent decades, SHASTA has shifted its activities into what Robin Blackburn has labelled "grey capitalism".[61] Pension fund assets—accumulated to support workers as they "grey" into retirement—are being increasingly invested in riskier, more volatile, and insecure "grey" financial assets that promise higher returns but conversely can be wiped out by economic crises. Before the 1979 revolution, the SSO held workers' pension contributions mostly in fixed long-term deposits. In 1989, nearly 80% of SSO's investment portfolio still remained in these low-risk deposits. By 2000, however, this share had decreased to 10%, while 70% of its total portfolio was composed of direct and indirect investments in the Iranian economy. In that same year, SSO-held companies produced 43% of the pharmaceutical and hygienic products, 36% of the cement, 35% of the televisions, 25% of the fireproof products, 31% of the refrigerators and freezers, and 35% of the rubber in Iran.[62] In 2012, after a further decade of expansion,

SSO's investments in the economy amounted to over US$15 billion (about 3.5% of GDP) in over 150 companies.[63]

In 2003, the World Bank criticised that Iran's pension benefits, by comparison with both European and other Middle Eastern countries, were overly generous. Fiscal pressure pushed the SSO to become more active in the acquisition of SOEs, both on the Tehran Stock Market and in negotiations over government debts to the fund. In 2001, for example, the government transferred assets worth $400 million to the SSO to cover constitutionally mandated obligations to pensioners. The SSO also purchased government bond issues and financed public infrastructure projects.[64] As of January 2010, the SSO head Ali Zabihi stated that over 27.5 million Iranians lived in SSO-enrolled households and warned that, even with high returns on these investments, future commitments to pensioners would surpass incoming revenues.[65] These fiscal pressures have been exacerbated. In 2011, SSO officials claimed the fund was owed nearly $24 billion by the government.[66]

Yet Iran's pension fund financialization shares characteristics with global trends. In the Chilean model of privatized Pension Fund Associations, the pension system for formal sector workers is utilized as a method of SOE privatization. In South Korea's National Pension Scheme, public pensions invest in both public sector bonds and financial sector assets.[67] The Turkish Army's pension fund invests in over sixty Turkish firms, and Saudi Arabia's General Social Insurance Fund holds stakes in the country's growing industrial sector.[68] The United States contains the largest low-risk bond-holding pension fund in the world (OASDI, known as Social Security) as well as California's public employees' retirement system (CalPERS), which invests two-thirds of its assets in global equities. As Blackburn writes, "those who dislike and distrust pension-fund capitalism must reckon with the fact that it is already hugely important and likely to become more so". De-scrambling the private-public mix of retirement funds, if even possible, would "scarcely be supported by those who hold funded pension entitlements".[69]

Given these types of institutional investors in wealthier countries, SSO officials defend the presence of pension funds in the market. Iran's current and—because of starkly reduced birth rates during the 1990s—final "baby boom" generation of working adults will never be subsequently replaced in full. Pensioners will hardly accept a selloff of SHASTA's investment portfolio to the private sector without major guarantees by the state on future entitlements. Pension financialization in the Islamic Republic has therefore created a sizeable interest group for pseudo-privatization—the Iranian middle class and the formal labour force. Funnelling public sector companies to the SSO and other pension funds is one method of outsourcing the state's direct welfare obligations. As with "grey capitalism" more generally, however, this strategy precariously rests on contradictory pressures of generating high profits against maintaining employment and wages in these very companies.[70]

Justice Shares

If SHASTA is pension fund capitalism for Iran's middle strata, could the new Justice Shares programme operate as "popular capitalism" for poorer classes? The reformist newspaper *Etemad* claimed, "Justice Shares are shares without profit", and conservative MPs alleged that payouts to nine million shareholders on the eve of the 2009 presidential elections were an illegal form of electioneering by Ahmadinejad.[71] Government supporters, however, assert that companies owned by Justice Share cooperatives are mostly profitable, and share values have substantially risen over the past several years. The Finance Minister Shams al-Din Husayni stated that buyers of privatized SOEs must agree to contracts whereby the firms maintain medium-term employment levels, and even claimed that his ministry's investigation of twenty-eight such firms showed that nearly all had increased employment levels.[72] Another inquiry showed, however, that in eight divested SOEs, profits that previously had been reinvested or sent to the treasury were mostly paid out as Justice Share dividends.[73] Parliament's reports on Article 44 also indicated numerous violations: companies divested without parliamentary approval, loss-making companies divested without attention to existing debts, and no accounting for the sources of share dividend profits.[74]

In other words, Justice Share-divested companies are torn between fiscal profitability and social obligations. Within sectors where reinvestment is crucial, this could lead to bankruptcy or collapse. Provincial Justice Share cooperatives could eventually act as trading entities on the stock market, adding powerful institutional investors to a diverse mix that may rationalize domestic industries towards more profitable activities.[75] This would also empower provincial elites in these cooperatives, generating new networks of influence linked to the heterogeneous "revolutionary" status groups and other households that possess these shares on paper. The outcome of this type of financialization is unpredictable. A common critique of Iran's Justice Shares programme harkens back to Russia's 1990s privatization voucher programme. Now seen by many Russians as a Ponzi scheme which led to the emergence of an oligarchic industrial class, Russia's version of "popular capitalism" allowed vouchers to be freely traded upon receipt. As journalist David Hoffman wrote, "millions were immediately exchanged for a bottle of vodka or sold for a song".[76] In post-Communist Hungary, as Michael Burawoy and János Lukács identified, popular reaction and protest against obvious illegalities in privatization of state property resulted in "bringing the state back in" to slow down the process.[77] Currently, Iran's Justice Shares cannot be sold by the original recipients, but a Russia-style scenario is not unthinkable in the future. The former director of the stock market, Allahverdi Rajai-Salmasi, now a managing director of Saman Bank, argued that individual selling and buying of Justice Shares would increase liquidity in Iran's capital market and create a "culture of investment".[78] If shares do become tradeable, via cooperatives or individuals, new market actors could quickly take over SOEs, whether in the private or the parastatal sector. The experience of Russia, though, where state linkages were never absent from the new capitalist oligarchy, illustrates that even privatization fully designed to shift assets to a "real" private sector can end up leading to a form of pseudo-privatization.

Parastatal subcontractors

Cooperatives, firms, and investment conglomerates affiliated with the IRGC and parastatal bodies do not signify a creeping militarization or "revolutionary" ideological subordination of Iran's economy so much as the commodification of bureaucratic privilege and status held by individuals in these organizations. The large engineering arm of the IRGC, Khatam al-Anbiya, has been awarded major infrastructural projects over the past decade, funded by the Ahmadinejad government. While this organization—analogous to the US Army Corps of Engineers—had been active during the Iran-Iraq war, use of military engineering contracts for infrastructural development stems from President Rafsanjani's decision to involve the IRGC in post-war reconstruction efforts. This was done partly to keep hundreds of thousands of IRGC cadres employed, and partly because a new generation of engineers and managers had been trained with useful skills. As Rafsanjani stated in May 1993, "in this way [the IRGC] earn an income, which they can use to maintain and repair their [military] machinery, while they are adding to the country's capacity for contractual work".[79] Yet Khatam al-Anbiya does not perform all these activities by itself; instead, it subcontracts out the work to hundreds of other companies, often in the domestic private sector. Over the past decade, IRGC-linked contracting firms have replaced foreign companies in the development of oil and gas fields, pipeline projects, and highway and tunnel construction. This preference for domestic companies is likely not due to nationalism, but to increased international sanctions against investment in the Iranian economy by foreign firms. After all, Khatam al-Anbiya has no problem with internationally based capital. It previously worked with European companies, as in the construction of the Godar-e Landar dam, and more recently with Chinese, Indian, and Russian firms on gas and oil projects.[80]

Yet as with the 2009 sale of Iran's main telecom company, many of these construction contracts are inked in murky, no-bid deals. The revolving door between contracting executives and government posts adds to suspicions of patronage politics. During Ahmadinejad's tenure, Parviz Fattah went from Minister of Energy to deputy commander of Khatam al-Anbiya and head of the IRGC Cooperative Foundation, while Rostam Qasemi inversely went from the top post in Khatam al-Anbiya to become Minister of Petroleum. This can be seen as either IRGC proficiency in capturing state largesse, or an exercise of technocratic legitimacy amidst a dearth of competitors in management and development; it is likely both. Still, even while IRGC contractors argue that they alone have the necessary economies of scale and accumulated technological experience to carry out thousands of development projects at lower costs than foreign firms brought in by local actors, they also boast how they subcontract out "sixty to seventy percent" of their projects to the "private sector".[81] While this figure seems exaggerated, it is still telling. The overall structure of these parastatal contractors more closely reflects a proliferation of networked layers of influence peddling achieved through the breakup of the public sector, not a transfer of infrastructural power and organizational capacity to the IRGC.

Parastatal subcontractors and military investment cooperatives are increasingly active in the domestic economy, to be sure, but they still end up competing with the economic activities of endowed foundations such as the Foundation of the Oppressed or the Imam Reza Shrine Foundation. These "NGOs" inherited Pahlavi-era industries, lands, and companies, acting as economic agents as well as minor social welfare organizations.[82] The Zam-Zam Soft Drink Company, for example, which belongs to the Foundation of the Oppressed, originated in the confiscation of pre-1979 Coca-Cola factories. Several major hotels in Tehran that formerly belonged to the Hilton Corporation also belong to this Foundation. Yet private sector enterprise still developed in these sectors, including subsidiaries of foreign capital. Pepsi and Coca-Cola soft drinks were eventually licensed for production and sale in Iran, sitting alongside Zam-Zam in corner grocery stores. Such parastatal forms of economic activities are common to middle-income countries under a variety of guises, and they do not necessarily crowd out private capital even though they may be uncompetitive outside a protected domestic market.[83]

Rather than economic centralization, then, the rise of military-linked contractors in Iran increasingly corresponds to the trajectory that Eastern European countries took in the post-Communist era, in which scholars such as Katherine Verdery argued that privatization often produced "new states" alongside the actual state. There, *apparatchiks* and firm managers easily converted themselves into "*entrepratchiks*". The valuation of public sector firms was "shot through with politics", and those who benefited the most were "the former bureaucratic and managerial apparatus of the party-state". These individuals could "create parasitic companies on the side" to syphon off assets, and then leverage political connections for maintaining advantageous economic positions.[84] The parallels with Russia can be observed here, also. Tehran's football team Ekbatan was a second rate club until it was bought by a former IRGC member, Hossein Hedayati, who renamed it after his company, Steel Azin. Hedayati then proceeded to buy up star players from domestic premier clubs as well as from foreign teams in order to make his name in the (even more prestigious than IRGC service) world of Iranian football.[85]

As I have described in this section, a variety of social actors exist within Iran's parastatal sector with opposing as well as overlapping interests regarding the distribution and privatization of state resources. The Islamic Republic remains embedded in these groups for a set of historical reasons—political factionalism, popular mobilization, post-war welfare policies, and projects of nationalist legitimation—that are intertwined with its post-revolutionary state formation. While parastatals may occupy superior positions to take advantage of the state's privatization agenda, the economic sphere is multilayered and multifaceted. 2011's board elections in the Tehran Chamber of Commerce, Industries and Mines, for example, featured surprisingly intense competition within and between both private and parastatal actors. Iran's business classes utilized the pro-private sector discourse of the state to extract concessions and split elite cohesion, exhibiting what Robert Bianchi described in Egypt as "unruly corporatism".[86] One unintended outcome of the past years of pseudo-privatization, therefore, was an emboldening of the private sector to act more definitively as a "class for itself". Especially after the Ahmadinejad administration lifted subsidies on fuel and electricity in 2010, private sector companies in manufacturing and trade have used the Chambers of Commerce as a centre for lobbying the state for protection and access to credit and other forms of capital in order to to lower operating costs. Today, nearly every issue of the main Iranian business daily, *World of Economy*, features a lengthy interview with a private sector representative who sets out a wish-list for economic policy. In other words, three decades after the revolutionary state fractured apart the domestic bourgeoisie, the Iranian private sector is coalescing as a social agent in response to threats from internal competitors as well as, of course, an increasingly hostile business environment outside the country's borders.[87] With seven different candidate lists put forward by Ahmadinejad supporters, mercantile traders, industrial associations, and various parastatal entities, the Tehran Chamber of Commerce election was a microcosm of the decades-long struggle over what form of capitalism will become dominant in the Islamic Republic.

Conclusion: in Iran, capitalism from where?

As Nazih Ayubi argued two decades ago, privatization in Middle Eastern states tended to produce "grey areas" between public and private sectors—spheres of activity separate in Western liberal thought, if not in practice. Ayubi noted it was common to witness "private businesses cream off public resources, and public officials 'parachute' on private companies".[88] Iran's privatization efforts, then, are not unique, but to situate the history outlined above more fruitfully in a broader comparative framework, we can use the three ideal-types that Iván Szelényi and his collaborators created to compare processes of capitalist development within post-Soviet Eastern Europe and socialist East Asia: capitalism from without, above, and below.[89]

In Poland, Hungary and the Czech Republic, a technocratic class within the state allied with reformist intellectuals and strong working classes to overpower pre-existing socialist bureaucracies. Easy access to Western capital and implementation of neoliberal prescriptions resulted in a "capitalism from without", whereby privatization was pursued along relatively Weberian rational-legal lines, and former *apparatchiks* were marginalized from the political means to manipulate the transfer of the public sector. In these countries, neoliberalism formed the "ideological cement" of the alliance between technocrats and dissident political entrepreneurs, but countervailing worker protest restrained new governments from enacting the most radical of anti-statist measures. The result by the late 1990s was a liberal democratic state, a fair amount of economic dynamism, and export-oriented, FDI-based methods of capital accumulation.

In Russia, Ukraine, Romania, and Serbia under Milošević, a patrimonial bureaucracy retained power and used the privileges of its offices and clients to amass private wealth. This is a form of capitalism that relies less on market exchange and more on political exchange (in Schumpeter's sense), resulting in "capitalism from above".[90] Communist officials turned private owners were less likely to pursue entrepreneurial activities than to maintain patrimonial links with their business partners, while Communist ideologies were abandoned in favour of extreme nationalist legitimation of new states. Rapid privatization without the bureaucratic-legal institutional setting for stable ownership rights led to a high degree of "asset stripping" of the SOE sector. The state remained large but its capacity to regulate the transition was almost non-existent. The emerging financial-industrial sector was parasitical in its relationship to the market, with little economic dynamism and few public goods available. The political outcome of capitalism from above was a multiparty authoritarian state with unfree and unfair elections.

In China and Vietnam, a technocratic class gained hegemony over economic policy and allied itself with a sui generis domestic bourgeoisie, but a state bureaucracy retained political power. This "capitalism from below" featured a class of small investors originating or reappearing in new spaces next to and within the interstices of a large state-owned industrial sector, often beginning in agricultural or petty commodity production. The bureaucracy and the technocracy checked each other's excesses towards extreme patrimonial or neoliberal policies, resulting in a hybrid system of capital accumulation and mixed forms of property (such as China's township-village enterprises). The political balance of power allowed space for a high amount of economic dynamism among non-elites, including workers and peasants. Patron-client relations still existed within market operations, but they did not prevent a state-led development which balanced the provision of public goods and infrastructure, technological upgrading of remaining SOEs, and selective utilization of foreign investment. The political outcome was a high capacity state that partially and gradually liberalized its authoritarian structures of governance.

These are, of course, ideal-types. Yet they allow us to frame the above-discussed shifts in Iran's post-revolutionary economic trajectory and to compare it with MENA neighbours. Rafsanjani's technocratic project, later allied with the reformists' dissident liberalism, was an attempt to construct an Iranian capitalism from without. These elite factions saw no problem with letting in foreign capital to help structure and rationalize a process of economic liberalization. This strategy was checked by fragmented state bureaucracies and oppositional elite factions, channelled into parastatal activity, and further curtailed by US-led sanctions from the mid-1990s onwards. This period in Iran stands in contrast to Turkey's AK Party, for instance, whose rise to power in 2002 after a long phase of political factionalism resulted in unprecedented privatization of Turkish SOEs to foreign capital.[91]

The temporary outcome of the stymied reformist project in Iran was, surprisingly, capitalism from below, as entrepreneurs in private sector banking and consumer goods industries spawned a dynamic and competitive market expansion which coexisted with the public sector. This was reinforced because the Iranian bourgeoisie was never fully expropriated after 1979, so that a dormant entrepreneurial habitus could re-emerge in the 1990s once avenues for capital accumulation in goods and services opened up. Of course, most of these entrepreneurs had public connections themselves, but utilized these networks of privilege within the private sector to outcompete public companies through organizational and market innovations. As in Tunisia and Kuwait, this economic pluralism did not, notably, result in a sustained push for democratization. Private capitalists in Iran had little structural power to break the factional deadlock of the political elite at this time, nor did they exhibit much inclination to try.[92]

Iran after 2005, however, most resembles capitalism from above, as wide and dispersed patrimonial networks came to dominate the technocratic agencies. As in the Egyptian state in the 1990s, privatization played an important "accumulative role ... among the acting and former members of the bureaucracy".[93] The result has not been centralization around any one state organization, but parasitic asset-stripping of the public sector on the one hand, and the emergence and expansion of subcontracted "new states" under the guise of parastatal and cooperative entities on the other. On the ideological plane, instead of technocratic neoliberalism, a resurgent nationalism rules the roost. If this process continues, the economic dynamism of these hybrid forms of property ownership, as much as they exist within the parastatal sector itself, will further become exhausted. This will have profound consequences on the subcontracted welfare functions of the parastatal sector unless the state constructs a more universalized welfare system in its place.

In sum, the politics of privatization in Iran, through a variety of agents and a wide array of recipients, was enmeshed within post-1979 internecine struggles among the political elite. Yet mass politics was also forcefully present, since various social classes and status groups formed the constituencies of competing parastatal organizations. This was the critical reason why the state never acquired the sufficient political insulation from below usually needed for technocratic liberalization. Even though all factions came to speak the same language of privatization, the structure and restructuring of political competition prevented the formation of an autonomous state apparatus that could implement such a plan, whether in clerical or military form. On the contrary, the Islamic Republic has neither achieved its privatization dreams nor enhanced its state capacity for other, equally transformational, projects. Yet the recent coalescing of a vocal private sector acting for itself portends that Iranian capitalism may be reshaped once again.

10

THE HOUND THAT DID NOT BARK

SOLVING THE MYSTERY OF BUSINESS WITHOUT VOICE IN EGYPT[1]

Robert Springborg

Since President Sadat's declaration in 1974 of a policy of economic *infitah* (opening), analysts of the Egyptian political economy have chronicled the rise of business influence, with some contending this has culminated in the emergence of a fully fledged business class.[2] During the Sadat era, such investigations focused not only on changes within intra-elite networks, including the emergence of crony capitalists (most notably Osman Ahmad Osman) but also on subjects that implied solidification of business as a self-conscious, collective actor. Evidence of business' growing economic and political power was seen, for example, in the formation and empowerment of organizations of businessmen, such as the Egyptian Businessmen's Association and the Egyptian-American Chamber of Commerce (AmCham), the growing representation of businessmen in the country's Parliament, the privatization of state owned enterprises (SOEs), and the alleged merger of ancien regime, Nasserist, and newly minted business elites into a unified, coherent and even intra-married class actor.[3]

The successor Hosni Mubarak's political economy was commonly depicted as the veritable apotheosis of business interests, legitimated and inspired by the new Washington Consensus of neo-liberalism. While much of the scholarly attention focused on the apex of the business elite,[4] some analysts chose to depict the "Whales of the Nile" not as mere crony capitalists dependent upon one or another of the Mubarak family, but as precursors, at least, of a true capitalist order. The broadening and deepening of capital markets, surging flows of foreign direct investment, further privatization of SOEs, signs of an expanding middle class such as new private primary, secondary and even tertiary educational institutions, and the growing number of Egyptian businessmen, led by the Sawiris family, with significant regional and even global economic interests, were seen as evidence that Egyptian capitalism had matured from its crony infancy.[5] The further influx of businessmen into Parliament, the emergence of an elite, neo-liberal think tank in the form of the Egyptian Centre for Economic Studies (ECES), and clear signs of business influence on public policy—whether over broad economic management, in specific areas such as tax, tariff and anti-monopoly laws, or regarding the establishment of new state institutions, such as the General Authority for Investment—all were read if not as market trumping state, at least as the beginning of more equal competition between them.[6] The World Bank's designation in 2008 and again in 2009 of Egypt as a "top reformer" on its "Ease of Doing Business" index, seemed to validate this view.[7]

The "coup-volution" of 25 January-11 February 2011 and subsequent dramatic events suggest that the relative coherence, power and autonomy of Egypt's business class may have been overstated.[8] The key piece of evidence, as in *Silver Blaze*, where Sherlock Holmes noted the significance of the dog not barking if the alleged murderer passing by it had indeed been a stranger, is that the allegedly powerful business community cum class appears to have collapsed virtually without a peep. The only physical resistance to protesters that has been traced to business actors was the so-called battle of the camels on 2 February, in which thugs on camels and horses, allegedly hired by Murtada Mansur, a Giza businessman, sought unsuccessfully to turn the tide in Tahrir Square. The ruling National Democratic Party (NDP), selected by Gamal Mubarak (younger son of Hosni Mubarak) as the political vehicle on which he would rise to the presidency, hence the organization within which his businessmen cronies were concentrated, collapsed in ignominy as its headquarter building adjacent to the Square went up in flames. Gamal's apparent efforts to induce the NDP to command the Ministry of Interior to unleash yet more force to quell the demonstrations were of no avail.[9]

Indeed, the key dramatis personae in the crucial events of January-February were the military and the Ministry of the Interior, organized Islamists and especially the Muslim Brotherhood, and young political activists networked through social media. Of these three, only the last could possibly be portrayed as being in some ways the product of business investments in socio-political capital. It would be too far a stretch, however, to contend that the "*facebookiyin*" youths in the streets represented or were the product of business interests, despite the key networker Wael Ghoneim's Silicon Valley connections. Moreover, as subsequent events demonstrated, while young, largely secular middle class protesters sparked the broader uprising, they lacked the socially broad, deeply organized support necessary to contend with the enduring elements of the deep state and/or organized Islamists. So, to the extent that business supported modern, secular civil society organization, which was not great even in its Mubarak heyday, its investments paid few immediate benefits, if indeed any over the longer haul. The same can be said of those governmental institutions in which business at least theoretically would have had the greatest interest if it had been actively and effectively seeking to consolidate its power vis-à-vis the state executive. Parliament played no role in the coup-volution and was easily captured by Islamists in the November 2011–January 2012 elections, before having its powers curtailed by *fiat* of the Supreme Council of the Armed Forces (SCAF) and then prorogued by a decision of the Supreme Constitutional Court in June, 2012. The legal-judicial system, including commercial courts whose strengthening had been advocated and supported by business interests, was similarly irrelevant in the uprising.[10] In its wake, when some judges sought to assert more independence, they and their courts were brought to heel or sidestepped by the SCAF, which both expanded the scope of the military's own legal-judicial system and, working with anti-Islamist judges, subordinated the Supreme Constitutional Court to its will.[11]

There is, in sum, little evidence of a business voice in the 2011 uprising, or of residual institutional legacies of the power of business within the state. This suggests that whatever power business exercised under

Sadat and Mubarak was almost exclusively through informal "networks of privilege" rather than being consolidated within state institutions or civil society organizations, or even in a widespread popular consensus on liberalism, whether economic or political.[12] Those "Whales of the Nile" unable to swim away from Egypt now languish in captivity, their former economic empires vulnerable objects of desire of the military, security services, officers of both, and Islamists. Revelations in courts and the media of the greed and excesses of Gamal's cronies discredit not only them, but in the eyes of many if not most Egyptians, business more generally, to say nothing of the creed of neo-liberalism they ostensibly represented.[13] Of the original long list of potential presidential candidates for the May-June 2012 elections, only one was a prominent businessman, with virtually all others being drawn from or connected to the deep state, various strands of the Islamist movement, tame political parties that had been nurtured by the deep state, or, at the very end of the list in terms of appeal, secular revolutionaries and those associated with them. The strength of Naguib Sawiris, the sole business magnate to even contemplate running for the office, was based not on his undisputed business acumen or his extensive support for civil society organizations, but on his appeal to fellow Copts. The same was true of the Reform and Development Party financed by the Christian businessman Rami Lakah.[14] It is not even clear that, had Gamal Mubarak succeeded his father, he and his cronies would have consolidated a business friendly regime. His personal power needs would have dictated preservation of the opaque network through which he generated politically relevant economic resources, as well as alliances with deep state actors. Those requirements in turn would have limited the scope for economic and political liberalization.

How then can we explain that business, assessed by many as having steadily expanded and consolidated its economic and political power over the almost forty years since the commencement of *infitah* in 1974, remained voiceless in the face of what appeared to be a mortal challenge to its interests in 2011? The answer lies neither in a deficiency nor in a surfeit of economic resources, conditions frequently invoked in explanations of Middle Eastern political economies. Egypt's ample hydrocarbon endowment, its strategic location close to key markets, abundant supply of human resources, its productive agriculture, and its easy access to (Arab) capital suggest that resource constraints cannot explain Egypt's economic underperformance or the failure of a dynamic, empowered capitalism to emerge.[15] Equally, while fuel exports accounted for about half the country's total exports in the years leading up to the coup-volution, the population/hydrocarbon wealth ratio was too low for a classic rentier state of the GCC variety to emerge, one in which allocation substitutes for participation, but which paradoxically may over time shift the balance of resources from state to business.[16]

The reason why Egypt's capitalists did not bark when faced with a mortal threat is political. It is the absence of democracy, an explanation which appears at first glance to border on the tautological. Indeed, it might be so if an empowered bourgeoisie is viewed as the only possible bearer of democracy, as some readings of its emergence in the West suggest:[17] no bourgeoisie, no democracy, and no democracy, no bourgeoisie. If, on the other hand, the emergence of democracy is viewed in instrumental political terms as the outcome of agreements reached between competitive political actors pursuing minimax political strategies, typically after maximalist ones have failed, then the hypothesized, essential link between the growth in the power of business and democratization is rendered moot.[18] Conceived as the independent rather than the dependent variable, the degree of democracy can be used to explain the relative power of business, as well as other non-state actors.[19] Egypt's praetorian authoritarian state accounts for both slow economic growth and the political weakness of business, as a closer look at the impediments the state places before private economic and political activity reveals.

By definition an authoritarian state seeks to limit the autonomy and capacity of independent political actors. The corollary is that primary political competition occurs within the state itself. In Republican Egypt power has been shared, and hence shifted constantly, between the person, family and office of the President, the military, the security services, the single/dominant political party, and some elements of the executive administration, especially those controlling local government, parliament and the courts. These institutionally based actors share an interest in preserving the power of the state over society, although occasionally the insiders reach out to societal actors to enhance their power vis-à-vis other contenders within the state. So, for example, Gamal Mubarak brought under his wing members of the business elite, who provided him with patronage resources in return for access to rents. Ahmad Ezz, for example, bankrolled NDP election campaigns for Gamal's preferred candidates out of the ample profits generated by his near monopoly over the steel industry, this market dominance being originally made possible and then protected by Gamal. During the Sadat era the President himself cultivated the Muslim Brotherhood (MB) as a counter to leftist political forces within and outside the state, before then turning on it when he perceived the Brothers to be insufficiently subordinate to his will. In the case of both Gamal Mubarak and Anwar al-Sadat, however, the principal objective was to neutralize the military, a task Gamal never accomplished and Sadat only partially, despite his constant purges of the officer corps.[20] The struggle between president, military, and security services, which commenced in the early Nasser era, has remained the central feature of Egyptian politics. Its logic demands of these key state actors and their ancillaries that they monopolize political resources to the greatest extent possible, while preventing societally based challengers from emerging.

The deterrent methods deployed are just as harmful for autonomous economic activity as they are for independent political activity. Information control with political intent imposes collateral damage on financial markets and the overall functioning of the economy, to say nothing of its contribution to corruption. A military seeking to augment its power by expanding its economic activities necessarily undermines both private sector competitors and public financial accountability. Preventing free and fair elections discourages political mobilization and support for it by autonomous businessmen. Surveillance and intimidation of civil society organizations similarly limits their appeal to potential donors. The overall lack of political competition, especially the absence of free and fair elections, reduces incentives for state actors to improve the performance of the state or the economy. A recent comparative study of Turkey and Egypt, for example, concludes that the successful overhaul of the Turkish state for the purpose of making it supportive of private exporters was driven by politicians' need to appeal to voters, while in Egypt no such overhaul occurred because state actors lacked the electoral incentive for it.[21] In this context it is worth noting that Egypt and Turkey's per capita exports of manufactured goods were essentially equal in 1980, fifteen years later democratic Turkey's were some fifteen times greater.[22]

To the extent that Egyptian state actors seek to encourage business, they are driven by their personal consumption desires and need for material resources in intra-state political struggles. This incentive structure causes those actors to exchange access to rents for patronage resources, rather than work towards creating an environment conducive to broad economic activity. Support for small and medium enterprises, for example, provides no direct political advantages to state actors, so those enterprises languish in the absence of supportive policies and institutions.[23] In addition, Omer Ali and Ibrahim Elbadawi have demonstrated empirically a related, negative incentive structure in the Arab world: while it is optimal for high natural resource per capita countries to expand public employment, for Arab countries with low per capita natural resource endowments the optimal strategy to perpetuate dictatorial rule "is to set up a repressive security apparatus and employ a smaller proportion of the population".[24] Egyptian politics, centred on the calculations of those competing for power within the state, is driven by the shared need to deter non-state political activity, and by rent seeking and appropriation of resources and markets. In the face of this logic, private autonomous business has few opportunities and faces innumerable threats.

Two questions remain to be answered. The first is why this comparatively primitive political economy, based on a predator state, has not been transformed, as in many similar cases, the second is what lies in store for Egypt in the wake of the coup-volution. The durability of Egypt's dysfunctional political economy can be accounted for both by the general factors that have impeded democratization, and by those specific to state-business relations. Since the latter are more directly related to the topic under consideration here, it is to those that we shall now turn.

First, the history and, even more importantly, the historiography of state-business relations may be relevant. If Egyptian business had a venerable history, bequeathing family and institutional legacies celebrated in a historiography that recorded the feats of the system and its leading lights, then it would be easier for contemporary business to kindle support were it to seek to assert itself against the state. Alas, Egyptian business is not well treated in the country's historiography; this reflects both the reality of state-business relations and popular perceptions of them.[25] Talaat Harb, financier-industrialist of the inter-war period, stands out as one of the few businessmen lionized in the Republican era. Yet it is less his business accomplishments than his alleged challenge to the imperialists that underpins his popular legacy.[26] The heroes of contemporary

Egyptian historiography are invariably men of the state, such as Ahmad Urabi and Gamal Abdel Nasser, or of popular movements, such as Saad Zaghloul and Hassan al Banna. Other than Talaat Harb, the name associated with business which is most fondly remembered by many contemporary Egyptians is that of Aziz Sidqy, "man of one thousand factories", who was Nasser's minister, credited with erecting public sector industry.[27] Businessmen who played vital roles in developing Egypt from the time of Muhammad Ali have typically been effaced from the historical record because they were *mutamassirin* (Egyptianized foreigners), amongst whom Jews and Christians were particularly prominent.[28] Ahmad Abboud, whose entrepreneurial activities were brought to an abrupt end by Nasser, is one of the few exceptions to this rule, but Abboud does not fare particularly well in Egyptian historiography; he is typically depicted as a monopolist in league with colonial and landowner interests.[29] Egyptians, in sum, are not taught to venerate their capitalists. If anything, prevailing historiography portrays them as self indulgent, agents of foreign powers and even enemies of the people and nation. Egypt, in sum, either has not produced or, more accurately, refuses to recognize that it has national equivalents to John D. Rockefeller, Andrew Carnegie, Henry Ford, or Steve Jobs.

The real history of state-business relations is not as one-sided as contemporary historiography suggests, but it is not particularly favourable to business either. Muhammad Ali's state building project presaged Nasser's in that it was state capitalist, with business being harnessed to the governing elite, whose political needs and personal whims took precedence over the views, skills and interests of entrepreneurs. During the colonial era business prospered, as did the country, but business was dominated by foreigners and *mutamassirin*, the vast majority of whom decamped as first nationalism, then nationalization rendered their situations untenable. While a few descendants of this former elite are still active in Egyptian business, they are not major players and survive through avoidance rather than embrace of government and politics. Business recovered after the disastrous Nasser years, but it remains top heavy, fundamentally malformed. At the overly large apex have been cronies, recruited from an admixture of those with backgrounds in the state, including the military, or particular business or professional communities, such as Copts and Alexandrines. *Mittelständler* are to be found, but in no area of industry or commerce have middle sized firms grown and agglomerated in something approaching the German or Italian model, notwithstanding the semi-integrated furniture manufacturers of Dumyat. The base of the pyramid is huge in terms of numbers of small and micro firms and those employed by them, but tiny in terms of capital and production. As the Mubarak era ground on, the top and bottom of the business pyramid expanded, the former in terms of fixed capital and output, the latter in numbers, while the middle remained essentially stagnant.[30] This malformation reflected the inability of small and micro enterprises to grow into medium sized firms, and the failure of medium sized companies to expand. Growth in output was at the top, as the increasing concentration of wealth reflected. So the actual history of business in Egypt provides little in the way of institutional or personal legacies, and not enough success stories for positive collective memories to be nurtured by a supportive historiography. While path dependency is not absolute, it is true that Egypt does not have legacy resources upon which to draw when and if it seeks to encourage the growth of business more independent from the state than it historically has been.

A second hindrance to capitalist transformation is the pre-eminence of security over development in the calculations of both domestic and relevant external actors. External and internal threats provide justification for the sprawling deep state anchored in the presidential bureaucracy, the Ministry of the Interior and the military. These institutions require resources, not only to perform their tasks, but to contest for power with one another. Experience in capturing and deploying resources in such institutional settings prepares officers and bureaucrats for parallel or subsequent private careers in "business".[31] The deep state thus impedes overall economic growth because it consumes national resources while deterring the development of private business, among other things, by competing with it on favourable terms. Access to land, capital and labour is provided by the deep state on a preferential basis, as utilization of conscript labour in military factories, privatization of land in military zones, and lack of civilian oversight of deep state finances attest. For many years Egypt has ranked high on the World Bank's embarrassing measure of "non performing loans", indicating that the country's banks, like those in Tunisia and Algeria, have been subject to pressure for capital from their deep states. Not surprisingly, Egyptian businessmen frequently cite access to capital as a principal constraint on their activities.[32] Another common complaint of owners of small and medium businesses is a shortage of land for business facilities.[33] So the deep state gobbles up capital and land, depriving private sector businessmen, other than regime cronies, of both, while transferring wage bills to taxpayers. Production costs are thus bound to be comparatively higher in the private sector. Amazingly the military remains the most popular institution in Egypt because its negative impacts on the country's finances and economy more generally are largely unknown, because it is the largest single employer in the country, hence creates dependencies, and because it claims to be providing national security.[34] Security, in sum, trumps development, so state trumps market. For security to serve as an incentive for effective industrialization, as some argue it did in East Asia, a precondition would be reduction if not liquidation of the military economy.[35] Since that economy's raison d'être is to ensure the loyalty of the officer corps, so long as the deep state remains in control, it will remain.

Egypt's principal foreign suitors have also been traditionally more interested in the country's geostrategic assets than in its economy. The Soviets tinkered with the communist economic model along the Nile, but their real concern was securing bases and other support, including ideological, that they deemed vital to their Cold War confrontation with the US. Washington, for its part, after it displaced the Soviets as Egypt's chief patron, provided nominal backing for economic liberalism, but the bulk of US funding and interest has been in the security relationship that ensures peace with Israel and access for US forces to the Gulf and East Africa.[36] The principal go-to man in Cairo for Washington in the last years of the Mubarak era was 'Omar Suleiman, head of General Intelligence. In the moment of truth following the coup-volution, when civilian political forces squared off against the military and the SCAF sought to demonstrate its nationalist credentials by having American NGO activists arrested, Washington swallowed the insult, abandoned the cause of its own civilian political actors, paid their $1 million in "bail", and handed over the military's annual aid "entitlement" of $1.3 billion.[37] Show trials of prominent businessmen, including the former Unilever executive Rashid Muhammad Rashid—the very man whom the SCAF invited to be its first prime minister but who turned them down and was then indicted, convicted and sentenced to several years in prison—have not been criticised by the US. When confronted with the choice of supporting economic and political liberalism in Egypt, or protecting its security assets by appeasing the deep state, the US delayed only briefly before opting for the latter.

Other foreign actors may be less tied to the deep state for security reasons, but they nevertheless prioritize relations with it in their economic calculations. Israel successfully pursued access to Egyptian gas through Hussein Salem, a former intelligence officer close to President Mubarak. Prince Walid bin Talal secured control over land in Toshka through dealings with President Mubarak himself.[38] Numerous touristic and mega residential real estate projects have resulted from partnerships between Arab investors and military/security officials. As Zeinab Abul Magd, Shana Marshal and Joshua Stacher have revealed, an increasing number of foreign companies operating in Egypt are doing so in partnership with the military, rather than with civilian businesses.[39] A growing share of the vital hydrocarbon sector, which invariably involves foreign investment, is falling under the control of military officers. Like the military itself, the budgets of the state's hydrocarbon sector and its component firms are not available for scrutiny by Parliament or state auditing agencies.[40]

The deep state, in sum, is a magnet for those seeking security assets, as well as for those pursuing economic gains, typically through rents. It therefore poses a substantial obstacle to the type of broad foreign direct and equity investment, frequently accompanied with technology transfer, which flowed into East Asian countries, especially China, and which underpinned economic "miracles" there and elsewhere, as in contemporary Brazil, India or Poland. It may be no coincidence that accelerating growth in China was accompanied by a scaling back of its military economy.[41] Even in Turkey, EU investment, which has commonly been accompanied by technology transfer, has bypassed the deep state to go directly into the private sector, reflecting the greater degree of democracy there.[42] Egypt's foreign suitors, by contrast, have been more supportive of state than market.

A third impediment facing business has been the deep state's steadfast resistance to efforts to convert economic into political power. The growth of Islamic finance in Egypt has lagged behind that in many other Muslim countries of comparative wealth, to say nothing of the rich GCC countries, primarily because of the deep state's suspicions that Islamists, especially the Muslim Brotherhood, could generate political leverage through it.[43] Not surprisingly, one of the initial announcements in the wake of the Brotherhood's triumph in the 2011–12 parliamentary elections was that Egypt would for the first time be issuing *sukuk* (Islamic bonds). The subsequent delay in preparing the issue was due in part to the erroneous assumption among Egyptian officials that they could be used for general budgetary support rather than just project financing—which indicates the comparatively primitive state of Islamic finance and knowledge about it in Egypt.[44] A particular target of the deep state was Khairat al-Shater, the "comptroller" of the Brotherhood's financial empire. He spent some twelve years in jail during the Mubarak era and had many if not all of his enterprises confiscated. He then emerged in 2012 as the principal challenger to the SCAF, only to be disqualified from standing for the presidency by the Presidential Election Committee, presumably responding to pressure from a SCAF wary of al-Shater forging an Islamic finance-Islamist nexus.

Although the true size of the Islamist economy is unknown, fragmentary evidence suggests that the deep state has managed to keep it in check, at least as compared with that in Turkey at its formative stage in the 1990s. Al-Shater's flagship Salsabil computer/electronics firm, combined with his other holdings, including companies that import furniture and clothing and produce pharmaceuticals and are assumed to have Brotherhood financial participation, have been estimated between LE50 and LE100 million in net worth, or some $9–18 million. LE80 million of assets was confiscated from him by the government in 2007. At that time Hassan Malek, another businessman Brother, had assets worth LE120 million seized.[45] If these figures provide an indication of the wealth of the vanguard of the Brotherhood bourgeoisie, it is a rather negligible financial force by comparison not only with Turkish Islamists in the 1990s, but also with the now beached "Whales of the Nile". Muhammad Mansour, for example, is estimated to still possess assets of between $500 million and $3 billion.[46] At the time of the coup-volution and before fleeing to London he employed in his various companies about 57,000 personnel; so both his net worth and his labour force could exceed the combined totals for the leading MB businessmen.[47] That organization's ability to mobilize capital, as witnessed in the 2011 and 2012 election campaigns, probably depends more on external linkages, whether to Egyptian expatriates or to Gulf Arabs, than on direct or indirect ownership of domestic businesses or other assets. This conclusion is reinforced by the findings of Emad Siam's careful study of

Islamist outreach organizations, which notes that a growing shortage of resources after the government's crackdown that intensified after 2000 undermined their ability to provide services, hence to gain new recruits, which in turn explains "the disconnect between the Islamists and the youth uprising".[48]

But the deep state under Mubarak did not target only direct economic-political linkages, especially if they were Islamist. It also impeded the formation of connections of marginal political relevance between secular businessmen and civil society. The businessmen's organizations that emerged in the wake of the *infitah*, including the Egyptian Businessmen's Association and AmCham, for example, were led by cronies tied to the regime, such as Shafiq Gabr, the perennial AmCham president closely linked to the military. The Egyptian Centre for Economic Studies (ECES), founded and funded by USAID to serve as a voice for economic reform, similarly fell under the influence of Gamal Mubarak's cronies and their point man, the prominent attorney Tahir Hilmy. Private universities that emerged from the 1990s were typically funded by businessmen, but these investors were careful to ensure that individuals trusted by the deep state were placed in prominent positions within them.[49] It was common knowledge among businessmen that funding NGOs risked retaliation from the deep state through a variety of means, such as refusing required licenses and permits or imposing fees or higher taxes. So the Turkish model of Islamist businessmen forging networks—culminating in the founding of MUSIAD as the rival business association to the regime's backed TUSIAD, and subsequently as the economic base for the AKP—was rendered impossible in Egypt.[50] The country was thus buffeted by a popular uprising before forces independent of the state were able to build and consolidate networks through which material resources could be channelled to political organizations. It is hardly surprising, therefore, that these forces, including business, have proven to be much weaker than the deep state *fulul* (remnants) of the ancien regime.

So what does the future hold in store for state-business relations in Egypt? Given their relatively unpromising history and the discouraging developments since February 2011, one is tempted to dismiss out of hand a rebalancing scenario in favour of business. That, however, would ignore the experiences of some other countries that have passed through bumpy transitions ending almost accidentally in more open political economies as a result of elite "pacting". This transition through political exhaustion scenario is based on the assumption that none of the contending political actors, whether military and the associated deep state, Islamists, secular liberals/revolutionaries, or indeed businessmen specifically, is sufficiently strong and united to impose its will. Each will learn through experience the limits to its power and will come to fear that it may fall victim to a coalition of other actors. For each actor, then, a sub-optimal outcome, in which it is protected from retribution, comes to be preferred over an optimizing, winning and taking it all strategy. Such protection is provided by democracy, which couples majority rule with protection of minority rights.[51] So, in this scenario, once even transitional democracy is established, greater economic freedoms are likely to follow, with the potential permanently to reform the state-business relationship, as has happened in Eastern Europe, Brazil, South Korea, Taiwan and elsewhere. A democracy flawed by inability to eradicate a deep state, such as that in Pakistan, will, however, continue to be plagued with corruption and cronyism.

This scenario of rebalanced state-business relations as an outcome of competing elites following minimax strategies in newly competitive political contexts has some resonance in today's Egypt. The rocky transition has already disabused liberal reformers and secular revolutionaries of the notion that they could single-handedly create new political and economic orders. The "Whales of the Nile" have swum away, have been incarcerated, or—in the case of several whose primary connection was with the military or security services, such as Ahmad Bahgat, Salah Diab, and Hassan Ratib—continue to exploit their "networks of privilege" with the deep state.[52] This leaves the Muslim Brotherhood, the military and the vital question of whether they too may have already come, or will soon come, to perceive their power as limited, and so to desire the democratic compromise; or whether one or the other or both will continue to believe they alone can prevail. In the compromise scenario each of the components of the now more pluralistic political elite has an incentive to foster broad business expansion to underpin its electoral appeal and capacities, as in Turkey since the 1980s. In the alternative winner take all scenario, whether it would be the MB or the military that triumphed, the victor's logic would be to exploit control of the state, probably in league with favoured cronies, to extend and expand patronage networks. President Mursi's purge of the SCAF in August

2012 did not resolve this issue, for he was able to remove Generals Tantawi and Anan only with the complicity of younger officers acting to preserve the reputation, privileges and power of the military. The result has been a re-partitioning of the state between the Brothers and the generals. The upgraded National Defence Council, in which the latter predominate, consecrates the military's continuing pre-eminence over national security policy, as well as over its internal organization and the military economy. But whether this two-legged system that excludes other civilian political forces will be stable enough to withstand mounting economic and political pressures remains to be seen.

While it remains uncertain whether Egypt is on the brink of a historic democratic compromise or consolidation of a new authoritarianism under the military or Islamists, in the meantime both the military and the MB are courting the remnants of big business. This competition between the MB and the military for the favour of business could provide an opportunity for business elites to exert some influence over the outcome of that contest, if not necessarily for more profound self assertion. Law 4 issued by the SCAF on 3 January 2012, just prior to the convening of the new Parliament, amended the investment incentive law of 1997 so as to permit investors charged with theft of state property, including land and privatized companies, to have charges dropped or sentences that have yet to reach the final stage of appeal waived in return for payment. More than sixty such cases have already been settled.[53] Parliament, for its part, once in session and under effective MB control, did not object in principle to this last minute decree by the SCAF, although it did call for the amount of compensation to be increased. That both the SCAF and the Brotherhood are signalling business-friendly intent is further reflected by Parliament's rejection in the spring of 2012 of a proposal to tax share dividends, and by the fact that neither the SCAF nor the Brotherhood has sought to compel the government to enforce administrative court decisions annulling contracts between businessmen and the Mubarak government.[54] The platform on which the MB entered the elections embraced substantial components of the neo-liberal "Washington Consensus".[55] In November 2012 the Brotherhood government signalled an accommodation with Ezz Steel, announcing that one of its wholly owned subsidiaries was being granted a new license to produce sponge iron. The previous year the mother company had been stripped of a license to produce billet ore and its owner, Gamal Mubarak intimate Ahmad Ezz, had been sentenced to ten years in jail and a LE330 million fine. Whether the announcement heralded Ezz's rehabilitation or simply an accommodation with those left in charge of his company remained unclear.[56]

If the military were to gain the upper hand against the Brotherhood it might seek more direct ownership and overall economic tutelage than it exercised under Mubarak, but would still be unlikely to launch an all-out attack on business. Indeed, the incumbent senior leadership of the military would be more likely to encourage it. Only if that leadership were to be replaced through a coup might business again become a direct target of radical officers. If the present cohabitation at the head of the state by the military and the Brotherhood continues, the former might well go along with the expansion of Islamic finance and the broader Islamist business sector, in part because it is consonant with the Minister of Defence Abd al-Fattah al-Sisi's mildly Islamist outlook.

Depending on the degrees of economic and political freedom that develop and the balance of power between political actors, the resulting political economy could resemble the Pakistani, the Turkish, or a yet more liberal political economy. In the case of the Pakistani model, which would be based on a politically ascendant military, a "Military, Inc" would form the core of the economy, with cronies at one remove and independent businessmen struggling out on the periphery.[57] At present this appears much less likely than emulation of the Turkish model resulting from the political cohabitation of the military and the Brotherhood. Some parallels can indeed already be drawn between the emergence of Turkey's quasi-Islamist economy and developments in Egypt. For example, the MB founded, in March 2012, its equivalent of MUSIAD in the form of the Egyptian Business Development Association, or EBDA (the acronym meaning "start" in Arabic). Its board of directors, chaired by a Brotherhood businessman and ally of Khairat al-Shater, Hassan Malek, includes several Islamist-inclined former members of the Mubarak business entourage, such as Safwan Thabet, owner of the Juhayna food products company, Mohamed Moamen of the Mo'men Group, and Abdel Rahman Seoudi of Seoudi Holding. Upon its founding EBDA's board signed a cooperation agreement with MUSIAD and received a delegation of MUSIAD affiliated Turkish businessmen, led by the Turkish ambassador.[58] It is interesting to note that a critical element in the implementation of the Turkish model was the post-1980 military-backed government sympathy for Islamism, most especially that of Prime Minister Turgut Ozal.[59] It could be that this "precondition" of at least tacit support for Islamism within the high command is currently present in Egypt, if indeed General al-Sisi's profoundly Islamic conception of political order reflects the views of his colleagues.[60] But even if that precondition is present, a Turkish model incorporating an Islamist business elite enjoying substantial autonomy from the military and the deep state more generally is unlikely to emerge quickly in Egypt. Despite the resources of tacit support by elements of the Turkish military-political elite, an active business community networked and represented by MUSIAD, and a long established democracy in which free and fair elections occurred, it required a generation for the political arm of the Turkish Islamist movement to gain the upper hand against the military. These preconditions are in their infancy in Egypt. So while the Turkish model might provide inspiration for many Egyptians and have some chance of ultimately prevailing, it is obvious that all of its prerequisites are yet to be found in the Egyptian situation.

Finally, a liberal, capitalist political order emerging in the wake of a pacted transition to democracy remains theoretically possible. The very fact that some 40% of the Egyptian population lives on less than $2 per day, however, renders it unlikely. Other features of the political economy, elsewhere described as "demographic democratic deficits", similarly suggest that this scenario is possible only over the very long haul.[61] Indeed, Egypt now confronts an economic crisis from which it will not quickly emerge and which could have profound political consequences. At some point, economic deprivation, exacerbated by renewed political authoritarianism, whether exercised by the military or even by the MB, could stimulate a real revolution by protestors mobilized from further down in the social order, or at least a renewal of widespread unrest. Such political violence might in fact be the precondition for a military exit, or even escape from Islamist authoritarianism. Alternatively, it might pave the way for a new authoritarianism. Another and probably equally likely outcome is a coup d'état conducted by officers inspired by military professionalism, nationalism, Islamism, contempt for the *fulul* of the Mubarak high command, or simply a fear of economic and political breakdown.

At present, however, both revolution and coup are but vague, distant threats to the key political competitors, who are focused on their struggle against one another, as reflected in the protracted delay in the constitution drafting process. Democracy through elite pacting remains possible, but it is unlikely to occur in the immediate future, if only because the Brotherhood and the military appear to continue to believe that their condominium is sufficiently powerful to prevail without the inclusion of other political forces. Structural change, dependent as it is on widening political inclusion, therefore seems destined to be delayed. Greater political freedom of expression, coupled with an enhanced power and autonomy for the legislative and judicial branches (if indeed this ever comes about), would over time pave the way for the incorporation and representation of interests, those of business included, as in Turkey. But this outcome is by no means preordained, even over the long haul. Business may find itself once again harnessed to or suppressed by an authoritarian political elite, paradoxically requiring another revolutionary upsurge to dislodge its grip. But any such renewal of mass protest would also threaten to sweep away business itself.

In conclusion, the coup-volution of 2011 demonstrated the structural weaknesses of big business, as manifested by its dependence on authoritarian elites and lack of effective linkages with civil and political societies. The coup-volution has shaken the balance of power within the state and provided access to it for the country's most powerful civilian political actor. But other civil and political society actors, deprived of enduring material linkages similar to those that networked Turkish businessmen and aspiring activists, remain comparatively weak, and even Islamist networks are a far cry from those of Turkey in, say, the 1980s. The "Second Republic" may come to resemble AKP Turkey, or it may fail to achieve sufficient legitimacy and develop enough governance capacity to provide business and the nation with the preconditions for economic success, and thus exacerbate underlying socio-economic deprivations that contributed to 2011's coup-volution.[62] In sum, the impact of Egypt's "Arab Spring" on state-business relations is yet to be clarified, and so their future remains essentially unknown. The coup-volution may have so weakened the deep state that business will be able to contribute effectively to building autonomous political resources while expanding its commercial reach. Alternatively, the deep state may regroup its forces under renewed covert or even overt military leadership, acting alone or in concert with Islamists. So whether Egypt is in transition to democracy, renewed praetorianism, mobilizational Islamism, or chaotic breakdown remains to be seen. Such uncertainty is certainly not advantageous to business, so for the immediate future it will be on the sidelines as the political struggle is played out by more powerful forces.

11

BUSINESSES AND THE REVOLUTION

Giacomo Luciani

"You, O King, went after the farms and took them away from their owners and cultivators. They are the people who pay the land tax and from whom one gets money. You gave their farms as fiefs to your entourage and servants and to sluggards. They did not cultivate them and did not heed the consequences. (They did not look for the things) that would be good for the farms. They were leniently treated with regard to the land tax (and were not asked to pay it), because they were close to the king. The remaining landowners who did pay the land tax and cultivated their farms had to carry an unjust burden. Therefore, they left their farms and abandoned their settlements. They took refuge in farms that were far away or difficult (of access), and lived on them".

(Ibn Khaldun, *Muqaddimah*: the Mobedhan addressing King Bahram b. Bahram of Persia)

Take Mohamed Bouazizi, the street vendor whose suicide started the Tunisian revolution. Why did he commit suicide? Because he didn't get property rights over the sidewalk, the license to operate his street vending operation. Now many people have actually immolated themselves to protest the regime in Tunis. But when this guy, who was a street vendor, did it, the whole region lit on fire because he happened to be of a certain social class.

Westerners and Americans don't like the phrase "social class" because it appears to be derived from Marxism, but the fact of the matter is that people do identify with other people based on their economic and social strata. So one of the reasons I'm sending a team to Tunisia now is we're trying to find out what the connection is between all of these places. Libya has clans and tribes, Egypt has nothing to do with clans and tribes, it's completely different. Yet they're all lighting up. And we believe it has to do with a social class that is not on a salary.

Bouazizi was not on a salary. The majority of Tunisians and Egyptians are not on a salary. They're earning their own incomes, they're very, very small entrepreneurs, albeit outside the law. And once we figure that one out, we'll find the course the revolution should take. It's all about who controls the assets and who controls transactions.

"This Land is Your Land—A conversation with Hernando De Soto",
World Policy Journal, Summer 2011

Introduction

The so-called "Arab Spring", the revolutionary movement that has seen unprecedented and irresistible popular participation and engulfed key Arab states one after the other, witnessed relatively limited participation by business. This may not be surprising, as the captains of industry and finance are seldom seen demonstrating with the masses; but beyond such a superficial level of analysis, the question remains, to what extent the revolution may have been helped and/or triggered by the actions or shortcomings of business actors.

The chapter proposes an analysis based on the fact that business is plural and diverse, and the behaviour and interests of the different components may diverge and conflict. We introduce a categorization in three broad groups: the crony capitalists, the outsiders and the marginalized;[1] and we discuss the political impact of their modus operandi in creating conditions for the revolution, in influencing the political outcome of the revolution, and finally in determining whether the revolution will successfully lead to more prosperous, just and democratic societies.

The plurality of business

The title of this chapter uses the plural "businesses" rather than the singular "business" or "private sector" because entrepreneurs are a very diverse category of analysis—ranging all the way from prominent capitalists, employing significant numbers of salaried workers in large-scale enterprises, to small and frequently impoverished self-employed individuals, sometimes commanding little or no capital worth speaking of, yet displaying considerable ingenuity to simply survive. It would be distorting to call this heterogeneous universe "the bourgeoisie", a term that should be reserved to the subset that commands enough capital to employ others and performs exclusively the role of owner-manager. Similarly, the concept of "middle class" is defined on the basis of income, and indicates that section of the population that is neither especially rich nor especially poor, but has sufficient means to be liberated from the daily fight for survival—while at the same time not belonging to society's elite. Our "businesses" include both people who definitely belong to the elite as well as individuals who are just above the survival threshold—and frequently below the poverty line.

Who, then, is not in any "business" at all? The obvious answer would involve: people who receive a salary and are more or less guaranteed employment. In advanced industrial societies, where unions are—or at least were—powerful, the salaried members of society frequently enjoy a relatively comfortable level of income that allows them to be members of the middle class. They do not engage in additional economic activities besides the one that earns their salary. We know that the condition of the salaried has been deteriorating in advanced societies: the share of national income accruing to dependent labour has been declining, job security is rarer and rarer, and the ranks of the middle class have been shrinking. In less developed countries, the plight of dependent workers is even worse, and many have in fact been obliged to take additional jobs, frequently as self-employed in more or less "informal" trades, thereby increasing the ranks of business broadly defined.

"Informal" means not officially recognized and/or recorded. In jurisdictions in which any value added generation is potentially a trigger for tax obligations, informality or invisibility is illegal. Informal therefore is also almost invariably illegal, although it does not need to be criminal: it can be a perfectly legitimate activity, except that it is kept hidden from the eyes of the state, or does not conform to all the laws and regulations that the state wishes to impose. Such rules and regulations are often extremely burdensome, and perfect compliance almost impossible. Excessive regulation is in fact functional to the state—at least to *some* states, and not exclusively Arab—because it opens the door to selective and more or less capricious enforcement, which in turn is a sure opportunity of private gain for the officer or civil servant charged with such enforcement. Informality therefore frequently comes in shades: ranging from the fully invisible and criminal, to the fully invisible but legitimate, to the partly invisible not quite in full respect of the rules. Big business is impossible to hide completely, although books can be cooked to cloud the true size of crucial metrics; nevertheless it is frequently "illegal" for this or that aspect, generally with the complicity of the state. It would then be equally misleading to assume that there is a clear-cut difference between formal and informal business, as all businesses are likely to be one and the other at the same time.

The title also includes the word "revolution". This is another historically abused term, through which those who were in fact military putschists (in Algeria, Egypt, Iraq, Libya, Syria) tried to give a veneer of ideological justification to their authoritarian and frequently very personal rule, which progressively evolved into the curious phenomenon of the hereditary Presidency of the Republic. But since 2010 and its inception in Tunisia, what we have witnessed in the Arab region unquestionably is a revolution, with widespread popular participation aimed at dislodging the incumbent power holders and achieving regime change. Though without any explicit attempt at regional projection, this revolution has nevertheless progressively engulfed the whole region, and probably will only stop spreading after all Arab countries are affected.

Our question is: what role did businesses play in the revolution? That includes not only the climax of the revolutionary movement, but also its incubation and, possibly even more important, its aftermath. Because revolutions may succeed or fail, and in the end their outcome is as important as their happening, or more.

Authoritarianism and economic liberalization

The revolution was a surprise for almost all analysts: for the past twenty or thirty years (depending on whether we want to take origin from the 1991 collapse of the Soviet Union or the post-1978 wave of democratization in Latin America) scholarship on the Middle East and North Africa was predominantly busy explaining the "Arab exception", that is, finding all kinds of arguments to explain the fact that the region seemed immune from any movement towards democratization.[2] Most explanations went too far: they tended to represent the roots of authoritarianism as immutable and unshakeable, rather than just a temporary phenomenon, the contingent delay of a process which was historically determined and would inevitably occur sooner or later.

The persistence of Arab authoritarianism could be explained in the case of the major oil-exporting countries, where oil rent provided the incumbent rulers with sufficient tools to gain the acceptance of their people. But it was more difficult to explain in the case of countries having only limited access to the oil rent, or none at all.[3] As fiscal difficulties forced these countries to progressively dismantle the apparatus of state control over the economy and liberalize, much orthodox thinking expected that their economies would grow, and pressure for political liberalization would emerge.

Economic liberalization was expected to lead to the emergence of new entrepreneurial forces—a latent national bourgeoisie. Exploiting new opportunities opened up by the liberalization process, the new, or newly empowered, bourgeoisie would—it was expected—invest in new projects and create employment to meet the challenge of a rapidly growing workforce. Liberalization would eventually benefit the majority of the population and lead to the emergence of a middle class, traditionally identified as the main actor of democratization.

But this scenario, which the Washington consensus expected to unfold following Asian precedents, did not play out as envisaged. In imposing state control over the economy, the incumbent regimes had destroyed or marginalized the old bourgeoisie, and there was no satisfactory replacement at hand.[4] Needing to favour the creation of a new entrepreneurial class, regimes ended up nurturing a crony bourgeoisie, that is, a bourgeoisie whose fortunes are contingent on access to the holders of political power and preferential treatment.

In itself the Arab regimes' tendency to nurture a class of crony capitalists is not so surprising, because all governments will inevitably favour economic actors that are perceived to be close to the government, and all entrepreneurs will try their best to be close to the government in order to receive favours. So the puzzle is not that the state nurtured a class of crony capitalists, but that this class failed to prosper and set economic growth in motion to an extent sufficient for creating a trickle-down effect.

One possible explanation is that the selection and fortunes of the cronies were guided more by concerns about security and loyalty than by genuine economic potential. John Waterbury has described the relationship between the regimes and the cronies as an "alliance for profits": "the tacit understanding has been that the bourgeoisie would renounce any overt political role and that it would follow the broad economic directives of the state in exchange for which it would be allowed to make significant profits".[5] The same, however, could well be said of, say, the relationship between the state and business in China, and yet China has experienced extraordinary economic growth.[6] Thus, the point is not just that the state bought the loyalty of the crony capitalists, but that the latter failed to deliver growth.

Another possible explanation is that cronies were chosen for their readiness to share profits with the key power holders. In this view, only entrepreneurs ready to let the clan of the President (Mubarak's sons, the Trabelsi family in Tunisia) directly benefit from their business were allowed to become established and/or survive. Thus, like King Bahram bin Bahram of Persia in Ibn Khaldun's narrative, the regime benefited good-for-nothings and discouraged the producers of real value added, who consequently "took refuge in farms that were far away or difficult"—going abroad or striving not to be visible.

The literature unanimously points to the fact that economic liberalization led to greater inequality of incomes and wealth, and specifically to an increase in the number of people living below the poverty level.[7] This outcome stood in contrast to the rhetoric of the regimes, which pretended to be supporting a growing role of the middle class—in Tunisia this was very evident.[8] This negative outcome was recorded alongside observations that the economy was and had been growing at relatively satisfactory rates over the past decades, and increasing oil prices were benefiting even the smaller oil exporters.

The growing income concentration that eventually led to the revolution can only be explained if we admit that the state was not able to mobilize the business sector around a development strategy capable of delivering higher growth and mobilizing broader resources in society. The state nurtured a class of crony capitalists and then steered them in a direction that did not allow them to truly prosper and become the engine moving the country's economic development. In fact, as we consider the fortunes of all the best-known crony capitalists, we see that very few managed to establish enterprises of any real significance. There are exceptions, but not many.

The crony capitalists

The lack of success of the crony capitalists is one of the key paradoxes in the failure of the authoritarian regimes outside the GCC. It should be stressed that in itself the nurturing of a class of crony capitalists is not unusual, indeed it is the norm rather than the exception in most countries.[9] It may very well become a successful strategy, as demonstrated by the positive outcome in several Asian countries—such as Indonesia—provided that the crony capitalists are able to "graduate" into large business entrepreneurs, capable of investing and pursuing opportunities beyond immediate profiteering from the spoils of the state. What we see in the experience of many countries in Asia, Latin America and the GCC, is that a process of natural selection takes place over time, and some of the businessmen who at some point have the opportunity to benefit from a favourable connection to political power eventually create sound bases for their business, and are able to prosper independently of privileged access to state resources, while others simply fade away.[10] It is in fact also normal that access to state resources does not last forever and rulers may get tired of their clients: any prudent businessman would expect this possibility and try to "graduate" as quickly as possible. Graduation takes place either through market diversification—notably gaining a foothold in export markets—or by performing a role which is recognized as being indispensible in the context of the country's development.

It is clear that graduation is not automatic. On the contrary, it requires some genuine business capabilities, which may or may not be there. We may say that the economic performance of a regime is largely dependent on its ability to select the right cronies—just as, more generally, the ability to select the right aides, and frequently these two coincide.[11] Personnel selection is crucial to the success of any organization, political regimes included. In this respect, it may be proposed that the shortcoming of some Arab authoritarian regimes has been not so much in their policies, as in the implementation of those policies.

Consideration of a few specific cases, notably from Egypt,[12] will clarify why I speak of failure. According to John Sfakianakis, in the early 2000s:

> some 32 businessmen comprised the established business elite of Egypt, with a large majority engaged mainly in import-substitution. The elite sector flour-

ished behind barriers of protection, was largely uncompetitive in the international market, and existed in large part due to rent-seeking operations. … By maintaining the system of privilege between certain businessmen and the state the former created a system in which it was extremely difficult for other, less-well-connected, businessman to penetrate the ranks of the 32.[13]

The image that we get from this passage is one of an entrenched, compact and immobile elite—pretty much paralleling the political elite. However, Sfakianakis also details various instances in which members of this small elite bitterly fought each other for the control of specific assets or markets; and he acknowledges that the privatization process "created opportunities for former bureaucrats to establish powerful networks of privilege that benefitted themselves and occasionally to compete with established private sector elites. … Overall, … a new set of powerful business actors created a set of networks or fortified previous ones that they could exploit to their own advantage".[14]

The existence of intra-elite competition and of newcomers is crucial in predicting the political inclination of the business elite, because the demand for an even playing field, better regulation and respect for the rule of law, more competitive markets, and so on, frequently originates from the inability of the holders of power to successfully arbitrate a growing number of intra-elite conflicts. No businessman loves competition, yet capitalist systems, ultimately, are systematically pushed towards greater competitiveness because the persistence of positions of rent negatively affects all except those enjoying such positions. We may attribute the stagnation and sclerosis of the Egyptian business environment to the lack of sufficient competition. The evidence provided by Sfakianakis indicates that the crony capitalists were far from being a monolithic entity, and were frequently in competition with each other; nevertheless, their ranks remained limited, and upward mobility of smaller business interests did not occur.

This is all the more surprising because, while the regime may have nurtured a number of inefficient rentier bureaucrats turned businessmen, not all that are normally considered cronies belong to this category. Some started off as businessmen, and emerged as such, being co-opted later as clients by the regime, simply because any government needs good businessmen to improve the management of the economy. Thus, not all large entrepreneurs in Egypt are cronies, and not all cronies are large entrepreneurs.

Osman Ahmed Osman

Osman Ahmed Osman, founder of Arab Contractors, is frequently listed as an example of cronyism. In fact, he is also recognized as one of the few genuine self-made entrepreneurs in Egypt.[15] He established a contracting enterprise in the 1940s; in 1950 he travelled to the Gulf, and was able to take advantage of the building boom which had been happening in the region—nothing like what came about in the 1970s, but still a major opportunity for a very small entrepreneur from Egypt. Hence, he first asserted himself abroad, and it is not clear that he enjoyed any "insider" privilege at that time. In 1958 he returned to Egypt, and won the contract to build the Aswan Dam. While this development automatically qualifies him as "insider", it is not clear that he got the contract because he was already an insider, rather, he became an insider because he obtained the contract.[16]

In 1961 his company, Arab Contractors, was nationalized by Nasser, but Osman stayed as top manager. The company's foreign business justified the fact that he was granted considerable managerial autonomy, allowing him a degree of bargaining power vis-à-vis the regime—which he continued to serve faithfully. After Nasser's death, Arab Contractors clearly benefited from Osman's personal proximity to Sadat, reinforced by marriage ties between their two families. The company was awarded major infrastructural work in connection with the reconstruction of the Suez Canal Zone after 1973, and Osman diversified into other lines of business.

Nevertheless, the key point which is often forgotten or ignored in the literature, is that Arab Contractors remains, to this date, wholly owned by the Egyptian government. After Osman Ahmed Osman's death, the post of CEO passed to his nephew Ismail Osman, who was then abruptly dismissed in 2001, ending the presence of the family in the company.[17] The family is no longer one of the leading Egyptian business families, and their name is nowhere in the list of Forbes' World billionaires (which has a total of 1,153 entries, including six Egyptians).[18] Thus Osman personally and Arab Contractors as a corporate entity may well have benefited from proximity to power, but the family is no longer important in the Egyptian business landscape, and the company is state owned.

The Sawiris family

In contrast, we should consider the trajectory of the Sawiris family. The founder, Onsi Sawiris, started from perhaps a slightly better social and economic position than Osman Ahmed Osman, but similarly established a contracting company, which was also nationalized under Nasser though he stayed on as CEO. However, in his case the decision to stay was imposed upon him, and he was deprived of his passport for a period of six years. When he finally got his passport back, he left for Libya, where he started his business again. He came back to Egypt after the launch of the *infitah* policies under Sadat and again entered business there, eventually branching out in different sectors of activity. Today, the Sawiris family's business interests are organized in three separate entities, each under one of the sons of Onsi Sawiris: contracting activity (Orascom Construction Industries) under Nassef Sawiris, the telecom business (Orascom Telecom) under Naguib Sawiris, and other miscellaneous activities (Orascom Development Holding) under Samih Sawiris. Nassef, Naguib and Onsi are in the 2011 list of Forbes' billionaires (respectively in positions 199, 367 and 401), while Samih's net worth is less than a billion but sufficient to have him listed as one of Africa's forty richest individuals. All three brothers were educated abroad: Naguib at ETH in Zurich, Samih at Berlin University and Nassef in Chicago.[19]

Obviously the Sawiris have benefited from proximity to power, but it may be argued convincingly that the latter was gained through business success, rather than the other way round. Beyond a certain point, a successful businessman will inevitably become visible in the eyes of power, and this encounter can be positive or negative: in the case of the Sawiris, it has been positive. Consider their telecom business: though it started with the acquisition of the state-owned monopoly cellular telephone business—Mobinil—Naguib Sawiris took over the company for the long haul. In contrast, in a majority of cases Egyptian businessmen who had an opportunity to acquire assets from the state in the wave of privatizations only clung to the acquired assets for a short time, and then sold on, frequently to foreign investors, at a considerable profit. This so-called QIQO (quick in quick out) strategy denotes an opportunistic mentality and approach. Naguib Sawiris, on the other hand, expanded rapidly and leveraged the dominant position of Mobinil in Egypt to invest internationally, including in more advanced markets, such as Italy, but primarily in high-growth high-risk markets such as sub-Saharan Africa or Iraq. Not all these gambles were successful—Orascom eventually sold out its operations in Iraq, considering that the situation was hopeless. But in any case it would be difficult to attribute Orascom Telecom's success exclusively or primarily to proximity to political power in Egypt.

Naguib Sawiris is especially interesting because of his openly expressed political opinions and, since the revolution, his active involvement in political life. In a very outspoken interview with Charlie Rose on 2 July 2008—well before the revolution—Naguib Sawiris clearly indicated that he believes in mobile communication because it is a tool for freedom, in contrast with the reality of suppression in most emerging markets and "in our part of the world"[20]. He also stated that "it is part of the revolution of the media … it has changed the political scene. Today you can't hide information, you can't prevent people from speaking". In fact, at that time, Sawiris was busy launching a mobile service in North Korea. Asked whether he thought mobile communications would have an impact on democracy, Naguib Sawiris said that they definitely would: "You can't shut up the people any longer, they talk to each other, they can communicate through SMS or Facebook, they can decide on a meeting, it goes like a blitz. …"; he noted on the role of SMS and mobiles in organizing demonstrations and protests. Concerning the situation in Egypt, he expressed satisfaction with the pace of economic reforms, but "on political reforms, I'd say we have not advanced much". He attributed this to the "fear of change" which he thought was ill advised because the resulting situation only benefited "fundamentalists and extremists" who are able to work underground.

Naguib was back on Charlie Rose's programme on 14 February 2011, and said that in his view the history of the region would be clearly divided into "before Tunisia and after Tunisia". He claimed he had predicted that the revolution was coming to Egypt because "we had a dictatorial regime, autocratic, denying its people all basic rights, freedom of speech and other basic human rights". He entered the political arena directly, establishing the Free Egyptians Party to fight against the Muslim Brotherhood and its political expression, the Freedom and Justice Party. The Party fought the parliamentary elections of November 2011 as part of the Egyptian Bloc, which scored rather poorly (obtaining thirty-five out of 508 seats, fourteen of these for Sawiris' party). Thus, Naguib Sawiris provides us with a case of an entrepreneur who has been close to the authoritarian regime but whose business success predates and justifies his close relationship to power, and whose fortune is largely independent of this relationship. He has also been openly critical of the regime, and is now politically active in the democratic opposition. Yet his case remains relatively isolated,[21] and this in itself is an indication of the regime's lack of success in nurturing a vigorous capitalist class.

Real estate developers

Also present on Forbes's billionaires' list is the Mansour family: Mohamed (number 764 on the list), Yasseen (804) and Youssef (854). The Mansours are primarily luxury real estate developers; their company, Palm Hills Development, has been accused of improperly buying public land for one of their developments.[22] The Mansours also are the representatives of GM cars in Egypt. They share ownership of Palm Hills with Mohamed al Maghrabi, who was Minister of Housing in the last government under Mubarak, and has been accused of being instrumental in allowing the company to misappropriate public land. Mohamed Mansour had been Minister of Tourism between 2004 and 2009. According to Amr Adly,[23] referring to documents leaked after the revolution, it appears that Alaa Mubarak, one of the sons of the President, was also a shareholder in Palm Hills, and made hefty profits out of partial sales of his shares to the remaining shareholders. Other names closely associated with the Mubarak family were also involved in the company.

It is clear, then, that the Mansours are much closer to the standard definition of crony capitalists. Adly documents other similar cases, notably the case of the Madinaty, an urban development scheme promoted by the Talaat Moustapha Group. The Group is active in construction, the development of high-end tourism projects (owning several hotels managed by Four Seasons) and urban development. The leader of the Group, Tarek Talaat Mustapha, has been a member of the National Assembly.[24] The sale of public land for the Madinaty project was annulled after the revolution because of administrative irregularities, although it was acknowledged that the price paid had not been low at all.[25] It appears that Gamal Mubarak was (or is) a hidden investor in the Talaat Mustapha Group (which is publicly traded on the Egyptian Stock Exchange) through two Cyprus based investment vehicles.[26]

Ahmed Ezz

A further significant case is that of Ahmed Ezz, whose steel company controlled 60% of the Egyptian steel market—all the more interesting because he was active in heavy industry. Ezz was arrested during the revolution and accused of various wrongdoings and, in September 2011, an Egyptian court sentenced him to ten years in jail on corruption charges.[27]

The military

Another case of cronyism, albeit sui generis, is the direct involvement of the army in economic activity and control of several business enterprises that are often totally unrelated to military affairs or defence interests.[28] The involvement of the army in business has a crony element, because the army is very much an insider. The fact that the generals and other high-ranking officers who are appointed to top managerial positions at the end of their military careers are just managers rather than owners, prevents them from acquiring the status of independent entrepreneurs, and impedes the companies they manage from evolving into competitive economic transformation actors.[29]

The broad picture that we may derive from these cases is one of a relatively small group of large business enterprises, distributed along a spectrum, ranging from predominant entrepreneurship to predominant cronyism and corruption. Proximity to power may predate business success, and facilitate or justify the latter; or business success may predate proximity to the power system, and similarly precipitate or justify the latter. It is clear that a successful large business can seek a degree of autonomy through international expansion, which is easier in certain sectors; or it can seek to leverage its privileged access to political decision-making cultivating domestic positions of rent seeking. Businessmen whose original fortune was made thanks to proximity to power may later evolve and become more entrepreneurial, and vice versa.

Picking losers

Proximity to power also means functionality to the projects and objectives that power holders pursue. In this respect, the outcome of the entrepreneur/crony capitalist dialectic is closely related to the nature of the economic projects that the state or power holders pursue. In the case of Egypt (but also Libya, Syria, Yemen, Tunisia) the lack of a clear and more decisive development strategy around which the private sector, crony or independent, could be mobilized and organized, has been an evident problem. Recent development literature has increasingly admitted that the state has an important role to play in guiding and mobilizing the private sector in pursuit of economic diversification. It is, in other words, not sufficient to simply open up the economy: the state must also "pick winners", that is, identify new industries and lines of production that do not exist yet or are just at an initial stage, but have potential for competitive success, and actively promote them.[30] This is a strategy that has proven extremely successful in many key Asian countries, as well as the Gulf.

In the GCC, governments have been prominently involved in "picking winners" and launching projects which were and are still predominantly implemented by state-owned enterprises or agencies, but around which the private sector has been able to organize, as partner or provider of a host of ancillary goods and services. Of course, this was facilitated by the availability of oil revenue—although Dubai and Bahrain have limited access to oil revenue, and Qatar has had to rely on foreign investment and debt to finance its LNG adventure. State entrepreneurship is important in guiding and mobilizing private sector participation and success.[31]

In contrast, in the rest of the Arab region, governments either have promoted the wrong industries or have not been effective in promoting the right ones. Tourism was promoted everywhere, and in fact some significant success stories were recorded. Tourism has one obvious problem, which is volatility: as soon as a negative event takes place, especially if it is a challenge to security, tourist flows are redirected, and the sector suffers catastrophic downturns. In other words, tourists are fickle customers. But apart from that there is no reason why tourism should not open the door to the establishment and prosperity of a large number of ancillary activities, acting as a growth engine for the entire economy.

However, apart from tourism, governments insisted in pursuing some very dubious options. Consider the case of Egypt: according to Roger Owen,[32] the "national" aims that the Egyptian regime publicly promoted were "food security" (primarily through the expansion of irrigated land) and other activities associated with developing desert areas such as Sinai or the New Valley, the creation of an Egyptian "Silicon

Valley", and the primacy of exports.[33] Many of the famously "crony" deals have been in connection with the development of desert areas—but none of them has turned any significant profit or succeeded in establishing a viable business. In these cases, the business receives extraordinary support from the government, and is privileged in this respect; however, the very concept of the venture is flawed and leads to no lasting value generation.

The incumbent regimes' inability to pick winners may be attributed to their giving priority to security over development,[34] but the situation did not improve even when business interests came to occupy a prominent direct role in government. In fact, progressively, the distance between the insider crony capitalists and political power simply disappeared. This was the result of two convergent movements: on the one hand, political power "forgot" its security-related origin and, through rampant corruption, became increasingly embroiled in business dealings; on the other hand, crony capitalists increasingly occupied positions of political responsibility.[35] In Egypt, the former process was encapsulated in the progressive rise of Gamal Mubarak and the prospect of a transition from father—who, after all, was an air force general—to son. The corruption of Mubarak's sons and their widespread participation in multiple business ventures was widely known. The literature is unanimous in identifying the appointment of Atif Ebeid as Prime Minister in 2004 as a turning point that signalled Gamal's predominant influence in policy making: Ebeid's cabinet was packed with business people, while Ahmed Ezz occupied the strategic post of Secretary General of Organizational Affairs of the ruling party, the NDP. Thus, it is clear that the business insiders were no longer simply close to political power, they held political power. This component of business was therefore very much involved with politics, and saw the preservation of the regime as functional to their interests. Dissenting voices were few and relatively isolated, the main example being the Sawiris.

In Tunisia, the state attempted to conduct an active policy of shaping a more competitive crony bourgeoisie through the so-called *Programme de Mise à Niveau*, meant to bring Tunisian industry to a level that would allow it to compete in the European and global market, following the EU-Tunisia Association Agreement. In this context, the Tunisian government encouraged the formation of larger enterprises through mergers and acquisitions, and found ways to officially recognize the role of leading entrepreneurs. "Some prominent figures of Tunisian entrepreneurship were ennobled, others were disgraced, and then, forgiven. Some were publicly accused of tax fraud (or *infraction économique*) and were granted, the ensuing year, preferential access to public urban projects".[36] Such tactics worked well to ensure that the major entrepreneurs would not dare to stand against the regime, but did not guarantee commercial success. In fact, no major industrial group has emerged in Tunisia, all remain marginal players in the global context. In the end, preoccupation with loyalty to the regime and the predatory attitude of the President's wife's clan prevailed over sound business and developmental rhetoric.

If, then, the state is not capable of mobilizing large business—whether entrepreneurial or crony—in the direction of valid investment projects, the practice of support from the state will not trigger faster economic growth, and may lead to a consolidation of the divide between large and small enterprises, frustrating the chances of smaller enterprises to grow and graduate to the category of large, politically relevant businesses.

The outsiders

The rigidity of the divide between insiders and outsiders has important political implications, because the outsiders will obviously feel excluded, and will attempt to develop alternative networks, which may turn into the social base of opposition movements.

Probably the most important tool for emerging entrepreneurs has been that of exit. Entrepreneurs and professionals have sought their fortune in a regional environment that offered opportunities, especially in the Gulf economies: we saw this already in the cases of Osman Ahmed Osman and Onsi Sawiris. A few moved to Europe or the United States, but the GCC option was certainly easier. The degree of success varied enormously: for one Hariri we have hundreds of thousands who simply managed to accumulate enough capital to buy a taxi or start some other form of individual business at home. The outsiders invested in their home countries but were not truly welcome. It is remarkable how there has been no serious effort on the part of the incumbent regimes to mobilize their respective expatriated entrepreneurs. Microenterprises set up with savings from working abroad had more to lose than to gain from encounters with the state. In his analysis of Tunisian "New Entrepreneurs" (all of them returnees from extended study or work experiences in Europe), Jean-Pierre Cassarino documents the mistrust they have towards officially backed institutions, including the Tunisian business association, UTICA:

"*Are you a member of the UTICA?*

No, I am not. If you're powerful, you can be a member of the UTICA. I run a small business concern; if I find a market opportunity, all the big fishes of the UTICA will know about it, and then, they'll pinch it. If I talk about it, they steal it. In Tunisia, we say that the Tunisians don't sleep during the night. Information is channeled very quickly. I don't want to be a member just out of caution. I don't want to belong to such a circle because, inevitably, they will ask me many questions, like "What's your job? With whom do you trade? That's it. I am not interested in the UTICA: I keep away from all that is political".[37]

It is interesting to note how the main business association is clearly perceived to be "something political", and the nature of the system predatory—even though the Tunisian regime was on paper officially supporting the emergence of new entrepreneurs and the prosperity of small businesses. In contrast, these entrepreneurs prefer to rely on alternative, informal networks. Asked the same question ("Are you a member of the UTICA?"), another entrepreneur answered:

"No, I am not. And I'm not a member of the RCD (the Party of the President) because it is too compromising"

"What do you mean?"

"That's it: it's too compromising. You never know what lies behind it. Well, I'm an entrepreneur".[38]

Thus official and unofficial or informal networks are mutually incompatible, and individual entrepreneurs feel the pressure of positioning themselves on either one or the other side of the divide.

The division of the business sector between a segment predominantly dependent on political access and privilege, and various segments relegated to different niches and not necessarily communicating with each other, has been the characterizing feature of business politics in the region for the past twenty years. The marginalized segments are composed primarily of small/medium or indeed micro enterprises, and are not well documented at all. For a variety of reasons, those active in these segments are not keen on publicity, and frequently hide their true respective financial and industrial capability. They tend to rely on informal networks, sometimes based on sect or geographical origin, but mostly on Islamic institutions.

Although explicit business political activism was not very visible, it is clear that outsider businesses not only existed, but also prospered to some extent and were able to support alternative networks, which also had a political intent and significance. Because the regimes mainly presented themselves as the bastion against Islamic politics, the insiders tended to be more secular in their message.[39] This contrasts with the experience of the Gulf, where a number of insiders are also prominent as promoters of Islamic business practices. In the Arab countries outside the Gulf, outsiders were thus mostly attracted or pushed to seeking solidarity in the Islamist circles that also represented the main opposition.[40] It would not be possible to clearly distinguish businessmen mainly motivated by religious conviction from those motivated by political inclinations or simply by the opportunistic search for supporting networks: what we can observe is that Islamist parties were able to survive and maintain a level of organization which eventually proved crucial not in the initiation, but certainly in the unfolding and aftermath of the revolution. This must have required access to continuing sources of finance, which allowed the Islamist parties to progressively expand their social support activities in the face of a retreating state, and cultivate popular support.

The emblematic case in this category may be that of Khairat al-Shater, de facto leader of Egypt's Muslim Brotherhood and initial candidate for the Presidency (later disqualified because he had been condemned and jailed under Mubarak; the Brotherhood then supported the candidacy of Mohammed Mursi, who was elected President). Al-Shater is reputed to be a medium-scale businessman,[41] but in fact not much is known about his business interests. He is said to own retail outlets that sell furniture and clothing imported from Turkey, but other businessmen close to the Brotherhood are representing the same companies. Zainab Abul-Magd claims that he started as a banker like Gamal Mubarak, and "the military trial of Brotherhood members in 2006 to 2007 was only the result of underlying competition between two groups that controlled capital in Egypt, namely between Gamal's group and the Brotherhood. All of those who stood trial were leading businessmen in the Brotherhood, the most important of whom was Khairat al-Shater".[42] According to Ahram Online,[43] on that occasion, al-Shater's fortune was estimated at LE80 million ($13 million), but this could be only the tip of the iceberg. In any case, the fact that seventy-two businesses close to the Brotherhood were confiscated in those trials, including al-Shater's, did not end his business career. "Despite repeated crackdowns on El-Shater's businesses by Egypt's former regime—starting in 1992 with the confiscation of his Salsabeel computer systems company, the sixty-one year-old seems to have survived, and even flourished, financially".[44]

Another well known Brotherhood businessman and partner of al-Shater is Hassan Malek, who, in association with al-Shater, runs the Egyptian branches of a Turkish furniture company, Istikbal, and a clothing brand called Sarar. In an interview he gave to Suzy Hansen of Bloomberg, Malek said: "They allowed me to reach a certain level, but there was a ceiling". Since the Brotherhood became the leading political party in post-revolution Egypt, Malek has been prominent in founding the Egyptian Business Development Association (EBDA), which aims at representing all the business ventures close to the Islamists that were disadvantaged until now.[45] The parallel with Turkey's MUSIAD, representing medium and small business that are a pillar of the support for the AKP government (as opposed to TUSIAD, representing primarily big business in Turkey, secular in orientation and closer to the military) is easily established, but may be premature.

Were the Brotherhood entrepreneurs excluded because they were Islamists, or did they become Islamists because they were excluded and frustrated with the regime? In the case of al-Shater and Malek it is clear that the former is the case: if anything, it may be surprising that the regime did not end up utterly destroying them, but simply limited their business ambitions. But what is true for them may not be true for all: possibly quite a few frustrated entrepreneurs did come closer to the Brotherhood in search of alternative networks of support, as they felt excluded from the official ones. Especially now that political power has passed to the Brotherhood, it is to be expected that many businesses will rush to become members of the EBDA, in the hope that the practice of favouritism will shift in their favour. Diane Zovighian details in Chapter Eight how the regime attempted to put in place policies in favour of small and medium enterprises, and how one specific NGO, the FEDA, has monopolized the support of foreign donors by claiming to represent SMEs. Was reliance on such an artificial representation a consequence of the fact that SMEs were typically not sufficiently loyal to the regime?

Was it the regime's inability to effectively reach out to SMEs (because it was mostly captured by big business?) that eventually contributed to the consolidation of the insider/outsider divide?

One thing is certain: the ranks of the outsiders were neither thin nor deprived of tools. Businesses closer to the opposition—primarily Islamic—were allowed to survive and prosper enough to be able to support the Brotherhood economically. This has proven crucially important, allowing the Brotherhood, as the only seriously organized force in Egypt, to be the main beneficiary of (or to steal, some would say) the revolution.

The marginalized

Thus, businesses have played multiple political roles, either directly in government, in advocating greater political openness while maintaining good relations with the government, or in actively supporting the opposition. But it is fairly clear that it was not the dialectic between insiders and outsiders among the capitalists that caused the revolution. Rather, it was sparked by the reaction of the much larger number of the marginalized, whether formally employed workers whose real incomes had been progressively eroded, or informal sector "entrepreneurs", for whom simple survival was a daily challenge.

The role of the workers has been highlighted in several contributions to the debate,[46] while others have focused on the activities of very small entrepreneurs and the informal sector.[47] Indeed, Hernando De Soto has argued that the common thread linking the revolutions in Tunisia, Libya and Egypt is the role of a new social class, which neither earns wages nor employs others. This class, represented by Mohamed Bouazizi, is a dominant phenomenon in the countries that experienced a liberalization process with rising inequality: "The majority of Tunisians and Egyptians are not on a salary. They're earning their own incomes, they're very, very small entrepreneurs, albeit outside the law".[48] Similarly, the President of the World Bank, Robert Zoellik, said: "it all started with—in a sense the red tape and the harassment of a small business person".[49]

Research on the marginalized or informal sector has mostly focused on the micro level, and it is difficult to gauge the aggregate importance of this component for the total economy. Estimates of the importance of the informal sector are always highly debatable, as the sector is invisible by definition. Nevertheless, it is clear that the marginalized have created their own informal networks, which have played a role in mutual support and notably finance. Diane Singerman has argued that the informal sector generates very large savings, which are circulated informally, hidden from taxation or control by the state.[50] Thus while the state controls the major, publicly owned banks, and channels funds to support the crony capitalists, and outsiders may to some extent create their own banks, the marginalized rely on savings club and self-organization to survive.

That the marginalized and the workers have played a leading role in the explosion of rage and indignation that set the Arab revolution in motion cannot be denied. But their typically micro organizational capability does not appear to have nurtured a lasting political force so far.

If we accept the view that marginalized, informal entrepreneurs are the potential engine of tomorrow's development, then the revolution can be depicted as an alliance between marginalized and outsider entrepreneurs to break the stranglehold on economic opportunities imposed by insiders. But this interpretation should be considered with great caution: in both Egypt and Tunisia the revolution was primarily made by the marginalized and a few tech-savvy liberals, and the outsiders came on board later, although their participation may have been essential for the positive outcome. Certainly, multiple other factors were at work, including non-economic factors. Eventually, the organizational weakness of the marginalized sector—as well as the workers and the smaller, technology savvy liberal bourgeoisie—led to their almost complete disappearance from the political scene, and the revolution turned into a contest between the outsiders, mostly represented by the moderate Islamic political forces, and the large crony bourgeoisie (in Egypt, closely allied with the military).

In conclusion

We have argued that the demise of the old regimes was caused or facilitated by their inability to set in motion a sufficiently inclusive process of economic growth. They nurtured a class of crony capitalists which, at least in the case of Egypt, eventually governed the economy directly rather than simply being favoured by the regime. Yet income inequality widened, absolute poverty increased, and the divide between cronies and outsiders or marginalized did not become more permeable. This outcome may be attributed to a combination of the dominant security preoccupation of the power holders, the corruption of their immediate entourage, and the monopolistic instincts of the cronies.

Will the collapse of the regimes be sufficient to open the door to more favourable results? Maybe the elimination of some of the cronies will create a more competitive and dynamic domestic market in some essential goods such as steel and other industrial sectors. But many of the cronies were real estate speculators or invested in questionable government-supported ventures such as the New Valley: their demise may not open very significant opportunities for greater competition.

Some old cronies will go, new cronies will emerge: it is possible that the new governments may be better at picking winners rather than losers, but, of course, there is no assurance of that. The reshuffling of the cards is positive in itself, as it facilitates the emergence of new entrepreneurs who may start as cronies and then become independent of state support, or may benefit from temporary state support to grow and be able to pursue more ambitious projects. However, realistically, the pursuit of the mythical "level playing field" is unlikely to reach its goal, because government interference will continue (as it does in even much bigger, industrial countries) and will inevitably favour some to the relative detriment of others.

Businesses have an important role to play in the aftermath of the revolution, putting the economy back on a growth path that will bring benefits to the marginalized majority, but the outcome is far from guaranteed. For things to evolve in the right direction, a substantial part of the informal business needs to emerge and become legal, in parallel with further selective privatization. In particular, military-controlled business must be civilianized and privatized, and diaspora entrepreneurs need to be called back. None of these things are easy to achieve.

More important, it is not clear that simply enlarging the scope for business participation will be enough to generate more equitable growth. In the end, the latter requires that the state plays a redistributive role through progressive taxation and the efficient provision of basic services, notably education, health services and affordable housing. The fiscal role of the state will need to be reconstructed and greater resources allocated to social services: whether the governments emerging from the revolution will in fact move in this direction is uncertain, but it may be expected that this agenda is unlikely to be popular with business. Yet governments will also need to stimulate investment and growth, including attracting foreign direct investment, thus maintaining a favourable investment climate. Much can be achieved in this respect through lighter administrative control, especially of new companies and projects, but in the end a balance will need to be struck between more effective taxation, on the one hand, and the need to attract investment and maintain the support of all businesses, on the other.

NOTES

1. INTRODUCTION: THE ROLE OF MENA BUSINESS IN POLICY MAKING AND POLITICAL TRANSITIONS

1. Stephen J. King, *The New Authoritarianism in the Middle East and North Africa* (Bloomington: Indiana University Press, 2009); Steven Heydemann, *Upgrading Authoritarianism in the Arab World*, Saban Center Analysis Paper (Washington: Brookings Institution, 2007).
2. Merih Celasun (ed.), *State-Owned Enterprises in the Middle East and North Africa: Privatization, Performance and Reform* (London: Routledge, 2001).
3. In the 2007 World Bank governance indicators, the GCC scores 0.3 on the scale from –2.5 to +2.5 for "government effectiveness", slightly above the global average of 0, but far below peers with comparable per capita GDP. The rest of the MENA region scores at –0.6, about 2/3 of a standard deviation below average.
4. The share of medium- to high-technology exports in total exports has stagnated around 20% since 1990, compared with 37% in Latin America and more than 50% in East Asia and the Pacific. See World Bank, *From Privilege to Competition: Unlocking Private-Led Growth in the Middle East and North Africa* (World Bank Publications, 2009), pp. 60ff.
5. On the shift away from authoritarian-populist distributional commitments see Laura Guazzone and Daniela Pioppi (eds), *The Arab State and Neo-Liberal Globalization: The Restructuring of State Power in the Middle East* (Reading: Ithaca Press, 2009); Anoushiravan Ehteshami and Emma C. Murphy, "Transformation of the Corporatist State in the Middle East", *Third World Quarterly* 17, no. 4 (1996), pp. 753–72; King, *The New Authoritarianism in the Middle East and North Africa*.
6. See World Bank, *From Privilege to Competition*, chapter five.
7. For country case studies on Arab crony capitalism, see Heydemann, *Networks of Privilege in the Middle East: The Politics of Economics Revisited.* (New York:Palgrave Macmillan, 2004).

8. For this argument specifically on the Saudi case, see Giacomo Luciani, "From Private Sector to National Bourgeoisie" in Paul Aarts and Gerd Nonneman (eds), *Saudi Arabia in the Balance: Political Economy, Society, Foreign Affairs*, (London: Hurst, 2005), pp. 144–84.
9. The lobbying of the export-oriented Moroccan apparel sector for customs streamlining and less onerous social security regulations in the 1990s might constitute one such exception: Melani Claire Cammett, *Globalization and Business Politics in Arab North Africa: A Comparative Perspective* (Cambridge University Press, 2010), pp. 185–8. Even there, however, it is not clear that business had a comprehensive reform vision.
10. Richard Doner et al., "Can Business Associations Contribute to Development and Democracy?" in Ann Bernstein and Peter L. Berger (eds), *Business and Democracy* (London: Continuum, 1998), pp. 126–47.
11. Heydemann, *Upgrading Authoritarianism in the Arab World.*
12. King, *The New Authoritarianism in the Middle East and North Africa*, p. 14.
13. Selvik's interview with Muhab Da'bul as cited in his chapter.
14. Interviews with Saudi and Emirati businessmen, 2009 to 2012.
15. I thank Marc Valeri for bringing this point to my attention.
16. Albert Hourani, "Ottoman Reform and the Politics of Notables", in William Polk and Richard Chambers (eds), *Beginnings of Modernization in the Middle East, the Nineteenth Century* (University of Chicago Press, 1968), pp. 41–68.
17. Jane Kinninmont, "The New and Old Economic Actors in North Africa", in Jane Kinninmont, Silvia Colombo, and Paola Caridi (eds), *New Socio-Political Actors in North Africa: A Transatlantic Perspective* Mediterranean Papers Series (Washington: German Marshall Fund, 2012), pp. 9–24.
18. For corroboration of this argument as well as a full classification of the political economies of MENA monarchies and different types of republican regimes, see Clement M. Henry and Robert Springborg, *Globalization and the Politics of Development in the Middle East* (Cambridge University Press, 2010).
19. The average score for the World Bank's "control of corruption" indicator is–0.46 for the republics Algeria, Egypt, Iran, Libya, Syria and Tunisia, while it is 0.16 for poor Jordan and Morocco and 0.69 for the rich Gulf monarchies.
20. James Liddell, "Notables, Clientelism and the Politics of Change in Morocco", *The Journal of North African Studies* 15, no. 3 (2010), pp. 315–31.
21. "Morocco protests will test regime's claims to liberalism", *Guardian*, 18 February 2011.
22. For more details on individual and collective organization, see Steffen Hertog and Giacomo Luciani, *Has Arab Business Ever Been, or Will it Be, a Player for Reform?*, Policy Paper for Arab Reform Initiative, October 2010.
23. For a survey on the role of business in North African transitions see Kinninmont, "The New and Old Economic Actors in North Africa", p. 15.

24. Ibid., pp. 16ff.
25. Ibid., p. 19.
26. Eva Bellin, *Stalled Democracy: Capital, Labor and the Paradox of State-Control Development* (Ithaca: Cornell University Press, 2002); Eva Bellin, "Contingent Democrats: Industrialists, Labor, and Democratization in Late-Developing Countries", *World Politics* 52, no. 2 (2000), pp. 175–205.
27. Jean-François Médard, "The Underdeveloped State in Africa: Political Clientelism or Neo-Patrimonialism" in Christopher Clapham (ed.), *Private Patronage and Public Power: Political Clientelism and the Modern State* (London: Frances Pinter, 1982), pp. 162–89.
28. Doner et al., "Can Business Associations Contribute".
29. Jill Crystal, *Oil and Politics in the Gulf: Rulers and Merchants in Kuwait and Qatar* (Cambridge University Press, 1995).
30. Discussions with various Kuwaiti merchants, Kuwait, September 2011.
31. Stephan Haggard and Robert R. Kaufman, *The Political Economy of Democratic Transitions* (Princeton University Press, 1995); Bellin, "Contingent Democrats".
32. Discussion with Syrian businessmen in the Gulf, October 2011.
33. "Fund Launched to Back Syrian Rebels", *Al Jazeera*, 6 June 2012, http://www.aljazeera.com/news/middleeast/2012/06/201266133319930526.html.
34. "Damascus Merchants Put up Shutters in Challenge to Assad", *The Daily Star—Lebanon*, 6 June 2012, http://www.dailystar.com.lb/News/Middle-East/2012/Jun-06/175840-damascus-merchants-put-up-shutters-in-challenge-to-assad.ashx.
35. Kinninmont, "The New and Old Economic Actors in North Africa", pp. 21ff.
36. David D. Kirkpatrick, "Ahmed Shafik counting on Egyptian elites' fears", *New York Times*, 25 May 2012, http://www.nytimes.com/2012/05/28/world/middleeast/ahmed-shafik-counting-on-egyptian-elites-fears.html.
37. Vali Nasr develops a similar argument about the potential of commerce and the Muslim middle class for political modernization; see Vali Nasr, *The Rise of Islamic Capitalism: Why the New Muslim Middle Class Is the Key to Defeating Extremism* (London: Free Press, 2010). The Arab uprisings suggest that the middle class for the time being is more important in this process than the commercial class.
38. David D. Kirkpatrick, "Muslim Brotherhood Leader Rises as Egypt's Decisive Voice", *New York Times*, 12 March 2012, http://www.nytimes.com/2012/03/12/world/middleeast/muslim-brotherhood-leader-rises-as-egypts-decisive-voice.html.
39. Haggard and Kaufman, *The Political Economy of Democratic Transition*, pp. 55–60.
40. Charles Kurzman and Erin Leahey, "Intellectuals and Democratization, 1905–1912 and 1989–1996", *American Journal of Sociology* 109, no. 4 (2004), pp. 937–86.

41. Peter B. Evans, *Embedded Autonomy* (Princeton University Press, 1995).
42. For analyses of lobbying, policy planning and self-regulation functions of business associations in the developing world, see Sylvia Maxfield and Ben Ross Schneider (eds), *Business and the State in Developing Countries* (Ithaca: Cornell University Press, 1997); Ben Ross Schneider, *Business Politics and the State in Twentieth-Century Latin America* (Cambridge University Press, 2004).
43. "Start-up Firms Bloom in Wake of Arab Spring", *Msnbc.com*, n.d., http://www.msnbc.msn.com/id/47016365/ns/business-us_business/t/start-up-firms-bloom-wake-arab-spring/; "In Arab Spring, Economic Gain May Trump Pain", *Jordan Times*, 18 January 2012, http://jordantimes.com/in-arab-spring-economic-gain-may-trump-pain; "Arab Spring Raises Hope for Era of Cleaner Business", *The Daily Star—Lebanon*, 9 November 2011, http://www.dailystar.com.lb/Business/Middle-East/2011/Nov-09/153523-arab-spring-raises-hope-for-era-of-cleaner-business.ashx.

2. OLIGARCHY VS. OLIGARCHY: BUSINESS AND POLITICS OF REFORM IN BAHRAIN AND OMAN

1. Referring to the role of the bourgeoisie under the French July Monarchy (1830–1848), in Alexis de Tocqueville, *The Recollections of Alexis de Tocqueville* (New York: Macmillan, 1896), p. 6.
2. Set of policies favouring employment of Omani nationals.
3. *The Financial Times*, 4 April 1990.
4. Jill Crystal, *Oil and Politics in the Gulf: Rulers and Merchants in Kuwait and Qatar* (Cambridge University Press, 1995).
5. Ibid., p. 195.
6. With the Basic Law promulgated in 1996, a serious obstacle to this mutual interference between business and politics has been settled; article 53 sets that no member of the Council of Ministers can combine its ministerial duty with the chair or membership to a board of any private company. Concretely, however, this decision did not lead to disruptions in government organization. Only two businessmen in the Cabinet left their positions in the following months: the Minister of Oil and Gas, Sa'id al-Shanfari, and the Minister of State for Development Muhammad al-Yusef. Some businessmen even entered the government after the promulgation of the Basic Law, like Juma'a bin 'Ali and Salim al-Khalili.
7. Eleven (out of twenty-four) ministerial portfolios are held by members of the Al Khalifa family, including Defence, Interior, Foreign Affairs, Justice and Finance.
8. Sayyid Haytham Al Sa'id is currently Minister of Heritage and Culture while Sayyid Fahd bin Mahmood has been the Deputy Prime Minister for Cabinet affairs since 1994. Several other ministers belong to collateral branches of the al-Busa'idi tribe but not to the royal family.

9. The Hawala are Sunnis who migrated to Bahrain from the nineteenth century from the Iranian coast but claim Arab origins. One example of these merchant families historically close to the Al Khalifa is the Kanoo family, who moved from southern Persia to Bahrain in the nineteenth century. Yusef Kanoo became in the 1920s and 1930s the largest banker on the island, and the Bahrain agent of companies like the Anglo-Persian Oil Company and Ford. The Kanoo group of companies is currently one of the largest family-owned groups of companies in the Gulf, while the family was estimated to be the fourteenth richest in the Arab world in 2011 (source: "Arabian Business Rich List 2011", http://richlist.arabianbusiness.com/profile/1298/). Khalid Kanoo, the current managing director of the Kanoo Group in Bahrain, was chairman of the Bahrain Chamber of Çommerce until 2005.
10. Graham E. Fuller and Rend Rahim Francke, *The Arab Shi'a: The Forgotten Muslims* (New York: St. Martin's Press, 1999), p. 125.
11. John E. Peterson, "Bahrain: Reform, Promise and Reality", in Joshua Teitelbaum (ed.) *Political Liberalization in the Persian Gulf* (London: Hurst, 2009), p. 158.
12. Peter Waldman, "'The Restive Sheihkdom", *Wall Street Journal*, 12 June 1995.
13. The Fakhro Group was founded in 1888. Yusef bin 'Abd al-Rahman (the minister's grandfather) and his five sons expanded the family business from the 1930s into a trade and economic empire spreading from Bahrain to India and Iraq.
14. Mohamed G. al-Rumaihi, *Bahrain. Social and Political Change since the First World War* (London: Bowker, 1976), p. 151.
15. Among the current board of directors are Nabil bin Khalid Kanoo; Ibrahim Zainal, chairman of MAZA Group of food business, founded in 1930 when his father came back from India where he was exporting rice, tea, clothes and construction material to the Persian Gulf; 'Adil al-Safar, a former district mayor of Manama and descendant of a merchant family already prosperous in the nineteenth century; and 'Abd al-Hamid al-Kooheji, chairman of AJM Kooheji Group, founded in 1890 as a textile trading company and now distributor in Bahrain of Bridgestone or LG products.
16. In 2011, Khalil al-Khonji, who is the chairman of Mohammed and Ahmed Al Khonji Group, a leading trading house of Muttrah founded in 1920, and also personally related by marriage alliance to Muhammad Zubayr, was reappointed chairman of the Chamber of Commerce by royal decree. Among the current board of directors are Khalid bin Muhammad Zubair and Shihab bin Yusef bin 'Alawi, son of the Minister responsible for Foreign Affairs.
17. Personal interview, Manama, 16 April 2009.
18. Two notable exceptions are the winning candidacies of Lujayna bint Muhsin al-Za'abi in Muscat (in 2000 and 2003), and in Sur in 2011 of Sa'ad Bahwan,

the chairman of OTE Group of Companies and youngest son of one of the leading Omani businessmen.

19. A former Deputy Chairman of the Chamber of Commerce (1975–93) and Minister of Commerce (1995–2006). In Oman, only eight individuals belonging to business families are members of the appointed current Majlis al-Dawla. The seventy-five member assembly is composed of a vast majority of tribal sheikhs and political elite originating from outside Muscat.
20. Maqbool al-Sultan, then Minister of Commerce and Industry, in *The Times of Oman* (Muscat), 17 August 2004.
21. For a detailed account of the events, see Munira Fakhro, "The Uprising in Bahrain: An Assessment", in Gary G. Sick and Lawrence G. Potter (eds), *The Persian Gulf at the Millennium: Essays in Politics, Economy, Security, and Religion* (New York: St. Martin's Press, 1997), pp. 167–88.
22. Fuller and Francke, *The Arab Shi'a*, p. 150.
23. Two of them were Deputy Prime Ministers, the others being the Ministers of the Prime Minister's Court, of Industry and Commerce, of Finance and of Oil and Gas Affairs.
24. Economic Development Board, *Developing Bahrain's Economy. Operating Review 2006* (2007), p. 18.
25. Economic Development Board, *Our Vision. From Regional Pioneer to Global Contender. The Economic Vision 2030 for Bahrain* (2008), p. 3.
26. Personal interview with an EDB communications department manager, Manama, 29 October 2010.
27. Economic Development Board, *Our Vision*, p. 5.
28. Laurence Louër, "The Political Impact of Labor Migration in Bahrain", *City and Society*, 20 (2008), p. 50.
29. The employer will not be granted any permit to hire a foreign worker until the Omanization targets of the branch are reached.
30. 1 Omani rial = US$2.6 (7 December 2012).
31. Personal interview, Muscat, 30 August 2005.
32. Personal interview, Muscat, 16 September 2003.
33. Personal interview, Muscat, 4 September 2005.
34. According to the previous system (in force since 2003), no tax was collected for companies registered in Oman earning below OR 5,000 profit. In the case of non-GCC foreign companies' branches established in Oman, profits beyond OR 5,000 could attract taxes up to 30%.
35. "Oman: Resolving a Taxing Issue", *Oxford Business Group*, 17 June 2009.
36. "World Investment Report 2009", United Nations Conference on Trade and Development, http://www.unctad.org/en/docs/wir2009_en.pdf; "Foreign Direct Investment Report 2009", United Nations Economic and Social Commission for Western Asia, http://www.escwa.un.org/information/publications/edit/upload/edgd-09-TP2.pdf

37. Haitham set himself up as a businessman in 1991 when he became one of the main shareholders, in partnership with Ahmed Makki and 'Umar al-Zawawi, of the newly-privatized *Sun Farms* agricultural company, one of the biggest owners of land in Batina and top vegetable producer in Oman. (See Calvin H. Allen and W. Lynn Rigsbee, *Oman under Qaboos. From Coup to Constitution, 1970–1996* (London: Frank Cass, 2000), p. 141.
38. As'ad was chairman of Oman Merchant Bank, established in 2007, in which he was one of the main shareholders, with the Gulf Merchant Bank, partially owned by Saudi Arabia's al-Rajhi family. But this project did not get off the ground, like the aborted sugar refinery project at Sohar port, in which As'ad was involved too.
39. In 2006, the average basic wage for Bahrainis working in the private sector was BD382 per month, compared with BD161 for non-Bahrainis. 46% of the expatriates working in the private sector, but only 1.1% of the nationals, earned less than BD100 per month (sources: http://blmi.lmra.bh/2011/03/data/lmr/Table_B.pdf; http://blmi.lmra.bh/otherdata/surveytables/mi_surveydata.xml, table 2.1.15.2; 1 Bahraini dinar = US$2.65).
40. Personal interview, Manama, 29 June 2008.
41. "Bahrain: Labor Dilemmas", *Oxford Business Group*, 2 October 2004.
42. Mohammed al-Garf, ''Businesses Protest Against Labour Fees', *Gulf Daily News*, 25 May 2010.
43. "Contractors Protest but LMRA Stands by Labour Fees", *Arabian Business*, 28 March 2009. Another demonstration, including members of the Council of Representatives, staged a mourning procession, with a black coffin symbolizing the death of small businesses in Bahrain (Rebecca Torr, '' 'Death' of Business Mourned", *Gulf Daily News*, 26 May 2010).
44. Rebecca Torr, ''Scrap LMRA Fees!", *Gulf Daily News*, 28 April 2010.
45. "CP Chairs EDB Meeting", *Bahrain News Agency*, 14 January 2008, http://www.bna.bh/portal/en/news/420622?date=2011–04–20
46. Personal interview with a former member of the Council of Representatives, 19 October 2008.
47. "The Crown Prince: Why Bahrain Needs Economic Reform", *Middle East Economic Digest*, 16 December 2008.
48. "New BCCI Strategies to Help SMEs", *Bahrain Chamber of Commerce*, 2 June 2009. http://www.bahrainchamber.org.bh/en/ViewNews.aspx?nid=257
49. Personal interview with a former member of the BCCI board, 16 April 2009.
50. Rebecca Torr, ''Business Leaders win BCCI Backing for Polls", *Gulf Daily News*, 25 November 2009.
51. The Minister of Labour stated that "[the decree] is the end of the sponsorship system, which does not differ much from slavery" (Habib Toumi, ''Bahrain's Decision to Scrap Sponsorship Rule Elicits Mixed Response", *Gulf News*, 5 May 2009).

52. Businessmen, like the BCCI board member 'Adil al-Maskati, even called for a two-year period. Interestingly, an amendment to the law forcing a foreign employee to complete at least one year before being allowed to switch his job was finally not adopted by the Council of Representatives. "Bahrain Council Rejects Jobs Switch Bill", *Trade Arabia*, 10 November 2009.
53. Since the 2008 financial crisis, 'Isam Janahi has suffered tremendous economic losses and his influence in Bahrain has dramatically weakened.
54. International Crisis Group, "Popular Protests in North Africa and the Middle East (III): the Bahrain Revolt", Middle East/North Africa Report 105 (6 April 2011), p. 6.
55. In March 2011, the proportion of Omanis employed in the private sector and earning less than the official monthly minimum wage was 70% (Supreme Council for Planning, www.moneoman.gov.om/book/mb/mar2011/T15.pdf).
56. Faisal Jawad is the CEO of Jawad Business Group (JBG), established in the 1950s. The group represents in Bahrain brands like Burger King, Costa Coffee and Mango. On a number of occasions since 2011 JBG stores were vandalized by pro-regime thugs (see Donna Abu-Nasr, "Torched Bank Warns Formula One Racing into Bahrain Violence", *Bloomberg* [19 April 2012]) and online campaigns were organized to boycott JBG products.
57. "BCCI's Call for Consolidated Efforts to Revive the Economy", *BCCI website*, http://www.bahrainchamber.org.bh/en/ViewNews.aspx?nid=601).
58. Sandeep Singh Grewal, 'Boycott Iranian Products' *Gulf Daily News*, 1 May 2011. The BCCI treasurer 'Uthman Sharif said this call "reflects an economic decision highlighting [the BCCI's] support to the Bahrain government and rulers".
59. 'HRH Premier Thanked by BCCI Chairman,' *LMRA Media Blog*, 26 March 2012, http://blog.lmra.bh/en/archives/1362.

3. PRIVATE SECTOR ACTORS IN THE UAE AND THEIR ROLE IN THE PROCESS OF ECONOMIC AND POLITICAL REFORM

1. Also called the Trucial States. This was the name given to the group of sheikhdoms that were British protectorates from 1892 until December 1971 and the establishment of the United Arab Emirates. In this paper the term Trucial States and Coast of Oman will be used interchangeably with UAE.
2. Jill Crystal, *Oil and Politics in the Gulf: Rulers and Merchants in Kuwait and Qatar* (Cambridge University Press, 1990), p. 8.
3. *UAE Yearbook 2009* (London: Trident Press, 2009), p. 58.
4. B.D. Augustine, "Index points to boost in non-oil sector", *Gulf News*, 4 May 2012.
5. Zaher Bitar, "Non-oil sector tops 71% of UAE GDP", *Gulf News*, 30 May 2010.

6. Commercial land was limited to those who were well connected to, or in alliance with the ruling families. The recent merchant families who emerged during the early 1970s have received wide-ranging support from the government which has provided them with commercial land and many other privileges. Much of their wealth began through the acquisition of such land, which was offered freely by the government. Others who were less well connected socially did not have similar chances.
7. Albadr S.S. Abu-Baker, "Political Economy of State Formation: The United Arab Emirates in Comparative Perspective", PhD dissertation, University of Michigan, 1995, p. 99.
8. This paper focuses on Arab and Persian merchants because of their dominance in the private sector as leading traders who managed to integrate with ruling families. As far as I am concerned, there are no leading Indian merchants who have been granted UAE citizenship.
9. Michael Herb, *All in the Family: Absolutism, Revolution, and Democracy in the Middle Eastern Monarchies* (Albany: State University of New York Press, 1999), p. 57.
10. John E. Peterson, "Rulers, Merchants and Sheikhs in the Gulf Politics: The Function of Family Networks", in Alanoud Alsharekh (ed.), *The Gulf Family: Kinship Policies and Modernity*, ed. (London: Saqi Books, 2007), p. 24.
11. Tribal elites are not necessarily separate from the merchant elites. Some merchant elites are intermarried with or members of tribal elites.
12. Abu-Baker, *Political Economy of State Formation*, p. 102.
13. Muhammad Morsy Abdullah, *The United Arab Emirates: A Modern History* (London: Croom Helm, 1978), p. 104. Among the major merchant figures were Bin Khalaf al-Otaiba and Hamid bin Buti in Abu Dhabi; bin Dalmuk, Sheikh Mani bin Rashid, Salim bin Misabbah, bin Bayat and bin Badur in Dubai; and bin Darwish, Humaid bin Kamil, and Ali al-Mahmud in Sharjah.
14. Abu-Baker, *Political Economy of State Formation*, p. 99.
15. Ragaei El Mallakh, *The Economic Development of the United Arab Emirates* (London: Croom Helm, 1981), p. 20.
16. Abu-Baker, *Political Economy of State Formation*, pp. 106–07.
17. As for the Indian merchants, who were under the protection of the British, they took advantage of this by expanding their trade in Dubai and asking for economic reforms. Therefore, the decline of the pearling industry led many Indian merchants to seek support from the British Political Resident in the Gulf to obtain repayment of their debts from leading Arab merchants.
18. The foreign merchants described here are those merchants who are originally not from the Arabian Peninsula, but later gained citizenship.
19. It should be noted here that sources explaining the roles of Persian merchants and those originating from the Indian subcontinent in the UAE are extremely limited.

20. Even though some of the current merchant elites, such as al-Ghurair and al-Futtaim, had participated in Dubai National Front in 1950s, they regained the trust of the al Maktoum after 1971.
21. Social elites are those families that are not as wealthy as merchant elites but have the same level of relations with ruling families. They are not necessarily well educated, but highly respected in the society by comparison with other tribes, such as the al-Qubaisat, al-Manaseer and al-Awamer. However, at present many of the social elites have become rich and involved strongly in the private sector.
22. Christopher Clapham, *Third World Politics: An Introduction* (Madison: University of Wisconsin Press, 1985), p. 48.
23. Herb, *All in the Family*, p. 15.
24. Elaborated from Abdulaziz Sager's examination of the private sector in the Arab world, Abdulaziz Sager, "The Private Sector in the Arab World—Road Map Towards Reform", *Arab Reform Initiative*, December 2007.
25. Some state-dominated companies are just major shareholders and have very limited management role.
26. European Commission, "Small and medium-sized enterprises (SMEs)", http://www.ec.europa.eu/enterprise/policies/sme.
27. Chris J. De Bruin, "Supporting SMEs 'Essential' for UAE growth", *Emirates 24/7*, 30 June 2010.
28. George Fahim, *Al-Emarat Al-Youm*, 22 April 2009.
29. Ibid.
30. "SME Law in Second half 2011: Mansouri", *Emirates 24/7*, 17 December 2010.
31. Abu-Baker, *Political Economy of State Formation*, p. 239.
32. When I submitted a special request to the Abu Dhabi Chamber of Commerce and Industry (ADCCI) for statistics concerning family corporations, I was told that these were highly sensitive matters and no access to the data was available. This reflects their close interrelation with the ruling families in all the Emirates.
33. Fareed Mohamedi, "Political Economy: State and Bourgeoisie in the Persian Gulf", *Middle East Report* 179 (1992), pp. 35–7.
34. Michael Field, *The Merchants: The Big Business Families of Saudi Arabia and the Gulf States* (Woodstock, NY: Overlook Press, 1985), p. 99.
35. For more detail see http://www.aljaber.ae
36. Field, *The Merchants*, pp. 249–51.
37. Ibid.
38. This is one of the leading banks in the UAE. It was established in 1979 in Abu Dhabi.
39. One of the Bani Yas tribes of Abu Dhabi.
50. Al-Fahim, *From Rags to Riches*, p. 50.
41. Ibid.
42. "The Rise of Abu Dhabi's Al Fahim Group", *AMEinfo*, 7 January 2004.

43. For more details on the specific industries see: http://www.alfahim.com.
44. James Paul, "The New Bourgeoisie of the Gulf", *Middle East Report* 142 (1986), pp. 18–22.
45. "Water tycoon 'Scotland's richest'" *BBC News*, 26 April 2009.
46. For more details see http://www.al-futtaim.ae
47. The Dubai National Front was a loose organization established in 1953 by Arab merchants of Dubai.
48. Christopher M. Davidson, *Dubai: The Vulnerability of Success* (New York: Columbia University Press, 2008), p. 208.
49. Abu-Baker, *Political Economy of State Formation*, p. 139.
50. Ibid., p. 140.
51. Ibid., p. 141.
52. Al-Futtaim's website, http://www.al-futtaim.ae
53. "UAE Economic growth to slow in 2012, says Standard Chartered", *AMEinfo*, 11 January 2012.

4. THE POLITICS OF SHI'I MERCHANTS IN KUWAIT

1. Rentier State Theory (RST) departs from the premise that the absence of a direct link between domestic production and public finance in most of the GCC states leads to an authoritarian neo-patrimonial state that—because of its riches—can act as a benevolent patriarch and co-opt societal forces through generous rent distribution. In the case of RST, the traditional extraction function of the state, through taxation, has been replaced with a state, primary engaged in allocation, through the redistribution of external rents. See Hazem Beblawi and Giacomo Luciani (eds), *The Rentier State* (London: Croom Helm, 1991).
2. The concept has traditionally been applied to urban politics in the modern history of the Levant.
3. Albert Hourani distinguishes three conditions propitious to the development of notable politics: personal dependence, a society dominated by urban notables (like old Venice) and the existence of some freedom of political action. Also see in this regard: Albert Hourani, "Ottoman Reform and the Politics of Notables" in William Polk and Richard L. Chambers (eds), *Beginnings of Modernization in the Middle East, The Nineteenth Century* (University of Chicago Press, 1968).
4. The small size of the city-state, a historical power-sharing agreement between the Al-Sabah and a Sunni merchant oligarchy, the early development of class relations due to a regional trade system, were all conducive to the crystallization of notable politics in Kuwait.
5. In his analyses of political modernization, Max Weber defines the political entrepreneur in opposition to the notable. The political entrepreneur is considered to be specialized in politics as a profession. Social position and economic resources

are not indispensable any more for succeeding in politics. The political entrepreneur—acting in a competitive environment—needs to mobilize other capacities (a political programme, political ideas) in order to gain the votes of the electorate. For a detailed analysis, see Max Weber, *Economie et Société II: l'organisation et les puissances de la société dans leur rapport avec l'économie* (Paris: Librairie Plon, 1971).

6. Also important is the intermediary function of the MP in Kuwait, who is in direct contact with his voters and whose daily activities consist of being an intermediary between voters and the government bureaucracy (*wasta* function). Also, the MPs' daily activities consist in visiting voters on occasions, such as attending funerals, marriages, etc. This is very different from the role of the MP in Western democracies.
7. Max Weber, *Economy and Society: An Outline of Interpretative Sociology* (New York: Bedminster Press, 1968). Max Weber distinguishes social relations on the basis of the orientation of social action. If social action is based upon a subjective feeling of belonging together—either affective or traditional—the social relation is called "communal" (*Vergemeinschaftung*).
8. Following its accession to power in 1926, the Pahlavi dynasty enacted a number of reforms, like land reform and compulsory military service, which severely hit the poor Iranians from rural backgrounds in the southern regions. See M. Reza Ghods, "Government and Society in Iran, 1926–1934", *Middle Eastern Studies* 27, 2 (1992), pp. 223–6.
9. Since this tendency combines legal reasoning with the insistence on mystical illumination as guidance towards salvation, Sheikhism has been criticized by traditional *usuli* scholars who consider it to be a deviant sect of Shi'ism. Juan R. Cole, "Shaykh Ahmad Al-Ahsa'i on the Sources of Religious Authority", in Linda S. Walbridge (ed.), *The Most Learned of the Shia: The Institution of the Marja' Taqlid* (Oxford University Press, 2001).
10. The first Sheikhi *marja'* who settled in Kuwait was Mirza 'Ali al-Ihqaqi, who left the Sheikhi community in al-Hasa because of a conflict with local *ulema*. Until today, the descendants of Mirza 'Ali al-Ihqaqi live in Kuwait and continue to lead the religious affairs of the Sheikhi community.
11. *Akhbari* scholars reject the *Usuli* school that considers the deductive reasoning (*'aql*) and the consensus (*'ijma*) of the *mujtaheds* as legitimate sources for elaborating Islamic law and complementing the Quran and the Akhbar.
12. Hourani distinguishes three conditions propitious to the development of notable politics: personal dependence, a society dominated by urban notables (like old Venice) and the existence of some freedom of political action. Hourani, "Ottoman Reform and the Politics of Notables".
13. See Laurence Louër, *Transnational Shia Politics: Religious and Political Networks in the Gulf* (London: Hurst, 2008), p. 122.

14. Interview, March 2009.
15. See in this regard Jacqueline Ismael, *Kuwait: Social Change in Historical Perspective* (Syracuse University Press, 1982).
16. Economic activity in al-Sharq was centred on the pearling industry. The Shi'i merchants were engaged in the same economic activities as their Sunni colleagues in the neighbourhood: pearl trading and dhow commerce.
17. Traditional *asabiyyat* refer to an esprit de corps based upon primordial factors such as kinship, tribalism and sect. We distinguish these traditional forms of social cohesion from more "modern" forms based upon broad-based interests (that is, ideologically driven/class-based interests) that transcend primordial cleavages in society. For a concise analysis, see J. Leca and Y. Shemeil, "Clientélisme et patrimonialisme dans le monde arabe", *International Political Science Review* 4 (1983).
18. Jill Crystal, *Oil and Politics in the Gulf: Rulers and Merchants in Kuwait and Qatar* (Cambridge and New York: Cambridge University Press, 1990).
19. Louër, *Transnational Shia Politics.*
20. See Saleh Mohammed 'Aischa 'Abdelrahman Al-Ghaz'ali, *al-jama'at al-siyasiyya al-kuwaytiyya fii qarn 1910–2007* [The political groups in Kuwait in the period of 1910–2007] (Kuwait: Sunduq Al-Barid, 2007), p. 321.
21. Sheikh Ghaz'al was the Shi'i ruler of Muhammara (Khoramshar) in the Iranian province of Khuzestan, which hosts an important Arab speaking population. From 1878 Sheikh Ghaz'al was under British protection, which enabled him to gain some autonomy from the Qajar dynasty. Mubarak was in a similar position, since the alignment with the British liberated him from the Ottoman yoke. See Ghaz'ali, *al-jama'at al-siyasiyya al-kuwaytiyya*, pp. 321–2.
22. Three representatives were present at the signature of the Protection Agreement between Sheikh Mubarak and the British Resident: two British diplomats and the Kuwaiti Shi'i merchant Al-Saffar. Ibid., p. 321.
23. Osman Salih, "The 1938 Kuwait Legislative Council", *Middle Eastern Studies* 28, 1 (1992), p. 83.
24. Historically, the old city-state was centred on two economic poles: al-Sharq and al-Qibla. The Shi'i families as well as the earliest sedentarized Sunni tribes from Basra and from Najd were to be found in al-Sharq. Al-Qibla represented a more homogeneous picture, as the Sunni merchant aristocracy was concentrated in this part of the old city. For detailed information on the urban geography of the old city-state, see F. Dazi-Héni, "La diwaniyya: entre changement social et recompositions politiques au Koweit au cours de la decennia 1981–1992", PhD dissertation, Institut d'Etudes Politiques, Paris, 1996, p. 101.
25. Interview, March 2009.
26. Ibid.
27. Some of these old Shi'i merchant families are: al-Naqqi, al-Wazzan, al-Shem-

ali, al-Mahmeed, Behbahani, Ma'rafi, Dashti, Abl, Abdal, Ghazal, al-Saffar, al-Arbasch, Mohammed-Ali, al-Sayegh and al-Qattan.

28. Interview, Jasem Qabazard, March 2009.
29. This period corresponds to the collapse of the natural pearl industry following the Japanese invention of cultured pearls. By the 1930s, the Japanese started to flood the market, as hundreds of Japanese farms were producing millions of pearls a year as cheap alternatives to the natural versions that were so hard and so expensive to harvest. The collapse of the pearl trade in the Gulf had devastating repercussions for the pearl merchants.
30. For a detailed account on the Assembly Movement, see Jill Crystal, *Kuwait: The Transformation of an Oil State* (Boulder: Westview Press, 1992), pp. 19–20.
31. Habib Hayaat, interview, March 2009. Hayaat is a former Minister of Communications and Public Works. He is the son of Hassan Jowhar Hayaat, who belonged to the old Shi'i merchant notability and had consistently been elected to Parliament between 1962 and 1975. Sayyid Jawad al-Qazwini was the brother of Mahdi al-Qazwini, the leading religious authority of the time. It was under their leadership that the Shi'a mobilized collectively and addressed their grievances to the British representative, asking for British citizenship to protect them against Arab nationalism. F. Al-Mdayris, *Al-harakat al-shi'iya fii al-Kuwayt* [The Shi'i Movement in Kuwait] (Kuwait: Dar Al-Qurtas, 1999), p. 14.
32. There exists a wide range of literature on the concept of the rentier state and its implications for state-society relations and class-politics. A state can be considered a rentier state when rentier revenues make up at least 40% of all government revenue, or when natural resource exports make up the bulk of GDP. See Giacomo Luciani, "Allocation vs. Production States: A Theoretical Framework", in Giacomo Luciani (ed.), *The Arab State* (Berkeley: University of California Press, 1990).
33. "Power" must be understood in its broad definition, including variables like access to central elite circles, support for Islamist movements, etc.
34. The term "*marja'iyya*" means "reference" in Arabic and refers to the centralization of religious authority in Shi'i Islam around the person of the *marja' al-taqlid* (the source of emulation). Ordinary scholars who have not reached the level of *ijtihad* are supposed to follow the opinions of a senior living *mujtahed* on a wide range of issues falling within the realm of religious law. The *marja' al-taqlid* is considered to be the most learned by the community of religious scholars of the *hawza*, a religious school for training Shi'i *ulema*. Since the nineteenth century, religious authority has become increasingly centralized around the Shi'i shrine cities in Iraq and Iran, whereby the *marja'* relies on a set of representatives (*wukala*) acting as his delegates in main centres of learning. Nowadays the *marja'iyya* is a form of centralized religious authority with transnational networks.

35. An example is Ali al-Korani, a Lebanese activist of al-Da'wa who, through his virulent speeches, would have an important impact on a young generation of Kuwaiti Shi'a. He was replaced by Sh. Mohammed Mahdi al-Asefi, an Iraqi of Iranian descent. The latter's arrival in Kuwait marked the arrival of political exiles to Kuwait following growing repression by the Ba'athist regime. See Louër, *Transnational Shia Politics*, pp. 110–20.
36. The system of the *marja'iyya*, whilst centralizing religious authority, does not recognize undisputed rules for designating a *marja'* and is therefore characterized by continuous factional struggles opposing contenders for religious authority. Al-Shirazi's claim to the *marja'iyya* was not recognized by the *mujtahed* of Iraq, Muhsin al-Hakim, because of his circumvention of several unwritten rules related to the *marja'iyya*. He was too young and did not frequent the Najafi seminars, being mostly educated in Karbala. For a detailed account of the problems within the centralization of clerical leadership in contemporary Shi'ism, see Abbas Amanat, "In Between the Madrasa and the Marketplace: The Designation of Clerical Leadership in Modern Shi'ism", in Said A. Arjomand (ed.), *Political Authority and Political Culture in Shi'ism* (Albany: State University of New York Press, 1988).
37. These Shi'a designated themselves as the Young Men (*Shabab*), in order to distinguish themselves politically from the older generation of notables, and were organized in the "*diwaniyya*" of the Young Men. See S.N. Al-Khaldi, *Al-ahzab al-islamiyya fii al-kuwayt: al-shi'a, al-ihwan wa al-salfiyyun* [The Islamic Movements in Kuwait: the Shi'a the Ikhwan and the Salafists] (Dar Al-Naba'li al-Nashra wa Al-Tawzi', 1999), pp. 102–04.
38. Max Weber, *Le savant et le politique* (Paris: Plon, 1959).
39. In countries where traditional *'asabiyyat* prevail, the structure of society tends to be "articulated" rather than "stratified". The literature on neo-patrimonialism analyzes these phenomena of weak horizontal integration from a systemic point of view, arguing that patronage and clientelism are at the heart of the neo-patrimonial state and enable the state to maintain its patriarchal domination over society.
40. The Social Society for Culture was established in 1963 by the dominant Shi'i merchant families, notably Qabazard, Ma'rafi, al-Kadhemi and Assiri. See Al-Khaldi, *Al-ahzab al-islamiyya fii al-kuwayt*, p. 105.
41. The dominant Shi'i merchant families, who also occupied positions in Parliament, all had a substantial part of their business concentrated in sectors relatively dependent on government patronage, such as real estate/lands and contracting. Some examples: the Ma'rafi family specializes in a broad range of activities, varying from trade to services, but concentrates on construction and real estate. The Al-Wazzan family is the main food supply contractor with the ministries of the Interior, Social Affairs and Health. Next to contracting, most

of the notables became commercial agents for foreign companies: Mercedes (al-Kadhemi), Panasonic (al-Youssefi), Porsche (Behbahani).

42. Al-Khaldi, *Al-ahzab al-islamiyya fii al-kuwayt*, p. 107.
43. Although exerting de facto leadership role within al-Mithaq (The Pact), Abdelwahhab Al-Wazzan does not have a formal role in the movement. The secretary general of the movement is 'Abd al-Hadi Saleh (ex-vice president of the Social Society for Culture in the 1980s).
44. Interview, Jasem Qabazard, March 2009.
45. Interview, Abdullilah Ma'arafi, March 2009.
46. For more information on the various terrorist attacks that swept the country in the 1980s see Lori P. Boghardt, *Kuwait amid War, Peace and Revolution: 1979–1991 and New Challenges* (Basingstoke: Palgrave Macmillan, 2006), p. 89.
47. Ibid., p. 100.
48. The two pro-government Shi'i deputies were Ya'coub Hayati (liberal and close to the Shiraziyyin) and Abbas Hussein Khudari (a "service deputy"). The only Shi'i pro-Iranian Islamist who succeeded in winning a seat in Parliament was Nasr Sarkhu. Other Islamist deputies like Adnan Abdelsamad and Abdelmohsin Jamal lost in the competition against other, government-supported candidates, like Abbas Khudari. See Linda L. Layne (ed.), *Elections in the Middle East: Implications of Recent Trends* (Boulder: Westview Press, 1987), p. 179.
49. Boghardt, *Kuwait amid War*, p. 133.
50. S. Eisenstadt, "Convergence and Divergence of Modern and Modernizing Societies: Indications from the Analysis of the Structuring of Social Hierarchies in Middle Eastern Societies", *International Journal of Middle Eastern Studies* 4.4 (1983). Also see in this regard Nazih Ayubi, *Over-stating the Arab State: Politics and Society in the Middle East* (London: I.B. Tauris, 1995).
51. See in this context the concept of "corporatism" as employed by Khaldoun al-Naqeeb in its analysis of state-society relations in the Gulf region: Khaldoun al-Naqeeb, *State and Society in the Gulf and Arab Peninsula: A Different Perspective* (London: Routledge, 1990).
52. Several authors (Shambayati, Ayubi, Ross) have argued that the nature of the rentier state inhibits the crystallization of class-based politics, thus leaving more space for the emergence of social movements based on moral (ascriptive and cultural) considerations.
53. See in this regard the study of E. Lust-Okar on elections and the role of parliamentarians in authoritarian MENA regimes, comparing it to a situation of "competitive clientelism": Ellen Lust-Okar, "Competitive Clientelism in the Middle East", *Journal of Democracy* 30, 3 (2009), pp. 122–35.
54. See in this context the distinction—formalized by Maurice Duverger—between "parties of cadres" and "parties of masses" related to the nature of political parties' legitimacy. Maurice Duverger, *Les partis politiques* (Paris: Le Seuil, coll. "Points Essais", 1992), p. 84.

55. Adnan Abdelsamad, Abdelmohsin Jamal, Nasr Sarkhu.
56. Hence the Sheikhi Shi'a are likely to vote for deputies of Tajammu'a Al-Risalat Al-Insaniyya (The Assembly of the Human Message).
57. We can think of Ahmed Lari (al-Tahaluf), Adnan Abdelsamad (al-Tahaluf), Hassan Jowhar (independent, but close to al-Tahaluf), Saleh Achour (al-Adala Wa-Salam), Abdelmohsin Jamal (al-Tahaluf). This information was collected during our fieldwork in Kuwait (March-April 2009).
58. The Shi'i deputies who are considered to be descendants from the Prophet: Sayyid Adnan Abdelsamad (al-Tahaluf), Sayyid Hussein al-Qallaf (independent, pro-government), Sayyid Youssef al-Zilzalla (al-Mithaq).
59. The ideological principles of the movement are justice, peace, Islamic unity, and consultation. Interview, Abdelhussein al-Sultan (secretary-general of the Shiraziyyin), March 2009.
60. After the death of Mirza al-Ha'iri al-Ihqaqi, there was a split with the Sheikhi-Hasawi community in Kuwait. One group recognizes his son, Abdallah al-Ihqaqi, as their new *marja'* and is associated with the Imam al-Sadiq mosque. Another group, not recognizing Abdallah al-Ihqaqi as its *marja'*, is associated with Majslis Abadar, under the direction of the merchant Hussein al-Qattan (Abu Bachar). Interviews, March and April 2009.
61. The charitable associations of the Shiraziyyin are Ahl al-Beyt, Sayyid al-Shuhada, Mohammed al-Ameen and Jama'iyyat al-Taqalin. Ibrahim al-Gholoom (director of the Shiraziyyin library "Rasol Al-Azam"): interview, March 2009.
62. Al-Anwar (The Lights) was created in 2003 and broadcast its programmes for the first time in 2005. The project of Mohammed al-Shirazi and his son, Mortadha Al-Shirazi, seems to have profited from the financial support of the affluent Shi'i merchants in Kuwait and in Saudi Arabia: interview, Abdelhussein Al-Sultan, March 2009.
63. Interview, Abdelwahhab al-Wazzan, March 2009.
64. The spokesmen of al-Mithaq are Abdelhadi al-Saleh (Minister of Parliamentary Affairs, 2006), Youssef al-Zilzalla (Minister of Commerce and Industry, 2006), Abdelwahhab al-Wazzan (Minister of Commerce and Industry, 1999), Jaber Behbahani (old mercantile elite close to Al-Sabah).
65. Because of his important role in the protection of Kuwait during the Iraqi invasion he profited from government's support on a number of occasions. He was appointed Minister of Commerce and Industry (1999) and currently heads the International Bank of Kuwait.
66. Louër, *Transnational Shia Politics*, p. 228.
67. Since 1999 four out of eight Shi'i ministers have been related to the group of Abdelwahhab al-Wazzan. There are three ministers affiliated with al-Mithaq: Abdelhadi al-Saleh, Abdelwahhab al-Wazzan, and Youssef al-Zilzalla. The fourth person is the current Minister of Finance, Mustafa al-Shemali, who is related by kinship ties to the Al-Wazzan family.

68. In this context the remark of Mustafa and Suleiman al-Wazzan on the role of family in politics is telling: "We are very low-profile, we do not want to show up. The worst for us is to come in public. We like to concentrate on daily works, but we have got two persons: Abdelwahhab al-Wazzan and also Mustafa al-Kharij. They represent us". Interview, Mustafa al-Wazzan and Suleiman al-Wazzan, March 2009.
69. The prominent urban-tribal tensions in Kuwaiti society have a strong class component, as the late-arrived tribal populations (*mutajanissin*)—essentially employed in public sector and dependent on government subsidies—challenge the prerogatives of the old commercial elites.
70. This is reinforced by the fact that the only limitation set by the Constitution is that power remains in the hands of the descendents of Sheikh Mubarak, of whom there are hundreds today.
71. For an in-depth analysis of this process of class-creation by the Saudi State, see Kiren Aziz Chaudhry, *The Price of Wealth: Economies and Institutions in the Middle East* (Ithaca: Cornell University Press, 1997), p. 172.
72. Interview, Jawaad Bukhamseen, March 2009.
73. In the elections of May 2008, an alliance was formed between Saleh Ashour, Anwar Bukhamseen and Khalil al-Saleh. The three deputies decided to work together in the first district for al-Adala Wa-Salam.
74. Tajamu'a al-Risalat al-Insaniyya is the first political movement of the Sheikhi community in Kuwait. The movement is organized around the Imam al-Sadiq mosque, led by the merchant Hussein al-Qattan. The group represents a couple of Hasawi families, related through intermarriage (such as al-Sayegh, al-Arbasch and al-Qattan). Among the political figures related to the movement are Ali al-Baghli (former Minister of Oil) and Abdel Azizi al-Qattan, both of liberal persuasion.
75. Al-I'tilaf al-Islami al-Watani (The National Islamic Coalition), uniting al-Tahaluf, al-Risalat al-Insaniyya and al-Mithaq participated in the election campaign. During the conference, Jawaad Bukhamseen insisted on the need for the Shi'a in Kuwait to be united and called upon the audience to support this national coalition in a "patriotic spirit": interview, Jawaad Bukhamseen, April 2009.
76. Al-Aqeelah was created by Hamad Khaaja in 2006. The investments of al-Aqeelah are multi-billion dollar projects in the shrine cities of Najaf, Karbala and Sayyida Zeinab in Syria. In 2008 Najaf airport was opened, a project which includes the building of villas, schools, and hotels in the city. The same is true for Sayyida Zeinab which is being transformed into a touristic pilgrimage hub.
77. "Al-Maliki: baladuna maftuhan amama al-Kuwaytiyiin Lilistithmar" [Al-Maliki: our country is open for Kuwaitis for investments], *Dar Al-Nahar*, 22 July 2007.
78. Interview, March 2009.
79. In the policy of land allocation, parcels of state land are distributed or "sold" at symbolic prices to select citizens, to be subsequently repurchased by the state

at a much higher price. It has been very important policy for creating state clienteles. See also Ghanim Al-Najjar, "The Decision-Making Process in Kuwait: The Land Acquisition Policy as a Case Study", PhD dissertation, Exeter University, 1984.

80. Interview, April 2009.
81. "I am someone neutral in the midst of all these people. I am original from Bahrain, but I support all the Shi'i movements and I am very close to the Emir. You know, they seem to be unified, but they are very dispersed, the Shi'is. At this moment we are trying to unite them". Interview, Ali al-Matruk, March 2009.
82. "Kuwait to mediate in Bahrain crisis", Reuters, 27 March 2011.
83. The Haider family holds 28% of shares in the Pearl of Kuwait Real Estate Company. See IPR Strategic Business Information Database, "Kuwait: Holding of Mahmud Haydar Family in the Kuwait Pearl Real Estate Company", 21 September 2003.
84. Interview, March 2009.
85. Furthermore, *Al-Dar* is planning to create a Shi'i satellite channel, in the same spirit as the al-Anwar station: interview, Mansur Haider, March 2009.
86. See Louër, *Transnational Shia Politics*, p. 249.
87. "Al-Tahaluf Al-Islami 'an al-waqf al-ja'fari: nuhadhdhiru al-hukuma min al al-istijabati li al dhughut al-kharijiyya" [The Islamic Coalition with regards to the Ja'fari waqf: we warn the government and we ask the government not to cede to external pressures], *Al-Rai Al-Aam*, 14 December 2001.
88. Interview, Hashem Al-Hashemi, March 2009: interview, Bin Nakhi, March 2009; interview, Hussein al-Ma'atuq, March 2009; interview, Ali al-Saleh, March 2009.
89. Interview, Ahmed al-Hussein, March 2009.
90. Interviews, March and April 2009.
91. *Al-Dar*, 28 July 2009.
92. Interview, Hussein al-Ma'atuq, April 2009.
93. In 2008 the Sunni Islamists still represented twenty-one seats, whereas they only attained eleven seats in the May 2009 elections.
94. See Rivka Azoulay, "Entre marchands, effendi et l'Etat: changement social et renouvellement des élites dans la communauté chiite koweitienne", MPhil thesis, Sciences Po, Paris, 2009, pp. 115–20.
95. Although some of the Shi'i deputies—notably the women (Rola Dashti, Ma'souma al-Mubarak)—did not run on a sectarian ticket, their success fits in the broader divide and rule policy as elaborated previously.

5. BREAKING LOOSE: REDUCED PRIVATE SECTOR DEPENDENCE ON GOVERNMENTS IN GCC ECONOMIES

1. I owe an intellectual debt for the development and evolution of this paper to Steffen Hertog, whose ideas on contrasting distribution in the two oil booms were

ultimately published in Steffen Hertog, "The Evolution of Rent Recycling During Two Booms in the Gulf Arab States: Business Dynamism and Societal Stagnation" in Metteo Legrenzi and Bessma Momani (eds), *Shifting Geo-Economic Power of the Gulf: Oil, Finance and Institutions* (Aldershot: Ashgate, 2011).

2. Giacomo Luciani, "From Private Sector to National Bourgeoisie: Saudi Arabian Business", in Paul Aarts and Gerd Nonneman (eds), *Saudi Arabia in the Balance: Political Economy, Society, Foreign Affairs* (New York: NYU Press, 2005), pp. 151–6. While Luciani is specifically referring to Saudi Arabia, wealth distribution schemes in other GCC countries used most if not all of these methods as well.
3. Giacomo Luciani, "Allocation vs. Production States: A Theoretical Framework", in Giacomo Luciani (ed.), *The Arab State* (Berkeley: University of California Press, 1990), p. 65.
4. The term "private sector" is ambiguous and fluid in the GCC context. One complication is that many large companies in GCC states are partially or entirely state-owned. For example, the Saudi Basic Industries Corporation (SABIC), which is the largest publicly traded company in the Middle East, is 70% state-owned. The situation is further complicated by the involvement of the ruling families in business, either in partnerships with private companies or independently. Any examination of the private sector in the GCC must at least identify these realities as issues to be addressed. Most of the sources of statistics make no mention of whether state-owned enterprises or businesses owned by ruling families are included in the "private sector" or the government sector, but it should be assumed that they are counted in the private sector, with all of the implications this has for analysis. For more on the definitional problems of the private sector in the Saudi context, see Luciani, "From Private Sector to National Bourgeoisie", pp. 144–8.
5. Also worth noting is that the structure of the capital sector is such that governments often use off-budget state agencies like Saudi Aramco or SABIC, which would not appear as government spending. Nonetheless, several new, large projects are at least partially in the hands of the private sector, and the government is careful not to crowd it out.
6. The value added of mining and utilities is used because it is the most complete, uniform data available. It serves as a relatively accurate approximation of hydrocarbon contributions to GDP. For all countries except Bahrain in recent years, the value added of utilities has typically been no more than 3% of that of mining, which makes it more or less negligible and does not change the analysis.
7. In 2010, the IMF estimated that the value of exported oil, gas, and petroleum products was US$66.8 billion while the value of re-exports was US$90.8 billion. IMF, *United Arab Emirates: 2011 Article IV Consultation, Country Report No. 11/111* (May 2011).
8. *EIU Country Profile Bahrain* (2009), pp. 20 and 26.

9. See Christopher M. Davidson, *Dubai: The Vulnerability of Success* (New York: Columbia University Press, 2008).
10. BP *Statistical Review of World Energy* (June 2011), pp. 6–8 and 20–22.
11. Ugo Fasano and Qing Wang, "Testing the Relationship Between Government Spending and Revenue: Evidence from GCC Countries", IMF Working Paper, WP/02/201 (2002), p. 18.
12. Ibid., p. 4.
13. Ibid.
14. United Nations Statistical Abstract of the ESCWA Region; various national reporting data; IMF Article IV Reports and Statistical Appendices.
15. Mary Gwen Okruhlik, "Debating Profits and Political Power: Private Business and Government in Saudi Arabia", PhD dissertation, University of Texas at Austin, 1992; Tim Niblock with Monica Malik, *The Political Economy of Saudi Arabia* (New York: Routledge, 2007), pp. 143–72.
16. National reporting data; IMF Article IV Reports and Statistical Appendices.
17. Ugo Fasano and Rishi Goyal, "Emerging Strains in GCC Labor Markets", IMF Working Paper, WP/04/71 (April 2004), p. 7.
18. "Gulf States: Private Sector Increasingly Independent", Oxford Analytica, 14 December 2009.
19. Ibid.
20. Ibid.
21. Since historical data on the breakdown of capital formation into public and private contributions are limited, I use government capital spending from government expenditure data rather than public sector contributions to capital formation. The use of these different categories explains why shares are above 100% in several cases. Data come primarily from the UN, although some recent data have been taken from national statistics agencies, ministries, and IMF Article IV reports. However, recent figures from Graph 15 do coincide quite well with the figures in Graph 14, which represent actual shares in fixed capital formation. The major exception is the UAE, but one must be cautious with UAE figures owing to the fragmented and unreliable nature of statistics in the federal system. There is little doubt that the direction of trends in the graph is correct, even if the estimate of absolute levels might be off in individual cases.
22. Hertog, "The Evolution of Rent Recycling During Two Booms in the Gulf Arab States", pp. 61–2.
23. As of November 2010, the Kingdom had US$624 billion worth of projects planned or under way, and Saudi Arabia was expected to award construction contracts worth US$86 billion in 2011: "Saudi Arabia to award $86b construction projects in 2011", *Saudi Gazette*, 23 November 2010.
24. Robert E. Looney, "Saudi Arabia: Measures of Transition from a Rentier State", in Joseph A. Kechichian (ed.), *Iran, Iraq, and the Arab Gulf States* (New York: Palgrave, 2001), pp. 140–41.

25. Ibid., p. 140.
26. Alexei Kireyev, "Key issues Concerning Non-Oil Sector Growth", in *Saudi Arabia's Recent Economic Developments and Selected Issues* (Washington: International Monetary Fund, 1998), pp. 29–33.
27. Volker Treichel, "Stance of Fiscal Policy and Non-Oil Economic Growth", in Ahsan Mansur and Volker Treichel (eds), *Oman Beyond the Oil Horizon: Policies Toward Sustainable Growth*, IMF Occasional Paper No. 185 (Washington: IMF, 1999).
28. Ugo Fasano and Qing Wang, "Fiscal Expenditure Policy and Non-Oil Economic Growth: Evidence from GCC Countries", IMF Working Paper, WP/01/195 (2001), p. 8.
29. K. Ghali and F. Al-Shamsi, "Fiscal Policy and Economic Growth: A Study Relating to the United Arab Emirates", *Economia Internazionale* 50, (1997), pp. 519–33.
30. Fasano and Wang, "Fiscal Expenditure Policy and Non-Oil Economic Growth".
31. ANIMA Investment Network, "The Mediterranean between Growth and Revolution: Foreign Direct Investments and Partnerships in MED Countries in 2010" (March 2011), p. 72.
32. ANIMA Investment Network, "Foreign Direct Investments in the Med Region in 2008: Facing the Crisis" (March 2009), pp. 26–7.
33. ANIMA Investment Network, "Mediterranean Investment Map: Sectoral Guidebook on Public Investment Policies in the Mediterranean" (January 2009), pp. 55 and 79.
34. Ibrahim Saif, "The Oil Boom in the GCC Countries, 2002–2008: Old Challenges, Changing Dynamics" (Washington: Carnegie Endowment for International Peace, March 2009), p. 14.
35. A list of structural reforms can be found in Ugo Fasano and Zubair Iqbal, "GCC countries: From Oil Dependence to Diversification" (Washington: International Monetary Fund, 2003), p. 10.
36. Kito de Boer *et al.*, "Perspectives on the Middle East, North Africa and South Asia (MENASA) Region", McKinsey and Company (July 2008), p. 51.
37. Saif, "The Oil Boom in the GCC Countries, 2002–2008", pp. 5–6.
38. Koba Gvenetadze, "Non-Oil Sector Supports Saudi Growth", *IMF Survey Magazine* (November 14, 2007).

6. CSR AND REPUTATION BUILDING IN SYRIA: CONTEXTUALIZING "THE BUSINESS CASE"

1. David Vogel, *The Market for Virtue: The Potential and Limits of Corporate Social Responsibility* (Washington: Brookings, 2005).
2. Charles Tilly, *Trust and Rule* (Cambridge University Press, 2005).
3. Interview, Muhab Da'bul, 1 April 2009.

4. D.J. Vogel describes how the greater emphasis on the business case in the post-Cold War revival of the CSR concept breaks with "old-style" conceptions of corporate responsibility wherein a company was supposed to behave virtuously for the sake of virtue itself. There has been a clear evolution, in the international CSR discourse, from doing good "to do good" to doing good "to do well". See Vogel, *The Market for Virtue.*
5. For more discussions of the merits of the business case see E. Kurucz, B. Colbert and D. Wheeler, "The Business Case for Corporate Social Responsibility", in A. Crane, A. McWilliams, D. Matten, J. Moon, and D. Siegel (eds), *The Oxford Handbook of Corporate Social Responsibility* (Oxford University Press, 2008), pp. 83–112, and A.B. Carroll; K.M. Shabana, "The Business Case for Corporate Social Responsibility: A Review of Concepts, Research, and Practice", *International Journal of Management Reviews* 12 (2010), pp. 85–105.
6. UNDP, "UN Global Compact Guide—JUNE 2010", http://www.undp.org.sy/files/UN%20Global%20Compact%20Guide%20-%20JUNE%202010.pdf.
7. United Nations, "UN SYRIA—Global Compact", http://www.un.org.sy/forms/pages/viewPage.php?id=52.
8. Quoted in Carroll and Shabana, "The Business Case for Corporate Social Responsibility", p. 99.
9. "For more on the Zakat vs. CSR models see Kjetil Selvik, "Business and social Responsibility in the Arab World: the Zakat vs. CSR models in Syria and Dubai", *Comparative Sociology* 12 (2013): 95–123.
10. The companies are listed in footnote 62. The remaining 12 members were NGOs and business chambers. UNDP, "UNDP Syria—Members' List", http://www.undp.org.sy/index.php/the-network/members-list-.
11. UNDP Democratic Governance Thematic Trust Fund, "Enchancing Civic Engagement in CSR through Inclusive Growth Based Civic-Private Sector Partnership", UNDP, http://www.bdpfunds.org/dgttf/files/dgttf…/APR-Syria.doc.
12. Steven Heydemann, *Authoritarianism in Syria: Institutions and Social Conflicts* (Ithaca: Cornell University Press, 1999), pp. 183–7.
13. Raymond Hinnebusch, *Syria: Revolution from Above* (London: Routledge, 2001).
14. As a consequence of the simultaneous fall in public expenditure and private sector expansion, the relative strength of the latter improved significantly. By 1990, gross private investment, which had dropped to less than 30% in the 1960s and ranged around one-third in the 1970s, exceeded that of the public sector. Volker Perthes, *The Political Economy of Syria under Asad* (London: I.B. Tauris, 1995), p. 59.
15. Interestingly, the liberalization of the finance sector also included Islamic Banks and insurance.
16. International Monetary Fund, "Syrian Arab Republic—IMF Article IV Con-

sultation Mission's Concluding Statement, May 14, 2006" http://www.imf.org/external/np/ms/2006/051406.htm

17. Syrian Ministry of Planning, "The Tenth Five-Year Development Plan 2006–2010, Chapter One", http://planning.gov.sy/files/file/FypChapter1En.pdf.
18. Michael Blowfield and Alan Murray, *Corporate Social Responsibility: A Critical Introduction* (Oxford University Press, 2008), pp. 252–77.
19. See Thomas Pierret and Kjetil Selvik, "Limits of Authoritarian Upgrading in Syria: Private Welfare, Islamic Charities, and the Rise of the Zayd Movement", *International Journal of Middle East Studies* 41, 4 (2009), pp. 595–614.
20. Interview, Said Hafez, 7 May 2008.
21. The Hafez family originally lived in Homs but moved to Damascus in 1936 to expand its business. At the time of the 1965 industry nationalizations in Syria it lost its first refrigerator producing plant and moved to Beirut. Following the outbreak of the Lebanese civil war and President Hafiz al-Asad's invitation to Syrian businessmen to repatriate, the family re-established itself in 1976 in Damascus where it experienced new commercial success from the 1990s.
22. As pointed out by Singer, *zakat* and *salat* appear inseparable in numerous Qur'anic *suras*. See Amy Singer, *Charity in Islamic Societies* (Cambridge University Press, 2008), p. 18.
23. See for instance Sheikh Sariya al-Rifa'i's speech to the merchants of Bab Srije quoted in Pierret and Selvik, "Limits of 'Authoritarian Upgrading' in Syria", p. 607.
24. A. Zysow, "Zakāt (a.)". in P. Bearman, Th. Bianquis, C.E. Bosworth, E. van Donzel and W.P. Heinrichs (eds), *Encyclopaedia of Islam, Second Edition* (Leiden: Brill, 2010), http://www.brillonline.nl/subscriber/entry?entry=islam_COM-1377.
25. Singer, *Charity in Islamic Societies*, p. 61.
26. According to a frequently cited verse in the Qur'an, *ayat al-sadaqa*, those entitled to receive *zakat* fall into eight categories: "the poor and the needy; those who work to collect [sadaqat], those whose hearts are brought together, the ransoming of slaves, debtors, in God's way, and the traveler". See Singer, *Charity in Islamic Societies*, p. 44.
27. Interview, Said Hafez and Amin Hafez, 30 March 2009.
28. Interview, Said Hafez, 7 May 2008.
29. Ibid.
30. Ibid.
31. John G. Ruggie, "The Global Compact: An Extraordinary Journey", http://www.wbcsd.org/web/publications/bar/rtbrugg.pdf.
32. Jean-Philippe Thérien and Vincent Pouliot, "The Global Compact: Shifting the Politics of International Development?" *Global Governance* 12 (2006).
33. UNDP, "UNDP Syria—UN Global Compact Syria", http://www.undp.org.sy/index.php?option=com_content&view=article&id=448&Itemid=128.

34. See for instance Oppenheim et al., "Shaping the New Rules of Competition: UN Global Compact Participant Mirror", McKinsey & Company, http://www.unglobalcompact.org/docs/news_events/8.1/McKinsey.pdf.
35. Gerald F. Davis, Marina V.N. Whitman and Mayer N. Zald, "The Responsibility Paradox", *Stanford Social Innovation Review* (2008), p. 32.
36. See United Nations General Assembly, "Business and Human Rights: Towards Operationalizing the 'Protect, Respect and Remedy' Framework", 22 April 2009, http://www2.ohchr.org/english/bodies/hrcouncil/docs/11session/A.RC.11.13.pdf.
37. Singer, *Charity in Islamic Societies*, p. 58.
38. *Forward Magazine*, March 2009, pp. 34–5.
39. AMEinfo, "World Economic Forum Names Syrian Entrepreneur as Young Global Leader", 7 March 2009, http://www.ameinfo.com/187479.html.
40. Interview, Abdulsalam Haykal, 26 May 2010.
41. For more on the discourse of entrepreneurship in Syria see Kjetil Selvik, "It's the Mentality, Stupid! Syria's Turn to the Private Sector", in Aurora Sottimano and Kjetil Selvik (eds), *Changing Regime Discourse and Reform in Syria* (Boulder: Lynne Rienner, 2008).
42. This again, according to Haykal, because the Security Council is perceived to serve the interests of the US and Israel.
43. The other representatives of the private sector in the council are Adib al-Fadel, Yasmina Azhari, Naji Chaoui, Sarhad Haffar, Bassel S. Hamwi, Ahmad Hashem, Abdulsalam Haykal, Ismail Jaroudi, and Mahdi Sajjad.
44. Global Compact Syria Network [Brochure].
45. Interview, Abdulsalam Haykal, 26 May 2010.
46. United Nations Global Compact, "Promoting Cross-Sectoral MDG'S Based Partnerships The Global Compact Network Syria", http://www.unglobalcompact.org/…/Microsoft_PowerPoint_-_SYRIA_CASE_Promotion_MDG_Based_Partnership_Projects.pdf.
47. Interview, Nader Kabbani, 26 May 2010.
48. According to Abdulsalam Haykal, MTN and Katakit are the sole Syrian companies to have separate CSR departments (interview, 26 May 2010). MTN has formulated an outline of its social sustainability philosophy on http://www.mtn.com.sy/index.php?option=com_content&task=view&id=108&Itemid=263
49. MTN, "MTN and UNDP to Establish Syria's First Cancer Research Centre", August 2009, http://www.itnewsafrica.com/pressoffices/mtn/0820.html.
50. UNDP, "August_Newsletter_UNGC[1]", http://undp.org.sy/files/August_Newsletter_UNGC%5B1%5D.pdf.
51. Emaar Syria, "Emaar: Syria", http://www.emaarsyria.co.sy/site/aamal.html.
52. Interview, Muhammad Agha, 18 June 2009.

53. See Pierre Bourdieu, "The Forms of Capital" in J.E. Richardson (ed.), *Handbook of Theory and Research for the Sociology of Education* (New York: Greenwood Press, 1986), pp. 241–58. See also Pierre Bourdieu, *Distinction: A Social Critique of the Judgement of Taste* (Cambridge, MA: Harvard University Press, 1984).
54. Pierre Bourdieu, "Les modes de domination", *Actes de la Recherche en Sciences Sociales* 2.2–3 (1976), p. 128.
55. Interview, Muhammad al-Sha'ir, 13 December 2007.
56. Interview, Muhammad al-Sha'ir, 7 May 2008.
57. Interview, Mounzer al-Bizreh, 1 April 2009.
58. Zysow, "Zakāt (a.)". *Encyclopaedia of Islam, Second Edition.*
59. Interview, Said Hafez and Amin Hafez, 30 March 2009.
60. Vogel, *The Market for Virtue.*
61. Interview, 'Adnan Abu Chaar, 26 May 2010.
62. Ibid.
63. The companies were Arabian Enterprises Company, KPMG Mejanni & Co. LLC Syria, Sawaf Institute for Medical Imaging, Transtek Systems, Bayan-Group, Salsabil Co Inc, Abu-Ghazaleh & Co. Consulting, Daaboul Industrial Group, ALFARES Pharmaceuticals, Earth Link and Advanced Resources Development (ELARD), Anwar Akkad Sons Company, University of Kalamoon, Direct Line, Sabree For Trade, Syrian International Academy, Banque Bemo Saudi Fransi, The Syrian Consulting Bureau, MAS Economic Group, Omrat EST., Boushra for Detergents and Soap Co., Y2Ad, AMARA Architecture, Byblos Bank Syria, Wafa Investing, LLC, SAMA GROUP—For International Trade Fairs & Conferences, MTN Syria, Alfadel Group, Bank Audi Syria, Emaar-Syria, Rayess Kingdom Group, Ganama, Gulfsands Petroleum, Rawasi Holding, Shell Petroleum, Syriatel, United Group, United Insurance Company, International Center for Human Construction.
64. Rateb al-Shallah is the president of the Damascus Chamber of Commerce and the son of Badr al-Din al-Shallah, who was instrumental in mediating between Hafiz al-Asad and the *souk* during the 1979–82 Islamic uprising; Abdulrahman al-Attar was one of three crony businessmen who dominated Syria's newly liberalized economy under Hafiz al-Asad; and Firas Tlass is the son of the former Defence Minister and long-time friend of Hafiz al-Asad Mustafa Tlass.
65. "Rami Makhlouf, De L'Affairisme à L'Illusionisme", *Le Monde*, 26 June 2011.
66. The Madar Group was founded by Muhammad Da'bul, its president, who shares responsibility of running the companies with his five sons, one of which is Hassan Da'bul.
67. Interview, Hassan Da'bul, 25 May 2010.
68. Interview, Muhab Da'bul, 1 April 2009.

7. SYRIA'S REFORMS UNDER BASHAR AL-ASAD: AN OPPORTUNITY FOR FOREIGN-EDUCATED ENTREPRENEURS TO MOVE INTO DECISION-MAKING?

1. Bashar al-Asad's inaugural speech had seemed to signal readiness to conduct not only economic but also political reforms, and political discussion forums mushroomed in Syria. For an informative overview of the beginning, events, and end of the Damascus Spring civil rights movement see Alan George, *Syria: Neither Bread nor Freedom* (London: Zed Books, 2003).
2. "Authoritarian upgrading" denotes authoritarian regimes' utilization of economic reforms, political competition, civil society organizations, modern communication technology, and international linkages to their own gain. Steven Heydemann, "Upgrading Authoritarianism in the Arab World", Saban Center for Middle East Policy, No. 13, October 2007, p. 5. During the 2000s, research on authoritarian survival/persistence/resilience/upgrading soared, seeking to explain how authoritarian systems act to enhance their legitimacy and "modern" credentials in order to stay in power. See Stephen J. King, *The New Authoritarianism in the Middle East and North Africa* (Bloomington: Indiana University Press, 2009). See also Andreas Schedler (ed.), *Electoral Authoritarianism. The Dynamics of Unfree Competition* (Boulder: Lynne Rienner, 2006). The author expects that, even after the Arab Spring, this concept will remain informative since (1) remaining authoritarian systems will step up their efforts of "upgrading" and (2) it helps to investigate the behaviour of actors privileged by authoritarian systems, even after they have been overthrown. See Steven Heydemann and Reinoud Leenders, "Authoritarian Learning and Authoritarian Resilience: Regime Responses to the 'Arab Awakening,'" *Globalizations* 8, 5 (2011), pp. 647–653.
3. See Volker Perthes (ed.), *Arab Elites: Negotiating the Politics of Change* (Boulder: Lynne Rienner, 2004). While in the 1970s the military careers of most Arab heads of states drew the attention of researchers, three successions in 1999 and 2000—Bashar al-Asad in Syria, Abdallah II of Jordan, and Muhammad VI of Morocco—gave the impression that a new generation of more cosmopolitan, "modern" leaders moved in.
4. For Syria see ibid., pp. 93ff.; Flynt Leverett, *Inheriting Syria. Bashar's Trial by Fire* (Washington: Brookings Institution Press, 2005), pp. 71–7; Eyal Zisser, *Commanding Syria. Bashar al-Asad and the First Years in Power* (London: I.B. Tauris, 2007), pp. 67 ff.
5. From the authoritarian regimes' point of view, foreign-educated persons can either be modernizers or, conversely, a source of disloyalty and foreign-inspired democracy promotion. Distrust affects highest government positions as well. Abdelnasser has remarked that foreign-educated Egyptians were "still not accepted at the core of power", illustrating this with the fact that US-educated Egyptian foreign ministers had been appointed when the country's foreign affairs were

mainly dealing with EU issues and vice versa, in order to prevent disloyalty. Gamal Abdelnasser, "Egypt: Succession Politics", in Perthes (ed.), *Arab Elites*, p. 124.

6. Antonio Spilimbergo, "Democracy and Foreign Education", CEPR Discussion Paper, No. 5934 (London: Centre for Economic Policy Research, 2006).
7. The statistics in SAR/MoHE constituted a very useful exception to the scarcity of quantitative data. During fieldwork for my PhD thesis, interviews with 65 persons were conducted in Damascus in March-May 2010. This paper is based in particular on the interviews with 12 foreign-educated businessmen and five foreign-educated economic consultants. Selected other interviews (at ministries, with employees of NGOs, banks, etc.), some of which were conducted for my Master's dissertation in the summer of 2007, were also used. All interviews are coded by their date to provide confidentiality. I want to express my gratitude to all my respondents, without whose hospitality and prompt willingness to contribute, this study would not have been possible. For my fieldwork expenses I thankfully received a Russell Trust Award from the University of St Andrews.
8. For a brief discussion see Charles Kurzman and Erin Leahey, "Intellectuals and Democratization, 1905–1912 and 1989–1996", *American Journal of Sociology* 109, 4 (2004), pp. 937–86, pp. 939ff. This includes Barrington Moore's well-known quote "no bourgeois, no democracy".
9. Giacomo Luciani, "Linking Economic and Political Reform in the Middle East. The Role of the Bourgeoisie" in Oliver Schlumberger (ed.), *Debating Arab Authoritarianism. Dynamics and Durability in Nondemocratic Regimes* (Stanford University Press, 2007), pp. 163–5.
10. Bassam Haddad, "The Social Context of State-Business Networks: Syria's New Upper Classes", Unpublished conference paper, Conference on Economic Reform in Syria. Centre for Syrian Studies, St Andrews, April 2008, pp. 40 ff.
11. For example, Haddad, "The Social Context of State-Business Networks"; Raymond Hinnebusch, *Revolution from Above* (London: Routledge, 2001).
12. Luciani, "Linking Economic and Political Reform in the Middle East"; Kjetil Selvik, "It's the Mentality, Stupid! Syria's Turn to the Private Sector" in Aurora Sottimano and Kjetil Selvik (eds), *Changing Regime Discourse and Reform in Syria* (Boulder: Lynne Rienner, 2008).
13. For the Tunisian case, see Eva Bellin, *Stalled Democracy: Capital, Labor, and the Paradox of State-Sponsored Development* (Ithaca: Cornell University Press, 2002).
14. This division is problematic insofar as the "crony bourgeoisie" might "overshoot" the regime's set reform goals. Thus, the diagram shows the businessmen's political motivation but not necessarily whether the regime is pleased by all their actions and demands.
15. However, personal traits and structural factors influence this "bourgeoisie-mid-

dle class divide": Not every formerly self-funded returnee, by a long way, is prepared to take risks or has the entrepreneurial skills to start a business, especially since structural factors, like the lack of infrastructure or overregulated market entry, hamper the establishment of successful businesses. Yet, the suggestion that there is a higher share of self-funded than state-sponsored graduates amongst entrepreneurs serves as an analytically clear starting point.

16. See Thomas Faist, "Migrants as Transnational Development Agents: An Inquiry into the Newest Round of the Migration-Development Nexus", *Population, Space and Place* 14 (2008), pp. 21–42.
17. This corresponds to frequent assessments that remittances are more likely to be turned into consumption—often of imported products—than into investment, and even more so if returnees return for retirement.
18. Spilimbergo, "Democracy and Foreign Education", p. 13.
19. Ibid., p. 29.
20. For Spilimbergo, foreign-educated persons who do not adopt democratization as a goal (for example, the Islamist radical thinker Sayyid Qutb) are treated as outlier cases and excluded from further analysis. Ibid., p. 4.
21. See Faist, "Migrants as Transnational Development Agents". The term "social capital" was introduced by Pierre Bourdieu and by James Coleman at approximately the same time. Bourdieu's terminology is especially useful since it delineates different kinds of capital (social, cultural, economic, symbolic) which add up to a person's behaviour and mentality, i.e. what Bourdieu calls *habitus*. Pierre Bourdieu, "The Forms of Capital", in J.E. Richardson (ed.), *Handbook of Theory and Research for the Sociology of Education*(New York: Greenwood Press, 1986), pp. 241–58.
22. See Laurie Brand, *Citizens Abroad. Emigration and the State in the Middle East and North Africa* (Cambridge University Press, 2006).
23. In Bourdieu's terms, (1) is persons' cultural capital, (2) their economic capital and the latter two constitute two dimensions of their social capital. Prestige and recognition gained by virtue of the capitals would be called symbolic capital.
24. While most Syrians would not consider graduates of Egyptian or Lebanese universities as foreign-educated, this study treats them as such since most of them studied at universities with Western curricula like the American University of Beirut (AUB) and the American University in Cairo (AUC) and had some exposure to "foreign" culture, though not as intensive as what other foreign-educated persons received.
25. There are two methodological reservations: Since group names carry normative connotations (e.g., the pejorative term "crony capitalist") and conceal differences between concerned individuals, they are only illustrative. Furthermore, this categorization cannot be quantified since assets are not easily measured and ranked; instead, interviewees were asked to play a "game of cards" to rank assets' significance (see below).

26. The diagram could also be helpful for investigating other groups of actors—whether with or without international education—but was developed for foreign-educated entrepreneurs in particular to enable comparison between their assets.
27. Post-populist authoritarianism (PPA) means an "authoritarianism from the left" which is, owing to economic vulnerabilities and pressures, forced to liberalize economically but successfully refrains from meaningful political liberalization. In contrast to authoritarianism from the right, in PPA the rise of crony capitalists is said to be virtually inevitable, since politics and economics had been closely intertwined during the populist era. Raymond Hinnebusch, "Authoritarian Persistence, Democratization Theory and the Middle East: An Overview and Critique", *Democratization* 13, 3 (2006), pp. 373–95, p. 384.
28. For good overviews see Selvik, "It's the Mentality, Stupid!" See also Oxford Business Group, *The Report. Syria 2010*; Samir Seifan, *Syria on the Path to Economic Reform* (Boulder: Lynne Rienner, 2010).
29. Selvik, "It's the Mentality, Stupid!", p. 48ff. For very illustrative case studies on the defects of state-market relations, see Søren Schmidt, "The Developmental Role of the State in the Middle East: Lessons from Syria" in Raymond Hinnebusch and Søren Schmidt (eds), *The State and the Political Economy of Reform in Syria* (Boulder: Lynne Rienner, 2009).
30. This, for example, was shown by businessmen's high-profile support for the presidential referendum in 2007. Pavilions staging *dabka* dance performances were set up in the street, mostly funded by local businessmen determined to show their loyalty: own observations; Joshua Landis, "The Presidential Plebiscite and Pageantry: What does it Mean?" *Syria Comment* blog, 4 June 2007, http://www.joshualandis.com/blog/?p=274. The same has been true for most businessmen's behaviour in the current uprising.
31. See Selvik, "It's the Mentality, Stupid!" This accumulation of businessmen as independent candidates can be explained by high campaigning costs that members of other social strata rarely can afford, by incentives such as prestige and publicity, and by attractive occasions for rent-seeking deals.
32. Bassam Haddad, "The Formation and Development of Economic Networks in Syria: Implications for Economic and Fiscal Reforms, 1986–2000", in Stephen Heydemann (ed.), *Networks of Privilege in the Middle East: The Politics of Economic Reform Revisited* (New York: Palgrave Macmillan, 2004), p. 48.
33. Before, integrated lists with eighteen candidates for the whole board would run for election; now places are divided into four business sectors and businessmen only vote for those posts on the board representing their sector. Board members are said to be more accountable now and voting turnout was higher than before. Interview, 5 April 2010.
34. Interviews, 5 April 2010 and 20 April 2011.

35. Despite assurances that STD is fully independent, it resembles a GONGO and is seen as such by the Syrian public. It includes NGOs initiated by the First Lady since 2001, i.e. Firdos, Massar, Shabab and Rawafed, working on rural, children's, youth, and cultural development respectively.
36. Tina Zintl, "Modernization Theory II: Western-Educated Syrians and the Authoritarian Upgrading of Civil Society", in Laura Ruiz de Elvira and Tina Zintl (eds), *Civil Society and the State in Syria: The Outsourcing of Social Responsibility* (Boulder: Lynne Rienner, 2012).
37. Interview, 5 April 2010.
38. Laura Guazzone and Daniela Pioppi (eds), *The Arab State and Neo-liberal Globalization: The Restructuring of State Power in the Middle East* (Reading: Ithaca, 2009). See also Zintl, "Modernization Theory II".
39. Hinnebusch, *Revolution from Above.*
40. Aurora Sottimano, "Ideology and Discourse in the Era of Ba'thist Reforms: Towards an Analysis of Authoritarian Governmentality" in Sottimano and Selvik (eds), *Changing Regime Discourse and Reform in Syria*, pp. 16 ff.
41. Haddad, "The Formation and Development of Economic Networks in Syria"; Hinnebusch, *Revolution from Above*; Sottimano, "Ideology and Discourse in the Era of Ba'thist Reforms".
42. They are: the old bourgeoisie (successful businessmen before the nationalizations of the 1960s, now emigrated or marginalized); the petty bourgeoisie (small urban shopkeepers with few if any relations to the regime, largely apolitical); the independent bourgeoisie (antagonistic towards the regime; backgrounds, size, and composition are rather unclear); the rentier bourgeoisie (formally independent businessmen living off favourable business deals with the regime); and the state bourgeoisie (a privileged or embourgeoised stratum of civil servants, see above). See Haddad, "The Social Context of State-Business Networks".
43. However, no equally well-known and outspoken businessman publicly joined the uprising in 2011.
44. Perthes (ed.), *Arab Elites*, p. 16.
45. Unfortunately, backgrounds of past ministers are not readily available; therefore, it is possible that the most "reformist" cabinets and ministers are overrepresented in the sources. Certainly, some foreign-educated ministers in Bashar al-Asad's first cabinet of December 2001 are referred to most often, e.g. Ghassan al-Rifai (Minister of Economy until 2004), Issam al-Zaim (Minister of Industry until 2003), Muhammad Atrash (Minister of Finance until 2003).
46. Their share slightly decreased in the cabinet of April 2011, to twelve foreign-educated ministers (of thirty-two posts), eight of them with Western degrees and also eight holding doctorates: SANA, "Al-Ra'is al-Asad Asdar Marsum Ta'lif al-Hukuma bi-Ri'assat Safar (President al-Asad issued decree on appointment of Safar Cabinet" *Ba'th*, 15 April 2011.

47. Perthes (ed.), *Arab Elites*, p. 93.
48. There had been one businessman-turned-minister in 2000–2001, but he seems to have been so politically insignificant that he remained unnamed and was not reappointed: ibid., p. 93. As far as data are available, later cabinets did not contain business representatives either.
49. A French-educated Minister of Higher Education, Rida Said—driving force behind the founding of Damascus University—"used government funds to send professors for training in France, Great Britain, and the United States": Sami Moubayed, *Steel & Silk: Men and Women who Shaped Syria 1900–2000* (Seattle: Cune Press, 2006), p. 456.
50. Approximately 28% were sent to Russia, 26% to France, 18% to Germany, 7% each to Poland and to the UK, 4% to the US, and 11% to destinations not further specified (excess due to rounding). Syrian Arabic Republic Ministry of Higher Education (SAR MoHE), "Achievements in Higher Education under the Glorious Correctionist Movement, 1970–1996" (Damascus: MoHE, n.d.), p. 70. According to respondents, most German-educated government delegates studied in the GDR, while self-funded study migrants chose the FRG: see ibid., p. 70. George, *Syria: Neither Bread nor Freedom*, p. 149.
51. Over 10,000 *ba'thāt 'ilmīyah* were funded but the majority received a scholarship for studying at Syrian universities and/or for undergraduate studies. For information on participating state institutions, host countries, and subjects studied see SAR MoHE, "Achievements in Higher Education", pp. 61–5.
52. Interview, Ministry of Higher Education, June 2007.
53. SAR MoHE, "Achievements in Higher Education", p. 61.
54. Men exempted from or having completed military service, as well as women, mostly did not register: interview, Ministry of Higher Education, June 2007.
55. See critical comments in George, *Syria: Neither Bread nor Freedom*, p. 149, and Selvik, "It's the Mentality, Stupid!" pp. 54ff., as well as by several interviewees. Degrees achieved in Western host countries were sometimes mockingly referred to as *"docteurs bpO"* (*"bon pour l'Orient"*), alluding to an allegedly higher willingness of Western institutions to award degrees to mediocre PhD candidates set to return to their native country, assuming that, in this case, lower academic quality would suffice.
56. Only 13% of university staff received their highest degrees within the Arab world; since many chose prestigious universities in Egypt or Lebanon, the share of Syrian-educated staff is extremely low. In comparison, most university staff studied in former Eastern Bloc countries (between 48% at Damascus University and 72% at Ba'th University, Homs), and up to a third went to Western universities (ranging from 16% at Ba'th University Homs to 35% at Aleppo University). German-educated Syrians were counted as Eastern Bloc graduates, since the GDR had been a much more common destination than Western Ger-

many. All figures are own calculations based on data from catalogues of Syria's four state universities, 2004/05 or 2005/06. Tina Zintl, "Modernisierungspolitik durch Kompetenztransfer? Syrische Remigranten mit deutschem Hochschulabschluss als Katalysatoren von Brain Gain in Syrien unter Bashar al-Assad", in Dieter Weiss and Steffen Wippel (eds), *Volkswirtschaftliche Diskussionspapiere* 104 (Berlin: Klaus Schwarz Verlag, 2009), p. 20.

57. More disturbingly, many chose to re-emigrate because of higher wages in the Gulf states. A state-controlled counter-measure was the temporary "lending" of Syrian university staff to Gulf institutions, organized by the Syrian Ministry of Higher Education itself. In this way, academic staff were allowed to accumulate higher wages during a period of up to five years before returning to their previous position in Syria. Interviews, May and June 2007.
58. The ministry was situated at the far end of the Damascus suburb of Dummar and employed only seventy-nine persons: Syrian Arabic Republic Central Bureau of Statistics, *Statistical Yearbook 2009, 62 edition* (Damascus: Syrian Central Bureau of Statistics, 2009), p. 72. Eventually, MoEX was merged into the Ministry for Foreign Affairs in April 2011 and thus ceased to exist as independent portfolio. See *Ba'th* op. cit., 15 April 2011.
59. See footnote 7 for details on the sample.
60. Some of the interviewees played the card game several times, e.g. to illustrate differences in the recruitment for the public vs. the private sector, or in different policy fields. The method was, as expected, a very useful point of entrance to more sensitive issues like corruption (several respondents emphasized this issue) or the favouring of specific religious groups (most declined this factor).
61. Their views on agency, i.e. whether foreign-educated persons are more "passively" recruited by superiors or whether they actively push for more influence, will be discussed in more detail below.
62. Interview, 6 April 2010.
63. Interview, 5 April 2010.
64. Interview, 27 March 2010.
65. Interview, 23 March 2010.
66. Interview, 9 May 2010.
67. Interview, 23 March 2010.
68. Interview, 6 April 2010.
69. Interview, 7 April 2010.
70. For foreign-educated public sector employees this might be different: a pilot study concentrating on German-educated Syrians showed that the vast majority of these persons—mostly former *mu'aidin* and now teaching at public universities—had put considerable effort into maintaining contacts with their former host country and saw them in an untarnished positive way. However, it might also be specific to Syrians educated in Germany (mostly the GDR), who

enjoy a surprisingly high reputation in Syria when compared with other graduates of the Eastern Bloc: it was inferred that they utilize their contacts with unified Germany, which now belongs to the much sought-after Western cooperation partners, in order to gain influence. See Zintl, "Modernisierungspolitik durch Kompetenztransfer?"

71. Interviews, 5 May 2010 and 18 May 2010. However, smaller producers who are less connected locally are less successful in doing so and often enlist the support of the Chamber of Commerce's Export Promotion Desk. Interview, 5 April 2010.
72. Interviews, 29 March 2010 and 31 March 2010.
73. Unfortunately, no figures on FDI by Syrian expatriates and repatriates are available (since "Arab investors" are taken as a joint category, thus including innumerable and often large-scale investors from the Gulf states). However, anecdotal evidence suggests that some Syrian repatriates, especially those returning from the Gulf, are investing in the private sector, especially in tourism/gastronomy.
74. To some extent this is only natural since establishing a successful business, especially in an economic environment such as the Syrian one, is hardly possible without local contacts and a comfortable financial allowance. So those with material support from their family will take the plunge from abroad more easily and successfully: often interviewees had gained local work experience in the family business before opening their own business, mostly in a related sector.
75. Interview, 18 March 2010.
76. Since asking for a respondent's religion (and receiving a helpful answer, i.e. not only distinguishing between Muslim and Christian but also between different Muslim denominations) was not feasible, estimates of the religious composition of foreign-educated persons and how this could influence their political clout were difficult.
77. For example, it is remarkable that most foreign-educated Syrian Business Council (SBC, see below) members disclosed the degree and subject of their studies but not their place of study in the SBC member's guide, which is based on a questionnaire completed by each member himself: Syrian Business Council (SBC), *Members' Guide 2008*; interview, 4 April 2010. Also, most interviewees, especially those active with NGOs, took care to stress the engagement and importance of non-foreign-educated persons: interviews, 5 April 2010 and 12 May 2010.
78. The issue of private primary and secondary education in international schools frequently came up in interviews. Interestingly, many of those who took their *baccalauréat* at a French school in Syria went to the UK or the US for studying, partly because of the additional foreign language and because admission was considered easier than to French universities, but also because of the higher status of education in those countries: interview, 1 April 2010.

79. Decision 3023 of 2009 established seventy-eight bi-national business councils and, at the same time, announced two chairpersons for each of them. They were selected from the well-connected businesspeople with the highest market shares in the respective country; degrees or working experience from those countries were not important.
80. In the SBC, at least sixteen of thirty founding members got their highest degree abroad (thirteen in Europe/North America, three in Lebanon, four in Syria, ten not indicated), while nine of the eleven current board members—all except one are founding members—are foreign-educated: Syrian Business Council (SBC), *Members' Guide 2008*; interview, 4 April 2010. Nine of the SYEA's eleven founding members are foreign-educated (six in the US or the UK, three in Lebanon): interview, 6 April 2010. The JCI was established by five foreign-educated persons (two in Canada, three in Lebanon) who had been invited to attend a course with the JCI Jordan financed through the International Chamber of Commerce: interview, 13 May 2010.
81. One interviewee who works in a family business in the Hariqa area of Damascus estimated that only 20–25% of families well established in the market sent their children abroad for studies: interview, 5 April 2010.
82. The SBC, for example, was initiated by members of Syria Holding, which was established in 2007 by the French-educated business tycoon Haytham Joud, who is also the SBC's chairman: interview, founding member of SBC, 12 May 2010. The SYEA was established by two US-educated friends and a Syrian-educated acquaintance after returning from a conference of Arab young entrepreneurs' associations in 1999: the over-representation of foreign-educated amongst the SYEA's founding members reflects the "network" of former university friends when these three persons searched in order to find the minimum eleven founding members for accrediting a Syrian NGO: interview, 6 April 2010.
83. Interview, 6 April 2010.
84. See SBC brochure 2010.
85. Interviews, 6 April 2010 and 1 April 2010.
86. Interview, 4 May 2010. *Forward Magazine*'s and *Syria Today*'s chief editors are foreign-educated and foreign respectively. Yet, in the media sector in general, salaries and other incentives are not high enough to attract foreign-educated persons back home. Interviews, 17 March 2010, 4 April 2010, and 4 May 2010.
87. While Attar and Haykal were born into old bourgeois families (the Attar family owns a large business empire; the Haykal Group, going back to 1939, is smaller but well-established), Suleiman is the son of one of the late Hafiz al-Asad's closest 'Alawite security advisers.
88. Interviews, economic consultants, 23 March 2010, 27 March 2010, 30 March 2010, 5 April 2010; interviews, lawyers, 9 May 2010.
89. Interviews, 7 March 2010, 31 March 2010, 5 April 2010, 9 May, 2010, and 20 May 2010.

90. Interview, 25 March 2010.
91. Ibid.
92. Moubayed, *Steel & Silk*, pp. 116 ff.
93. Interviews, 1 April 2010, 5 April 2010.
94. Interview, 12 May 2010.
95. Interview, 1 April 2010.
96. Interviews, 5 May 2010 and 18 May 2010.
97. One of these businessmen was however educated at a foreign secondary school in Damascus, and was president of the Damascus Chamber's mixed business council linked with the one country his father had already been having relations with. This shows that international contacts also are passed on in business families from one generation to the other, independently of university education gained abroad. Interview, 18 May 2010.
98. Interview, 4 April 2010.
99. Interview, 12 May 2010. The impression that the SBC is more linked to nouveaux riches crony capitalists than the Chambers, which are more representative of traditional Damascene merchants, is further illustrated by the fact that these institutions and interviewed members' offices were located in different parts of Damascus: the SBC and many of its members are clustered in prestigious New City locations like Malki, Rawda, or Abou Roumaneh while the Damascus Chambers of Commerce and Industry are in Hariqa/Old City, where many members have their shops, if not in Shallan/New City or the outskirts.
100. Interview, 4 April 2010.
101. Ibid.
102. Interview, 12 May 2010.
103. Interview, 26 April 2010.
104. Several interviews plus quotations from interviews with businessmen in Selvik, "It's the Mentality, Stupid!" pp. 54–6.
105. This causes a self-fulfilling prophecy, as ambitious civil servants tend to quit their jobs and switch to international organizations or GONGOs, or emigrate.
106. This discourse might, in some instances, be more rhetorical if the same person rejects certain reforms in order to protect his own business from unwanted competition.
107. Interview, 31 March 2010.
108. Conversely, it might be that only those who were summoned by the regime had the elbow room to leave an impact and were visible to the outside observer.
109. While this is because of common business interests and not the common experience of having studied abroad, it could be argued that this similarity in their biographies furthers their cooperation and the willingness to engage in such an association.

110. For obvious reasons it has often been said that Syria follows a Chinese model of development, and it is possible that parallels between the two countries include the issue of highly-skilled returnees. See Ellen Lust-Okar, "Reform in Syria: Steering between the Chinese Model and Regime Change", Carnegie Endowment for International Peace papers, No. 69, July 2006. See also various speeches and interviews with Bashar al-Asad. Beijing also started to attract Chinese overseas students back home and political positions are increasingly filled with returnees who enjoy a reputation as competent technocrats; yet these are recruited predominantly from former scholarship holders of the regime or "princeling' returnees", i.e. offspring of the elites. He Li, "Returned Students and Political Change in China", *Asian Perspective* 30.2 (2006), pp. 5–29, 23. If other returnees wield political influence it is not directly through holding political ranks, but rather indirectly via consultancy, and is restricted to specific issue areas. The situation in Syria seems to be quite similar, except that there is a short supply of Syrians with state-sponsored Western education, while China has financed large delegations to the US since 1978. Cheng Li (ed.), *Bridging Minds across the Pacific. U.S.-China Educational Exchanges, 1978–2003* (Lanham, MD: Lexington Books, 2005).

8. THE POLITICS OF "GOOD GOVERNANCE" IN MUBARAK'S EGYPT: WESTERN DONORS AND SME POLITICS UNDER AUTHORITARIAN RULE

1. According to the World Bank, "Good governance is epitomized by predictable, open and enlightened policy-making, a bureaucracy imbued with a professional ethos acting in furtherance of the public good, the rule of law, transparent processes, and a strong civil society participating in public affairs". See World Bank, *Governance: The World Bank's Experience* (Washington: World Bank, 1994), p. vii.
2. This refers to a set of administrative, economic and regulatory reforms that aim to facilitate the development of SMEs.
3. Micro, small and medium enterprises are generally defined according to two criteria: the number of workers and the enterprise's fixed assets. The various Egyptian ministries have adopted different definitions. The enterprises comprising between one to fifty workers are the object of this paper.
4. Established by then Minister of Economy Youssef Boutros Ghali, the SME Development Unit was a technical unit attached to the minister himself, which was moved from one ministry to another, following Boutros Ghali. Boutros Ghali was a central figure of the Mubarak regime, and a key actor in the development and implementation of economic reforms. A former IMF official, he was well acquainted with Western development institutions and known for his capacity to secure foreign funding for development projects. The centrality of the figure

of Boutros Ghali and his personal involvement in and takeover of the Unit point to the patrimonial nature of development politics in Mubarak's Egypt. In the aftermath of Mubarak's fall, Boutros Ghali was sentenced in absentia to thirty years' imprisonment.

5. Other governmental and semi-governmental agencies have been involved, to a lesser extent, in SME development policy. This has allowed for concurrent policy initiatives to emerge and has complicated the development and implementation of reforms. The SME Development Unit's main competitor has been the Social Fund for Development (SFD) which was given by Law 141/2004 a mandate over micro and small enterprises.
6. Republic of Egypt, Ministry of Finance, "Enhancing Competitiveness for SMEs, General Framework and Action Plan", 2004.
7. Before and after the 2004 policy document, a number of additional thematic reports were published by the SME Development Unit on a wide array of topics: SME definition, export, credit, leasing, finance.
8. Steven Heydemann (ed.), *Networks of Privilege in the Middle East: The Politics of Economic Reform Revisited* (New York: Palgrave Macmillan, 2004).
9. Tamer El Meehy, "Guidelines for the Development of an M/SME Policy Framework in Egypt", Submitted to the Ministry of Foreign Trade, May 2002, p. 18.
10. The services they provide to SMEs range from capacity-building, training, commercial services, financial and technical counselling, loans, etc.
11. Political participation is defined by Huntington and Nelson as an "activity by private citizens designed to influence governmental decision-making". Samuel Huntington and Joan Nelson, *No Easy Choice: Political Participation in Developing Countries* (Cambridge, MA: Harvard University Press, 1976), p. 4; see also Holgar Albrecht, "The Nature of Political Participation" in Ellen Lust-Okar and Saloua Zerhouni (eds), *Political Participation in the Middle East* (Boulder: Lynne Rienner, 2008), p. 15.
12. "Advocacy groups" refers to civil society organizations involved in the promotion of reform in health, education, human rights, environmental issues, and other socio-economic issues.
13. Interview, March 2009.
14. In contrast, bilateral and multilateral agencies tend to work with the government, as the CIDA and IDRC do. For a discussion of the activities and profiles of funding and implementing agencies supporting democratization projects in the Arab world since the early 1990s, see Sheila Carapico, "Foreign Aid for Promoting Democracy in the Arab World", *Middle East Journal* 56, 3 (2002), pp. 379–95. While these "democracy brokers" initially focused on groups working on political reforms, they have "increasingly reachrede NGOs whose advocacy work aims at social and economic issues rather than specifically political ones". See Thomas Carothers and Marina Ottaway (eds), *Funding Virtue, Civil*

Society Aid and Democracy Promotion (Washington: Carnegie Endowment for International Peace, 2000), p. 12.

15. See Carapico, "Foreign Aid for Promoting Democracy". Thomas Carothers, "Choosing a Strategy" in Thomas Carothers and Marina (eds), *Uncharted Journey, Promoting Democracy in the Middle East* (Washington: Carnegie Endowment for International Peace, 2005).
16. Interview, March 2009.
17. Ibid.
18. The Social Fund for Development is a semi-governmental agency that was established by presidential decree in 1991 with funds from the UNDP and the World Bank. The primary purpose of the Fund was to act as an "economic and social safety net" to compensate for the negative effects of the structural adjustment programmes on the Egyptian population. Its mission has evolved since then and its core activity is now the development of micro and small enterprises through the provision of financial and non-financial services.
19. The FEDA's president and board members openly acknowledge this.
20. Interview, March 2009.
21. See, for example, Fouad Thabet, *Advocacy, Networking and Civil Society Organizations: Practical Cases*, [in Arabic] Friedrich Ebert Stiftung, Federation of Economic Development Associations, November 2004.
22. From the 1980s to the mid-1990s, foreign donors did assist a number of projects aiming to empower unions and cooperatives, for example the FES and CIPE.
23. Interviews, March and April 2009.
24. http://www.fedamisr.net/about2.asp?id=1
25. This expression is borrowed from John Sfakianakis' work but is used here with a different meaning. It was originally elaborated to describe the close interpersonal relationships developed by private sector actors with state bureaucrats during the economic reforms and the privatization of the 1990s in order to secure access to rents. See John Sfakianakis, "The Whales of the Nile" in Steven Heydemann (ed.), *Networks of Privilege in the Middle East: The Politics of Economic Reform Revisited* (New York: Palgrave Macmillan, 2004).
26. Interview, foreign donors, April 2009.
27. Marina Ottaway, for example, stresses the existence of this missing constituency for democratic reform in the Middle East, including Egypt. See Marina Ottaway, "The Missing Constituency for Democratic Reform" in Thomas Carothers and Marina Ottaway (eds), *Uncharted Journey, Promoting Democracy in the Middle East*, (Washington: Carnegie Endowment for International Peace, 2005). For the case of Egyptian SMEs, see El Meehy, "Guidelines for the Development of an M/SME Policy Framework in Egypt".
28. Social capital in Bourdieu's definition amounts to "the aggregate of the actual

or potential resources which are linked to possession of a durable network of more or less institutionalized relationships of mutual acquaintance and recognition". See Pierre Bourdieu, "The Forms of Capital" in J.E. Richardson (ed.), *Handbook of Theory and Research for the Sociology of Education* (New York: Greenwood Press, 1986).

29. See, for example, Mona El-Fiqi, "The Building Blocks", *Al Ahram Weekly*, 28 September—4 October 2008; Sherine Nasr, "Putting the Books in Order", *Al Ahram Weekly*, 30 March—5 April 2006. "SME Owners Complain of "Poor" Services", *Daily News* (Egypt), 21 December 2006.
30. Pierre Bourdieu, "The Forms of Capital".
31. Interview, April 2009.
32. Though foreign donors insist on transparency and internal governance, it is not clear how FEDA's, and in general, NGOs' budgets are audited.
33. For a detailed study of patron-client relations, see S.N. Eisenstadt and Luis Roniger, *Patrons, Clients and Friends, Interpersonal Relations and the Structure of Trust in Society* (Cambridge University Press, 1984).
34. Diego Gambetta (ed.), *Trust: Making and Breaking Cooperative Relations* (New York: B. Blackwell, 1988).
35. Lemarchand and Legg, "Political Clientelism and Development, A Preliminary Analysis", in Norman Provizer (ed.), *Analyzing the Third World, Essays from Comparative Politics* (Cambridge, MA: Schenkman, 1978), p. 123.
36. Eisenstadt and Roniger, *Patrons, Clients and Friends*. Patron client relations can differ in their organizational features. They can be collective or individual-based, short-term or long-term, ongoing or unstable, informal or institutionalized. The resources exchanged can also vary. A patron can provide political or economic resources; a client can provide loyalty, support, vote, etc. The degree of coerciveness used by the patron and the client's level of dependency also vary.
37. Maha Abdelrahman describes the restrictions imposed on civil society organizations in Egypt. See Maha Abdelrahman, *Civil Society Exposed: The Politics of NGOs in Egypt* (London: Tauris Academic, 2004).
38. For more information on the limitations of donors' assistance to NGOs see, for example, Oliver Schlumberger, "Dancing with Wolves: Dilemmas of Democracy Promotion in Authoritarian Contexts", in Dietrich Jung (ed.), *Democratization and Development: New Political Strategies for the Middle East* (New York: Palgrave Macmillan, 2006).
39. Mustapha Al-Sayyid, "A Clash of Values; U.S. Civil Society Aid and Islam in Egypt" in Thomas Carothers and Marina Ottaway (eds), *Funding Virtue, Civil Society Aid and Democracy Promotion* (Washington: Carnegie Endowment for International Peace, 2000).
40. In the case of SMEs in Egypt, the existence of a SME sub-donor might have facilitated the flow of information on FEDA, though this remains unclear.

41. Republic of Egypt, Development Unit of the Ministry of Foreign Trade, Small, Medium and Micro Enterprise Policy Development Project, *Procedures and Guidelines for the Policy Development Process, A Policy Formulation Manual*, August 2003.
42. Schmitter contrasts "state corporatism" with "societal corporatism". See Philippe Schmitter, "Still the Century of Corporatism?" *Review of Politics* 36, 1 (1974), pp. 85–131.
43. Ibid., pp. 93–4.
44. See for example, Howard Wiarda, *Civil Society, The American Model and Third World Developmen*t (Boulder: Westview Press, 2003).
45. Interview, March 2009.
46. More generally, the fact that, in Egypt, many advocacy NGO figures have been involved with or directly working with the government points to their weak autonomy and might be considered a condition facilitating the corporatization of their NGOs.
47. Eight characteristics of a "typical corporatist arrangement in Egypt" can be identified in his work: a typical corporatist arrangement 1) "is created by statute;" 2) "is endowed with a formal monopoly of representation for all who work in its field of jurisdiction;" 3) "its membership is compulsory…if not in law, providing the group with a guaranteed income that is supplemented by government subsidies;" 4) its "organizational structure is almost always hierarchical;" 5) its "local units are tied to functional and regional branches which are centralized under a national confederation with headquarters in the capital city;" 6) "the confederation, in turn, is linked with a parent ministry that supervises its finances and activities, consults with its leaders on public policy and delegates quasi-governmental powers of economic regulation and professional discipline;" 7) its "association leaders are generally selected through a combination of appointment and elections;" 8) "many confederation councils also have special seats reserved for ministry appointees making them more like "mixed commissions" than elected board of directors". See Robert Bianchi, *Unruly Corporatism: Associational Life in Twentieth-Century Egypt* (New York: Oxford University Press, 1989).
48. These appointed board members included one SFD official, one MOSA official, one official from the Ministry of Industry, one official from the Central Bank and a journalist from *Al Ahram Economy*.
49. Interview, April 2009.
50. Interview, March 2009.
51. Ibid.
52. Ibid.
53. Interview, April 2009.
54. http://www.fedamisr.net/files/pdf/11.pdf

55. Interview, March 2009.
56. Schmitter, "Still the Century of Corporatism?" p. 104.
57. Ibid.
58. See Amin Allal and Florian Kohstall, "Opposition within the State: Governance in Egypt, Morocco and Tunisia", in Holger Albrecht (ed.), *Contentious Politics in the Middle East* (Gainesville: University Press of Florida, 2010).
59. Statement of the Federation of Economic Development Associations on January 25 Revolution in Egypt, 3 February 2011. Available at http://www.cipe.org/publications/detail/statement-federation-economic development-associations-january-25-revolution.

9. VECTORS OF IRANIAN CAPITALISM: PRIVATIZATION POLITICS IN THE ISLAMIC REPUBLIC

1. *Tehran Times*, 20 February 2007. In this chapter I keep the common transliterations for presidents and supreme jurists in the Islamic Republic—e.g. Khomeini, Ahmadinejad. For all other proper nouns in Persian, I use a simplified transliteration scheme.
2. *The Business Year: Iran*, http://www.thebusinessyear.com/publication_detail.php?publication=9.
3. *Khorasan*, 26 December 2010.
4. Miles Kahler, "Orthodoxy and its Alternatives: Explaining Approaches to Stabilization and Adjustment", in Joan Nelson (ed.), *Economic Crisis and Policy Choice: The Politics of Adjustment in the Third World* (Princeton University Press, 1990).
5. Michael Mann, *The Sources of Social Power*, Vol. 2 (Cambridge University Press, 1993).
6. Kiren Chaudhry, "The Myths of the Market and the Common History of Late Developers", *Politics and Society* 21, 3 (1993), pp. 245–74, p. 249.
7. Stephan Haggard and Robert Kaufman, "Institutions and Economic Adjustment" in Stephan Haggard and Robert Kaufman (eds), *The Politics of Economic Adjustment: International Constraints, Distributive Conflicts, and the State* (Princeton University Press, 1992), p. 25.
8. Peter Evans, *Embedded Autonomy: States and Industrial Transformation* (Princeton University Press, 1995); John Waterbury, *Exposed to Innumerable Delusions: Public Enterprise and State Power in Egypt, India, Mexico, and Turkey* (Cambridge University Press, 1993).
9. Dag MacLeod, *Downsizing the State: Privatization and the Limits of Neoliberal Reform in Mexico* (University Park: Pennsylvania State University Press, 2004) points out that Skocpol's use of "autonomy" in the literature on revolutions was addressed to the Marxian debates of the 1970s, which questions whether states could be independent from the dominant class. This is the operating definition

of autonomy for Hamilton's case study of the Mexican state: for instance, Nora Hamilton, *The Limits of State Autonomy* (Princeton University Press, 1982). Evans, however, evokes the Weberian version of autonomy to illustrate how the state can support a domestic capitalist class, not oppose it: Evans, *Embedded Autonomy*. This has led the Marxist sociologist Michael Burawoy to joke that Evans' study, *Embedded Autonomy* should instead be called ''In Bed with Autonomy": Presentation at the XVII International Sociological Association World Congress, Gothenburg, Sweden, 11–17 July 2010.

10. Przeworski argued, in the cases of Eastern Europe and Latin America, that governments which enact economic liberalization programmes must either seek "the broadest possible support" from trade unions and other popular groups with social power, or "they must work to weaken these organizations". See Adam Przeworski, *Democracy and the Market: Political and Economic Reforms in Eastern Europe and Latin America* (Cambridge University Press, 1991), p. 182.
11. Melani Cammett, *Globalization and Business Politics in Arab North Africa: A Comparative Perspective* (Cambridge University Press, 2007).
12. Steven Solnick, *Stealing the State: Control and Collapse in Soviet Institutions* (Cambridge, MA: Harvard University Press, 1998), p. 7.
13. Steven Heydemann, "Networks of Privilege: Rethinking the Politics of Economic Reform in the Middle East", in Stephen Heydemann (ed.), *Networks of Privilege in the Middle East: The Politics of Economic Reform Revisited* (New York: Palgrave Macmillan, 2004), p. 24.
14. Ha-Joon Chang and Ilene Grabel, *Reclaiming Development: An Alternative Economic Policy Manual* (London: Zed Books, 2004), p. 90.
15. Steffen Hertog, "Defying the Resource Curse: Explaining Successful State-Owned Enterprises in Rentier States", *World Politics* 62, 2 (2010), pp. 261–301, p. 285. One can add to the list here China's partial success in promoting SOEs as domestic market leaders in a variety of high value-added sectors; see the various chapters in Olivier Cattaneo, Gary Gereffi and Cornelia Staritz (eds), *Global Value Chains in a Postcrisis World: A Development Perspective* (Washington: The World Bank, 2010).
16. Bahman Amouee, *Political Economy of the Islamic Republic* [in Persian] (Tehran: Gam-e No Press, 2002), pp. 42–3. Beheshti and Bahonar were assassinated in 1981, while Alviri went on to become a main supporter of Hashemi Rafsanjani and shifted his views towards economic liberalism.
17. Ibid., pp. 27–31. Sahabi later said the new government had made a huge mistake by nationalizing the banking sector. Only afterwards did they realize the extent of nonperforming loans left over from the Pahlavi period. By nationalizing the banks, they assumed responsibility for the debt. It would have been better to allow bankruptcies and create new national banks, as Bazargan and his liberal allies had argued at the time, but the politics of the day demanded nationalization as a symbolic act.

18. Amir Mehryar, "Shi'ite Teachings, Pragmatism and Fertility Change in Iran" in Gavin Jones and Mehtab Karim (eds), *Islam, the State and Population* (London: Hurst, 2005), p. 141.
19. Amouee, *Political Economy of the Islamic Republic*, p. 161. Also Sohrab Behdad, "The Political Economy of Islamic Planning in Iran" in Hooshang Amirahmadi and Manoucher Parvin (eds), *Post-Revolutionary Iran* (Boulder: Westview Press, 1988).
20. On the IKRC, see Kevan Harris, "The Imam's Blue Boxes", *Middle East Report* 257 (2010), pp. 22–3.
21. Kaveh Ehsani, "The Urban Provincial Periphery in Iran: Revolution and War in Ramhormoz" in Ali Gheissari (ed.), *Contemporary Iran: Economy, Society, Politics* (Oxford University Press, 2009), p. 45.
22. Shaul Bakhash, "The Politics of Land, Law, and Social Justice in Iran", *Middle East Journal* 43, 2 (1989), pp. 186–201; Ahmad Ashraf, "There is a Feeling that the Regime Owes Something to the People", interview in *Middle East Report* 156 (1989), pp. 13–18.
23. Anoushiravan Ehteshami, *After Khomeini: The Iranian Second Republic* (London: Routledge, 1995), p. 92.
24. Mehrdad Valibeigi, "The Private Sector in Iran's Post-Revolutionary Economy", *Journal of South Asian and Middle East Studies* 17, 3 (1994), pp. 1–18, 10–11. Karimi suggests that over 300,000 female carpet weaving jobs in rural areas were lost because of US sanctions on the Iranian carpet trade in the 1980s. Zahra Karimi, "The Effects of International Trade on Gender Inequality in Iran: The Case of Women Carpet Weavers" in Roksana Bahramitash and Hadi Salehi Esfahani (eds), *Veiled Unemployment: Islamism and the Political Economy of Women's Employment in Iran* (Syracuse University Press, 2011), p. 173.
25. Arang Keshavarzian, *Bazaar and State in Iran: Politics of the Tehran Marketplace* (Cambridge University Press, 2007). Perhaps the most vocal proponent of domestic *laissez-faire* policies was the Qom-based Ayatollah Ahmad Azari-Qomi, who wrote numerous editorials in the newspaper *Resalat* on Islamic justifications for supporting private enterprise.
26. Kamal Athari, "The Housing Sector in Iran: Market or Planning?" in Thierry Coville (ed.), *The Economy of Islamic Iran: Between State and Market* (Louvain: Peeters, 1994), p. 255.
27. Amouee, *Political Economy of the Islamic Republic*, pp. 271–4.
28. Jahangir Amuzegar, *Iran's Economy Under The Islamic Republic* (London: I.B. Tauris, 1993), p. 137.
29. The Persian term is *isargaran*, which is used officially of those who have given their own or a loved one's life defending the Islamic Republic. The Parliament's move stipulated that if 80% of the company's new shareholders belonged to preferential groups, then 10% of the value needed to be paid in cash and the

rest in instalments over five years. If shareholders did not fall into these categories, 40% of the shares were to be bought with cash and the rest delivered within three months.

30. Ahmad Meydari, "Political Circumstances and the Structure of Ownership Over the Last Three Decades in Iran" [in Persian], *Goftogu* 56 (2010), pp. 29–47; Firouzeh Khalatbari, "The Tehran Stock Exchange and Privatisation" in Thierry Coville (ed.), *The Economy of Islamic Iran: Between State and Market* (Louvain: Peeters, 1994).
31. Behnam Moradi, "Dimensions of Privatization and its Impact on Private Investment (Case of Iran)" [in Persian], *Political-Economic Information* 213/4 (2005), pp. 180–199, p. 193.
32. Amouee, *Political Economy of the Islamic Republic*, p. 272.
33. The lack of regulatory fixity in housing construction is satirized by Dariush Mehrjui's 1986 film *The Lodgers*.
34. Kaveh Ehsani, "Privatization of Public Goods in the Islamic Republic", *Middle East Report* 250 (2009), pp. 26–33, pp. 29–30.
35. This market competition in dairy goods, for example, expanded remarkably the range of products produced domestically to suit consumer tastes. For decades, only two types of cheese were available in Tehran markets—sheep feta and processed cheese spread. Today the dairy conglomerate Kaleh makes domestic versions of Mozzarella, smoked Gouda, blue cheese, and Camembert.
36. The Iranian currency (10 rials = 1 toman) over the 2000s slowly declined relative to the US dollar, from about 700 tomans down to 1,000 tomans= 1 USD by the end of the decade.
37. Information in this paragraph is compiled from Meydari, "Political Circumstances and the Structure of Ownership".
38. Ibid., p. 39.
39. Bijan Khajepour, "Domestic Political Reforms and Private Sector Activity in Iran", *Social Research* 67, 2 (2000), pp. 577–98, p. 590.
40. For the battle over foreign investment during this period, where conservatives borrow the language of economic nationalism in order to attack reformist economic proposals, effectively switching places with each other, see Evaleila Pesaran, *Iran's Struggle for Economic Independence: Reform and Counter-Reform in the Post-Revolutionary Era* (London: Routledge, 2011).
41. Atieh Associates Newsletter, October 2004. This did not mean that Rafsanjani, who had been subjected to heavy criticisms and accusations of corruption by reformist newspapers during the 1990s, approved of all of Khatami's measures. The Expediency Council often sided with the Guardian Council in its opposition to the social and political reforms proposed by Khatami's government and passed by a then reformist-controlled Parliament.
42. *Donyâ-ye Eqtesâd*, 27 June 2010.

43. For more on how Ahmadinejad was perceived in the 2005 election, even by some reformist commentators, see Kevan Harris, "The Politics of Subsidy Reform in Iran", *Middle East Report* 254 (2010), pp. 36–9.
44. Meydari, "Political Circumstances and the Structure of Ownership". Mehdi Karroubi, former Parliament speaker and notable reformist politician, also ran for president in 2005, and promised 50 US dollars to every Iranian if elected. It is misleading, therefore, to state that Ahmadinejad was the only presidential candidate who engaged in populist promises. Aloof technocratic discourse does not function well in the competitive field of Iranian politics, and populism is therefore embedded in the entire political arena.
45. Kevan Harris, "Lineages of the Iranian Welfare State: Dual Institutionalism and Social Policy in the Islamic Republic of Iran", *Social Policy & Administration* 44, 6 (2010), pp. 727–45.
46. Data and details in Meydari, "Political Circumstances and the Structure of Ownership", pp. 41–4.
47. IRIN Channel 2, 29 November 2009.
48. *The Economist*, 12 July 2001. Petropars was sold in 2009 to a consortium of investors including Mashhad's wealthy Imam Reza religious foundation, *Jam-e Jam*, 28 April 2009.
49. *Etemad*, 28 September 2009.
50. *Etemad*, 7 October 2009, IRIN Channel 2, 29 November 2009.
51. *Etemad*, 4 July 2009, emphasis by author.
52. *Alef*, 27 September 2009.
53. For example, Abbas Milani stated that the IRGC was akin to a "military junta" which controlled "minimally about sixty percent of the economy". (See Abbas Milani, "Taking Tehran's Temperature: One Year On", Panel at The Carnegie Endowment for International Peace, 8 June 2009. Transcript at http://carnegieendowment.org/files/0609carnegie-tehran.pdf.) Said Arjomand wrote that the IRGC's "economic empire" was at the commanding heights of a "military-industrial-commercial complex". See Said Arjomand, *After Khomeini: Iran Under His Successors* (Oxford University Press, 2009), p. 60.
54. *Etemad*, 25 November 2009.
55. *Khorasan*, 26 December 2010.
56. *Donya-ye Eqtesad*, 27 June 2010.
57. e.g. Stephen Kotkin, *Magnetic Mountain: Stalinism as a Civilization* (Berkeley: University of California Press, 1995); Joel Andreas, *Rise of the Red Engineers: The Cultural Revolution and the Origins of China's New Class* (Stanford University Press, 2009).
58. While still unpublished, Boroujerdi's findings are summarized at http://pomed.org/blog/2010/03/pomed-notes-analyzing-the-political-elite-of-the-islamic-republic-of-iran.html/. On the provincial origins of 1979's new class, see Ehsani, "The Urban Provincial Periphery in Iran".

59. Walter Korpi, "Welfare-State Regress in Western Europe: Politics, Institutions, Globalization, and Europeanization", *Annual Review of Sociology* 29 (2003), pp. 589–609, p. 598.
60. *Jam-e Jam*, 19 January 2011.
61. Robin Blackburn, "The New Collectivism: Pension Reform, Grey Capitalism and Complex Socialism", *New Left Review* I/233 (1999), pp. 3–65.
62. World Bank, *The Pension System in Iran: Challenges and Opportunities*, 2 vols., Middle East and North Africa Social and Human Development Group (Washington: The World Bank, 2003), pp. 25–6.
63. *BBC Persian*, 8 June 2011; *Shargh*, 4 April 2012.
64. World Bank, *The Pension System in Iran*, p. 35. Most Iranians are unaware of the role of the SSO in the economy, even while millions of them benefit from the fund's monthly cheques and health insurance coverage.
65. *Etemad*, 7 January 2010.
66. *BBC Persian*, 8 June 2011.
67. See Hugo Fazio and Manuel Riesco, "The Chilean Pension Fund Associations", *New Left Review* I/223 (1997), pp. 90–100; Chang Lyui Jung and Alan Walker, "The Impact of Neo-liberalism on South Korea's Public Pension: A Political Economy of Pension Reform", *Social Policy & Administration* 43, 5 (2009), pp. 425–44.
68. Thomas Siebert, "Turkey's Military has a Stake in 60 Companies", *The National*, 19 October 2010; Mourad Haroutunian, "Saoudi Gosi, Pension Fund Invest in Al Sawfa Cement, Riyadh says", *Bloomberg News*, 14 February 2012.
69. Blackburn, "The New Collectivism", p. 25.
70. For instance, the Tabriz Workers' House—an official state union—has complained that pseudo-privatization has led to further subcontracting by firms once they are sold to the parastatal sector, often leading to violations of labour contract law, overtime abuses, sub-minimum wages, and lack of pension payments *Mahd-e Azadi*, 27 April 2010. Tabriz Tractor Manufacturing, one of the main employers in the city and the sponsor of the city's popular football club, was privatized in 2010. Its two main shareholders are the vehicle SOE Saipa and the parastatal Basij Mehr Credit Institution.
71. *Etemad*, 18 July 2009, *Khabar Online*, 26 May 2011.
72. *Iran*, 30 October 2010, *Khabar Online* 21 March 2011.
73. Meydari, "Political Circumstances and the Structure of Ownership".
74. *Shargh*, 29 November 2010.
75. *Donya-ye Eqtesad*, 23 July 2011.
76. David Hoffman, *The Oligarchs: Wealth and Power in the New Russia* (New York: Public Affairs, 2002), p. 196.
77. Michael Burawoy and János Lukács, *The Radiant Past: Ideology and Reality in Hungary's Road to Capitalism* (University of Chicago Press, 1992).

78. *Jomhuri-yeEslami*, 17 September 2009.
79. Daily Report, Near East South Asia, FBIS-NES-93–103, 1 June 1993, p. 59.
80. Thanks to Farideh Farhi for this point.
81. *Iranian Students News Agency*, 13 December 2011.
82. Not all foundations (*bonyads*) are religious, and not all of them are parastatal. The Foundation for Martyrs and Devotee Affairs, for example, used to be a parastatal but now is directly run by the executive branch. The pre-1979 Pahlavi Foundation, conversely, was avowedly secular. *Bonyads* were also heavily criticized during the 1990s for lack of transparency, misuse of funds, and the blurring between economic production and welfare redistribution—a perfect target for the economic liberals of the Rafsanjani era as well as the political liberals of the Khatami era. One of the main goals of the Khatami administration was to fold the welfare functions of *bonyads* and other parallel institutions into the executive branch. This was correctly seen by the conservative faction as an attempt to centralize the state and remove veto points for conservatives' ability to hold up state policy they did not like; see Suzanne Maloney, "Islamism and Iran's Postrevolutionary Economy: The Case of the Bonyads" in Mary Ann Tetreault and Robert Denemark (eds), *Gods, Guns, and Globalization: Religious Radicalism and International Political Economy* (Boulder: Lynne Rienner, 2004); Ali Saeidi, "The Accountability of Para-governmental Organizations (bonyads): The Case of Iranian Foundations", *Iranian Studies* 37, 3 (2004), pp. 479–98.
83. Conceptually, these large foundations might be explained as a form of what Ben Ross Schneider calls "diversified business groups" common to middle-income countries. Ben Ross Schneider, "A Comparative Political Economy of Diversified Business Groups, or How States Organize Big Business", *Review of International Political Economy* 16, 2 (2009), pp. 178–201.
84. Katherine Verdery, *What Was Socialism, and What Comes Next?* (Princeton University Press, 1996), pp. 212–13.
85. *RFE/RL*, 10 October 2010.
86. Robert Bianchi, *Unruly Corporatism: Associational Life in Twentieth-Century Egypt* (New York: Oxford University Press, 1989).
87. This outcome resembles Melani Cammett's findings in North Africa, wherein states that privilege one faction of industrialists over another during periods of liberalization tend to create aggrieved segments of the business class which then collectively mobilize in lobbying efforts. Loud business protests and the perception of an autonomous private sector, in other words, surprisingly appear in countries where the state has tight and privileged relations with one segment of the business class. Melani Cammett, *Globalization and Business Politics in Arab North Africa: A Comparative Perspective* (Cambridge University Press, 2007).
88. Nazih Ayubi, "Political Correlates of Privatization Programs in the Middle East", *Arab Studies Quarterly* 14, 2/3 (1992), pp. 39–56.

89. This conclusion draws from Eyal, Szelényi and Townsley and from King and Szelényi: Gil Eyal, Iván Szelényi, and Eleanor Townsley, *Making Capitalism without Capitalists* (London: Verso, 1998); Lawrence King and Iván Szelényi, "Post-Communist Economic Systems" in Neil Smelser and Richard Swedberg (eds), *The Handbook of Economic Sociology* (second edition) (New York: Russell Sage Foundation, 2005).
90. Schumpeter argued that, in instances of stunted capitalist development, "without protection by some non-bourgeois group, the bourgeoisie is politically helpless and unable not only to lead its nation but even to take care of its particular class interest. Which amounts to saying that it needs a master". See Joseph Schumpeter, *Capitalism, Socialism, and Democracy* (fifth edition) (London: Routledge, 1994), p. 138.
91. On Turkish SOE privatization, see Mehmet Güran, "The Political Economy of Privatization in Turkey: An Evaluation" in Tamer Çetin and Fuat Oğuz (eds), *The Political Economy of Regulation in Turkey* (New York: Springer, 2011). On how the AKP constructed a neoliberal "capitalism from without" see Cihan Tuğal, *Passive Revolution: Absorbing the Islamic Challenge to Capitalism* (Stanford University Press, 2009).
92. See Eva Bellin, *Stalled Democracy: Capital, Labor, and the Paradox of State-Sponsored Development* (Ithaca: Cornell University Press, 2002); Pete Moore, *Doing Business in the Middle East: Politics and Economic Crisis in Jordan and Kuwait* (Cambridge University Press, 2004).
93. John Sfakianakis, "The Whales of the Nile: Networks, Businessmen, and Bureaucrats During the Era of Privatization in Egypt" in Steven Heydemann (ed.), *Networks of Privilege in the Middle East: The Politics of Economic Reform Revisited* (New York: Palgrave Macmillan, 2004), p. 79.

10. THE HOUND THAT DID NOT BARK: SOLVING THE MYSTERY OF BUSINESS WITHOUT VOICE IN EGYPT

1. The author would like to thank Amr Adly and Steffen Hertog for commenting on an earlier draft of this chapter.
2. For the interpretation of business constituting a class, see Malak Zaalouk, *Power, Class, and Foreign Capital in Egypt: The Rise of the New Bourgeoisie* (London: Zed Books, 1989); and Ibrahim G. Aoude, "From National Bourgeois Development to Infitah: Egypt 1952–1992", *Arab Studies Quarterly* (Winter, 1994), http://findarticles.com/p/articles/mi_m2501/is_n1_v16/ai_16082325/?tag=content;col1. For descriptions of the rise of business, see Raymond A. Hinnebusch, "The Politics of Economic Reform in Egypt", *Third World Quarterly* 14, 1 (1993), pp. 159–71; and Robert Springborg, "The Arab Bourgeoisie: A Revisionist Interpretation", *Arab Studies Quarterly* 15, 1 (Winter 1993), pp. 13–39.

3. Raymond A. Hinnebusch, "Children of the Elite: Political Attitudes of the Westernized Elite in Contemporary Egypt", *The Middle East* Journal, 36, 4 (Autumn, 1982), pp. 535–61; Robert Bianchi, "Businessmen's Associations in Egypt and Turkey", *Annals of the American Academy of Political and Social Science*, 482 (November 1985), pp. 147–59; Noha El Mikawy and Ramy Mohsen, *Civil Society Participation in the Law Making Process in Egypt* (Bonn: ZEF) (January 2005) http://www.zef.de/fileadmin/webfiles/downloads/projects/politicalreform/Civil_Society_Participation_Egypt.pdf; Sufyan Alissa, "The Political Economy of Reform in Egypt: Understanding the Role of Institutions", *Carnegie Papers*, 5 (October 2007) http://carnegieendowment.org/files/cmec5_alissa_egypt_final.pdf; Heba Handoussa *et al., Egypt Human Development Report 2008: The Role of Civil Society* (Cairo: United Nations Development Programme).
4. John Sfakianakis, "The Whales of the Nile: Networks, Businessmen, and Bureaucrats during the Era of Privatization in Egypt", in Steven Heydeman (ed.), *Networks of Privilege in the Middle East* (New York: Palgrave Macmillan, 2004), pp. 77–100.
5. That these trends existed and were supportive of an emerging liberalism was, for example, the thesis of Bruce K. Rutherford, *Egypt After Mubarak: Liberalism, Islam and Democracy in the Arab World* (Princeton University Press, 2004).
6. See for example Lisa Blaydes, *Elections and Distributive Politics in Mubarak's Egypt*, Cambridge University Press, 2011. On ECES and US support for it see James V. Grimaldi and Robert O'Harrow, "In Egypt: corruption cases had an American root", *Washington Post,* 20 October 2011, http://www.washingtonpost.com/investigations/in-egypt-corruption-had-an-american-root/2011/10/07/gIQAApWoyL_story.html. On the role of businessmen in Parliament see Marwa Hussein, "Greater Business Leverage in Egyptian Parliament", *Ahramonline*, 23 December 2010 http://english.ahram.org.eg/NewsContent/3/0/2458/Business/Greater-business-leverage-in-Egyptian-parliament-.aspx
7. http://www.doingbusiness.org/reforms/top-reformers-2009. For an explanation of how this improved ranking may have occurred, see Robert Springborg, "Egypt" in Abbas Kadhim (ed.), *Governance in the Arab World* (New York: Routledge, forthcoming).
8. The term "coup-volution" was coined by Nathan W. Toronto, "Egypt's Coup-volution", *Middle East Insight*, 6 (6 February 2011), http://blog.nus.edu.sg/middleeastinstitute/2011/02/16/egypts-coup-volution/
9. Esam al Amin, "Mubarak's last gasps", *Counterpunch*, 4–6 February 2011, http://www.counterpunch.org/2011/02/04/mubarak-s-last-gasps/; Sameh Naguib, "Egyptian Revolution", *Socialistworkeronline*, 2 July 2011, http://www.socialistworker.co.uk/art.php?id=25245
10. The legal/judicial strengthening project supported by USAID for more than a

decade from the mid-1990s, and focused on commercial courts, both responded to and articulated a demand by the business community.

11. Nathan J. Brown, "Egypt's Judges in a Revolutionary Age", *The Carnegie Papers*, Middle East (February 2012). For a description of how the SCAF worked behind the scenes with judges, see David D. Kirkpatrick, "Judge helped Egypt's military to cement power", *New York Times*, 4 July 2012, pp. A1, A10.
12. This apt term is from Steven Heydemann, *Networks of Privilege in the Middle East.*
13. For an insightful review of this evidence, see Amr Adly, "Mubarak 1990–2011: The State of Corruption", *Arab Reform Initiative Thematic Study* (March 2011) http://www.arab-reform.net/IMG/pdf/Mubarak_1990–2011_The_State_of_Corruption.pdf
14. Lakah appealed to Copts although he is a Syro-Lebanese Greek Catholic.
15. For a review of the comparative economic importance of hydrocarbon and other resources, see Robert Springborg, "Gas and Oil in Egypt's Development" in Robert Looney (ed.), *Handbook of Oil Politics*. (New York: Routledge, 2011), pp. 295–311.
16. Nathan Hodson's chapter in this book documents this process.
17. For an analysis of the comparison between Europe and Egypt in this regard, see Robert Springborg, "Agrarian Bourgeoisie, Semiproletarians, and the Egyptian State: Lessons for Liberalization", *International Journal of Middle East* Studies, 22 (1990), pp. 447–72.
18. This is the logic underlying "pacted" transitions. See Guillermo O'Donnell, Phillipe C. Schmitter and Laurence Whitehead (eds), *Transitions from Authoritarian* Rule (Baltimore: Johns Hopkins University Press, 1986). For a review of the literature on pacted transitions and assessment of its utility, see "Workshop on Regime Transitions: Transitions from Communist Rule in Comparative Perspective", The Center for Democracy, Development, and the Rule of Law, Stanford University (15–16 November 2002) http://iis-db.stanford.edu/pubs/20263/RegimeTransitions%5B1%5D.workshopreport.1–30–04.pdf For an application of the model in the Arab world, see Lisa Anderson, "Political Pacts, Liberalism, and Democracy: The Tunisian National Pact of 1988", *Government and Opposition*, 26, 2 (April 1991), pp. 244–60.
19. This is the argument for example in Clement M. Henry and Robert Springborg, *Globalization and the Politics of Development in the Middle East* (Cambridge University Press, 2010).
20. Sadat's failure to fully subordinate the military is attested by his assassination by elements of the military, possibly with the complicity of some members of the senior officer corps. The most thorough investigation of the on-going struggle for power between the military and Egypt's presidents is Hazem Kandil, *Soldiers, Spies and Statesmen: Egypt's Road to Revolt* (London: Verso, 2012).

21. Amr Adly, "Politically Embedded Cronyism: The Case of Post-Liberalization Egypt", *Business and Politics*, 11, 4 (August 2009) http://www.bepress.com/bap/vol11/iss4/art3; and Amr Adly, *Politics and Economics of State Reform and Development in the Middle East: Turkey and Egypt in the Post-liberalization Era (1980–2010)* (London: Routledge, 2012). A global empirical study of the relationships between incentive structures in democracies, quality of governance and economic growth also supports this argument. See Nicholas Charron and Victor Lapuente, "Does Democracy Produce Quality of Government?" *European Journal of Political Research*, 49 (2010), pp. 443–70.
22. Amr Adly, "The Political Economy of Trade Liberalization: Turkey and Egypt in the Post-Liberalization Era", unpublished PhD thesis, Department of Political and Social Sciences, European University Institute (September 2010), p. 11.
23. Nihal el-Megharbel, "Enhancing Linkages between SMEs and Large Enterprises in Egyptian Industry", Egyptian Center for Economic Studies, *Working Paper 140* (October 2008) http://www.eces.org.eg/publications/View_Pub.asp?p_id=10&p_detail_id=264&logout=1
24. Omer Ali and Ibrahim Elbadawi, "The Political Economy of Public Employment in Resource Dependent Countries", *Economic Research Forum Working Paper 673* (May 2012) http://www.erf.org.eg/CMS/uploads/pdf/673.pdf
25. Anthony Gorman, *Historians, State and Politics in Twentieth Century Egypt: Contesting the Nation* (London: Routledge Curzon, 2003).
26. His accomplishments have in fact probably been overstated in nationalist historiography, for his financial empire based on Bank Misr had crumbled by the outset of World War II. See Eric Davis, *Challenging Colonialism: Bank Misr and Egyptian Industrialization, 1920–1941* (Princeton University Press, 1983).
27. For oral histories of Sidqy and others involved in business and economic policy making in Egypt, see *The Chronicles*, the periodical publication of the Economic and Business History Research Center of The American University in Cairo. http://www.aucegypt.edu/research/ebhrc/publications/Pages/TheChronicles.aspx
28. Robert L. Tignor, *State, Private Enterprise, and Economic Change in Egypt, 1918–1952* (Princeton University Press, 1984); Robert L. Tignor, "Decolonization and Business: The Case of Egypt", *The Journal of Modern* History, 59, 3 (September 1987), pp. 479–505; Gorman, *op. cit.*, pp. 174–95; and Marius Deeb, "The Socioeconomic Role of the Local Foreign Minorities in Modern Egypt, 1805–1961", *International Journal of Middle East* Studies, 9 (1978), pp. 11–22.
29. Robert Vitalis, *When Capitalists Collide: Business Conflict and the End of Empire in Egypt* (Berkeley: University of California Press, 1995); and Robert Vitalis, "On the Theory and Practice of Compradors: The Role of 'Abbud Pasha in the Egyptian Political Economy", *International Journal of Middle East Studies*, 22, 3 (1990), pp. 291–315.

30. On the distribution of labour by size of firms, see Alia El Mahdi and Ali Rashed, "The Changing Economic Environment and the Development of Micro and Small Enterprises in Egypt, 2006", in Ragui Assaad, *The Egyptian Labor Market Revisited* (Cairo: American University in Cairo Press, 2009), pp. 83–116.
31. Zeinab Abul-Magd, "The Egyptian Republic of Retired Generals", *Foreign Policy*, 8 May 2012, http://mideast.foreignpolicy.com/posts/2012/05/08/the_egyptian_republic_of_retired_generals. On the expansion of security and intelligence services under Mubarak, see Samer Soliman, *The Autumn of Dictatorship: Fiscal Crisis and Political Change in Egypt* (Palo Alto: Stanford University Press), pp. 54–75.
32. For a comparative review of Egyptian data on non-performing loans, see Henry and Springborg, op. cit., pp. 162–211. For an evaluation of access to credit, see Khaled Abdel-Kader, "Private Sector Access to Credit in Egypt: Evidence from Survey Data", Egyptian Center for Economic Studies, *Working Paper* 111 (July 2006) http://www.eces.org.eg/Uploaded_Files/%7B7533AF5C-D50E-401F-A5C0-C9805817DE11%7D_ECESWP111e.pdf The "Islah 2 Index", which compares ease of doing business in Cairo with Alexandria and is compiled annually by the Alexandria Business Association with the assistance of the International Finance Corporation and Alexandria University, in 2012 identified access to credit, along with bureaucracy and centralization, as the three principle obstacles to doing business in Egypt. See Nesma Nowar, "Business Hurdles", *al-Ahram Weekly*, 14 June 2012, http://weekly.ahram.org.eg/2012/1102/ec3.htm
33. Heba Handoussa *et al.*, "Youth in Egypt: Building Our Future, *Egypt Human Development Report 2010*. Cairo: UNDP, 2010; and Mary Kraetsch, "Youth in Focus", *Middle East Youth Initiative*, 27 June 2010, http://www.shababinclusion.org/userfiles/file/Interview%20with%20Heba%20Handoussa%20FINAL.pdf
34. Robert Springborg, "Is Tantawi Reading the Public's Pulse Correctly?" *Egypt Independent*, 6 December 2011, http://www.egyptindependent.com/opinion/tantawi-reading-public%E2%80%99s-pulse-correctly Robert Springborg, "Resilient Praetorianism in Egypt", in Thomas C. Bruneau and Cristiana Matei (eds), *Handbook of Civil-Military Relations* (London: Routledge, 2012).
35. Richard F. Doner, Bryan K. Ritchie and Dan Slater, "Systemic Vulnerability and the Origins of Developmental States: Northeast and Southeast Asia in Comparative Perspective", *International Organization*, 59 (2005), pp. 327–61.
36. Jason Brownlee, *Democracy Prevention: The Politics of the U.S-Egyptian Alliance* (Cambridge University Press, 2012).
37. Robert Springborg, "The US Response to the Arab Spring: Leadership Missing", in Riccardo Alcaro and Miguel Haubrich-Seco (eds), *Re-thinking Western Policies in Light of the Arab Uprisings* (Rome: Italian Institute of International Affairs, Research Paper 4, February 2012). http://www.iai.it/content.asp?langid=2&contentid=+739&ritorno

38. Amr Adly, "Mubarak (1990–2011): The State of Corruption", op. cit.
39. Shana Marshall and Joshua Stacher, "Egypt's Generals and Transnational Capital", *Middle East Report*, 262 (Spring 2012), pp. 12–18; Shana Marshall, "Egypt's other revolution: modernizing the military-industrial complex", *Jadaliyaa* (February 10, 2012); Zeinab Abul-Magd, "The Generals' Secret: Egypt's Ambivalent Market", *Sada* (Washington: Carnegie Endowment, February 2012); and Zeinab Abul-Magd, "The army and the economy in Egypt", *Jadaliyya* (23 December 2011),
40. Zeinab Abul-Magd, "The Egyptian Republic of Retired Generals", op. cit.
41. Tai Ming Cheung, "Disarmament and Development in China: The Relationship between National Defense and Economic Development", *Asian Survey*, 28, 7 (July 1988), pp. 757–74.
42. Sinan Ulgen, "Turkish Business and EU Accession", *Essays* (London: Centre for European Reform, 2006), http://www.edam.org.tr/document/ulgen_cer_essay_dec06.pdf
43. Samer Soliman, "The Rise and Decline of the Islamic Banking Model in Egypt" in Clement M. Henry and Rodney Wilson (eds), *The Politics of Islamic Finance* (Edinburgh University Press, 2004), pp. 265–85.
44. "Government prepares to sell $2 bn in Islamic Bonds, Says Scholar", *Egypt Independent*, 14 February 2012 http://www.egyptindependent.com/news/government-prepares-sell-us2-bn-islamic-bonds-says-scholar; "A new chance in Egypt for Islamic Finance", *Egypt Independent*, 21 April 2011 http://www.egyptindependent.com/news/new-chance-egypt-islamic-finance
45. Zeinab Abul Magd, "The Brotherhood's businessmen", *Egypt Independent*, 13 February 2012; "Asharq Al-Awsat talks to Muslim Brotherhood presidential hopeful Khairat El-Shater), http://www.egyptindependent.com/opinion/brotherhoods-businessmen" *Asharq Al-Awsat*, 13 April 2012, http://www.asharq-e.com/news.asp?section=3&id=29236; and Ahmad Feteha, "Muslims Inc: How Rich is Khairat el-Shater?" *Ahram Online*, 3 April 2012, http://english.ahram.org.eg/News/38278.aspx
46. Upon being named Minister of Transport in December 2005, Muhammad Mansour resigned his fifty-eight company directorships and chairmanships, most of which were in companies that had long standing agency agreements with such leading US-based multinationals as General Motors, Caterpillar, Marlboro, and McDonald's. Ibtessam Zayed and Salma Hussein, "Mohamad Mansour: ATarnished Captain of Industry", *ahramonline*, 10 March 2011, http://english.ahram.org.eg/NewsContentP/3/6724/Business/Mohamed-Mansour-A-tarnished-captain-of-industry.aspx
47. The lower figure was provided by a well informed banker (interview, London, 11 May 2012), the higher by a former Western diplomat with personal knowledge of Mansour's assets (personal communication, 1 June 2012).

48. Emad Siam, "The Islamist vs the Islamic in Welfare Outreach", *IDS Bulletin* 43, 1 (December 2011), pp. 87–93.
49. Mustafa al Fiqi, for example, long time chairman of the parliamentary foreign affairs committee, intimate of the Mubaraks and beneficiary of particularly egregious security service interventions on behalf of his NDP parliamentary election campaigns in 2005 and 2010, was made president of the British University of Egypt, a post he held until shortly after the coup-volution.
50. Sebnem Gumuscu, "Class, Status and Party: The Changing Face of Political Islam in Turkey and Egypt", *Comparative Political Studies*, 43, 7 (2010), pp. 835–61; Mustafa Akyol, "The Turkish Model", *The Cairo Review of Global Affairs*, 4 (Winter 2012) http://www.aucegypt.edu/GAPP/CairoReview/Pages/articleDetails.aspx?aid=150
51. This is a paraphrase of the argument of the literature referenced in note 18.
52. Amr Adly, personal communication (18 May 2012).
53. *Muthakrat bisha'n marsum al maglis al 'askary bi'gaazit al tassahluh fii gara'im al 'udwaan 'ala al maal al 'aam* (Memorandum Regarding the Directive of the Military Council to Permit Reconciliation in Crimes Pertaining to Misappropriation of Public Funds), Egyptian Initiative for Human Rights February 2012 (http://eipr.org/sites/default/files/pressreleases/pdf/eipr_memo_law4_2012.pdf).
54. Ibid., and Amr Adly, "Mubarak (1990–2011): The State of Corruption", op. cit.
55. Ibrahim Saif, "The Economic Agenda of the Islamist Parties", *Carnegie Paper* (May 2012), http://carnegie-mec.org/publications/?fa=48187
56. "Ezz Steel Awarded new Expansion License", *Ahram Online* (November 19, 2012), http://english.ahram.org.eg/NewsContent/3/12/58573/Business/Economy/Ezz-Steel-awarded-new-expansion-licence-.aspx
57. Ayesha Siddiqa, *Military, Inc.: Inside Pakistan's Military Economy* (Oxford University Press, 2007).
58. "The Turkish Ambassador Meets with EBDA Board of Directors", EBDA website (http://www.ebda-egypt.com/index.php?option=com_k2&view=item&id=28:the-turkish-ambassador-meeting-with-ebda-board-of-directors&Itemid=309; Nadine Maroushi, "Senior Brotherhood member launches Egyptian Business Association, *Egypt Independent*, 26 March 2012.
59. Banu Eligur, *The Mobilization of Political Islam in Turkey* (Cambridge University Press, 2010).
60. This interpretation is based on a reading of General al-Sisi's writings at the US Army War College, Carlisle, Pennsylvania, March 2005, and discussions with US military personnel.
61. Robert Springborg, "The Precarious Economics of Arab Springs", *Survival*, 53, 6 (December 2011–January 2012), pp. 85–104.
62. For an assessment of the military's mishandling of the transition and its prob-

able consequences, see “Lost in Transition: The World According to Egypt’s SCAF”, *Middle East Report 121* (24 April 2012), International Crisis Group.

11. BUSINESSES AND THE REVOLUTION

1. This categorization closely relates to the division between large, small and medium, and microenterprises that Robert Springborg uses in chapter ten in this volume.
2. Quoting just a few of the most recent titles: Ibrahim Elbadawi and Samir Makdisi (eds), *Democracy in the Arab World: Explaining the Deficit* (London: Routledge, 2011); Laura Guazzone and Daniela Pioppi (eds), *The Arab State and Neo-Liberal Globalization: The Restructuring of State Power in the Middle East* (Reading: Ithaca, 2009); Eberhard Kienle (ed.), *Democracy Building and Democracy Erosion: Political Change North and South of the Mediterranean* (London: Saqi, 2009); Oliver Schlumberger (ed.), *Debating Arab Authoritarianism: Dynamics and Durability in Nondemocratic Regimes* (Stanford University Press, 2007).
3. In my earlier work I indeed argued that the Arab non-rentier states should be expected to democratize because of their fiscal crisis (“Economic Foundations of Democracy and Authoritarianism,” *Arab Studies Quarterly* 10 [1988], pp. 457–75). I saw this expectation supported by developments in the late 1980s, notably in Algeria, Egypt and Jordan. See “The Oil Rent, the Fiscal Crisis of the State and Democratization” in Ghassan Salamé (ed.), *Democracy without Democrats? The Revival of Politics in the Muslim World*, (London: I.B. Tauris, 1994), pp. 130–55; “Resources, Revenue and Authoritarianism in the Arab World: Beyond the Rentier State?” in Rex Brynen, Bahgat Korany and Paul Noble (eds), *Political Liberalization and Democratization in the Arab World* (London: Lynne Rienner, 1995), pp. 211–28, although the catastrophic outcome of the attempted democratization process in Algeria had the effect of discouraging democratic transitions everywhere in the region. The bloody civil war into which Syria has fallen at the time of writing may have a similar discouraging effect on the current revolutionary wave.
4. I have discussed the impact of the weakness of the national bourgeoisie in the Arab countries outside the GCC in “Linking Economic and Political Reform in the Middle East: The Role of the Bourgeoisie” in Schlumberger (ed.), *Debating Arab Authoritarianism*, pp. 161–76; see also Lisa Anderson, “Liberalization in the Arab World”, Discussion paper for the Mellon Seminar, Near Eastern Studies Department, Princeton University, 14 February 1992.
5. John Waterbury, “Democracy without Democrats? The Potential for Political Liberalization in the Middle East” in Salamé (ed.), *Democracy without Democrats*, p. 27.
6. Indeed, Waterbury adds: “None of this is peculiar to the Middle East” (ibid.).

7. Cilja Harders, "The Informal Social Pact: The State and the Urban Poor in Cairo", in Eberhard Kienle (ed.), *Politics from Above, Politics from Below: The Middle East in the Age of Economic Reform* (London: Saqi, 2003), pp. 194–7; Ahmad El Sayyed El-Naggar, "Economic Policy: from State Control to Decay and Corruption", in Rabab El-Mahdi and Philip Marfleet (eds), *Egypt: the Moment of Change* (London: Zed Books, 2009), pp. 41–3; Ahmad El Sayyed El-Naggar, "Massaging the Figures", *Al Ahram Weekly* 772 (8–14 December 2005), http://weekly.ahram.org.eg/print/2005/772/ec1.htm.
8. Hamza Meddeb, "La Tunisie, pays émergent?" *Societés Politiques Comparées* 29 (2010), http://www.fasopo.org/reasopo/n29/article.pdf.
9. See for example D.C. Kang, *Crony Capitalism: Corruption and Development in South Korea and the Philippines* (Cambridge University Press, 2002).
10. I developed this point in "From Private Sector to National Bourgeoisie: Saudi Arabian Business," in Paul Aarts and Gerd Nonneman (eds), *Saudi Arabia in the Balance: Politics, Economics & International Relations* (London: Hurst, 2005), pp. 144–84; and in *Linking Economic and Political Reform in the Middle East.*
11. On the coincidence of crony capitalists and key government aides see the chapters two (Valeri) and three (Almezaini) in this volume.
12. The discussion in this chapter is based almost exclusively on evidence from Egypt, the country for which we have the best information on several business entities of all sizes.
13. John Sfakianakis, "The Whales of the Nile: Networks, Businessmen and Bureaucrats during the Era of Privatization in Egypt" in Steven Heydemann (ed.), *Networks of Privilege in the Middle East: The Politics of Economic Reform Revisited* (London: Palgrave Macmillan, 2004), p. 79.
14. Ibid., p. 80.
15. Yahya M. Sadowski *Political Vegetables: Businessmen and Bureaucrats in the Development of Egyptian Agriculture* (Washinton: Brookings Institution, 1991).
16. The corporate histories of Binladen and Saudi Oger (Hariri) in Saudi Arabia present very similar cases of ambiguity in the interplay between business savvy and political access.
17. Aziza Sami, "Enjoying Bad News", *Al Ahram Weekly* 564, 13–19 December 2001.
18. "2011 World's Billionaires", *Forbes.*
19. On the potential impact of international education see chapter seven by Tina Zintl in this volume.
20. For more information please visit http://www.charlierose.com/view/interview/9157.
21. Jane Kinninmont also quotes a second case of political activism, that of Ahmed Heikal, son of Mohammed Hassanien Heikal, who was an adviser to President Gamal Abdel Nasser; see Jane Kinninmont, "The New and Old Economic

Actors in North Africa", in Jane Kinninmont, Silvia Colombo, and Paola Caridi (eds), *New Socio-Political Actors in North Africa: A Transatlantic Perspective*, Mediterranean Papers Series (Washington: German Marshall Fund, 2012), p. 22. Mohammed Heikal's proximity to power waned after the death of Nasser. Ahmed Heikal is the CEO of Citadel Capital, a private equity firm, while his brother Hassan has been the CEO of the investment bank EFG-Hermes since 2007; he joined the bank in 1995, having previously worked for Goldman Sachs.

22. Zina Moukheiber, "Billionaire Egyptian Family Faces Potential Blow To Reputation", *Forbes*, 25 April 2011.
23. Amr Adly, "Mubarak 1990–2011: The State of Corruption", *Arab Reform Initiative Thematic Study*, March 2011, http://www.arab-reform.net/IMG/pdf/Mubarak_1990–2011_The_State_of_Corruption.pdf.
24. His brother Hisham was appointed by Mubarak as member of the Shura Council, until 2008 when he was arrested in connection with the murder of his former lover, the Lebanese singer Suzanne Tamim, in Dubai. Hisham Talaat Mustapha was initially condemned to death, but later the sentence was reduced to fifteen years in prison, which he is serving. This of course has little to do with the business of the company, except for showing the arrogance of someone who believes he is above the law.
25. Adly, *Mubarak 1990–2011*, p. 9.
26. Ibid.
27. Richard Leiby, "The Rise and Fall of Egypt's Most Despised Billionaire, Ahmed Ezz", *Washington Post*, 9 April 2011.
28. According to Zeinab Abul Magd, "There are three major military bodies engaged in civilian production: the Ministry of Military Production, running eight factories; the Arab Organization for Industrialization, running twelve factories; and the National Service Products Organization, running fifteen factories, companies, and farms". (See "The Egyptian Republic of Retired Generals", *Foreign Policy*, 8 May 2012, http://mideast.foreignpolicy.com/posts/2012/05/08/the_egyptian_republic_of_retired_generals).
29. The negative implications of the economic role of the military and the "deep state" are discussed in detail by Robert Springborg in Chapter ten in this volume.
30. This is the line promoted by the so-called "New Structural Economics". See Justin Yifu Lin, *New Structural Economics* (Washington: The World Bank, 2012).
31. Steffen Hertog, "Public Industry as Tool of Rentier Economy Diversification: The GCC Case", in Giacomo Luciani (ed.), *Resources Blessed: Diversification and the Gulf Development Model* (Berlin: Gerlach, 2012, forthcoming).
32. Roger Owen, "What Constitutes Business Rationality in Egypt at the End of the Twentieth Century: a Political Economy Approach", in Kienle (ed.), *Politics from Above, Politics from Below*, pp. 157–66.

33. Emphasis on exports has been typical of developmental states and has succeeded well in Asia. In the Arab countries it has been paid mostly lip service, with only limited real support provided, and exports of products other than hydrocarbons have not improved much.
34. As discussed in detail by Robert Springborg in Chapter ten in this volume.
35. In contrast, Springborg argues that the "deep state" that is ultimately in control in Egypt never abandoned its priority to security, and business representatives in government did not wield any real power.
36. Jean-Pierre Cassarino, *Tunisian New Entrepreneurs and their Past Experiences of Migration in Europe* (Aldershot: Ashgate, 2000), pp. 142–3.
37. Interview with Maruan, October 1996, in Cassarino, *Tunisian New Entrepreneurs*, pp. 89–90.
38. Interview with Selim, June 1996, in Ibid., pp. 198–9.
39. In some cases, this was also because individual entrepreneurial families are members of religious minorities: e.g. the Sawiris are Copts. Another case of business politics being influenced by religious minority status is that of Shi'a business in Kuwait, discussed by Rivka Azoulay in chapter three in this volume.
40. John Waterbury (*Democracy without Democrats*, p. 27) saw this already in 1994, when he wrote: "For a transition to begin some segments of the bourgeoisie, with substantial resources, has to be ready to ally with forces outside the state's patronage network. It may be that Islamic business groups, most prominent in Egypt, have begun to make such a move. But there is equally compelling evidence that Islamic business interests are thickly intertwined with state economic interests, state functionaries, and the military".
41. It is in fact not altogether clear whether Shater is still an active businessman or is simply a partner in some business ventures run by others, while he devotes himself to political action.
42. Zainab Abul-Magd, "The Brotherhood's Businessmen", *AlMasry AlYoum*, 13 February 2012.
43. Ahmed Feteha, "Muslims Inc: How Rich is Khairat El-Shater?" *Ahram Online*, 3 April 2012, http://english.ahram.org.eg/NewsContentPrint/36/0/38278/Presidential-elections-/0/Muslims-Inc-How-rich-is-Khairat-ElShater.aspx.
44. Ibid.
45. Suzy Hansen, "The Economic Vision of Egypt's Muslim Brotherhood Millionaires", *Bloomberg Businessweek*, 19 April 2012, http://www.businessweek.com/articles/2012–04–19/the-economic-vision-of-egypts-muslim-brotherhood-millionaires.
46. Joel Beinin, "Workers and Egypt's January 25 Revolution", *International Labor and Working Class History* 80 (2011), pp. 189–96; and "Workers' Struggles under "Socialism" and Neo-Liberalism", in El-Mahdi and Marfleet (eds), *Egypt: the Moment of Change*, pp. 68–86; Emil P. Totonchi, "Laboring a Democratic

Spring: the Past, Present and Future of Free Trade Unions in Egypt", *Working USA* 14, 3 (2011), pp. 259–83.

47. Works on the informal sector predate the revolution. They describe the condition of the marginalized, not necessarily with respect to organized political resistance: see Harders, *The Informal Social Pact*; Julia Eliacahar, *Markets of Dispossession: NGOs, Economic Development and the State in Cairo* (London: Duke University Press, 2005); Béatrice Hibou, *La force de l'obéissance* (Paris: La Découverte, 2006).
48. "This Land is Your Land—A conversation with Hernando De Soto", *World Policy Journal* 28, 2 (2011), http://www.worldpolicy.org/journal/summer2011/this-land-is-your-land.
49. See http://blogs.reuters.com/trnewsmaker/2011/04/06/full-transcript-of-robert-zoellick-newsmaker/. See also Jane Kinninmont, *The New and Old Economic Actors*.
50. Diane Singerman, *Avenues of Participation* (Princeton University Press, 1995), pp. 179ff.

BIBLIOGRAPHY

Abdelrahman, Maha M. *Civil Society Exposed: The Politics of NGOs in Egypt*. London: Tauris Academic, 2004.

Abdullah, Muhammad Morsy. *The United Arab Emirates: A Modern History*. London: Croom Helm, 1978.

Abu-Baker, Albadr S.S. "Political Economy of State Formation: The United Arab Emirates in Comparative Perspective", PhD dissertation, University of Michigan, 1995.

Adly, Amr. "The Political Economy of Trade Liberalization: Turkey and Egypt in the Post-Liberalization Era", PhD dissertation, European University Institute, 2010. If Adly's references ordered chornologically, items need to be switched round.

———. *Politics and Economics of State Reform and Development in the Middle East: Turkey and Egypt in the Post-liberalization Era* (1980–2010). London: Routledge, 2012.

Akyol, Mustafa. "The Turkish Model", *The Cairo Review of Global Affairs*, 4 (2012), 68–83.

Al Fahim, Mohammed. *From Rags to Riches: A Story of Abu Dhabi*. London: I.B. Tauris, 1998.

Al-Ghaz'ali, Saleh Mohammed 'Aischa 'Abdelrahman. *Al-Jama'at al-Siyasiyya al-Kuwaytiyya fi Qarn 1910–2007* [The Political Groups in Kuwait in the Period 1910–2007]. Kuwait: Sunduq Al-Barid, 2007.

Al-Khaldi, Sami Nasir. *Al-Ahzab al-Islamiyya fi al-Kuwayt: al-Shi'a, al-Ihwan wa al-Salfiyyun* [The Islamic Movements in Kuwait: the Shi'a the Ikhwan and the Salafists]. Kuwait: Dar Al-Naba' li al-Nashra wa al-Tawzi', 1999.

Al-Mdayris, Falah. *Al-Harakat al-Shi'iya fi al-Kuwayt* [The Shi'i Movement in Kuwait]. Kuwait: Dar Al-Qurtas, 1999.

Al-Najjar, Ghanim. "The Decision-Making Process in Kuwait: The Land Acquisition Policy as a Case Study", PhD dissertation, Exeter University, 1984.

BIBLIOGRAPHY

Al-Naqeeb, Khaldoun. *State and Society in the Gulf and Arab Peninsula: A Different Perspective*. London: Routledge, 1990.

Al-Sayyid, Mustapha. "A Clash of Values: U.S. Civil Society Aid and Islam in Egypt", in Thomas Carothers and Marina Ottaway (eds), *Funding Virtue, Civil Society Aid and Democracy Promotion*. Washington: Carnegie Endowment for International Peace, 2000.

Albrecht, Holgar. "The Nature of Political Participation", in Ellen Lust-Okar and Saloua Zerhouni (eds), *Political Participation in the Middle East*. Boulder: Lynne Rienner, 2008.

Allal, Amin and Florian Kohstall. "Opposition within the State: Governance in Egypt, Morocco and Tunisia", in Holger Albrecht (ed.), *Contentious Politics in the Middle East*. Gainesville: University Press of Florida, 2010.

Allen, Calvin H. and W. Lynn Rigsbee. *Oman under Qaboos. From Coup to Constitution*. London: Frank Cass, 2000.

Amanat, Abbas. "In Between the Madrasa and the Marketplace: The Designation of Clerical Leadership in Modern Shi'ism", in Said A. Arjomand (ed.), *Political Authority and Political Culture in Shi'ism*. Albany: State University of New York Press, 1988.

Amouee, Bahman. *Political Economy of the Islamic Republic* [in Persian].Tehran: Gam-e No Press, 2002.

Amuzegar, Jahangir. *Iran's Economy under the Islamic Republic*. London: I.B. Tauris, 1993.

Anderson, Lisa. "Political Pacts, Liberalism, and Democracy: The Tunisian National Pact of 1988", *Government and Opposition*, 26, 2 (1991), 244–60.

Andreas, Joel. *Rise of the Red Engineers: The Cultural Revolution and the Origins of China's New Class*. Stanford University Press, 2009.

Aoude, Ibrahim G. "From National Bourgeois Development to Infitah: Egypt 1952–1992", *Arab Studies Quarterly* 16, 1 (1994), 1–23.

Arjomand, Said Amir. *After Khomeini: Iran under His Successors*. Oxford University Press, 2009.

Ashraf, Ahmad. "There is a Feeling that the Regime Owes Something to the People", *Middle East Report* 156 (1989), 13–18.

Athari, Kamal. "The Housing Sector in Iran: Market or Planning?" in Thierry Coville (ed.), *The Economy of Islamic Iran: Between State and Market*. Louvain: Peeters, 1994.

Ayubi, Nazih. "Political Correlates of Privatization Programs in the Middle East", *Arab Studies Quarterly* 14, 2/3 (1992), 39–56. Same problem as Adly, the earlier refernece should be listed first.

———. *Over-Stating the Arab State: Politics and Society in the Middle East*. London: I.B. Tauris, 1995.

Azoulay, Rivka. "Entre marchands, effendi et l'Etat: changement social et renouvellement des élites dans la communauté chiite koweitienne", MPhil thesis, Sciences Po, Paris, 2009.

Bakhash, Shaul. "The Politics of Land, Law, and Social Justice in Iran", *Middle East Journal* 43, 2 (1989), 186–201.

Beblawi, Hazem and Giacomo Luciani. *The Rentier State: Nation, State, and Integration in the Arab World*. London: Croom Helm, 1987.

Behdad, Sohrab. "The Political Economy of Islamic Planning in Iran", in Hooshang Amirahmadi and Manoucher Parvin (eds), *Post-Revolutionary Iran*. Boulder: Westview Press, 1988.

Beinin, Joel. "Workers' Struggles under "Socialism" and Neo-Liberalism", in Rabab El-Mahdi and Philip Marfleet (eds), *Egypt: the Moment of Change*. London: Zed Books, 2009.

———. "Workers and Egypt's January 25 Revolution", *International Labor and Working Class History* 80 (2011), 189–96.

Bellin, Eva. "Contingent Democrats: Industrialists, Labor, and Democratization in Late-Developing Countries". *World Politics* 52, 2 (2000), 175–205.

———. *Stalled Democracy: Capital, Labor, and the Paradox of State-Sponsored Development*. Ithaca: Cornell University Press, 2002.

Bianchi, Robert. "Businessmen's Associations in Egypt and Turkey", *Annals of the American Academy of Political and Social Science* 482 (1985), 147–59.

———. *Unruly Corporatism: Associational Life in Twentieth-Century Egypt*. New York: Oxford University Press, 1989.

Blackburn, Robin. "The New Collectivism: Pension Reform, Grey Capitalism and Complex Socialism", *New Left Review* I/233 (1999), 3–65.

Blaydes, Lisa. *Elections and Distributive Politics in Mubarak's Egypt*. Cambridge University Press, 2011.

Boghardt, Lori Plotkin. *Kuwait Amid War, Peace and Revolution: 1979–1991 and New Challenges*. Basingstoke: Palgrave Macmillan, 2006.

Bourdieu, Pierre. *Distinction: A Social Critique of the Judgment of Taste*. Cambridge, MA: Harvard University Press, 1984.

———. "The Forms of Capital", in J.E. Richardson (ed.), *Handbook of Theory and Research for the Sociology of Education*. New York: Greenwood Press, 1986.

———. "Les modes de domination". *Actes de la Recherche en Sciences Sociales* 2, 2–3 (2009).

Brand, Laurie A. *Citizens Abroad. Emigration and the State in the Middle East and North Africa*. Cambridge University Press, 2006.

Brownlee, Jason. *Democracy Prevention: The Politics of the U.S-Egyptian Alliance*. Cambridge University Press, 2012.

Burawoy, Michael and János Lukács. *The Radiant Past: Ideology and Reality in Hungary's Road to Capitalism*. University of Chicago Press, 1992.

Cammett, Melani Claire. *Globalization and Business Politics in Arab North Africa: A Comparative Perspective*. Cambridge University Press, 2007.

Carapico, Sheila. "Foreign Aid for Promoting Democracy in the Arab World", *Middle East Journal* 56,3 (2002), 379–95.

Carothers, Thomas. "Choosing a Strategy", in Thomas Carothers and Marina (eds), *Uncharted Journey, Promoting Democracy in the Middle East*. Washington: Carnegie Endowment for International Peace, 2005.

Carothers, Thomas and Marina Ottaway (eds). *Funding Virtue, Civil Society Aid and Democracy Promotion*. Washington: Carnegie Endowment for International Peace, 2000.

Carroll, Archie B. and Kareem M. Shabana. "The Business Case for Corporate Social Responsibility: A Review of Concepts, Research and Practice". *International Journal of Management Reviews* 12 (2010), 85–105.

Cassarino, Jean-Pierre. *Tunisian New Entrepreneurs and their Past Experiences of Migration in Europe*. Aldershot: Ashgate, 2000.

Cattaneo, Olivier, Gary Gereffi and Cornelia Staritz. *Global Value Chains in a Postcrisis World: A Development Perspective*. Washington: World Bank, 2010.

Celasun, Merih (ed.). *State-Owned Enterprises in the Middle East and North Africa: Privatization, Performance and Reform*. London: Routledge, 2001.

Chang, Ha-Joon and Ilene Grabel. *Reclaiming Development: An Alternative Economic Policy Manual*. London: Zed Books, 2004.

Charron, Nicholas and Victor Lapuente. "Does Democracy Produce Quality of Government?" *European Journal of Political Research*. 49 (2010), 443–70.

Chaudhry, Kiren. "The Myths of the Market and the Common History of Late Developers", *Politics and Society* 21, 3 (1993), 245–74.

———. *The Price of Wealth: Economies and Institutions in the Middle East*. Ithaca: Cornell University Press, 1997.

Cheung, Tai Ming. "Disarmament and Development in China: The Relationship between National Defense and Economic Development", *Asian Survey* 28, 7 (1988), 757–74.

Clapham, Christopher S. *Third World Politics: An Introduction*. Madison: University of Wisconsin Press, 1985.

Cole, Juan R. "Shaykh Ahmad Al-Ahsa'i on the Sources of Religious Authority", in Linda S. Walbridge (ed.), *The Most Learned of the Shia: The Institution of the Marja' Taqlid*. Oxford University Press, 2001.

Crane, Andrew *et al.* (eds). *The Oxford Handbook of Corporate Social Responsibility*. Oxford University Press, 2008.

Crystal, Jill. *Oil and Politics in the Gulf: Rulers and Merchants in Kuwait and Qatar*. Cambridge University Press, 1990.

———. *Kuwait: The Transformation of an Oil State*. Boulder: Westview Press, 1992.

Davidson, Christopher M. *Dubai: The Vulnerability of Success*. New York: Columbia University Press, 2008.

Davis, Eric. *Challenging Colonialism: Bank Misr and Egyptian Industrialization, 1920–1941*. Princeton University Press, 1983.

Davis, Gerald F., Marina V.N. Whitman and Mayer N. Zald. "The Responsibility Paradox". *Stanford Social Innovation Review* (Winter 2008).

Deeb, Marius. "The Socioeconomic Role of the Local Foreign Minorities in Modern Egypt, 1805–1961", *International Journal of Middle East Studies* 9 (1978), 11–22.

Doner, Richard F., Bryan K. Ritchie and Dan Slater, "Systemic Vulnerability and the Origins of Developmental States: Northeast and Southeast Asia in Comparative Perspective", *International Organization*. 59 (2005), 327–61.

Doner, Richard F. et al. "Can Business Associations Contribute to Development and Democracy?" in Ann Bernstein and Peter L. Berger (eds), *Business and Democracy*. London: Continuum, 1998.

Duverger, Maurice. *Les partis politiques*. Paris: Le Seuil, coll. "Points Essais", 1992.

Ehsani, Kaveh. "Privatization of Public Goods in the Islamic Republic", *Middle East Report* 250 (2009), 26–33.

———. "The Urban Provincial Periphery in Iran: Revolution and War in Ramhormoz", in Ali Gheissari (ed.), *Contemporary Iran: Economy, Society, Politics*. Oxford University Press, 2009.

Ehteshami, Anoushiravan. *After Khomeini: The Iranian Second Republic*. London: Routledge, 1995.

Ehteshami, Anoushiravan and Emma C. Murphy. "Transformation of the Corporatist State in the Middle East", *Third World Quarterly* 17, 4 (1996), 753–72.

Eisenstadt, S. N. "Convergence and Divergence of Modern and Modernizing Societies: Indications from the Analysis of the Structuring of Social Hierarchies in Middle Eastern Societies", *International Journal of Middle Eastern Studies* 8, 1 (1983), 1–27.

Eisenstadt, S.N., and Luis Roniger. *Patrons, Clients and Friends, Interpersonal Relations and the Structure of Trust in Society*. Cambridge University Press, 1984.

El Mahdi, Alia and Ali Rashed, "The Changing Economic Environment and the Development of Micro and Small Enterprises in Egypt, 2006", in Ragui Assaad (ed.), *The Egyptian Labor Market Revisited*. Cairo: American University in Cairo Press, 2009.

El Mallakh, Ragaei. *The Economic Development of the United Arab Emirates*. London: Croom Helm, 1981.

El Mikawy, Noha and Ramy Mohsen. *Civil Society Participation in the Law Making Process in Egypt*. Bonn: ZEF, 2005.

El Sayyed El-Naggar, Ahmad. "Economic Policy: from State Control to Decay and Corruption", in Rabab El-Mahdi and Philip Marfleet (eds), *Egypt: the Moment of Change*. London: Zed Books, 2009.

Elbadawi, Ibrahim and Samir Makdisi (eds). *Democracy in the Arab World: Explaining the Deficit*. London: Routledge, 2011.

Eliacahar, Julia. *Markets of Dispossession: NGOs, Economic Development and the State in Cairo*. London: Duke University Press, 2005.

Eligur, Banu. *The Mobilization of Political Islam in Turkey*. Cambridge University Press, 2010.

Evans, Peter B. *Embedded Autonomy: States and Industrial Transformation*. Princeton University Press, 1995.

Eyal, Gil, Iván Szelényi and Eleanor R. Townsley. *Making Capitalism without Capitalists: Class Formation and Elite Struggles in Post-Communist Central Europe*. London: Verso, 1998.

Faist, Thomas. "Migrants as Transnational Development Agents: An Inquiry into the Newest Round of the Migration-Development Nexus", *Population, Space and Place* 14 (2008), 21–42.

Fakhro, Munira. "The Uprising in Bahrain: An Assessment", in Gary G. Sick and Lawrence G. Potter (eds), *The Persian Gulf at the Millennium: Essays in Politics, Economy, Security, and Religion*. New York: St. Martin's Press, 1997.

Fasano, Ugo and Rishi Goyal. "Emerging Strains in GCC Labor Markets", IMF Working Paper, WP/04/71 (April 2004).

Fasano, Ugo and Qing Wang. "Fiscal Expenditure Policy and Non-Oil Economic Growth: Evidence from GCC Countries", IMF Working Paper, WP/01/195 (2001).

Fazio, Hugo and Manuel Riesco. "The Chilean Pension Fund Associations", *New Left Review* I/223 (1997), 90–100.

———. "Testing the Relationship Between Government Spending and Revenue: Evidence from GCC Countries", IMF Working Paper, WP/02/201 (2002).

Field, Michael. *The Merchants: The Big Business Families of Saudi Arabia and the Gulf States*. Woodstock, NY: Overlook Press, 1985.

Fuller, Graham E. and Rend Rahim Francke. *The Arab Shi'a: The Forgotten Muslims*. New York: St. Martin's Press, 1999.

Gambetta, Diego. *Trust: Making and Breaking Cooperative Relations*. New York: B. Blackwell, 1988.

George, Alan. *Syria: Neither Bread nor Freedom*. London: Zed Books, 2003.

Ghali, Khalifa H. and Fatima Al-Shamsi. "Fiscal Policy and Economic Growth: A Study Relating to the United Arab Emirates", *Economia Internazionale* 50 (1997), 519–33.

Ghods, M. Reza. "Government and Society in Iran, 1926–1934", *Middle Eastern Studies* 27, 2 (1992), 218–30.

Gorman, Anthony. *Historians, State and Politics in Twentieth Century Egypt: Contesting the Nation*. London: Routledge Curzon, 2003.

Guazzone, Laura and Daniela Pioppi (eds). *The Arab State and Neo-Liberal Globalization: The Restructuring of State Power in the Middle East*. Reading, UK: Ithaca, 2009.

Gumuscu, Sebnem. "Class, Status and Party: The Changing Face of Political Islam in Turkey and Egypt", *Comparative Political Studies*. 43, 7 (2010), 835–61.

Güran, Mehmet. "The Political Economy of Privatization in Turkey: An Evaluation", in Tamer Çetin and Fuat Oğuz (eds), *The Political Economy of Regulation in Turkey*. New York: Springer, 2011.

Haddad, Bassam. "The Formation and Development of Economic Networks in Syria: Implications for Economic and Fiscal Reforms, 1986–2000", in Steven Heydemann (ed.), *Networks of Privilege in the Middle East: The Politics of Economic Reform Revisited*. New York: Palgrave Macmillan, 2004.

Haggard, Stephan and Robert Kaufman. *The Politics of Economic Adjustment: International Constraints, Distributive Conflicts, and the State*. Princeton University Press, 1992.

———. *The Political Economy of Democratic Transitions*. Princeton University Press, 1995.

Hamilton, Nora. *The Limits of State Autonomy: Post-Revolutionary Mexico*. Princeton University Press, 1982.

Harders, Cilja. "The Informal Social Pact: The State and the Urban Poor in Cairo", in Eberhard Kienle (ed.), *Politics from Above, Politics from Below: The Middle East in the Age of Economic Reform*. London: Saqi, 2003.

Harris, Kevan. "The Imam's Blue Boxes", *Middle East Report* 257 (2010).

———. "Lineages of the Iranian Welfare State: Dual Institutionalism and Social Policy in the Islamic Republic of Iran", *Social Policy & Administration* 44, 6 (2010), 727–45.

———. "The Politics of Subsidy Reform in Iran", *Middle East Report* 254 (2010), 36–9.

Henry, Clement M. and Robert Springborg. *Globalization and the Politics of Development in the Middle East*. Cambridge University Press, 2010.

Herb, Michael. *All in the Family: Absolutism, Revolution, and Democracy in the Middle Eastern Monarchies*. Albany: State University of New York Press, 1999.

Hertog, Steffen. "Defying the Resource Curse: Explaining Successful State-Owned Enterprises in Rentier States", *World Politics* 62, 2 (2010), 261–301.

———. "The Evolution of Rent Recycling During Two Booms in the Gulf Arab States: Business Dynamism and Societal Stagnation", in Matteo

Legrenzi and Bessma Momani (eds), *Shifting Geo-Economic Power of the Gulf: Oil, Finance and Institutions*. Aldershot: Ashgate, 2011.

———. "Public Industry as Tool of Rentier Economy Diversification: The GCC Case", in Giacomo Luciani (ed.), *Resources Blessed: Diversification and the Gulf Development Model*. Berlin: Gerlach, 2012.

Heydemann, Steven. *Authoritarianism in Syria: Institutions and Social Conflict, 1946–1970*. Ithaca: Cornell University Press, 1999.

———. "Networks of Privilege: Rethinking the Politics of Economic Reform in the Middle East", in Steven Heydemann (ed.), *Networks of Privilege in the Middle East: The Politics of Economic Reform Revisited*. New York: Palgrave Macmillan, 2004.

———. "Upgrading Authoritarianism in the Arab World", Saban Center for Middle East Policy, No. 13, October 2007.

Heydemann, Steven and Reinoud Leenders. "Authoritarian Learning and Authoritarian Resilience: Regime Responses to the 'Arab Awakening.'" *Globalizations* 8, 5 (2011), 647–53.

Hibou, Béatrice. *La force de l'obéissance*. Paris: La Découverte, 2006.

Hinnebusch, Raymond. "Children of the Elite: Political Attitudes of the Westernized Elite in Contemporary Egypt", *Middle East Journal* 36, 4 (1982), 535–61.

———. "The Politics of Economic Reform in Egypt", *Third World Quarterly* 14, 1 (1993), 159–71.

———. *Syria: Revolution from Above*. London: Routledge, 2001.

———. "Authoritarian Persistence, Democratization Theory and the Middle East: An Overview and Critique", *Democratization* 13, 3 (2006), 373–95.

Hoffman, David. *The Oligarchs: Wealth and Power in the New Russia*. New York: Public Affairs, 2002.

Hourani, Albert. "Ottoman Reform and the Politics of Notables", in William Polk and Richard L. Chambers (eds), *Beginnings of Modernization in the Middle East, The Nineteenth Century*. University of Chicago Press, 1968.

Huntington, Samuel P., and Joan M. Nelson. *No Easy Choice: Political Participation in Developing Countries*. Cambridge, MA: Harvard University Press, 1976.

Ibrahimipour, Hossein *et al.* "A Qualitative Study of the Difficulties in Reaching Sustainable Universal Health Insurance Coverage in Iran", *Health Policy and Planning* 26 (2011), 485–95.

Ismael, Jacqueline S. *Kuwait: Social Change in Historical Perspective*. Syracuse University Press, 1982.

Jung, Chang Lyui and Alan Walker. "The Impact of Neo-liberalism on South Korea's Public Pension: A Political Economy of Pension Reform", *Social Policy & Administration* 43, 5 (2009), 425–44.

Kahler, Miles. "Orthodoxy and its Alternatives: Explaining Approaches to Stabilization and Adjustment", in Joan Nelson (ed.), *Economic Crisis and Policy Choice: The Politics of Adjustment in the Third World*. Princeton University Press, 1990.

Kandil, Hazem. *Soldiers, Spies and Statesmen: Egypt's Road to Revolt*. London: Verso, forthcoming.

Kang, D.C. *Crony Capitalism: Corruption and Development in South Korea and the Philippines*. Cambridge University Press, 2002.

Karimi, Zahra. "The Effects of International Trade on Gender Inequality in Iran: The Case of Women Carpet Weavers", in Roksana Bahramitash and Hadi Salehi Esfahani (eds), *Veiled Unemployment: Islamism and the Political Economy of Women's Employment in Iran*. Syracuse University Press, 2011.

Keshavarzian, Arang. *Bazaar and State in Iran: Politics of the Tehran Marketplace*. Cambridge University Press, 2007.

Khajepour, Bijan. "Domestic Political Reforms and Private Sector Activity in Iran", *Social Research* 67, 2 (2000), 577–98.

Khalatbari, Firouzeh. "The Tehran Stock Exchange and Privatisation", in Thierry Coville (ed.), *The Economy of Islamic Iran: Between State and Market*. Louvain: Peeters, 1994.

Kienle, Eberhard (ed.). *Democracy Building and Democracy Erosion: Political Change North and South of the Mediterranean*. London: Saqi, 2009.

King, Lawrence and Iván Szelényi. "Post-Communist Economic Systems", in Neil Smelser and Richard Swedberg (eds), *The Handbook of Economic Sociology (Second Edition)*. New York: Russell Sage Foundation, 2005.

King, Stephen J. *The New Authoritarianism in the Middle East and North Africa*. Bloomington: Indiana University Press, 2009.

Kinninmont, Jane. "The New and Old Economic Actors in North Africa", in Jane Kinninmont, Silvia Colombo and Paola Caridi (eds), *New Socio-Political Actors in North Africa: A Transatlantic Perspective*, Mediterranean Papers Series. Washington: German Marshall Fund, 2012.

Kireyev, Alexei. "Key Issues Concerning Non-Oil Sector Growth", in *Saudi Arabia's Recent Economic Developments and Selected Issues*. Washington: International Monetary Fund, 1998.

Korpi, Walter. "Welfare-State Regress in Western Europe: Politics, Institutions, Globalization, and Europeanization", *Annual Review of Sociology* 29 (2003), 589–609.

Kotkin, Stephen. *Magnetic Mountain: Stalinism as a Civilization*. Berkeley: University of California Press, 1995.

Kurucz, Elizabeth C., Colbert, Barry A. and Wheeler, D. "The Business Case for Corporate Social Responsibility", in Andrew Crane, Abigail McWilliams, Dirk Matten, Jeremy Moon, and Donald Siegel (eds), *The Oxford Handbook of Corporate Social Responsibility*. Oxford University Press, 2008.

Kurzman, Charles and Erin Leahey. "Intellectuals and Democratization, 1905–1912 and 1989–1996", *American Journal of Sociology* 109, 4 (2004), 937–86.

Layne, Linda L. *Elections in the Middle East: Implications of Recent Trends*. Boulder: Westview Press, 1987.

Leca, Jean and Yves Schemeil. "Clientélisme et patrimonialisme dans le monde arabe", *International Political Science Review* 4 (1983), 455–94.

Lemarchand, René and Keith Legg. "Political Clientelism and Development, A Preliminary Analysis", in Norman Provizer (ed.), *Analyzing the Third World: Essays from Comparative Politics*. Cambridge, MA: Schenkman, 1978.

Lesch, Anne. "Egypt's Spring: Causes of the Revolution", *Middle East Policy* 18, 3 (2011), 35–48.

Leverett, Flynt Lawrence. *Inheriting Syria: Bashar's Trial by Fire*. Washington: Brookings Institution Press, 2005.

Li, Cheng. *Bridging Minds across the Pacific. U.S.-China Educational Exchanges, 1978–2003*. Lanham, MD: Lexington Books, 2005.

Li, He. "Returned Students and Political Change in China", *Asian Perspective* 30, 2 (2006), 5–29.

Liddell, James. "Notables, Clientelism and the Politics of Change in Morocco", *The Journal of North African Studies* 15, 3 (2010), 315–31.

Looney, Robert E. "Saudi Arabia: Measures of Transition from a Rentier State", in Joseph A. Kechichian (ed.), *Iran, Iraq, and the Arab Gulf States*. New York: Palgrave, 2001.

Louër, Laurence. *Transnational Shia Politics: Religious and Political Networks in the Gulf.* London: Hurst, 2008.

———. "The Political Impact of Labor Migration in Bahrain", *City and Society* 20 (2008), 32–53.

Luciani, Giacomo. "Economic Foundations of Democracy and Authoritarianism", *Arab Studies Quarterly* 10 (1988), 457–75.

———. "Allocation vs. Production States: A Theoretical Framework", in Giacomo Luciani (ed.), *The Arab State*. Berkeley: University of California Press, 1990.

———. "The Oil Rent, the Fiscal Crisis of the State and Democratization", in Ghassan Salamé (ed.), *Democracy without Democrats? The Revival of Politics in the Muslim World*. London: I.B. Tauris, 1994.

———. "Resources, Revenue and Authoritarianism in the Arab World: Beyond the Rentier State?" in Rex Brynen, Bahgat Korany and Paul Noble (eds), *Political Liberalization and Democratization in the Arab World*. London: Lynne Rienner, 1995.

———. "From Private Sector to National Bourgeoisie: Saudi Arabian Business", in Paul Aarts and Gerd Nonneman (eds), *Saudi Arabia in the Balance: Political Economy, Society, Foreign Affairs*. New York: NYU Press, 2005.

———. "Linking Economic and Political Reform in the Middle East. The Role of the Bourgeoisie", in Oliver Schlumberger (ed.), *Debating Arab Authoritarianism. Dynamics and Durability in Nondemocratic Regimes*. Stanford University Press, 2007.

Lust-Okar, Ellen. "Reform in Syria: Steering between the Chinese Model and Regime Change", Carnegie Endowment for International Peace papers, No. 69, July 2006. The Lust-Okar references need to listed in reverse order (earlier references first).

———. "Competitive Clientelism in the Middle East", *Journal of Democracy* 30, 3 (2009), 122–35.

MacLeod, Dag. *Downsizing the State: Privatization and the Limits of Neoliberal Reform in Mexico*. University Park: Pennsylvania State University Press, 2004.

Maloney, Suzanne. "Islamism and Iran's Postrevolutionary Economy: The Case of the Bonyads", in Mary Ann Tetreault and Robert Denemark (eds), *Gods, Guns, and Globalization: Religious Radicalism and International Political Economy*. Boulder: Lynne Rienner Publishers, 2004.

Mann, Michael. *The Sources of Social Power, Vol. 2*. Cambridge University Press, 1993.

Marshall, Shana, and Joshua Stacher, "Egypt's Generals and Transnational Capital", *Middle East Report* 262 (2012), 12–18.

Maxfield, Sylvia and Ben Ross Schneider (eds). *Business and the State in Developing Countries*. Ithaca: Cornell University Press, 1997.

Médard, Jean-François. "The Underdeveloped State in Africa: Political Clientelism or Neo-Patrimonialism" in Christopher Clapham (ed.), *Private Patronage and Public Power: Political Clientelism and the Modern State*. London: Frances Pinter, 1982.

Meddeb, Hamza. "La Tunisie, pays émergent?" *Sociétés Politiques Comparées* 29 (2010).

Mehryar, Amir. "Shi'ite Teachings, Pragmatism and Fertility Change in Iran", in Gavin Jones and Mehtab Karim (eds), *Islam, the State and Population*. London: Hurst, 2005.

Meydari, Ahmad. "Political Circumstances and the Structure of Ownership Over the Last Three Decades in Iran" [in Persian], *Goftogu* 56 (2010), 29–47.

Mohamedi, Fareed. "Political Economy: State and Bourgeoisie in the Persian Gulf", *Middle East Report* 179 (1992), 35–7.

Moore, Pete W. *Doing Business in the Middle East: Politics and Economic Crisis in Jordan and Kuwait*. Cambridge University Press, 2004.

Moradi, Behnam. "Dimensions of Privatization and its Impact on Private Investment (Case of Iran)" [in Persian], *Political-Economic Information* 213/4 (2005), 180–99.

Moubayed, Sami M. *Steel & Silk: Men and Women Who Shaped Syria 1900–2000*. Seattle: Cune, 2006.

Murray, Alan and Michael Blowfield. *Corporate Social Responsibility: A Critical Introduction*. Oxford University Press, 2008.

Nasr, Vali. *The Rise of Islamic Capitalism: Why the New Muslim Middle Class Is the Key to Defeating Extremism*. London: Free Press, 2010.

Niblock, Tim and Monica Malik. *The Political Economy of Saudi Arabia*. New York: Routledge, 2007.

O'Donnell, Guillermo, Philippe C. Schmitter and Laurence Whitehead (eds). *Transitions from Authoritarian Rule*. Baltimore: Johns Hopkins University Press, 1986.

Okruhlik, Mary Gwen. "Debating Profits and Political Power: Private Business and Government in Saudi Arabia", PhD dissertation, University of Texas at Austin, 1992.

Ottaway, Marina. "The Missing Constituency for Democratic Reform", in Thomas Carothers and Marina Ottaway (eds), *Uncharted Journey, Promoting Democracy in the Middle East*. Washington: Carnegie Endowment for International Peace, 2005.

Owen, Roger. "What Constitutes Business Rationality in Egypt at the End of the Twentieth Century: a Political Economy Approach", in Eberhard Kienle (ed.), *Politics from Above, Politics from Below: The Middle East in the Age of Economic Reform*. London: Saqi, 2003.

Paul, James. "The New Bourgeoisie of the Gulf", *Middle East Report* 142 (1986), 18–22.

Perthes, Volker. *The Political Economy of Syria under Asad*. London: I.B. Tauris, 1995.

———. *Arab Elites: Negotiating the Politics of Change*. Boulder: Lynne Rienner, 2004.

Pesaran, Evaleila. *Iran's Struggle for Economic Independence: Reform and Counter-Reform in the Post-Revolutionary Era*. London: Routledge, 2011.

Peterson, John E. "Rulers, Merchants and Sheikhs in the Gulf Politics: The Function of Family Networks", in Alanoud Alsharekh (ed.), *The Gulf Family: Kinship Policies and Modernity*. London: Saqi Books, 2007.

———. "Bahrain: Reform, Promise and Reality", in Joshua Teitelbaum (ed.), *Political Liberalization in the Persian Gulf*. London: Hurst, 2009.

Pierret, Thomas and Kjetil Selvik. "Limits of Authoritarian Upgrading in Syria: Private Welfare, Islamic Charities, and the Rise of the Zayd Movement", *International Journal of Middle East Studies* 41, 4 (2009), 595–614.

Przeworski, Adam. *Democracy and the Market: Political and Economic Reforms in Eastern Europe and Latin America*. Cambridge University Press, 1991.

Richardson, John G. *Handbook of Theory and Research for the Sociology of Education*. New York: Greenwood Press, 1986.

Rumaihi, Mohamed G. *Bahrain. Social and Political Change since the First World War*. London: Bowker, 1976.

Rutherford, Bruce K. *Egypt After Mubarak: Liberalism, Islam and Democracy in the Arab World*. Princeton University Press, 2004.

Saeidi, Ali. "The Accountability of Para-governmental Organizations (bonyads): The Case of Iranian Foundations", *Iranian Studies* 37, 3 (2004), 479–98.

Saif, Ibrahim. "The Oil Boom in the GCC Countries, 2002–2008: Old Challenges, Changing Dynamics". Washington: Carnegie Endowment for International Peace, March 2009.

Salih, Osman. "The 1938 Kuwait Legislative Council", *Middle Eastern Studies* 28, 1 (1992), 66–100.

Schedler, Andreas. *Electoral Authoritarianism: The Dynamics of Unfree Competition*. Boulder: Lynne Rienner, 2006.

Schlumberger, Oliver. "Dancing with Wolves: Dilemmas of Democracy Promotion in Authoritarian Contexts", in Dietrich Jung (ed.), *Democratization and Development: New Political Strategies for the Middle East*. New York: Palgrave MacMillan, 2006.

——— (ed.). *Debating Arab Authoritarianism: Dynamics and Durability in Nondemocratic Regimes*. Stanford University Press, 2007.

Schmidt, Søren. "The Developmental Role of the State in the Middle East: Lessons from Syria", in Raymond Hinnebusch and Søren Schmidt (eds), *The State and the Political Economy of Reform in Syria*. Boulder: Lynne Rienner, 2009.

Schneider, Ben Ross. *Business Politics and the State in Twentieth-Century Latin America*. Cambridge University Press, 2004.

———. "A Comparative Political Economy of Diversified Business Groups, or How States Organize Big Business", *Review of International Political Economy* 16, 2 (2009), 178–201.

Schumpeter, Joseph Alois. *Capitalism, Socialism, and Democracy*. London: Routledge, 1994.

Seifan, Samir. *Syria on the Path to Economic Reform*. Boulder: Lynne Rienner, 2010.

Selvik, Kjetil. "It's the Mentality, Stupid! Syria's Turn to the Private Sector", in Aurora Sottimano and Kjetil Selvik (eds), *Changing Regime Discourse and Reform in Syria*. Boulder: Lynne Rienner, 2008. "Business and Social Responsibility in the Arab World: the Zakat vs. CSR Models in Syria and Dubai", *Comparative Sociology* 12 (2013): 1–29.

"Business and Social Responsibility in the Arab World: the Zakat vs. CSR Models in Syria and Dubai", *Comparative Sociology* 12 (2013): 1–29.

Sfakianiakis, John. "The Whales of the Nile: Networks, Businessmen, and Bureaucrats During the Era of Privatization in Egypt", in Steven Heydemann (ed.), *Networks of Privilege in the Middle East: The Politics of Economic Reform Revisited*. New York: Palgrave Macmillan, 2004.

Siddiqa, Ayesha. *Military, Inc.: Inside Pakistan's Military Economy*. Oxford University Press, 2007.

Singer, Amy. *Charity in Islamic Societies*. Cambridge University Press, 2008.

Singerman, Diane. *Avenues of Participation*. Princeton University Press, 1995.

Skocpol, Theda. *States and Social Revolutions: A Comparative Analysis of France, Russia, and China*. Cambridge University Press, 1979.

Soliman, Samer. *The Autumn of Dictatorship: Fiscal Crisis and Political Change in Egypt*. Palo Alto: Stanford University Press, 2011.

———. "The Rise and Decline of the Islamic Banking Model in Egypt", in Clement M. Henry and Rodney Wilson (eds), *The Politics of Islamic Finance*. Edinburgh University Press, 2004.

Solnick, Steven Lee. *Stealing the State: Control and Collapse in Soviet Institutions*. Cambridge, MA: Harvard University Press, 1998.

Sottimano, Aurora. "Ideology and Discourse in the Era of Ba'thist Reforms: Towards an Analysis of Authoritarian Governmentality", in Aurora Sottimano and Kjetil Selvik (eds), *Changing Regime Discourse and Reform in Syria*. Boulder: Lynne Rienner, 2008.

Sottimano, Aurora and Kjetil Selvik. *Changing Regime Discourse and Reform in Syria*. Boulder: Lynne Rienner, 2008.

Spilimbergo, Antonio. "Democracy and Foreign Education", CEPR Discussion Paper, No. 5934. London: Centre for Economic Policy Research, 2006.

Springborg, Robert. "Agrarian Bourgeoisie, Semiproletarians, and the Egyptian State: Lessons for Liberalization", *International Journal of Middle East Studies* 22 (1990), 447–72. References for Springborg should be listed in reverse order, with earliest listed first.

———. "The Arab Bourgeoisie: A Revisionist Interpretation", *Arab Studies Quarterly* 15, 1 (1993), 13–39.

———. "Gas and Oil in Egypt's Development", in Robert Looney (ed.), *Handbook of Oil Politics*. New York: Routledge, 2011.

———. "The Precarious Economics of Arab Springs", *Survival* 53, 6 (2011–2012), 85–104.

———. "Resilient Praetorianism in Egypt", in Thomas C. Bruneau and Cristiana Matei (eds), *Handbook of Civil-Military Relations*. London: Routledge, 2012.

Thérien, Jean-Philippe and Vincent Pouliot. "The Global Compact: Shifting the Politics of International Development?" *Global Governance* 12 (2006), 55–75.

Tignor, Robert L. *State, Private Enterprise, and Economic Change in Egypt, 1918–1952*. Princeton University Press, 1984.

———. "Decolonization and Business: The Case of Egypt", *The Journal of Modern History* 59, 3 (1987), 479–505.

Tilly, Charles. *Trust and Rule*. New York: Cambridge University Press, 2005.

Tocqueville, Alexis de. *The Recollections of Alexis de Tocqueville*. New York: Macmillan, 1896.

Totonchi, Emil P. "Laboring a Democratic Spring: the Past, Present and Future of Free Trade Unions in Egypt", *Working USA* 14, 3 (2011), 259–83.

Treichel, Volker. "Stance of Fiscal Policy and Non-Oil Economic Growth", in Ahsan Mansur and Volker Treichel (eds), *Oman Beyond the Oil Horizon: Policies Toward Sustainable Growth*, IMF Occasional Paper No. 185. Washington: IMF, 1999.

Tuğal, Cihan. *Passive Revolution: Absorbing the Islamic Challenge to Capitalism*. Stanford University Press, 2009.

Valibeigi, Mehrdad. "The Private Sector in Iran's Post-Revolutionary Economy", *Journal of South Asian and Middle East Studies* 17, 3 (1994), 1–18.

Verdery, Katherine. *What Was Socialism, and What Comes Next?* Princeton University Press, 1996.

Vitalis, Robert. "On the Theory and Practice of Compradors: The Role of 'Abbud Pasha in the Egyptian Political Economy", *International Journal of Middle East Studies* 22, 3 (1990), 291–315.

———. *When Capitalists Collide: Business Conflict and the End of Empire in Egypt*. Berkeley: University of California Press, 1995.

Vogel, David. *The Market for Virtue: The Potential and Limits of Corporate Social Responsibility*. Washington: Brookings Institution Press, 2005.

Waterbury, John. *Exposed to Innumerable Delusions: Public Enterprise and State Power in Egypt, India, Mexico, and Turkey*. Cambridge University Press, 1993.

———. "Democracy without Democrats? The Potential for Political Liberalization in the Middle East", in Ghassan Salamé (ed.), *Democracy without Democrats*. London: I.B. Tauris, 1994.

Weber, Max. *Le savant et le politique*. Paris: Plon, 1959.

———. *Economy and Society: An Outline of Interpretative Sociology*. 3 vols. New York: Bedminster Press, 1968.

———. *Economie et société II: L'organisation et les puissances de la société dans leur rapport avec l'économie*. Paris: Plon, 1971.

Wiarda, Howard J. *Civil Society, the American Model and Third World Development*. Boulder: Westview Press, 2003.

World Bank. *Governance: The World Bank's Experience*. Washington: The World Bank, 1994.

———. *The Pension System in Iran: Challenges and Opportunities*. 2 vols. Middle East and North Africa Social and Human Development Group. Washington The World Bank, 2003.

Zaakouk, Malak. *Power, Class, and Foreign Capital in Egypt: The Rise of the New Bourgeoisie*. London: Zed Books, 1989.

Zintl, Tina. "Modernization Theory II: Western-Educated Syrians and the Authoritarian Upgrading of Civil Society", in Laura Ruiz de Elvira and Tina Zintl (eds), *Civil Society and the State in Syria: The Outsourcing of Social Responsibility*. Boulder: Lynne Rienner, 2012.

Ziser, Eyal. *Commanding Syria: Bashar Al-Asad and the First Years in Power*. London: I.B. Tauris, 2007.

INDEX